Structural Change and Exchange Rat

Paul J. J. Welfens
Anna Wziątek-Kubiak
Editors

Structural Change and Exchange Rate Dynamics

The Economics of EU Eastern Enlargement

With 36 Figures and 58 Tables

Springer

Professor Dr. Paul J. J. Welfens
University of Wuppertal
EIIW – European Institute for International
Economic Relations
Rainer-Gruenter-Straße 21
42119 Wuppertal
Germany
welfens@eiiw.uni-wuppertal.de
www.euroeiiw.de; www.econ.international.net

Professor Dr. Anna Wziątek-Kubiak
Polish Academy of Science
Institute of Economics
Palac Staszica
ul. Nowy Swiat 72
00-330 Warsaw
Poland
hkubiak@inepan.waw.pl

Cataloging-in-Publication Data

ISBN 978-3-642-06608-5 e-ISBN 978-3-540-28526-7

Springer is a part of Springer Science+Business Media

springeronline.com

Printed in Germany

Hardcover-Design: Erich Kirchner, Heidelberg

Contents

Introduction **1**

Changes in Competitive Advantages of Transition Economies: Measurement and Factors **9**
Anna Wziątek-Kubiak and Dariusz Winek

Comment 33
Dieter Schumacher

EU Export Specialization Patterns in Selected Accession Countries **37**
Dora Borbély

Comment 73
Kerstin Schneider

Sectoral Change and Economic Integration: Theoretical and Empirical Aspects of the Eastern Enlargement of the European Union **79**
Roland Döhrn and Ullrich Heilemann

Comment 97
Paul J.J. Welfens

Structural Change and Economic Dynamics in Transition Economies **101**
Albrecht Kauffmann

Comment 117
Christopher Schumann

Patterns of Industrial Specialization and Concentration in CEECs: Theoretical Explanations and their Empirical Relevance **119**
Antje Hildebrandt and Julia Wörz

Comment 147
Simon Görtz

The Absence of Technology Spillovers from Foreign Direct Investment in Transition Economies **149**
Jutta Günther

Comment 167
Federico Foders

Innovations, Technological Specialization and Economic Convergence in the EU **171**
Andre Jungmittag

Comment 201
Andreas Pyka

Equilibrium Exchange Rates in the Transition: The Tradable Price-Based Real Appreciation and Estimation Uncertainty **205**
Balázs Égert and Kirsten Lommatzsch

Comment 241
Bernd Kempa

Innovation, Structural Change and Exchange Rate Dynamics in Catching-up Countries **245**
Paul J.J. Welfens

Comment 279
Krzysztof Marczewski

List of Contributors **281**

Index **283**

Introduction

After the initial transformational recession in Eastern Europe factor allocation quickly became influenced by restructuring, competition and economic opening up. The old socialist central planning system had been driven predominantly by non-market priorities and had been marked by distortions in demand-supply linkages and biased preferences of state planners. Within a few years new market economy institutions were created and privatization of industry widely accomplished but the new institutions and the restructured firms – including state-owned firms in certain sectors – had to cope over many years with distortions from the old system. At the same time foreign economic relations became embedded in international organizations, that is the rules of the WTO, the IMF and the BIS – this gave impulses to trade policy, capital market liberalization and monetary policy regimes in Eastern Europe. Moreover, many transition countries have tried to anticipate EU membership as have foreign investors from Europe, the US and Asia. Changing international economic links in combination with structural change, real income growth and monetary policies influenced the nominal and real exchange rate, and the latter clearly had a feedback effect on the allocation of resources.

Changes in relative sectoral productivity plus product innovations and shifts on the demand side have caused major changes in the composition of output. EU accession countries have responded in different ways to the new domestic and international framework. Taking into account the single EU market it is obvious that major structural shifts and a rise in per capita income in the transition countries (with 75 million inhabitants) cannot leave the structure of output and economic growth in western Europe unaffected. Massive EU15 foreign direct investment in eastern Europe and rapidly growing east-west trade within the enlarged EU – in line with the logic of the gravity equation – have changed the composition of output and employment in the whole of Europe.

Structural change was enormous in the new EU member countries as postsocialist economies' transition to a market economy implied that former ideological emphasis on industry and the lack of resources for the services sector were no longer relevant. Rather outsourcing in the context of a competitive market economy and trade brought impulses for efficiency-enhancing outsourcing of services; at the same time suppliers in the services sector increasingly adjusted to the consumers' revealed preferences and the gradual growth of the demand for services along with rising real income in the medium run. In the EU accession countries the anticipated pressure from the EU single market supported the process of economic modernization and contributed to both trade creation and foreign direct investment (FDI) creation: Relative trade links between eastern European accession countries and EU15 countries have increased; with respect to foreign direct investment flows the dynamics were, of course, rather asymmetrical, the extent of FDI flows to eastern Europe partly depending on the type of privatization strategy pursued. FDI, investment by domestic firms and trade all are expected to contribute to growth and structural change.

Structural change has four elements: (i) the changes in the sectoral composition of industry and (ii) changes in the structure of trade; (iii) the relative increase of the services sector as restructuring brings about outsourcing of industrial services – the latter is part of a long term relative rise in the nominal demand for nontradable goods which goes along with a relative rise in the nontradables price; and these structural dynamics in turn are linked to changes in the real exchange rate. Facing a long term real appreciation in countries which are catching up economically producers in the tradables sector have to adjust in terms of process innovations and product innovations.

Eastern Europe's institutional modernization and economic catching up with more EU15 countries necessarily involved overcoming distortions from the former socialist system. This can be seen as a kind of "smoothing out" of inherited and distorted structures, thus allowing the emergence of new structures based on and driven by technological progress and adjustments to changing relative prices and the changing international environment. The opening up and liberalisation of the CEECs in the direction of the EU both facilitated and stimulated exchanges of knowledge, diffusions of new technology and flows of goods and factors. It was also accompanied by massive reallocation of production and resources and this fundamentally shaped the ongoing structural changes.

A large shift in the structure of GDP and employment brought the CEECs' economic structures closer to those in the EU. Manufacturing experienced a radical opening-up when faced with such intense international competition as exists, although trade and investment flows have experienced much greater structural changes than any other sectors of the economy. In terms of gross value added, the share of industry in most of the new member states is now similar to that in the EU. However, in 2001 the eight CEECs accounted only for 4.6% of total manufacturing of the enlarged EU (the EU-15 plus the eight CEECs). In terms of purchasing power parity this share exceeded 9%. In 2004 total GDP of EU accession countries was about 5% of EU-15 GDP, however, on the basis of purchasing power parity figures their share was 10%.

The magnitude of the CEECs' shift away from the structures inherited from the central planning model has been, ironic perhaps, rather advantageous in their process of catching up. However, since the inherited distortions may have been disproportionally manifested in different types of economic structure it is reasonable to analyse different aspects of the structural changes from various points of view. It may be helpful in identifying the new opportunities and challenges. This is all the more important given that theory has failed to date to provide an ideal structure that is indispensable for a fast process of catching up.

For the immediate future of the new member states the balance between real and nominal convergence (that is to say, compliance with the Maastricht criteria) is important. Since structural changes are a prerequisite for real convergence the dual obligation to implement the Copenhagen criteria and Lisbon strategy on the one hand and the Maastricht convergence requirements on the other may create new challenges for the new member states. The problem of finding an optimum balance between the benefits stemming from real convergence and the costs attributable to the process of maintaining price stability and pursuing effective control over measures of nominal convergence (interest rates and exchange rates) is only just emerging.

The fifteenth anniversary of the breakthrough in the region offers an excellent opportunity to look back and examine the features of the structural changes that have taken place in these economies compared to the incumbent EU countries and the factors that have driven them and been driven by them.

The purpose of this book is to provide systemic analysis of the structural changes that have taken and are taking place in the new member states and to explain how they interact in particular with exchange rate dynamics. The book deals directly with three issues. Firstly, the character, driving factors and scope of the structural changes themselves that have been taking place in the new member states. Secondly, the usefulness of previous experiences of new member states catching up within the EU, as well as economic theories that help identification of the main factors and trends shaping structural change and the real process of catching up for transition economies. Thirdly, the links and interdependencies between structural changes, which imply changes in supply capacity and in the quality of tradable goods and exchange rate dynamics. This deals with identifying the key factors influencing exchange rate dynamics in the new member states and the implications of this analysis for both exchange rate theory and modelling.

All of the papers here with the exception of one are empirical analyses based on a single panel of data used to analyse each country at least as far back as the medium-term. Each refers to a multiplicity of theoretical frameworks helping to explain structural change and identifying the forces underlying patterns. Some papers overlap in their use of theoretical models, although each adopts a distinctive approach or deals with different subject matter..

The book's nine chapters mainly focus on aspects of competitiveness and structural changes: spatial allocation of resources, trade, market structure and exchange rate dynamics of the economy. Each paper employs its own measures and different evaluation methods are used. Several authors look into the interdependences between structural change, innovation processes and exchange rate changes. There are new insights from both modelling and empirical analysis.

Defining competitiveness as the ability to compete, Anna Wziatek-Kubiak and Dariusz Winek evaluate changes in the competitiveness of Polish and Hungarian manufacturing from 1996 to 2000. Distinguishing between the ability to compete (measured by factors of competitiveness) and the effect of competition (market shares) makes it possible to test the relevance of changes in market shares of transition economies as a measure of changes in respective sectoral competitiveness. Based on the criteria of changes in trends in both the domestic and EU market shares, four areas of the transition countries' manufacturing sectors were selected as were three factors indicating the ability of products to compete in each area. Each was subsequently evaluated. The findings of the analysis show improvements in the competitiveness of Polish manufacturing in 1998-2000 as compared to 1996-1998. With EU enlargement in 2004, anticipated by many investors in both eastern Europe and the EU-15, it is clear that there are incentives from changes in the division of labour in Europe, and this certainly has a spatial dimension, too.

Assuming the main source and intensity of technology to be domestic R&D, Dora Borbély focuses on the links between technological intensity across various manufacturing sectors and patterns of export specialisation in the Czech Republic, Hungary and Poland in relation to the EU in the years 1995-2001. The analysis of export specialisation and export performance based on three measures – coverage ratio, revealed comparative advantage (Balassa) and Grubel-Lloyd index of intra-industry trade – appears to contradict traditional trade theory, which suggests that accession countries will tend to specialise in labour intensive goods. Borbély also questions whether the distinction between the EU-15 and the new member states in terms of skill levels of the labour force reveals specific conclusions for each of these groups of countries. These doubts oblige Borbély to question the assumptions underpinning the new economic geography view that less mature products will tend to be provided by the new member states, and more mature products by the previously incumbent EU members. Analysis of the R&D intensity of manufacturing of the three above-selected new member states indicates that in terms of sectoral distribution they are similar to Germany. However, these similarities go hand-in-hand with differences in export specialisation patterns by technological intensity. Either domestic R&D is not the main source of new technology in all of these new three member states or there are large differences in the use of R&D results in production and in the efficiency of activity of R&D sectors among these countries.

The paper by Roland Döhrn and Ullrich Heilemann apply the Chenery hypothesis of structural change to the post-socialist transition countries. The innovative model explains the sectoral composition of output in eastern Europe and also refers to a comparative perspective of a normal market economy allocation. The empirical model fits reality in the accession countries rather well and thus allows us to better understand shifts in the sectoral composition of output. Moreover, some new aspects are discussed, including the role of foreign direct investment which has different impacts in the various sectors.

Albrecht Kauffmann first takes a brief look at the distortions of the socialist command economies and then gives a short overview of alternative theoretical approaches to structural change. Starting from the familiar three-sector approach he proceeds by pointing out basic models of structural change for both closed economies and open economies. He also considers the issue of economic catching up.

Using panel estimation techniques, two measures of geographic concentration (absolute and relative) and two measures for the size of industry (employment and production), Antje Hildebrandt and Julia Wörz show changes in the pattern of location of manufacturing activity within the ten CEECs in the years 1993-2000 and the key factors influencing them. Comparing theese with those found in the EU-15 during the 1980s allows an identification of the sequence of changes in the location of manufacturing accompanying economic integration. As traditional trade theories suggest, integration initially induces an increase in concentration. However, the authors expect that in the near future deepening integration will result in the emergence of de-concentration trends within the CEECs, as took place in the EU in the 1990s. Based on new economic geography models Hildebrandt and

Wörz also identify the driving forces behind the concentration of industry within the CEECs. Their conclusion that relative concentration patterns are strongly influenced by relative productivity, location of demand and FDI contradicts the hypothesis put forth by new economic geography models. They found that relative productivity levels determine the CEECs' share of output in a given industry's total output, whereas the influence of FDI and export orientation towards the EU was important only for a handful of industries. This throws new light on the analysis of the role of domestic factors in shaping the pattern of industry location in the CEECs.

Jutta Günther's contribution concerns the economic effects of technology spillovers from FDI on the catching up economies and their domestic firms' productivity and dual economic structures. Focusing on four main channels of technology spillover, namely via demonstration, labour mobility, suppliers and customer support, and based on field studies carried out in the Hungarian economy using qualitative interviews with representatives of foreign and domestic companies; she concludes that foreign subsidiaries contribute to the overall modernisation of the transition economies. However, as they co-operate mainly among themselves, their activity leads to a dual economic structure. As long as domestic firms do not improve their competitiveness the gap between them and foreign subsidiaries increases and they operate in separate spheres within the host economy. In effect, innovation stimulating spillover between the two sides becomes increasingly difficult. In Günther's opinion, government support for domestic small and medium sized enterprises seems the best solution to the problems.

Andre Jungmittag analyses the effect of innovation, technological specialisation, diffusion and the usual production factors on long term growth as well as convergence of labour productivity in the EU-15 between 1969 and 1998. He shows that although growth of capital stock and technological diffusion were the most important driving forces behind long term development and the convergence of labour productivity among the EU-15 countries, there were some differences here between those EU countries that had to catch up and those EU countries that initially lead the way. While the level of relative R&D technological specialisation was a driving force for growth in the countries that led initially, technological diffusion and imitation was the key factor for growth in the catching up countries. He emphasises that due to technological transfers and imitation some of the EU countries that negatively specialised in R&D intensive technology and in cutting-edge technology managed to achieve high growth dynamics. Technology transfers and imitation in countries that were catching up had a trade-off effect in terms of negative specialisation in R&D intensive and cutting edge sectors. This means that increases in efficiency enabled by technological transfers and imitation are important preliminary stages in establishing own innovative capacity in R&D intensive areas in the catch up countries. On the other hand, Jungmittag shows that countries with structural changes that shifted toward R&D intensive industries tended to experience higher growth. The need to support this type of structural change and cross-border technology diffusion and knowledge spillover by government policy seems therefore justified. Jungmittag calls on the EU to encourage the catch up new members to participate in the emerging EU innovation system and to introduce selective R&D policies. Accession countries will benefit from EU innovation policy and rising FDI inflows from western Europe, at the same time there will be shadow effects from Euro zone and new exchange rate regimes.

The exchange rate is one of the most important factors affecting structural change in the economy, its geographical location of production, trade flows, specialisation and market structure. Overvaluation causes loss of competitiveness, harms growth and real convergence. An undervalued exchange rate parity makes attaining low inflation and ERM-II entry difficult. However, since the new member states do not have opt-out clauses from the obligation to adopt the euro in the future, assessments of the equilibrium exchange rate of their currencies is worthy of some attention, and was provided by Balász Ègert and Kirsten Lommatzsch. They performed a reduced form estimation of the real exchange rate for the Czech Republic, Hungary, Poland, Slovenia and Slovakia in the 1990s. They focused on a comparison of the results of different estimation methods rather than on different theoretical approaches and showed that estimates of equilibrium real exchanges rates are sensitive to whatever econometric methods, periods and model specification are selected and to differences in their variables. The employment of a number of time series and panel cointegration methods enables a comparison of the equilibrium RER of the five above-mentioned new member states as well as pin points the uncertainty surrounding estimates and the size of real misalignment. Ègert and Lommatzsch point out that equilibrium appreciation of the RER in transition economies is based not only on higher service prices (the Balassa-Samuelson effect) but also on higher prices of domestically produced tradable goods. During the catch up process improvements in competitiveness and quality of goods may result in appreciation of the RER. It was found that labour productivity was the most stable determinant of inflation-based RER, while other variables differed considerably across the analysed countries. Their estimations represent average long-term coefficients for the panel members and other factors. Some conflicting results between time series and panel estimation concerning the real misalignment may be due to country specific factors.

The growing number of Polish manufacturing product groups increased competitive pressure on EU products. The multinomial logit estimate for the probability of a given product group being in a particular manufacturing sector according to the value of three factors of competitiveness outlined above indicates that of the three selected factors influencing changes in market shares, relative unit labour costs (of both countries as compared to the EU average) played the major role. The basis for the increase in market shares of both countries was the improvement in relative unit labour costs. The analysis of relative unit intermediate costs and relative unit export values reveals that on the EU market Poland's products surpassed – in competition – mainly low quality EU and non-EU products, while in the Hungarian case it was high quality products as well. However, in an increasing number of high quality product groups Poland increased its competitive pressure on the EU product market as well.

A modern macroeconomic model has to take into account the short, medium- and long-term links between technology/growth and exchange rates dynamics. The contribution by Paul Welfens is the first new effort in this direction. By including product innovation and innovation processes in his analysis of the determinants of nominal and real exchanges rates in the long-, medium- and very short-term exchanges rate models, he adds interesting refinements and improvements to the existing theory; the approach shows that product innovations bring about a real appreciation. In his analysis of the determinants of nominal and real exchange rates Welfens brings in four innovations: the role of innovation in a modified Balassa-Samuelson model of the real exchanges rate; the link between the stock market and foreign bond and money markets, which additionally integrate technological catching up in both stock markets and exchange rate dynamics. As a theoretical progress he incorporates product innovation into the Mundell-Fleming model and links Schumpeterian forces to the long-term equilibrium real exchange rate. His analysis leads to important conclusions from a policy point of view. Welfens points out, firstly, that increasing product innovation is accompanied by medium-term appreciation. Secondly, he shows that the economic and technological catching up which accompany short- and medium-term appreciation of the currency create the risk of a rise in unemployment, mainly of unskilled workers. The retraining of unskilled labour and higher expenditures on education are crucial, he argues. Thirdly, if high unemployment rates become a sustainable problem, political instability increases alongside reductions in net capital inflows. In a system of flexible exchange rates the risk of exchange rate overshooting might also arise.

Among the major findings of this paper, three deserve particular attention. The first is the interaction between structural changes, catching up and exchange rate dynamics. Those factors, namely labour productivity and innovation, that determine structural changes impact exchange rate dynamics very strongly. This suggests the need to introduce innovation to the exchange rate model, as Welfens has done.

Second, the shift from concentration to de-concentration trends in industry within the CEECs, which accompanies the increased role of inter-industry specialisation, may result in increasing competition among members of the enlarged EU for FDI, whose role in location of industry would then increase. This would be accompanied by an increase in competitive pressure from the new member states' product groups on the EU product market. At the same time, however, appreciation of new member states' currencies, which tends to accompany the catching up of their economies, would reduce their competitive pressure on EU products.

Third, examples of catching up EU incumbent countries reveal that for years the main source of technology of new member states is likely to be technological diffusion and imitation. However, the improvements in efficiency of the new member states which tend to accompany catching up should force them to develop their R&D sectors. Neglecting the role of the R&D sector in technological development would imply a bottleneck of some new member states in the catching up process.

Most papers presented in this volume are from the EU project "Changes in Industrial Competitiveness as a Factor of Integration: Identifying Challenges of the Enlarged Single European Market" in the EU 5th Framework Programme (Contract No. HPSE-CT-2002-00148).

The editors are quite grateful to Dieter Schumacher, Kerstin Schneider, Christopher Schumann, Simon Görtz, Federico Foders, Andreas Pyka, Bernd Kempa and Krzysztof Marczewski for their comments. They have shed additional light on the complex and important issues of structural change, catching-up and exchange rate dynamics.

We appreciate the organization of a workshop on Structural Change and Exchange Rate Dynamics in Wuppertal in early 2004 where the preparatory work was mainly done by Dora Borbély from EIIW. The smooth cooperation with colleagues from CASE in Warsaw and the contributions from so many other colleagues from Europe is very much appreciated. We finally express our gratitude to Michael Agner, Stephanie Kullmann and Jens Perret (EIIW) who put much effort into the editing process and the index as well.

April 2005, Wuppertal and Warsaw
Paul J.J. Welfens and Anna Wziątek-Kubiak

Changes in Competitive Advantages of Transition Economies: Measurement and Factors

Anna Wziątek-Kubiak and Dariusz Winek[1]

Contents

1 Introduction 10
2 Nature of Competitiveness 11
3 Market Share Changes as an Indicator of Changes in Competitiveness 13
4 Changes in Market Performance of Polish and Hungarian Manufacturing 16
4.1 Data and Methodology 16
4.2 Changes in Market Performance of Poland's and Hungarian Manufacturing 17
5 Factors Influencing Changes in Market Performance of the Polish and Hungarian Manufacturing (Ability to Compete versus Effect of Competition) 22
6 Do Polish and Hungarian Product Groups Compete with the EU Ones? 28
7 Conclusions 30
References 31

---

[1] The following paper is a result of the project 'Changes in Industrial Competitiveness as a Factor of Integration: Identifying Challenges of the Enlarged Single European Market' funded from the 5th Framework Programme of the European Community (Ref. HPSE-CT-2002-00148). The authors are solely responsible for the content of the paper. It does not represent the opinion of the Community and the Community is not responsible for any use that might be made of data appearing therein.

1 Introduction

Competitiveness is an ambiguous notion. In literature there are many approaches to competitiveness and many ways of measuring it. It partly results from the fact that competitiveness "is not a concept invented by theorists but by those with a practical approach, connected with creation of politics" (Fagerberg 1996, p.56) and has a business rather than a theoretical origin.

Literature reveals three main approaches to competitiveness: macro, trade and micro. The macro approach narrows the definition of competitiveness to economic growth. In the trade approach, competitiveness is evaluated on the basis of trade performance and specialisation. The micro approach links competitiveness to the process of competition. Its changes are assessed on the grounds of changes in productivity and market shares. The micro approach is explored in this paper.

The definition of competitiveness as an ability to sell on the market (Balassa 1963, p.29 and Artto's 1987, p.47) indicates that changes in competitiveness reflect changes in ability of firms to compete. Such an understatement has far reaching consequences. Primarily, it emphasizes that competitiveness is a relative and international category. It implies that while assessing competitiveness the capacity of rivals to compete needs to be taken into consideration. Secondly, such a definition touches upon the issue of differences between the ability to compete and its consequences. In other words, there is a problem of whether it is sufficient in assessing competitiveness to evaluate the ability to compete or should the effect of competition (pushing out of the market and strengthening of position on the market) be exposed as well. Thirdly, the question about the measures to evaluate the ability to compete (by prices, cost and productivity) and competition effects becomes pressing. Fourthly, there is a question of how to ensure that the research includes product truly competing on a given market, both in terms of goods and geography. Producers of a given product in one country can perform at a different quality range than producers of other countries. The distance between these producers along the quality spectrum therefore determines to what extent they are competitors on a given product market.

Using the examples of Hungary and Poland in this study, the above-mentioned issues are analysed. Comparing the effect of competition of these transition economies on both the domestic and EU market (changes in their share on both markets) with factors of competition, the relevance of changes in market shares as a measure of changes in competitiveness of the transition economies is put forward in this paper.

This paper consists of 6 sections. The first section presents an understanding of competitiveness specific for this paper. The second shows the advantages and disadvantages of market shares as a measure of assessment of changes in competitiveness. In the third section basing on the criterion of changes of the Hungarian and Polish manufacturing in domestic and EU market shares, four parts of manufacturing have been distinguished: product groups which strengthened their position on both markets, product groups which have been pushed out from the markets, and products groups whose share in both markets diverged. The following section then verifies whether changes in market shares in economies in transition (i.e., that is the competition effects) reflects changes in their capacity to compete, measured by relative unit labour costs, relative intensity of investment and relative cash flow. The last section searches for those segments at different quality ranges, in which the products of both countries pushed out EU producers from the EU market. This study is crowned with conclusions.

2 Nature of Competitiveness

Although competitiveness is a frequently-used category and is implicitly contained in many theories, there are no theoretical bases to analyse it as there is no formalised theory of competitiveness. Competitiveness is a category used more in business and management than in economics. In business and management, it has become synonymous with competitive advantage, as opposed to comparative advantage as it is seen in the context of means of winning the competition on the microeconomic level.

In economics, competitiveness is understood in various ways. It is limited to signify growth, or even an economic situation, foreign trade performance and efficiency. This category is attached to theories of economic growth and trade, although none of these theories have ever used competitiveness as an explanatory variable (Gomory, Baumol, 2000,ch.1). Each of these theories mark the boundaries of analysis which are reflected in the ways of understanding competitiveness and methods of its research. These approaches to competitiveness are so strikingly diverse that it often seems that the subject of analysis is entirely different, though related by name. In international economics textbooks, the comparative advantage category is used – frequently mistaken for competitiveness – as Balassa (1989) pointed out. In effect, the notion of competitiveness is often used in the analysis of trade performance. It is not taken into account that trade theories focus on optimalization issues. These theories do not consider nor develop the competitive aspect of trade as they do not take into account that "there are in fact conflicts in international trade" (Gomory and Baumwall, 2000, p.4). Neither do they consider the fact that trade is an effect of competition within a given country (among its producers) as well as in foreign markets.

This paper is based on the assumption that competitiveness derives from competition and thus directly reflects a rivalry between individuals. Such assumption implies that:

- competitiveness is dependent on carrying out competition targets,
- the range of research on competitiveness is marked by the area, scope and methods of competition which are reflected in methods of changes in competitiveness,
- competitiveness is a relative term. To evaluate its changes one needs to take into account changes which a competitor undergoes as juxtaposed to other competitors.

Competitiveness helps to achieve the aims of the competition struggle – the growth of market share. Competition pertains to situations in which the sides, while aiming to achieve the same but effectively the opposite target, find themselves in conflict. Competition spans the process of firms pushing other firms out of the market (and by the same token the goods produced by them). By reflecting the firms' ability to act under pressure of competition, competitiveness reveals "the ability of exporting industries, or those competing against the country's import, to sustain their market shares" (Feenstra 1989, p. 1), that is across foreign markets (exporting industries) and domestic markets (competing against import and other domestic producers). By serving to outdo rivals (Peng 2000, s. 85), competitiveness enables competitive firms to stay on the market. Results of competitive struggle among companies reflecting "the seizure of certain firms by others" (Reynauld, Vidal 1998, p.59) result in changes to market position (Frischtak 1999, p.86) and eventually changes in market structure. A growing market share of a firm confirms its winning position in the competition struggle and demonstrates improving of its competitiveness. Thus, these results demonstrate the companies' ability to meet the consumers' demand (Kirzner, 2000).

Since competitiveness reflects competition, its boundaries, the area of its occurrence and its subject remain the same as for competition. The research on competitiveness concentrates on companies (the actual and potential market participants) which aim to place themselves on a given product market, strengthen their position and eliminate competitors. The subject of the research is, however, the product market, its segments and goods produced by various companies, not the structure of production of a given (domestic or foreign) business. The latter demonstrates specialisation, which is evaluated by the extra-market – not intra-market – comparisons (Porter 1990, p.84). Thus, when analysing competitiveness, one uses the rules of partial equilibrium analysis and not, as it is done in case of specialisation, general equilibrium analysis.

The evaluation of the competitiveness of firms concerns results of competition between groups of firms selected on the bases on various criteria such as size, form of ownership and location of production (domestic and foreign). When evaluating competitiveness of a product one in fact evaluates the competitiveness of a product manufactured by a given group of firms against other firms. Thus, when speaking of the competitiveness of domestic products, one means competitiveness of products produced in one country by firms performing in its territory as opposed to products produced by firms acting abroad against which the domestic product competes both on domestic and foreign markets. There is no such notion as product competitiveness but only competitiveness of products produced by selected firms against their competitors (Branson 1980, p.193 onwards).

Market participants produce uncompetitive (price does not cover production cost) and competitive goods, with different competitiveness levels. Competition takes place between all market participants. Competition benefits come across as lower costs and product differentiation (Porter 1990, p.10, 29; 1986, p.20) for ensuring profits. Competition allows only some competitors to survive: those who increase profits by improving their use of resources or by creating new ones. The profits in turn enable a firm to improve its market position, which reflects an ongoing and never-ending struggle (Porter 1990, p.34). Although only goods produced with profit may be labelled competitive, uncompetitive businesses also join the competition. With time, their products are eliminated from the market. The selection of producers of a given product is reflected in pushing goods with low competitiveness or those entirely uncompetitive out of the market. This process takes place on both the domestic (between local producers as well as between local and foreign ones) and foreign markets.

The evaluation of product competitiveness does not translate into firm competitiveness. In evaluating product competitiveness, sales results and not net financial results are used. Firm competitiveness reflects the firms' overall performance, including non-production related activities (Wziątek-Kubiak, 2001).

Reflecting competition, competitiveness is a relative and international category. In its evaluation, one compares the competitiveness of one product manufactured by a producer fighting to take control of as large a part of the market for this product as possible (Galli, Pelkmans, 2000, p.9) – both domestically and internationally. Since the product's competitiveness is verified both on the domestic and the foreign market, an evaluation of competitiveness of domestic production based on export has only limited research capabilities (Casson 1999, p.X). Additionally, improving productivity alone does not have to imply the rise of the company's competitiveness, since another company, foreign or domestic, may increase its production productivity by a wider margin. In such a case, the improvement of a firm's or product's productivity may be accompanied by a drop in its international competitiveness.

Since competitiveness reflects the competition struggle of markets, it is fair to say that methods used in this struggle are the methods used to change competitiveness. Two types of competitiveness (price and non-price) reflect two basic methods of competition. However, several issues arise. Are competition methods a measure of competitiveness evaluation? How does one assess changes in competitiveness if companies do not compete based on price? Does competitiveness reveal itself through a high or low price?

In this paper, perceiving competition as an ongoing process as opposed to the equilibrium analysis implies that the Schumpeterian approach is employed. This concept is grounded in costs and quality advantages, which for Schumpeter were more important than the price competition of the traditional theory. As a result of competition threat from competitors, entrepreneurs introduce innovations resulting in changes of firms' internal productivity. In this way, these processes are the basis for the process of selection or "creative destruction".

Price competition takes place only in selected markets although it is of key importance in the competition struggle of the economies in transition's companies. In the 1990s, the firms in these economies were undergoing restructuring which affected their productivity. Thus, the productivity described their capacity to compete.

3 Market Share Changes as an Indicator of Changes in Competitiveness

Competition is a zero sum game. On a stable as well as on a quickly growing market, the improvement of firm's position is accompanied by another firm's fall. Changes in competitiveness illustrate a firm's ability to stay on the market. Due to this fact, one often finds market share to be synonymous with resultant or performance competitiveness across literature (Meeksen, Rayp 2000, p. 275; Hall, Smith, Tsoukalis 2001, p. 109; Competitiveness... 1990, p.2).

Market participants aim to improve their position on the markets where their goods are sold, both domestic and foreign. Changes in competitiveness of exported products are therefore described by the changes in foreign markets share. Changes in competitiveness of domestic-based products competing against imports are reflected in a change of their share on the domestic market (Feenstera 1989, p. 1). Therefore, changes in a share on domestic and foreign markets can be treated as an indicator of change in a competitive position on these markets, which is defined as follows:

$$CP_D = 1 - \frac{Im}{Ps - Ex + Im} = \frac{Ps - Ex}{Ps - Ex + Im} = \frac{Ps - Ex}{TD_D} \tag{1}$$

$$CP_F = \frac{Ex}{TD_F} \tag{2}$$

where:
CP_D – competitive position on domestic market,
CP_F – competitive position on foreign market,
Ex – export,
Im – import,
Ps – sold production,
TD_D – total demand (apparent consumption) on domestic market,
TD_F – total demand (apparent consumption) on foreign market.

The approach presented in this paper, which limits evaluation of competitiveness to the analysis of both domestic and foreign market share, differs from the commonly used approach. In this generally used method, competitiveness is limited to evaluation of exports market share. It is also assumed in this approach that firms are dealing with open economies, and thus virtually all country's production is exportable. Since there are no differences between competitiveness of production exported and that sold on the domestic market, the entire production can be said to have a similar level of competitiveness[2]. This assumption does not comply with the conditions of the analysed countries. It is because in those countries one still finds a large number of companies with very low competitiveness (Wziątek-Kubiak, 2001). Besides, the economies in transition of the analyzed period were only beginning to open and were certainly not as open as the developed market economies.

Using market share as an indicator of changes in competitiveness, one should keep in mind some limitation of these indicators. Since it can reflect a number of different factors, such an indicator should be interpreted with caution while its limits are well understood. Several points illustrate this discussion.

As the first point, one needs to consider the following situation. On one hand, since in Poland a major part of production is conducted on the domestic market,

[2] Export market share neglects competition by the domestic producers who do not export.

changes in the domestic market share are an important part of the competitiveness changes analysis. On the other hand, however, foreign trade performance influences changes in the domestic market share. These changes are the result not only of alterations in size of domestic production but shifts of export and import as well (equation 1). A greater rate of growth of export and import compared with domestic production results in a fall of the domestic production share in the domestic market. Although it may be the effect of export's growth dynamics overtaking growth of production sold on the domestic market, this change does not necessarily have to mean a worsening competitiveness in domestic production. It may be accompanied by a rising share of export on foreign markets, which would in turn suggest improvement in competitiveness.

As the second point, it would be worthwhile to take into account the problems with interpretation of changes in competitiveness when changes in domestic and foreign markets shares diverge. Whenever the share of production in a given country rises on both the domestic and foreign markets, there are no doubts that improvement in the production competitiveness takes place. Falling market shares on both markets show that production competitiveness is decreasing. The most ambiguous is the evaluation of changes in production competitiveness, in which changes in domestic and foreign markets diverge. Such can be the result of reorientation of production between the domestic and the foreign market as well as, on the one hand, an effect of improvement of position of competitive firms on foreign market and simultaneously on the other hand, a deterioration of position of low competitive and non-competitive firms on the domestic market, which were never exported.

As a third point it needs to be noted that changes in companies' activity both on the domestic and foreign markets are influenced by differences in dynamics of demand between them. Greater dynamics of the domestic rather than the foreign demand encourage local producers to develop sales on the domestic market. It may be accompanied by decelerating dynamics of export growth, implying stabilisation or even a reduction in export market share.

As a fourth point, one should state that market shares are dependent upon the size of a country. Larger countries with significant domestic markets will, as a rule, have a larger domestic market share ratio. However, even within a group of large countries there are quite large differences in domestic market shares (Italy versus UK) as well as in intensity of exports. Thus a question arises whether the specifics of large countries do or do not influence different methods of assessing changes in their competitiveness compared with smaller countries.

As a fifth point it should be decided if domestic market shares reflect the nature of the product being traded with some products more tradable than others.

Last but not least, the classification problem should be considered. When looking from a perspective of an international comparison, the problems increase because a harmonised product coding system does not exist. This means that the results of the analysis should be considered with caution.

4 Changes in Market Performance of Polish and Hungarian Manufacturing

Assuming that in the process of competition more able firms are selected and separating this process from its results, this study evaluates and compares the capacity of product groups manufactured in Hungary and Poland to compete while looking at the results of competition in the form of changes in market shares. Thus this paper acknowledges the fundamental assumptions behind changes in market shares.

4.1 Data and Methodology

In this paper, the Comex, NewCronos, as well as German (for 1996-1998)[3], Polish and Hungarian national databases are used. Due to the limited availability of reliable data for the EU countries before 1996, the years 1996-2000 are the main point of focus within this study. The data for 1996 is estimated in case of Austria. Evaluating the changes of the Polish and Hungarian shares on the domestic and EU markets, the markets outside the EU, which are the recipients of over one-third of the export value in countries discussed here, are disregarded.

The definition of the market share indicators is straightforward. EU market share is based on the Polish and Hungarian exports to the EU in the EU apparent consumption (equation 2). The indicator of the domestic market share has been calculated as the ratio of coverage of transition country domestic sales of manufactured product groups to its apparent consumption (equation 1). A decline of this indicator means that a transition country supplies less to its home market and thus loses the domestic market share.

As a market share is a relative indicator of competitiveness, three factors influencing ability to compete as a relative indicator are used as well. These are unit labour costs, unit investment intensity and unit cash flows. The transition countries indicators are compared with the EU average.

Comparing the Polish and Hungarian indicators of competitiveness with those of EU indicators, it is worthwhile to consider whether firms from these countries really compete with each other. Products from the discussed countries differ in quality from the EU products, which is reflected in the scope of competition between the transition economies and the EU. As the measure of product similarity, and to be more precise their belonging to a quality group, a unit intermediate costs has been assumed.

Labour unit costs are derived by dividing the wages and social contribution of a given product group by its total sales. Intensity of investment (relation of investment to the sales) and cash flow (a ratio of profit sum and depreciation and revenue from sales) are the additional variables used in this paper. The former variable depicts the ability and effort to increase and upgrade the production; as in transition countries, investment is a major factor of technological change and a source

---

[3] which were not available in NewCronos database

of differentiation of production. The latter variable shows the effect of improvement in the use of resources and the creation of new resources.

4.2 Changes in Market Performance of Poland's and Hungarian Manufacturing

Market shares are used as a measure of changes in competition results. The first difficulty in assessing changes in market share is the lack of reliable statistical data, which is a result of differing times of introducing the NACE rev.1 classification in Hungary (1998) and Poland (1994). The differences between NACE and CPA classification present a second problem. A closer look at the input-output table suggests that in Poland, data are not reliable for about 15% of total number of manufacturing product groups.

In the analysed period both countries had a small share of the apparent consumption in the EU, not exceeding 1% (table 1). Their respective shares in apparent consumption were similar, amounting to 0.5%. Hungary has achieved greater progress in strengthening its position on the EU market than Poland. As far as the entire manufacturing sector is concerned, however, differences in changes between the two countries could be the result of a varying export structure and changing dynamics in particular commodity markets and not only a success in the competition for this market.

Changes in Poland's and Hungary's export market share on the EU market were the result of their manufacturers' competition with the EU and non-EU producers. The results of competing against the latter were reflected in changes in the share of Polish and Hungarian exports to the EU in the external imports of the EU. As table 1 shows both countries were successful in "pushing out" non-EU suppliers from the EU market and were taking over their market share. Such an occurrence suggests an improvement in competitiveness compared to non-EU countries. The greatest growth was experienced by Hungary. Compared to Hungary, Poland's export to the EU is much more prone to vary across time. One reason for this is the difference in product structure between goods exported by Poland as compared to Hungary.

Before 1990, domestic demand in most of the transition countries was mainly met by the domestic production. The opening of these economies significantly impacts the changes in the position of domestic supplies on the domestic market. This process has been taking place since the late 1980s and has continued into the 1990s. Between 1995 and 2000, the share of the Polish supply in the domestic markets fell quite substantially (table 1). However, in many product groups the position of Polish deliveries to the domestic market was still much higher than in the most EU countries. If the position of Polish manufacturers on the Polish market is substantial (although falling), their position on the EU market is very weak (although increasing)[4]. As far as the Polish manufacturing in the domestic and EU

[4] Only in the case of 10 out of 94 groups, the share of Polish deliveries to the EU exceeded 1% of the EU apparent consumption (the share of 13 groups range between 0.5% and 1%).

markets is concerned, divergence in trends seems to indicate that some important changes took place in the Polish manufacturing.

Table 1. Share of Hungarian and Polish exports to the EU in the EU imports and EU apparent consumption and in domestic apparent consumption (in percentage)

Type of market share	1996	1997	1998	1999	2000
Share of Hungarian manufacturing exports to the EU in the EU external imports of manufacturing	1.74	2.02	2.34	2.56	2.64
Share of Polish manufacturing exports to the EU in the EU external imports of manufacturing (a)	2.12	2.11	2.36	2.37	2.58
Share of Hungarian exports of manufacturing to the EU in the EU apparent consumption of manufacturing	0.34	0.44	0.51	0.42	0.5
Share of Polish exports of manufacturing to the EU in the EU apparent consumption of manufacturing (a)	0.29	0.30	0.35	0.36	0.47
Share of EU exports to Hungary in Hungarian apparent consumption of manufacturing	n.a.	n.a.	30.7	33.27	31.64
Share of EU exports to Poland in Polish apparent consumption of manufacturing (e)	25.4	27.4	28.3	29.7	30.4
Share of Hungarian manufacturing suppliers to the domestic market in Hungarian apparent consumption	n.a.	n.a.	50.4	45.2	38.5
Share of Polish manufacturing suppliers to the domestic market in Polish apparent consumption (b), (d) (e) F-01	65.5	62.1	60.2	58.7	58.1
Share of Polish manufacturing suppliers to the domestic market in Polish apparent consumption (a), (c) (e)	62.2	58.3	56.0	54.3	53.5

a) 93 commodity groups (without 300 and 333),
b) data on exports extracted from data on F-01, data for 90 groups (without 233,272,273,333,335)
c) data on exports extracted from SAD statistics
d) 90 commodity groups (without 233, 272, 273, 333, 335)
e) Apparent consumption concerns only the enterprises which fill F-01 forms. Production of small enterprises is not included, which causes the Polish apparent consumption to be underestimated.

Source: Own calculations

When analysing changes in the transition economies, the important arising problem is the period of analysis. Since economies of this type restructure rapidly, short-term changes can differ from those in the medium-term. When applying a medium-term approach, one faces the risk that major trends which emerged in the economy disappear.

In this paper the basic timeframe of analysis is 1996-2000, which is important to remember because the specified period precedes the moment of accession of the analysed countries to the EU. Basing on changes in the external and the domestic environment, two sub-periods were identified: from 1996 to 1998 and from 1998 onwards. In the first period, although a strong external protection of the domestic market and producers was gradually reduced, the favourable external environment and expanding imports supported dynamic economic growth. The second sub-period emerged as an effect of external turbulence. Russian and Asian crises were followed by a downswing in the EU market. The external disequilibrium, as an effect of a high current account deficit, was a basis for a tightening of the macroeconomic policy and accompanied a slowdown in the economic activity.

With respect to the changes in the share of the Polish and Hungarian manufacturing, there was a divergence in market share trends (i.e., between the EU as compared to the domestic market)[5]. While most Polish product groups managed to improve their position on the EU market, such was not the case for the domestic market. In 2000 only 33 out of 94 Polish product groups improved their position on the domestic market which they held in 1996, while 81 improved their position on the EU market. This observation prompts the question as to which markets reflect the changes in competitiveness. Are the changes in the domestic market share a more relevant indicator of changes in competitiveness than foreign market share changes? The use of EU market share as an indicator of changes in competitiveness leads to the conclusion that most Polish product groups have improved their competitiveness. However, if one assumes that the domestic market is a major indicator of changes in competitiveness, the conclusion is not the same. In the search for answers to the above-mentioned questions, both criteria to distinguish 4 parts of both transition countries manufacturing are used concurrently. The first part contains product groups, the share of which increased over a given period in both the domestic and EU markets, while in the fourth these shares declined. In case of the second and third parts, changes in the share of product groups on both markets diverged (table 2).

In the year 2000, only 27 Polish product groups recovered and strengthened their positions on both markets in comparison to 1996[6]. Eight groups lost their position on both markets. For the majority (52 groups), the trends in changes in market shares were divergent.

---

[5] Classifying product groups according to changes in market shares, it is assumed that a market position of a given product group deteriorates if the share in both markets declines by more than 5%. The remaining groups are recognised groups whose market position has improved.

[6] 7 product groups out of 27 were foodstuff, 4 – wood and paper products and 3 non-metallic mineral products

Table 2. Classification of Polish manufacturing according to changes in position on domestic and EU market (1996-1998) (by NACE rev.1)

	Increased share in EU market	Decreased share in EU market	Data not available
	I part (25 product groups)	II part (5 product groups)	
Increased share in domestic market	151, 153, 156, 157, 158, 159, 183, 201, 203, 205, 212, 221, 222, 231, 232, 245, 252, 264, 267, 332, 342, 352, 362, 364, 366	155, 265, 266, 296, 351	160
	III part (47 product groups)	IV part (9 product groups)	
Decreased sharein domestic market	152, 172, 174, 175, 176, 177, 181, 182, 191, 202, 204, 211, 241, 242, 243, 247, 251, 261, 262, 263, 268, 271, 281, 282, 287, 291, 292, 293, 294, 295, 297, 311, 312, 313, 314, 315, 316, 321, 322, 323, 331, 341, 343, 353, 354, 361, 365	154, 171, 192, 193, 244, 246, 300, 355, 363	274, 283, 284, 334
Data not available	233, 286, 335	272, 273	173, 223, 275, 285, 333

Source: Own calculations

In both sub-periods, as a result of a shift of product groups between the four distinguished parts of the Polish manufacturing, the size of these parts changed considerably. 27 out of 86 product groups for which data is available improved their position continuously throughout both sub-periods on both markets. In the case of most remaining product groups, an earlier deterioration of the position on the domestic market was offset by improvements between 1998 and 2000.

Within 8 product groups whose position deteriorated on both markets (part IV) in 2000 as compared to 1996, a continuous process of deterioration took place in the case of only 2 groups. In the case of the remaining 6 product groups, the earlier trend was altered.

The third part of the Polish manufacturing was the largest. However, 23 out of 47 groups held the same position in both sub-periods. The position of most product groups on the domestic market weakened, but only the position of three groups deteriorated entirely on the EU market.

Table 3. Classification of Polish manufacturing according to changes in position on domestic and EU market (1998-2000)

	Increased share in EU market	Decreased share in EU market	Data not available
	I part (43 product groups)	II part (4 product groups)	
Increased share in domestic market	151, 152, 153, 154, 156, 157, 158, 159, 193, 201, 202, 203, 205, 212, 221, 222, 232, 242, 245, 252, 261, 262, 263, 266, 267, 268, 281, 282, 283, 292, 294, 295, 300, 313, 314, 316, 331, 342, 343, 355, 361, 365, 366	155, 231, 244, 265	160, 334
	III part (33 product groups)	IV part (8 product groups	
Decreased Share in domestic market	171, 172, 174, 175, 176, 177, 181, 183, 191, 204, 211, 241, 243, 246, 247, 251, 271, 274, 287, 291, 293, 297, 312, 315, 322, 323, 332, 341, 351, 352, 353, 354, 364	182, 192, 264, 296, 311, 321, 362, 363	284
Data not available	173, 233, 272, 286	273, 335	223, 275, 285, 333

Source: Own calculations

The comparison of Tables 3 and 4 shows the differentiation of production orientation between the Polish and Hungarian manufacturing. Much of the product groups in Hungary were characterized by an outward orientation.

The question why the position of so many groups on the domestic market deteriorated has risen. Was it the effect of changes in international specialisation, changes in orientation (from inward to outward) or a decrease in competitiveness? As the domestic producers were more sheltered on the domestic market, it was much easier for them to hold their position there rather than on the EU market.

Table 4. Classification of Hungarian manufacturing according to changes in position on domestic and EU apparent consumption (1998-2000).

	Increased share in EU market	Decreased share in EU market	Data not available
	I part (31 product groups)	II part (10 product groups)	
Increased share in domestic market	151, 153, 155, 156, 157, 159, 172, 177, 203, 204, 221, 222, 241, 261, 262, 265, 266, 267, 271, 272, 281, 283, 287, 315, 323, 332, 342, 343, 354, 355, 363	158, 174, 182, 211, 243, 247, 263, 264, 294, 366	160, 173, 223, 275, 284, 335
	III part (43 product groups)	IV part (6 product groups)	
Decreased Share in domestic market	152, 154, 171, 175, 176, 183, 192, 193, 201, 212, 232, 244, 245, 246, 251, 252, 268, 273, 274, 282, 286, 291, 292, 293, 295, 296, 297, 300, 311, 312, 313, 314, 316, 322, 331, 341, 351, 352, 353, 361, 362, 364, 365	181, 191, 202, 205, 242, 321	285, 333, 334
Data not available	231, 233		

Source: Own calculations

5 Factors Influencing Changes in Market Performance of the Polish and Hungarian Manufacturing (Ability to Compete versus Effect of Competition)

Based on the introduced division of the Polish and Hungarian manufacturing into four parts, this section presents the relation between an average level of each of three selected factors for a given period and changes in market shares. The choice of factors was limited by the accessibility of EU data.

Firstly, since a relatively cheap and a quite well educated labour force, as well a low level of capital per employee makes labour costs commonly recognised as a major factor of transition economies' competitive advantages, relative unit labour costs (RULC) (i.e., unit labour costs (ULC) of the transition country as compared to the EU average) are evaluated. ULC, as a relation between labour costs and sales, shows whether changes in productivity are compensated by changes in wages. Whenever RULC is above one (ULC in a given transition country is higher than in the EU), the efficiency of use of the labour force in Poland and Hungary is lower than in the EU.

Secondly, intensity of gross investment in tangible goods is explored in the transition country as compared to the EU (RII). It is defined as a relation of total investment during the reference period in all tangible goods to sales. In a transition country, investment not only allows increasing production capacity but is the major source of technological progress as well. Being a major channel introducing new products and processes of innovation, it serves as an improvement in competitiveness.

The last but not the least factor of changes in competitiveness is a relative unit cash flow (RUCF). It is the most ambiguous indicator of changes in competitiveness and its interpretation is the most ambiguous. A high RUCF may, therefore, have many causes such as high profits, high depreciation rate, a low degree of assets use and implementation of a high profit-low turnover strategy. On the other hand, high profit/low turnover strategy of firms translates into RUCF decline although it results in an increase in productivity of fixed assets.

With the EU manufacturing as a backdrop, the Polish one was distinguished by two characteristics. Primarily, it had a lower capacity to compete as measured by RULC but with a much higher investment intensity and cash flow. High RUCF (when depreciation rate is considerably higher in the EU than it is in Poland) suggests that in analysed countries, assets have been used to a lower degree and the production potential was lower, or exhibited a narrower implementation of pro-market strategy than in the EU. Secondly, both the Polish and Hungarian manufacturing are characterized by a very high differentiation of the three analyzed indicators across product groups. It indicates that an intense process of structural reshaping took place, while competitive advantages were forming.

Mid-term changes hide the dynamics of short-term changes thus concealing the significant variation in time of the adjustment processes and the capacity to compete by the countries in question. If in the period of a Polish economic slowdown, especially until 1999, there was a deterioration of RULC of manufacturing, then the dynamics and the direction of changes in each of the four selected parts were different. In the mid and short-term the product groups which increased their domestic and EU market share (part I) were characterized with the smallest RULC and RUCF and the largest RII. At the same time, the groups whose situation on both markets was deteriorating (part IV) had the highest RULC. It may be surprising that product groups which were loosing the domestic market but at the same time were improving their position on the EU market (part III) were characterized by an unfavourable and worsening RULC and RII (table 5 and 6). Yet, in this part of Polish manufacturing, both indicators increasingly varied across product groups. Such a situation reflects, to a large extent, changes in the composition of this part. The slowing down of the increase in the share of most product groups of this part on the EU market confirms the deteriorating capacity to compete on the part of some groups. It can be expected that without radical changes in productivity, many groups of this part will begin loosing their capacity to compete.

Table 5. RULC, RII and RUCF of Polish manufacturing by parts in 1996-1998

Relative index	Descriptive statistics	I part	II part	III part	IV part	Overall Polish manufacturing
ULC	average	0.945	1.151	1.032	1.270	1.038
	standard deviation	0.285	0.267	0.353	0.307	0.324
Intensity of investment	average	2.172	1.810	1.997	2.088	2.032
	standard deviation	1.366	0.461	0.688	1.333	0.988
Cash flow	average	1.282	1.836	1.432	1.260	1.403
	standard deviation	0.681	1.379	0.406	0.306	0.602

I part contains product groups, the share of which increased over a given period in both the domestic and EU markets
II part contains product groups, the share of which increased in the Polish market and declined in the EU market
III part contains product groups, the share of which decreased in the Polish market and increased in the EU market
IV part contains product groups, the share of which declined in both the domestic and EU market over a given period

Source: Own estimations

The four parts, established on the bases of altering trends in the domestic and EU shares, differed not only with respect to the level of RULC but also by the capacity to adjust to the shifting conditions in the economy. In a slowdown period, product groups of part I strengthened their position on the market by lowering RULC (table 5 and 6). The situation was opposite in the case of part IV. In the analysed sub-periods, the differences in RULC between part I and IV increased from 33% to 49%. Simultaneously, within part I a process of homogenisation of RULC was taking place, as opposed to part IV. Thus a conclusion comes to mind that the level and changes in RULC reflect the changes in the capacity to compete by the Polish firms, which in turn had a high impact on the changes of their market position.

In the years 1998 – 2000, the competitiveness of the Hungarian manufacturing, measured in RULC, was substantially higher than that observed of Poland. On the other hand, however, the Polish and Hungarian manufacturing were linked by a number of common characteristics.

Table 6. RULC, RII and RUCF of Polish and Hungarian manufacturing by selected parts in 1998-2000.

Relative index	Country	Descriptive statistics	I part	II part	III part	IV part	Overall Polish manufacturing
RULC	Poland	average	0.934	1.034	1.108	1.392	1.049
		standard deviation	0.242	0.210	0.440	0.386	0.361
	Hungary	average	0.765	0.950	0.923	1.400	0.908
		standard deviation	0.237	0.328	0.421	0.779	0.460
RII	Poland	average	1.876	2.224	1.867	2.174	1.913
		standard deviation	0.806	0.941	0.701	1.699	0.800
	Hungary	average	1.662	1.339	1.719	2.027	1.670
		standard deviation	0.909	0.428	1.284	1.449	1.093
RCF	Poland	average	1.283	1.414	1.292	1.442	1.301
		standard deviation	0.414	0.555	0.608	0.825	0.545
	Hungary	average	1.662	1.339	1.719	2.027	1.670
		standard deviation	0.909	0.428	1.284	1.449	1.093

Source: Own estimations

Firstly, the differentiation of RULC, RII and RUCF across the Hungarian product groups was very high, even higher than in the case of Poland (table 6). It suggests that in both countries the process of emerging new competitive advantages is intense. Secondly, in both countries the analysed indicators differed substantially among the four parts. The competitive part (part I) was characterized by the lowest RULC and the differences between part I and IV were very large. At the same time, part I was most homogeneous in terms of RULC, although it was more varied than the EU counterpart. Its relatively small intensity of investment was accompanied by a small RUCF, which suggests that the assets were used more adequately than in the case of groups in other parts. Thirdly, it is surprising that the level of RULC is similar across the parts different in terms of sales orientation (parts II and III). The varying level of RULC was significant within part III, whose product groups increased the share in the EU market but were pushed out from the domestic market. Similarly to the Polish manufacturing, in this part of Hungarian manufacturing there were product groups of both very low and very high RULC. However, unlike the Polish part, the Hungarian was characterized by a very high but exceptionally varied intensity of investment across the product groups. Thus it seems that within part III of manufacturing in both countries there is a strong differentiation of capacity to compete. In the future, such a situation may lead to an exiting by some product groups from this part.

To identify the key factors responsible for improvements in the competitive positions, a statistical and econometric analysis was performed. At the start, the ANOVA approach was applied, the differences between values of the three indicators described above in four parts were tested. Secondly, the multinomial logit model to explain the market performance of product groups was applied.

The results of the statistical analysis presented in table 7 suggest that in the Polish and Hungarian cases, RULC are statistically different between the distinguished parts, which is not the case for RUCF and RII. However, RII have a different variance between the distinguished parts.

Applying the Tukey's Multiple Comparison Test (to test differences between means of particular two groups) and the Dunn's Multiple Comparison Test (to test differences between medians of particular two groups), it was found that the statistically significant differences exist only between means and medians of relative unit labour costs in part I and IV. Such was the case both for Polish and Hungarian manufacturing. Even though the number of groups in the sample in part IV was rather small (in the case of Poland it consisted of only 9 observations, in the case of Hungary, 6), the power of the test showing significant statistical difference between the means of relative unit labour costs in parts I and IV was high enough to treat these results as reliable (it was more than 95 % in the Polish case and around 90% in the Hungarian case).

Table 7. Test for statistical significance of relative ULC, investment intensity and cash flows of Polish and Hungarian manufacturing between distinguish parts in 1998-2000 (*p* values in appropriate test).

Country	Index	Test for statistical significance of difference between: Variances a)	Means b)	Medians c)
		in four distinguish parts		
Poland	RULC	0.0000	0.0065	0.0095
	RII	0.0000	0.7418	0.8710
	RUCF	0.0001	0.8709	0.9420
Hungary	RULC	0.0002	0.0837	0.0423
	RII	0.0036	0.6422	0.9261
	RUCF	0.6407	0.4839	0.4081

a) Difference in variances tested by corrected Bartlett's statistics.
b) Difference in means tested by F statistics from modified ANOVA for unequal sample sizes.
c) Difference in medians tested by Kruskal-Wallis ANOVA.
Source: Own estimations

Furthermore, the multinomial logit model to explain market performance of product groups was applied. As the endogenous variable a variable classifying a given product group in a particular part of the Polish and Hungarian manufacturing was chosen. Part IV of manufacturing in both countries (diminishing shares in both domestic and EU markets) was classified as base category and labelled "0". Hence, part I (an improved position on both domestic and EU markets) was consistently labelled "3". Values of relative indicators for a given product group were chosen as a vector of exogenous variables (**x**). The multinomial logit model, where there are probabilities that i^{th} product group falls into a distinguished j^{th} category, was specified by equation (3) and (4) as follows:

$$P_{ij} = \frac{\exp\{\mathbf{x}_i'\beta_j\}}{1+\sum_{k=1}^{3}\exp\{\mathbf{x}_i'\beta_k\}} \text{ for } j=1,2,3 \qquad (3)$$

and

$$P_{i0} = \frac{1}{1+\sum_{k=1}^{3}\exp\{\mathbf{x}_i'\beta_k\}} \qquad (4)$$

For the vector of exogenous variables (**x**), three discussed factors potentially responsible for the competitive position: RULC, RII and RUCF have been chosen. The results of the multinomial logit model estimation are shown in Table 8.

Table 8. Results of the multinomial logit estimation for probability of including given product group to the particular part of Polish and Hungarian manufacturing according to the value of RULC, RII and RUCF in 1998-2000 (number of product groups in both countries 176).

Change from 4th to j-th part	Estimation results	Constant	RULC	RII	RUCF
1 part	Coefficient	5.09	-2.43	-0.17	-0.32
	t-value	3.77	-2.54	-0.70	-1.07
2 part	Coefficient	2.81	-1.87	-0.46	-0.01
	t-value	1.50	-1.31	-1.13	-0.03
3 part	Coefficient	3.08	-1.14	-0.19	0.11
	t-value	2.50	-1.35	-0.81	0.41
	log-likelihood = -191.80, AIC = 407.61, AIC/n = 2.32				

Source: Own estimations

The results confirm the outcomes previously obtained in the statistical analysis. The only statistically significant factor able to explain the market performance of a given product group, especially showing a shift from the fourth (worst) to first (best) performing part of manufacturing, was relative unit labour costs. The results indicate that decimal decline in the index for a given product group would increase the probability odds of shifting this product group from part IV (worst performing) to part I (best one) by 0.24. In all equations (for each part), negative coefficients show that the decline in RULC increase probability odds of achiving a better market position in a given product group. In the estimated multinomial logit model coefficients for both RII and RUCF were not statistically significant, and their sign could not be clearly interpreted.

The performed analyses suggest that the basis for the increase in market shares of both countries was the improvement in capacity to compete measured by the level of RULC and its changes.

6 Do Polish and Hungarian Product Groups Compete with the EU Ones?

If many Polish and Hungarian product groups increased their share in the EU market, it needs to be explored in which of the EU market segments they would exert the strongest competitive pressure quality-wise. In this section, quality as an element of product differentiation is treated, and its relevance to competition is explored.

In the literature, product differentiation is analysed from both the demand and supply side. On the demand side, product differentiation presupposes a differentiated market demand. On the supply side, different varieties of the same products may be associated with identical technologies. Demand differentiation and differentiation with regard to production technology are associated with the subdivision of product differentiation into vertical (quality) and horizontal differentiation. The first one is linked to difference in prices and technology, the second to equal prices and identical technologies. In the case of international division of labour along the spectrum of vertical differentiation, the transition countries are positioned at the lower end of quality range, while the EU countries are at the higher end. Therefore, the distance between both groups of countries along the quality spectrum will determine the extent to which they are competitors. In a context dynamic due to economic development, the changes in demand and production will induce changes in specialisation with regard to quality level of commodity groups. Based upon such an observation, one would expect transition countries to move up the quality ladder.

This paper assumes that relative unit intermediate costs (RUIC) indicate differences in quality of products. A higher share of input and higher intensity of use of external services indicates a higher quality of products. Differences in RUIC imply differences in quality of product groups between countries.

To support the hypothesis that RUIC is a measure to assess product quality, RUIC has been compared with relative unit export value (RUEV) in Hungary and Poland (ratio to EU mean). The comparison supports the hypothesis. Between 1998 and 2000, both values were similar in the case of Hungary, while in Poland the differences between them were approaching 17% (RUIC was 0.81 while RUEV – 0.67). Such differences could have resulted from a fact that RUIC are calculated for the entire production, both for export and local sale, while RUEV is measured for export to the EU. In Poland, the majority of production is done on the domestic market; these numbers are higher than in Hungary. Besides, the Polish manufacturing sector includes many firms which present a very low level of competitiveness and do not export as well as firms which produce high quality products and have a high level of competitiveness and export dynamically (Wziątek-Kubiak 2001). Such a situation is most certainly reflected in the differences between RUEV and RUIC in the Polish manufacturing. At the same time, neither RUEV nor RUIC changed significantly in the years 1996-2000, while the direction in their changes was the same.

Furthermore, the proportions between the two indicators were similar for the competitive groups (part I) and non-competitive groups (part IV) in both countries. For the former, both numbers were comparatively highest, while for the latter, the lowest. Similarly, the competitive groups and the increasing pressure of competitiveness by the EU products on both markets were characterized by a rather high (although usually lower than in the EU) quality of sold goods. The products pushed out from the EU market were of the lowest quality.

Table 9. RUIC of Polish and Hungarian manufacturing by parts during 1996-2000

Country	Period	Descriptive statistics	I part	II part	III part	IV part	Overall Polish manufacturing
Poland	1996-2000	average	0.831	0.895	0.804	0.721	0.809
		standard deviation	0.122	0.080	0.110	0.085	0.115
	1996-1998	average	0.807	0.881	0.810	0.775	0.808
		standard deviation	0.144	0.096	0.101	0.071	0.114
	1998-2000	average	0.816	0.913	0.808	0.740	0.808
		standard deviation	0.115	0.220	0.113	0.088	0.123
Hungary	1998-2000	average	1.00	0.962	0.923	0.881	0.971
		standard deviation	0.079	0.099	0.177	0.159	0.122

Source: Own estimations

Table 9 shows that there were rather substantial differences in the quality range between the product groups of Poland as compared to Hungary and the EU. On the other hand, the table depicts quite few differences between the Hungarian and the EU product groups. The competitive Hungarian groups (part I) were characterized by a rather high level of quality close to the EU level. This level was significantly higher than in the Polish competitive groups. The increased homogeneity of this part of the Hungarian manufacturing, as compared to the Polish manufacturing, shows that within the Polish part one could find groups of a high quality level.

The differences between the quality of Polish and Hungarian export products is partially a result of a lower presence of foreign capital in the Polish manufacturing and a lower export orientation than in Hungary and partially a result of the differences in the export structure. Nonetheless, the Polish product groups exerted less competition pressure on the EU producers of high quality products than did the Hungarian product groups.

7 Conclusions

To evaluate changes in the competitiveness of Hungarian and Polish manufacturing, competitiveness in this paper is derived from the process of competition, rivalry between transition economies' and foreign companies on both domestic and the EU markets.

Comparing the ability to compete (measured by relative unit labour cost, relative unit investment intensity and relative unit cash flow) with the effect of competition (changes in market shares), the paper raised the issue of relevance of changes in market shares of transition economies as a measure of changes in their competitiveness. Based on criteria of changes in trends in both the domestic and the EU market share, four parts of manufacturing of both transition economies were selected; similarly, a level and changes in three factors showing ability to compete of products of each part were evaluated. The analysis shows that in the period from 1998 to 2000, a considerable increase in the number of product groups of Polish manufacturing took place when compared to that seen between 1996 and 1998. The growing number of Polish manufacturing groups has been increasing the competitive pressure on the EU market. Secondly, among three selected factors changes in market shares of both transition economies, unit labour costs played the major role. Thirdly, the analysis of a relative unit intermediate costs and relative unit export value reveals that on the EU market the Polish products surpassed in competition mainly the low quality EU and non-EU products, while the Hungarian supassed the high quality products as well. In other words, changes in Polish manufacturing in market shares were the result of high and increasing competitiveness of low quality products, while Hungarian changes were the result of high quality changes as well. However, the above differences between these two transition economies do not undermine the conclusion that unit labour costs have been the main factor responsible for changes in competitive advantages of both countries.

References

Balassa, B. (1989), Comparative Advantage, Trade Policy and Economic Development, New York, Harvester Wheatshcaf.

Branson, W. H. (1980), Trends in United State, International Trade and Investment, in: Feldstein,M.,ed., *The American Economy in Transition*, Chicago, The University of Chicago Press.

Casson , M., ed., (1999), *International Competitiveness*, London, Routledge.

Competitiveness and its Measurement, (1990), *Forward Strategy 1991-1993*, IDB, Northern Ireland.

Feenstra, R. C., ed., (1989), *Introduction, in Trade Policies for International Competitiveness*, Chicago, The University of Chicago Press.

Frischtak, C., (1999), Manufacturing, Competitiveness: Concept, Measurement Policies, in F. Sercovich, Ch.-Y. Ahn, C. Frischtak, C., Mrak, M., Huegge, H., Peres, W., Wangwe, S.,ed., *Competition and the World Economy UNIDO*, Cheltenham, Edward Elgar.

Galli, G., Pelkmans, J., (2000), *Regulatory Reform and Competitiveness in Europe*, vol. 2, Cheltenham, Edward Elgar.

Gomory, R..E., Baumol, W. J., (2000), *Global Trade and Conflicting National Interests*, Cambridge, Massachusetts, London, England, The MIT Press.

Hall, R., Smith, A., Tsoukalis, L., ed., (2001), *Competitiveness and Cohesion in EU* Policies, Oxford, Oxford University Press.

Howell, D. C., (1995), *Fundamental Statistics for the Behavioural Sciences*, Belmont, California, Duxbury Press.

Kirzner, I., (2000), Competition and the market process some doctrinal milestones, in Krafft, J., ed., *The Process Competition*, Chaltenham, Edward Elgar.

Maddala, G. S., (1983), *Limited Dependent and Qualitative Variables in Econometrics*, New York, Cambridge University Press.

Meeusen, W., Rayp, G., (2000), Patents and Trademarks as Indication of International Competitiveness, in P. Buigues,P., Jacquemin, A., and Marchipont, J..F., ed., *Competitiveness and Value of Intangible Assets*, Cheltenham, Edwards Elgar.

Peng, M. W., (2000), *Business Strategies in Transition Economies*, London, IBS International Business Series.

Porter, M. E., (1986), *Competition in Global Industries*, Harvard Business School Press, Boston.

Porter, M. E., (1990), *The Competitive Advantage of Nations*, The Macmillan Press Ltd, Houndmills.

Raynauld, A., Vidal, J. P., (1998), Labour Standards and International Competitiveness. A Comparative Analysis of Developing and Industrialized Countries, Cheltenham, Edward Elgar.

Wziątek-Kubiak, A., (2001), Restrukturyzacja sektora eksportowego, in Maczynska, E., *Procesy restrukturyzacji dużych przedsiębiorstw w okresie transformacji*, Warszawa, DiG.

Comment on: Changes in Competitive Advantages of Transition Economies: Measurement and Factors

Dieter Schumacher

The paper presents changes in market shares (i) on the EU market and (ii) on the domestic market as a measure of changes in competitiveness of transition countries and applies figures for Poland and Hungary. The main findings are

- in most product groups the share of Polish and Hungarian supplies in the EU market as well as the domestic market increased,
- in Poland this is true mainly for low-quality products, in Hungary for high-quality products as well,
- unit labour costs played the major role as a cause of these changes among several factors considered in the analysis.

It is difficult, indeed, to assess the overall competitiveness of a national economy. The notion of "competitiveness" is taken from the analysis of individual enterprises and, in the above paper as well as in many other studies, microeconomic indicators such as market shares or unit labour costs are applied at the level of the overall economy. A number of economists, however, think that the notion of competitiveness should not be applied at all at the economy-wide level (e.g., Paul Krugman (1994) on competitiveness as a dangerous obsession). Other economists take a different view on the competitiveness of an economy and argue that it is not only the ability to sell which is important but also the ability to earn. For example, the US President's Commission on Industrial Competitiveness (1985, p. 7) defines the following: "Competitiveness for a nation is the degree to which it can, under free and fair market conditions, produce goods and services that meet the test of international markets while simultaneously maintaining and expanding the real income of citizens." Similar definitions are used by the US Competitiveness Policy Council (e.g., 1994) and are in line with the regular reporting of a number of German research institutes on the technological performance of the German economy commissioned by the Federal Ministry of Education and Research (see Belitz, Schumacher, Straßberger and Trabold 1998 or Federal Ministry of Education and Research 2002).

The decisive question is therefore not how high the world market shares are and how they change, but whether in the long-term an economy can maintain as high a level of real income as possible and achieve as high an increase in income as possible. Taking this view, indicators such as GDP per capita or labour productivity are proposed to describe the market success of a country and investment in human capital, R&D expenditure and investment in physical capital are suggested as important factors behind that success. Against this background, it is not the share in foreign or domestic markets which counts but the structure of production and exports concentrating more on high-tech, high-quality, high-price goods than low-tech, low-quality, low-price goods.

Following international trade theory the aim is not to export as much as possible, the aim of exports is to finance the import of goods which can be domestically produced only at a higher price. A higher share of exports in foreign markets is, therefore, accompanied by a higher share of imports on the domestic market (which should not be interpreted as declining competitiveness). And it is also important to export goods at the highest possible price in order to achieve high terms of trade and, thus, a large increase of real income arising from the international division of labour. Decreasing unit labour costs give a higher price competitiveness to a country. On the other hand, however, it means a deterioration of the terms of trade and, hence, a smaller contribution of foreign trade to real income.

Taking a broader view and applying indicators such as those mentioned above to transition countries we would also conclude that Hungary and Poland improved their competitiveness in the second half of the 1990's. In the Table, summarising statistics are compiled on GDP and on the structural position of the two countries in manufacturing trade of the EU(15). After 1995, the GDP per capita of Poland and Hungary grew much faster than the EU average. And the exports of both countries increased in particular in human-capital intensive, high-tech goods changing the pattern of supply from labour-intensive consumption goods to more human-capital intensive investment goods and consumer durables. These exports are to a large extent due to foreign direct investment in the motor vehicles, electrical and general machinery industries. In these sectors especially German firms very quickly integrated the transition countries in central and eastern Europe into their intra-firm division of labour. The expenditure on R&D in Poland and Hungary is considerably lower than the average level of the old EU countries, whereas their expenditure on education is in line with the OECD average (for more details see Krawczyk, Frietsch and Schumacher 2002).

As such, our assessment of the economic success of Poland and Hungary in the 1990's is by and large positive as in the paper by Wziątek-Kubiak and Winek, however, for different reasons. Taking market shares as an indicator an increase for some countries always implies a decrease for other countries. Do the old EU countries become less competitive when transition countries increase their market shares? For the German economy, for instance, you may even argue that it became more competitive due to higher imports of cheaper intermediate goods from transition countries. The point is that increasing international trade is not a zero-sum game but a positive-sum game, assuming the ability to structurally adjust all countries gain, at least with regard to allocative efficiency. Thus, competition among national economies differs from competition among firms. The further catching-up process in transition economies in terms of real income requires above-average growth rates and also implies additional integration into the world economy and, hence, increasing shares of both their exports on foreign markets and their imports on the domestic market.

Table 1. Indicators of the competitive position of Poland and Hungary, 1995 and 2002

	Poland		Hungary	
	1995	**2002**	**1995**	**2002**
GDP per capita, EU(15) = 100, at PPP	37	42	45	54
Relative share in imports of EU(15) [1)]				
R&D-intensive goods	-71	-29	-11	18
Cutting-edge technology	-178	-119	-75	9
Advanced technology	-47	-2	7	23
Non R&D-intensive goods	50	34	12	-39
Total manufacturing goods	0	0	0	0
Revealed comparative advantage in trade with EU(15) [2)]				
R&D-intensive goods	-68	-30	-15	10
Cutting-edge technology	-121	-75	-43	17
Advanced technology	-60	-20	-9	7
Non R&D-intensive goods	47	35	18	-23
Total manufacturing goods	0	0	0	0

[1)] 100*ln(mi / Mi), mi is the share of commodity group i in EU(15) imports from Poland or Hungary, respectively,Mi is the share of commodity group i in total imports of EU(15). A positive (negative) value indicates that the share of that commodity group in imports from Poland or Hungary is larger (smaller) than in total EU imports.
[2)] 100*ln(mi / xi), mi and xi are the share of commodity group i in EU(15) imports and exports in trade with Poland or Hungary, respectively. A positive (negative) value indicates that the share of that commodity group in imports from Poland or Hungary is larger (smaller) than in exports to Poland or Hungary.

Source: DIW Foreign Trade Data. – OECD, National Accounts of OECD Countries, Paris 2005. – Own calculations.

References

Belitz, H., D. Schumacher, F. Straßberger and H. Trabold (1998), The Long-Term Technological Strength of the German Economy, DIW Berlin.

Competitiveness Policy Council (1994), Promoting Long-Term Prosperity. Third Report to the President and Congress, U.S. Government Printing Office, Washington, D.C.

Federal Ministry of Education and Research (2002), Germany's Technological Performance 2001, Bonn.

Krawczyk, O., R. Frietsch and D. Schumacher (2002), Indikatorenbericht zur technologischen Leistungsfähigkeit Deutschlands 2000/2001. Aufhol-Länder im weltweiten Technologiewettbewerb, Gutachten im Auftrag des BMBF, Hannover/ Berlin/ Karlsruhe.

Krugman, P. (1994), Competitiveness: A Dangerous Obsession, in: Foreign Affairs, Vol. 73, No. 2, pp. 28 – 44.

President's Commission on Industrial Competitiveness (1985), Global Competition. The New Reality, Vol. I and II, U.S. Government Printing Office, Washington, D.C.

EU Export Specialization Patterns in Selected Accession Countries

Dora Borbély[1]

Contents

1 Introduction 38
2 Theoretical Background 39
3 Empirical Analysis 40
3.1 Aggregated Exports of Three Accession Countries to the EU15 40
3.2 Analysing R&D Expenditure 44
3.3 Analysing Specialization Patterns in Manufacturing Exports 48
4 Conclusion and Future Research 59
Annex 1 60
Annex 2 64
Annex 3 66
Annex 4 69
References 71

[1] EIIW Working Paper No. 116. This research is part of the project "Changes in Industrial Competitiveness as a Factor of Integration: Identifying Challenges of the Enlarged Single European Market" in the EU 5th Framework Programme (Contract No. HPSE-CT-2002-00148). The author is solely responsible for the contents, which might not represent the opinion of the Community. The Community is not responsible for any use that might be made of data appearing in this publication. For valuable comments the author is grateful to Paul J.J. Welfens.

1 Introduction

In the last few decades, integration of goods, capital and financial markets has proceeded on a global scale. In particular, international trade and foreign investment flows have increased enormously since the second half of the eighties. Globalisation and internationalisation have been driven by lower trade barriers and transportation costs, reduced restrictions on FDI and improvements in communication technologies, facilitating the utilisation of scale economies and a deeper division of labour. These impulses are expected to be part of the driving forces for structural changes in the economy, and for changes in competitiveness. Changes in relative factor prices and technological upgrading will also be crucial.

Western Europe, in particular, faces a much tougher competitive environment, mainly due to the opening-up of Eastern Europe and to some extent to the emergence of Asian competitors. Since the theoretical literature does not present a consistent picture of evidence on the outcome of internalisation and globalisation on specialization patterns, this empirical paper aims to draw first conclusions on structural change in the export industry for three Eastern European countries: Hungary, Poland and the Czech Republic at a disaggregated level.

One may anticipate accelerated structural change in eastern European accession countries in the late 1990s as the impulses from system transformation and from anticipated EU membership have stimulated a dynamic adjustment process, including a shift in specializations in particular countries. These impulses included trade liberalization and rising FDI inflows from EU countries. This process should be accompanied by shifts in revealed comparative advantage. Moreover, it is widely accepted that the regional trade orientation of eastern European countries shifted strongly towards the EU in the 1990s. It is therefore clear that major changes in sectoral specialization in Western Europe will reflect major changes in EU accession countries.

As this analysis looks into Hungary, Poland and the Czech Republic in the 1990s it is clear that different developments in the respective country's sectoral R&D expenditure can affect specialization patterns. In order to ascertain whether specialization has taken place in low, middle or high technology sectors, this paper aims to find a connection between R&D expenditure and three indicators measuring foreign trade performance at a disaggregated sectoral level: Trade Coverage Index, Revealed Comparative Advantage and the Grubel-Lloyd Index for Intra-Industry Trade.

In section 2 the paper looks at the theoretical background of structural change in open economies. The statistical analysis is done in section 3 on the basis of NACE 2-digit (partially NACE 3-digit) level of aggregation. Three indicators mentioned above are being calculated to analyze the performance of three accession countries in their trade with the EU15. Finally, section 4 concludes and provides suggestions for further complementary research.

2 Theoretical Background

The "Traditional Trade Theory" emphasizes the role of physical geography and endowments of natural resources when explaining foreign trade structures. According to Ricardo (1817), locational patterns are driven by relative differences in technology observed as differences in relative production costs termed "comparative advantage". According to the Heckscher-Ohlin model (Heckscher 1949, Ohlin 1933) uneven spatial distribution of production – specialization – emerges, if countries display pronounced differences in factor endowments. The "Traditional Trade Theory" predicts that a general economic opening up induces activities to concentrate in countries with matching comparative advantages. However, these theories do not explain why IIT takes place: A large part of trade comprises the exchange of differentiated goods that fall into the same product category and takes place between industrialised countries with similar factor endowments and production technologies.

"New Trade Theory" models include scale economies, product differentiation (preference variety) and imperfect competition as main ingredients to explain IIT. The major conclusion of the "New Trade Theory" is that the share of IIT in total trade is opposed to the share of inter-industry trade, and is positively related to the similarities of demand and production characteristics (Love of Variety Approach). Demand characteristics and market structure thus play a crucial role in these kinds of models. More modern "New Trade Theory" models distinguish further between horizontal and vertical product differentiation (Greenaway, Hine and Milner 1995). The "New Trade Theory" is, however, no complete theory of economic geography. One question remains unanswered: Why can ex-ante similar countries develop divergent production and trade structures? The "New Economic Geography" helps to understand such real world developments.

The literature of the "New Economic Geography" adds transportation costs and their implications for specialization patterns to "New Trade Theory" models (Krugman and Venables 1995). The "New Economic Geography" focuses particularly on two main agglomeration mechanisms: (1) interregional and inter-sectoral labour mobility (Krugman 1991, Puga 1998) and (2) mobility of firms demanding intermediate products (Venables 1996). These two factors lead to an endogenous differentiation process of initially similar regions. "New Economic Geography" models tend to show that at early stages of integration, concentration forces dominate and due to reduced trade costs industry tends to cluster, but further integration promotes a re-dispersion of industries towards the periphery due to lower factor costs. Furthermore, Venables (1998) points out - investigating the relationship between agglomeration and specialization within the increasing returns to scale activity - that the resulting division between the core region and the periphery is not unique and is not necessary in line with comparative advantages. The more mature the product, the less important are fixed costs of production e.g. R&D expenditure, and the greater is the scale of production (Brülhard 1995). A country that has the most beneficial endowments for fixed costs, e.g. much skilled labour and equipment, will attract production of new goods. Old goods will be produced where factor endowment is favourable with respect to variable costs of production, such as a low share of skilled labour.

To summarize, what does the theory tell us about the EU export specialization patterns of accession countries? "Traditional Trade Theory" predicts that the accession countries will export mainly labour and possibly resource intensive goods, because therein lies their initial comparative advantage. The "New Trade Theory" indicates that the extent of intra-industry trade in accession countries will depend on country characteristics, such as demand characteristics. Thus the share of IIT will be high, if demand characteristics place emphasis on product differentiation indicating a high level of economic integration of the respective country. The "New Economic Geography" shows that for mature products the importance of fixed costs e.g. R&D expenditure is less relevant, so that mature products tend to be produced and exported by countries richly endowed with skilled workers and physical capital, e.g. the EU15. "Old" products, referring to non-innovative products, will therefore be rather exported by the accession countries. The following empirical analysis aims to test these assumptions by calculating simple indicators to shed some light on the foreign trade specialization patterns of some accession countries as compared to the EU15.

3 Empirical Analysis

In this paper we use three different indicators, the *Trade Coverage Index*, the *Revealed Comparative Advantage Index* and the *Grubel-Lloyd Index of Intra-Industry Trade* to measure foreign trade performance - at a disaggregated level - of three accession countries, Poland, the Czech Republic and Hungary, towards the current EU15 countries. We will, however, first take a look at aggregated exports.

3.1 Aggregated Exports of Three Accession Countries to the EU15

To give an insight into the development of exports, we first take a look at the export flows at an aggregated level[2]. Therefore we use the SITC rev.3. Classification (Table 1).

Throughout the paper, only that part of total manufacturing exports (imports) of the three accession countries considered is dealt with, which is imported (exported) by the EU15. Since we are interested in structural change especially compared to the structure of the economies in the EU15, these variables seem to be appropriate to explain the main findings. Besides, trade with the EU15 comprises the greatest part of trade activities in these countries. In the year 2001 export ratios of EU exports to total exports amounted for 69.2% in Poland, 68.9% in the Czech Republic, and 74.3 % in Hungary. The ratio of imports stemming from the EU15

[2] Data comes from the COMEX-Database of the European Commission.

was a bit lower with 61.4% in Poland, 61.8% in the Czech Republic, and 57.8% in Hungary.[3]

Table 1. SITC rev. 3. Classification

CODE	CONTENT
0	Food and live animals
1	Beverages and Tobacco
2	Crude Materials, Excluding Fuels
3	Mineral Fuels etc.
4	Animal, Vegetable oil and fat
5	Chemicals
6	Basic Manufactures
7	Machines, Transport Equipment
8	Miscellaneous Manufactures Goods
9	Goods not classified by kind

Figure 1 shows the logarithm of the exports of Hungary, Poland and the Czech Republic to the EU15 in the years 1993 and 2001, the first and last year of our observation period. The use of logarithms allows us to compare the relative volumes between the countries rather easily.

The first striking result is that exports in the categories "beverages and tobacco" (1) and "animal, vegetable oil and fat" (4) are relatively low compared to the categories "basic manufactures" (6), "machines and transport equipment" (7) and "miscellaneous manufactured goods" (8). Manufacturing thus seems to be one of the main export ingredients of the accession countries to the EU15.

Comparing the years 1993 and 2001 seems to show similar results for all three countries. Export volumes to the EU15 were considerably higher in 2001 than in 1993, except for "animal and vegetable oils and fats" (4), where volumes have hardly changed. Contrasting the export flows of the two years does not, however, say anything about the development of exports in the years between, which this paper will now turn to. In order to reveal specialization patterns in the export structure it is important to outline the relative shares of the exports of each category to total (EU15) exports. Figures 2-4 show the respective shares for the three accession countries on a yearly average for the period 1992-2001.

The results are quite clear: In all three countries, exports to the EU15 are dominated by "Machines and Transport Equipment" (7). This holds especially for Hungary, where category 7 makes up more than 60% of total exports to the EU. In Poland and the Czech Republic "Basic Manufactures" (6) and "Miscellaneous Manufactured Goods" (8) also play an important role. In Poland the shares of these three branches are relatively equally distributed with roughly 25-30 % respectively. In the Czech Republic, the importance of categories 6 and 8 has decreased continuously since 1996. In Hungary this has been the case since 1995.

[3] See Borbély and Gern (2003)

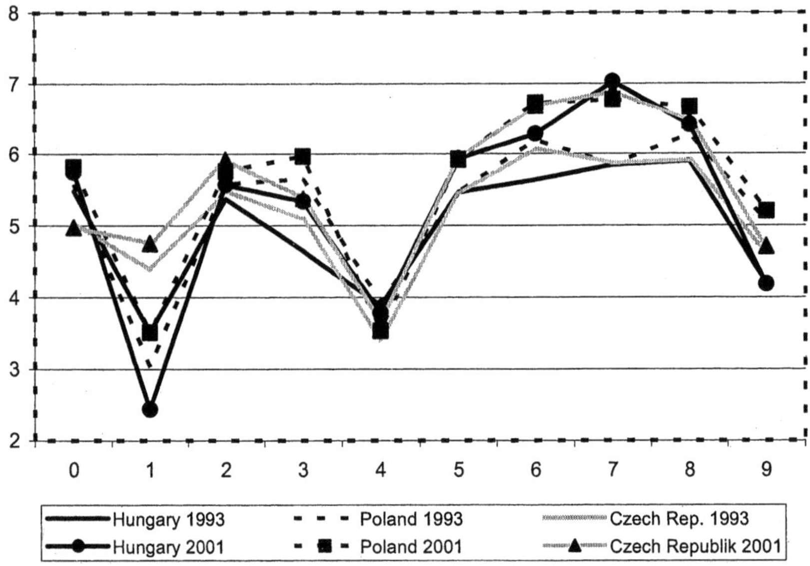

Fig. 1. Logarithm of Exports to the EU15 in the 9 main SITC rev.3. categories

Machines and Manufacturing are the single most important export branches for these countries. All the other branches remained mostly under 10% in the initial period and no longer exceed 5 % in the second half of the 1990s. The outstanding role of manufacturing in the export structure of the accession countries is not surprising. This is in line with the outcome of the "Traditional Trade Theory" and the "New Economic Geography" models, if we assume that many of the manufactured goods are labour intensive in production and do not require high endowments in capital, skilled work, technology, or R&D activities.[4]

However, within the branch of manufacturing, there are, as a matter of course, great differences in the intensity of inputs required. In the next step, we will focus solely on manufacturing in great detail and attempt to identify specialization or dispersion patterns among the countries. We therefore use foreign trade data on manufacturing at a 3-digit level.[5]

[4] If the parent company – e.g. in the computer sector - gives a blueprint of a computer to a foreign subsidiary in eastern Europe, the product can be a medium technology product but it nevertheless can be produced by low skilled workers using a sophisticated electronic assembly line.

[5] Data is extracted from the COMEX database of the European Commission. Only trade data between the accession countries and the EU15, and intra-EU trade data are used.

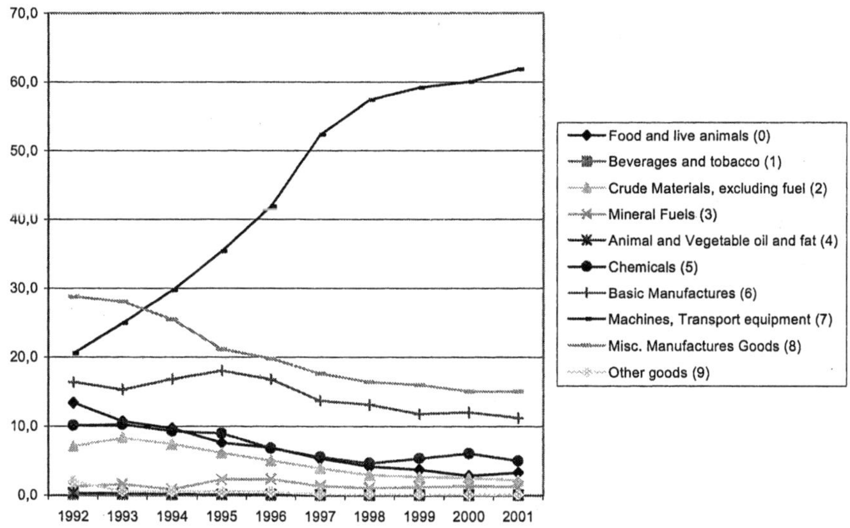

Fig. 2. Shares of branches in exports to the EU-15 in Hungary

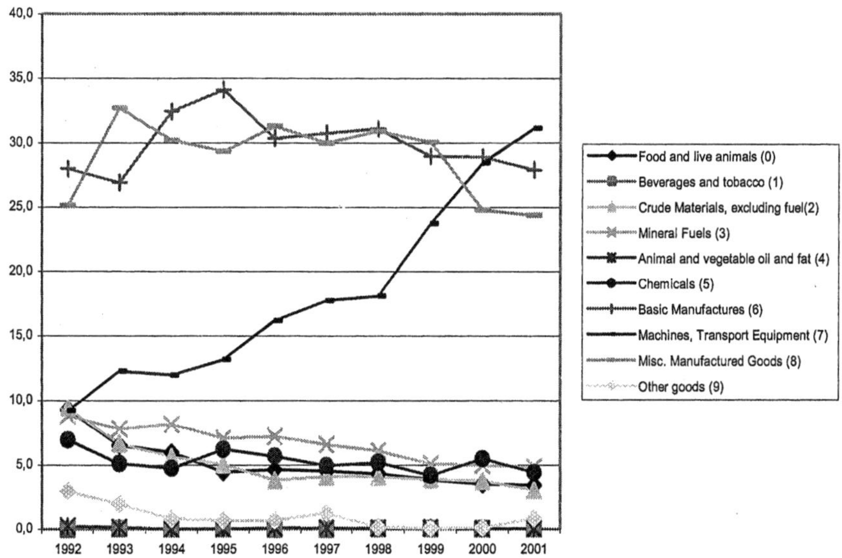

Fig. 3. Shares of branches in exports to the EU-15 in Poland

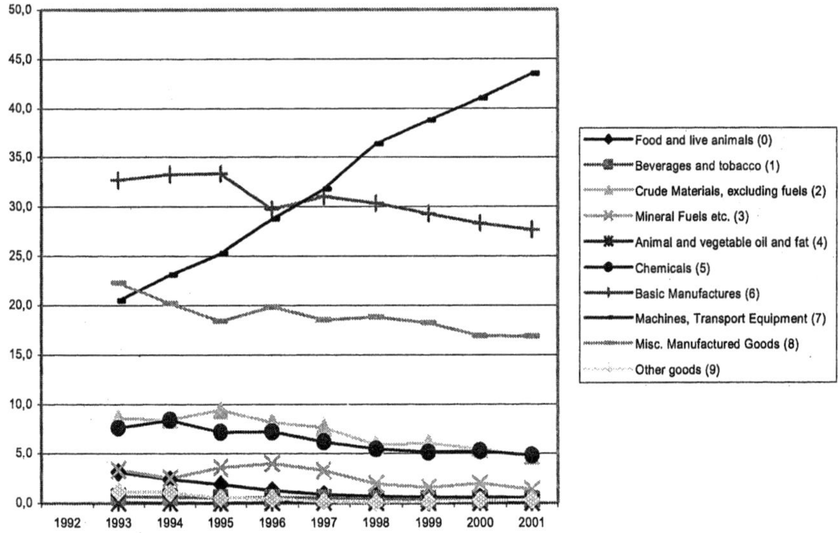

Fig. 4. Shares of branches in exports to the EU-15 in the Czech Republic

3.2 Analysing R&D Expenditure

Different measures can be applied to categorize product groups according to their technology level. The most commonly used distinction is between low, medium (medium-low and medium-high) and high technology industries. This distinction is, however, not detailed enough for our purposes. In the following we will use R&D expenditure, which is available at a more disaggregated level, as a proxy for technology intensity.

According to the Schumpeterian point of view, technology intensity of goods plays an important role in specialization patterns. Schumpeterian goods – which are defined as technology intensive goods – can be divided into two categories: immobile Schumpeterian goods require high R&D activities and R&D and production must be located together at the same geographical location. On the contrary, for mobile Schumpeterian goods production and R&D activity can be located at different places. In the course of catching up the question arises, in the exportation of what kinds of goods do accession countries gain more comparative advantage and in the exportation of what kind of goods do they lose comparative advantage? According to the "climbing-up-the-ladder-strategy", technological catching-up first takes place in low-tech industries. Under the assumption that these are likely to be more labour-intensive and less capital-intensive industrial sectors, the outcome is consistent with the classical Heckscher-Ohlin model. Countries will specialise in labour-intensive goods, with the result that catching up first takes place in those industries. As a result we should observe that the EU15 specialize more in R&D and human capital- intensive goods exportation, whereas the accession countries specialize in labour-intensive goods exportation. In the course of integration, however, accession countries should experience a rise in exports in the low and middle technology fields and in the later stages of integration also of higher technology products.

Here it is assumed that technology and R&D intensity are positively correlated. The two variables are of course no perfect substitutes, however, for the purpose of this analysis they can be used as alternatives. Other possible measures for technology intensity would be the use of data on capital stock or total factor productivity. However, here we face severe data availability problems for the accession countries.[6]

Figures 5, 6 and 7 show the R&D intensity in different industrial sectors for Poland, the Czech Republic and Hungary. Figure 8 represents the according figures for Germany, as an example of the current EU15 countries.

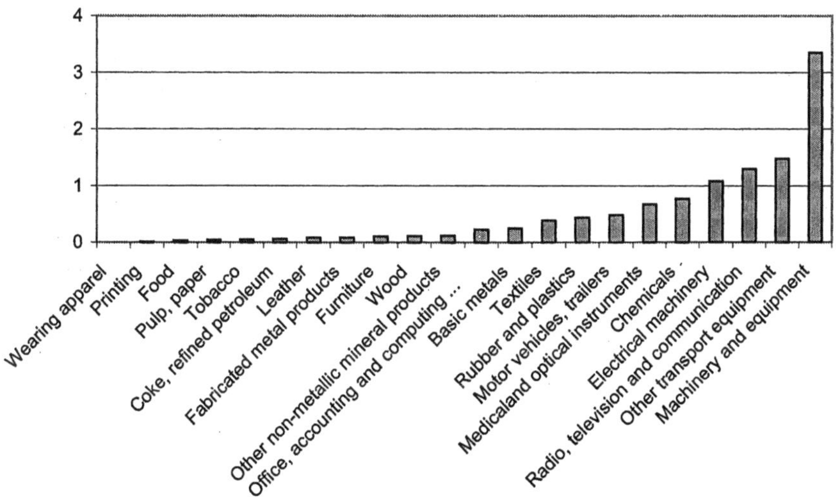

Fig. 5. R&D intensity in Poland, average of 1995-2000, in %

[6] For many accession countries – in particular for Poland –, also FDI and imports of goods can be seen as main sources of technology spill-over. Analysing FDI should be a target for future research. Imports as a source of technology are, however, very hard to measure.

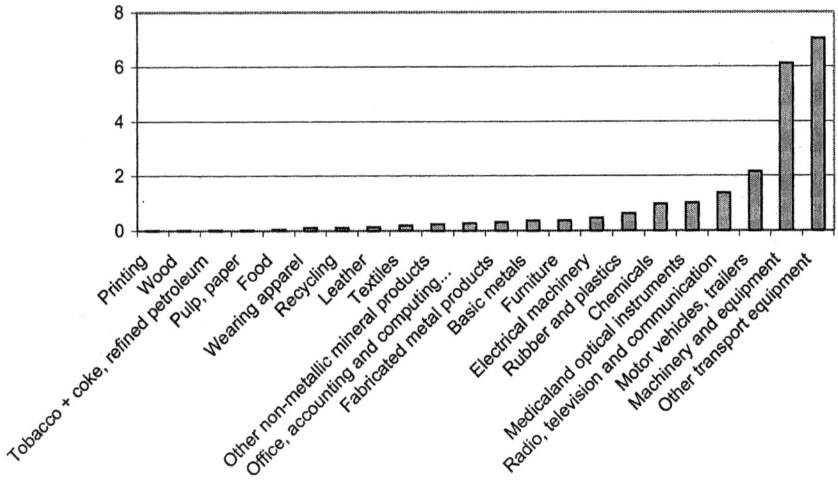

Fig. 6. R&D intensity in the Czech Republic, average of 1997-2000, in %

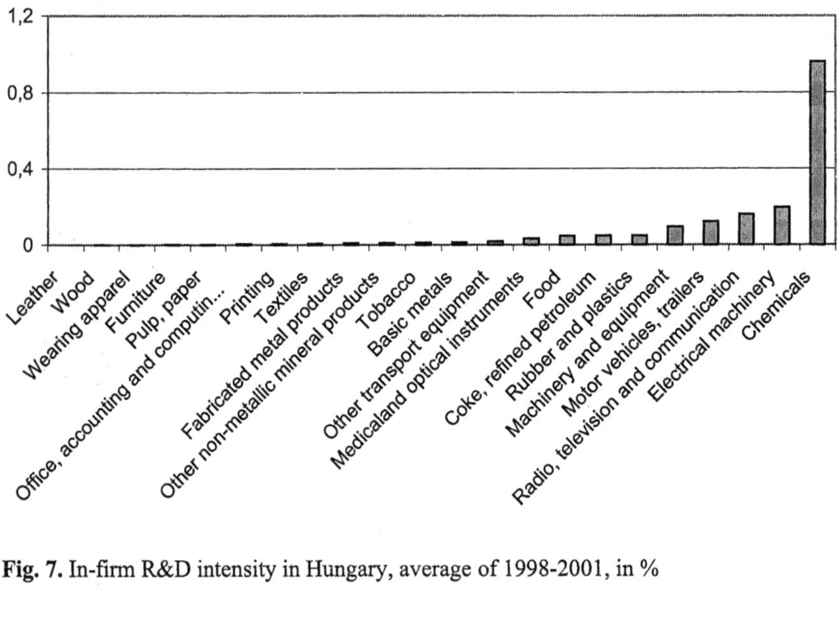

Fig. 7. In-firm R&D intensity in Hungary, average of 1998-2001, in %

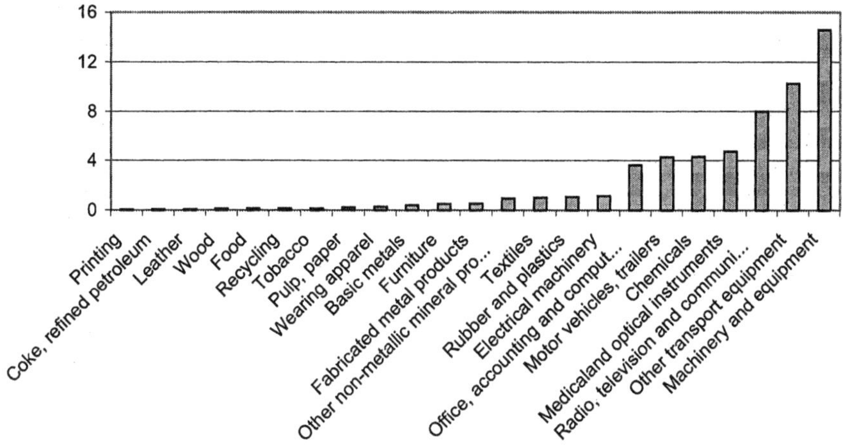

Fig. 8. R&D intensity in Germany in the year 2000, (in %)

The R&D ratio is measured as the relation between sectoral R&D expenditure and sectoral turnover.[7] Note, that the underlying figures are not fully comparable with each other. While R&D expenditure for Poland, the Czech Republic and Germany represent total figures, the Hungarian data contains – due to problems with data availability – only in-firm R&D expenditure. R&D expenditure of Hungarian research institutes or Hungarian universities e.g. are not covered. This probably accounts for Hungary's R&D intensity being considerably lower than in the other two accession countries.

In the accession countries there is hardly any R&D expenditure in most industrial sectors. In Poland and Hungary there is merely one sector each, namely machinery and equipment in Poland, and chemicals in Hungary, and in the Czech Republic two sectors, namely machinery and equipment and other transport equipment, which have significantly higher R&D expenditure ratios. As already mentioned above, the Hungarian figure is not comparable to the other countries, therefore we have to interpret it carefully. The highest in-firm R&D ratio in Hungary does not exceed 1%, while in most sectors it lies beyond 0.2 % of turnover, which is rather negligible. However, it is noteworthy that chemicals are at the top of the R&D list in Hungary. Although R&D expenditure represents total figures in the Czech Republic and Poland, only a few sectors far exceed the 1% R&D ratio. In contrast, in Germany, in almost half of the sectors, the R&D ratio exceeds 1%. The absolute ratio is also far higher in Western Europe: while Germany invests more than 14% of turnover in R&D in the highest R&D intensive sector, invest-

[7] Data on turnover for Germany and on R&D expenditure in Hungary is taken from Eurostat. Turnover in the accession countries has kindly been provided by the National Statistical Offices. R&D expenditure in Germany, Poland and the Czech Republic are taken from the OECD's Anbert database.

ment is only 7% in the Czech Republic and not even 3,5% in Poland. However, the distribution of R&D expenditure across the sectors is similar if one compares accession countries and Germany. In all of the countries some of the most R&D intensive sectors are radio, television and communication and machinery and other transport equipment. However, one should not ignore that in some branches of manufacturing the source of differentiation in specialisation might not (only) be domestic R&D, but other sources like transfer of technology and imitation.

Next we aim to establish whether manufacturing foreign trade patterns, especially exports, in accession countries at a disaggregated level are connected to technology intensity in the respective manufacturing sector. To corroborate this hypothesis we will order the results of all calculated indicators of NACE 2-digit-level classified products according to the national R&D intensity. We will calculate some indicators also for the NACE 3-digit level; these figures can be found in the annexes of the paper.

3.3 Analysing Specialization Patterns in Manufacturing Exports

Data on exports and imports to the EU15 in the manufacturing sector are available for all three accession countries at a 3-digit-level.[8] Data is classified by NACE rev.1.1. The list of variables can be found in Annex 1. We will now apply three different measures of trade performance to shed some light on the specialization patterns of manufacturing foreign trade, especially exports, in Hungary, Poland and the Czech Republic. We will calculate firstly the Trade Coverage Index, secondly the Revealed Comparative Advantage Index by Balassa and thirdly the Grubel-Llyod-Index of Intra-Industry Trade.

3.3.1 Trade Coverage Index

The Trade Coverage Index (TCI) reveals the ratio of exports (X) to imports (M).

$$TCI_i^t = \frac{X_i^t}{M_i^t} \tag{1}$$

i can stand for e.g. total manufacturing or for a certain product group.

For a first insight, we calculate the Trade Coverage Index for total manufacturing in different years. Table 2 shows the results.

[8] Most of the data has been kindly provided by the National Statistical Offices of Hungary, Poland and the Czech Republic. Otherwise it is taken from the COMEX database.

Table 2. TCI for total manufacturing

TCI	1997	1998	1999	2000	2001	2002
Poland	0.57	0.59	0.63	0.74	0.80	
Czech Rep.	0.78	0.91	1.00	0.99	1.01	1.07
Hungary			1.42	1.50	1.58	

Poland's foreign trade structure concerning total manufacturing differs from the other two accession countries. While Poland imports more than it exports in manufacturing, although this trend has been decreasing throughout the second half of the 1990s, the Czech Republic and Hungary export more than they import, with the result that their TCI exceeds 1 most of the time. However, all three countries have rising TCI values in common.

It is of utmost importance to analyse whether the countries import and export rather low or high quality products. According to the "New Economic Geography" models, the accession countries would, in the initial stages of integration, rather specialize in low R&D intensity product groups, later on also in higher technology products. Figures 9, 10 and 11 display the development of the sectoral TCIs, ordered according to the country's own R&D intensity.

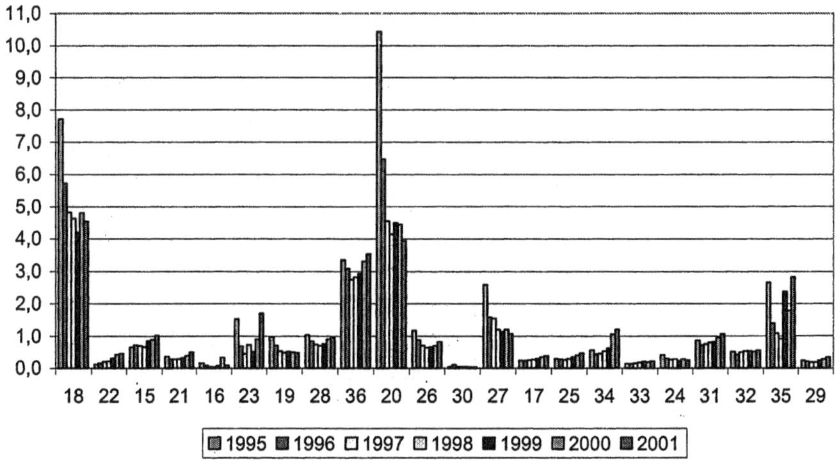

Fig. 9. Trade Coverage Index in Poland, according to R&D intensity, 1995-2001

In the case of Poland, product categories 18, 36 and 20 dominate the figure. The TCIs for wearing apparel (18) and manufacture of wood and its products (20) amount for values around four – however decreasing from eight or ten – in the respective time horizon, for furniture it accounts for a TCI value of three. That means that Poland exports roughly four times more wearing apparel and wood and three times more furniture to the EU15 than it imports from it. The rest of the figure underlines the trend that has already been shown by total manufacturing: the foreign trade position of Poland in manufacturing is not bright, but shows slight changes for the better. TCIs are slowly increasing in many product groups, however in the majority of manufacturing product groups Poland's imports relatively more than it exports. Except for the three categories mentioned above, TCIs do not significantly differ according to R&D intensity. To sum up, it can be stated that TCIs in the low and middle technology sectors are higher than in the high technology sectors in the Polish economy.

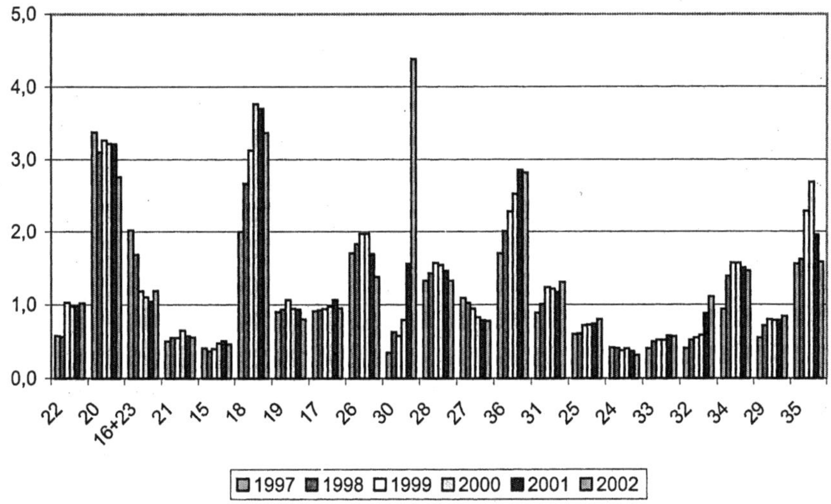

Fig. 10. Trade Coverage Index in the Czech Republic, according to R&D intensity, 1997-2002

The situation is a little different in the Czech Republic: the respective TCIs are presented in figure 10. As indicated by the TCIs for total manufacturing, sectoral TCIs are also often larger than one, meaning exports exceeding imports in the respective manufacturing sector. We can find sectors with exports being up to two or three times higher than imports in basically all technology levels: low R&D intensity (wood and cork products (20), wearing apparel (18)), middle R&D intensity (office machinery and computers (30) and furniture (36)) and high R&D intensity (other transport equipment (35)). There has been an extraordinary increase in TCI in the manufacture of office machinery and computers (30). This is a rather strong indicator for the Czech Republic's foreign trade specialization in middle and higher technology products.

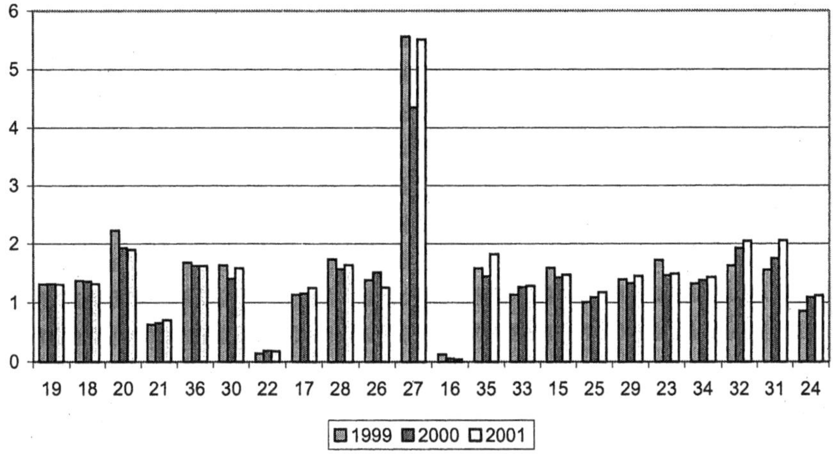

Fig. 11. Trade Coverage Index in Hungary, according to R&D intensity, 1999-2001

Figure 11 shows the sectoral TCIs for Hungary, and clearly reflects the total manufacturing TCIs. Except for pulp and paper (21), publishing and printing (22) and tobacco (16) all TCIs exceed unity. Especially in the manufacture of basic metals (27), Hungary clearly exports more to the EU15 than it imports from it. Otherwise TCIs are relatively evenly distributed, and volatility is rather low. The very short time horizon of only 3 three years plays, of course, a role in the low volatility. Despite the short time horizon, the trend of rising TCIs seems to be most pronounced in the middle (35, 33, 25) and especially in high technology sectors (32, 31, 24). Obviously, exports to the EU15 play a major role in the Hungarian economy, at least in comparison to Poland and the Czech Republic.

To conclude, the Polish economy imports more from the EU15 than it exports to the EU15 in most of the manufacturing product groups. TCIs exceed one mainly in certain low and middle technology product groups. Positive net exports to the EU15 play a more important role in the Czech Republic, where large TCIs can be found in all technology sectors. A high rise in net exports has in particular taken place in the manufacturing of office machinery and computers. With three exceptions, Hungary experiences positive net exports to the EU15 in all product groups. Sectoral TCIs seem to be the most evenly distributed in Hungary.

In the next stage we will focus more on exports and analyse in which product groups the accession countries have a relative comparative advantage or disadvantage as compared to the current EU member states.

3.3.2 RCA-Balassa

The specialization indicator used here is a modification of the classical Revealed Comparative Advantage (RCA) index, invented by Balassa (1965). The modification reveals the relative comparative advantage of an industry within a country by comparing the share of that particular industry in the country's total exports to the share of that industry in total world exports at a certain point in time.[9] Since we are interested in the question, whether an accession country has a comparative advantage as compared to the EU15[10], we take the respective accession countries' exports to the EU15 instead of total exports, and intra-EU15 exports instead of worldwide exports. RCA-Balassa for country i at time t is as follows:

$$RCA_i^t = \frac{\left(\frac{x_i}{\sum_k x_{ik}}\right)}{\left(\frac{x_j}{\sum_k x_{jk}}\right)} \tag{2}$$

Where k stands for commodities in total, j stands for the EU15 and i for an accession country. RCA-Balassa has a minimum value of 0 and a maximum value of infinity. If $RCA_i > 1$, the accession country i has a comparative advantage in that commodity as compared to the EU15. If $RCA_i < 1$, there is a comparative disadvantage of the accession country i. X can stand for different variables, mostly used for exports, patents or value added. In this analysis it stands for exports.

Annex 2 displays the RCA-Balassa values for the NACE classification at the 3-digit level for Poland, annex 3 for the Czech Republic and annex 4 for Hungary. In all three countries there are several branches with RCA values close or equal to zero. In Poland, these comprise for instance exports of grain mill products (156), tobacco (160), or ceramic products (263). The Czech Republic has a very strong comparative disadvantage in the exportation of for instance fish (152), grain mill products (156), or animal feeds (157) and Hungary for instance publishing (221), nuclear fuel (233), or paints (243). On the contrary, very strong comparative advantages exist in Poland concerning the export of wood and its products (205) and coke oven products (231); in the Czech Republic of wooden containers (204) and also coke oven products (231) and in Hungary of textile articles (174), leather clothes (181) and electrical equipment (316). To enable us to characterise the export structure more distinctly, the analysis will now turn to a NACE 2-digit-level consideration. Unfortunately, R&D expenditure data was not available at the 3-digit-level.

Subsequently we wish to establish whether, in the course of integration, high R&D intensity (standing for technology intensity) leads to a higher RCA-Balassa value. Do accession countries still have a stronger comparative advantage in sectors with lower technology intensity than in sectors with higher intensity? To put it differently: Do accession countries still have a comparative disadvantage in sec-

9 Whereas the classical RCA-Balassa reveals a country's sectoral export-import relation divided by the export-import relation of its total economy.

10 Greece is missing in the database due to data availability problems, so it is actually EU14, which we consider.

tors with high technology intensity? For the initial periods of transition we would expect a clear negative relationship between the two variables: higher technology intensity accompanied by lower RCA-Balassa value for accession countries. However, in the course of European integration we would expect the R&D expenditures to rise in accession countries and also the share of products with higher R&D intensities to rise. This could lead to a rise in the number of sectors with an RCA-Balassa value >1, meaning that accession countries may gain comparative advantages compared to EU15 in more and more product categories; alternatively, RCAs in certain sectors could rise over time so that the sector is likely to gain importance in economic terms. On the other hand, this would mean, that in other product categories they might lose comparative advantage. If specialization takes place, we should see clear upwards and downwards movements in the RCA-Balassa values. Furthermore, in the course of European integration, we should gradually see a positive relationship between R&D expenditure and RCA-Balassa values in accession countries.

In order to get an idea of the technology intensity of export products, figures 12, 13 and 14 show the RCAs of exports of each product group at NACE 2-digit-level listed according to the national R&D intensity for Poland, the Czech Republic and Hungary. Intensity is increasing as moving from the left to the right of the figure (according to figures 5, 6 and 7), and RCA is again calculated as compared to the EU15 countries. To demonstrate the economic importance of the product groups, the percentage of the respective group's exports to total manufacturing exports is also shown in the figure. It is represented by the line, which belongs to the right scale in the figure.

Figure 12 shows an interesting picture for Poland. Less than half of the product groups show a comparative advantage of Poland as compared to the EU15. These are mainly found in rather high labour intensive and low or middle R&D and technology intensive sectors. RCAs are by far the highest for wearing apparel (18) – the lowest technology intensive sector – as well as for furniture (36) and wood or wooden products (20). However, Poland has improved its comparative position towards the EU15 in many product groups. Some of those belong not only to lower, but also to middle or even higher technology intensive groups. According to this development, it does not seem unlikely that Poland could gain a comparative advantage in some more middle and higher technology product group in the next years. Moreover, it is losing comparative relatively significantly in some low technology product groups, in particular in wearing apparel (18), in which it had performed much better in the middle of the 1990s.

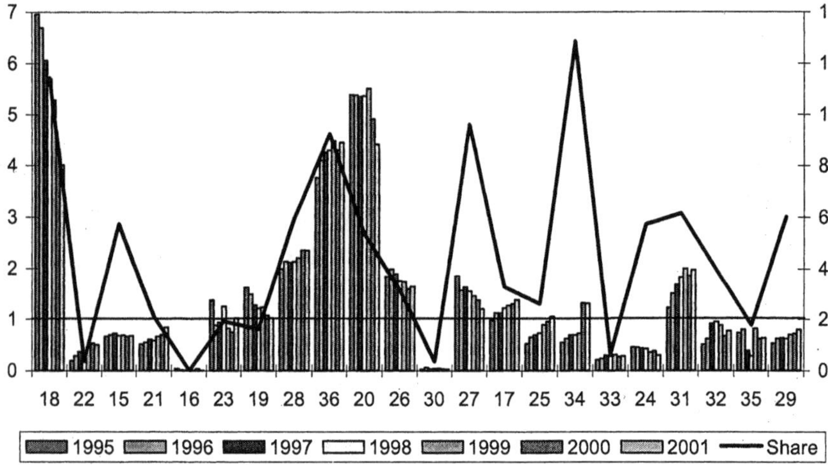

Fig. 12. Poland, RCA of exports according to R&D intensity

The share of exports within total manufacturing exports is highest in Poland in wearing apparel (18) and motor vehicles (34) with approximately 12% each, followed by furniture (36) and basic metals (27) with around 10% respectively. These four sectors account for almost half of total manufacturing exports. Interestingly, these four sectors comprise both low and middle technology intensities. The export volumes seem rather evenly distributed along the technology ladder.

The picture presented for the Czech Republic is slightly different. First of all, the absolute number of product groups with a comparative advantage is higher than in Poland. Furthermore, the Czech Republic has an increasing comparative advantage in the middle and higher technology intensive sectors, while the export position in the low technology fields seems to have deteriorated since 1997. With the exception of wood or wood products (20) and printing and publishing (20), all product groups, which reveal a comparative advantage in exports compared to the EU15 lie in middle and higher technology sectors.

To underline the meaning of middle and high technology sectors in the Czech Republic, the line indicating the share of the products groups' exports in total manufacturing exports seems to have an upward slope as moving from lower to higher technology sectors. Thus export shares are highest in high and lowest in low technology industries.

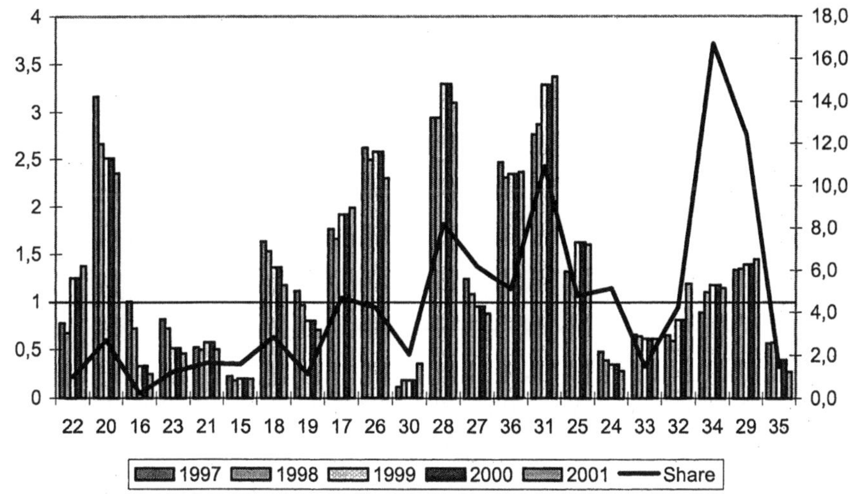

Fig. 13. Czech Republic, RCA of exports according to R&D intensity

Hungarian manufacturing's export position is shown in figure 14. There are two low technology sectors, namely leather (19) and wearing apparel (18) with a strong comparative advantage, and three high technology sectors: motor vehicles (34), radio, television and communication equipment (32) and electrical machinery and apparatus (31). Since RCA's in the high technology sectors exceed RCAs in the low technology sectors by far, Hungary's relative export advantage seems to mainly lie in high technology product groups. Since the time horizon of three years is again very short, one should be cautious with formulating statements on the development; however, comparative advantages in the high R&D intensive sectors seem rather to be increasing – or at least they are steadily high over time – while some RCAs in the low technology sectors are decreasing.

The distribution of the product groups' shares undermines the statement of specialization in high technology exports. Clearly the export of R&D intensive products dominates the picture. More than half of manufacturing exports belong to high technology sectors.

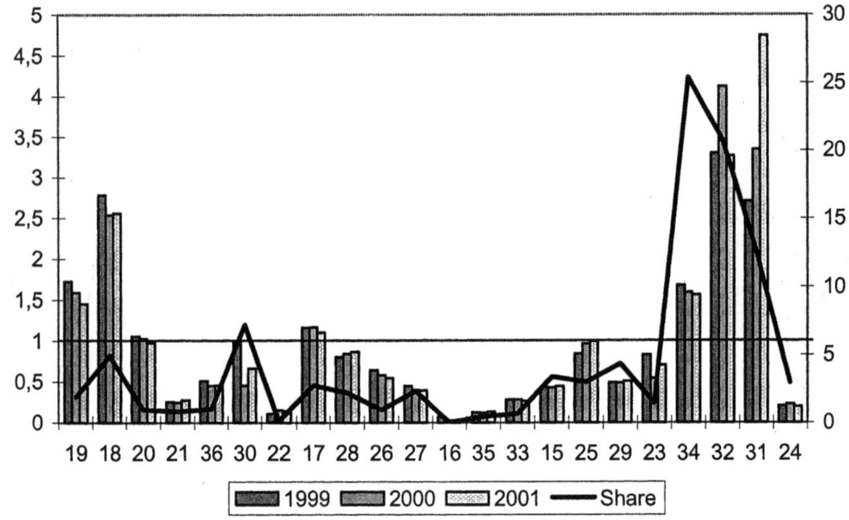

Fig. 14. Hungary, RCA of exports according to in-firm R&D intensity

To sum up, there are dynamic patterns of specialization in accession countries: while Poland specializes mainly in rather low or middle R&D intensive sectors, the Czech Republic gains comparative advantages in the middle and higher R&D intensive sectors and Hungary has a strong tendency to specialize in very high – and in some very low – technology sectors. From a theoretical perspective one may expect that certain fields of low, medium or high technology intensities will be reinforced over time as a result of reinforcement of specialization; in such a dynamic view it is not so much important that modified RCA exceeds unity but that the RCA indicator is rising. Indeed, the empirical findings suggest that especially the Czech Republic and Hungary – with rising RCAs in many sectors – have a broader field of competence and might find it easier than Poland to upgrade the overall economy in technological terms over time.

After having analysed, which product linkages exist in the trade between the EU15 and the accession countries, we will now focus on the total extent of economic integration between eastern and western European countries.

3.3.3 The Grubel-Lloyd Index of Intra-Industry Trade

According to the "New Trade Theory", intra-industry trade is determined by country characteristics such as demand differences. The size of intra-industry trade indicates the extent of the economic integration of a country, also influencing the relative per capita income. Taking into consideration that a large part of foreign trade takes place within the same industries, we will now turn to analysing the ratio of intra-industry trade in accession countries. Again, we will only use that part of foreign trade of the accession countries, which is associated with the EU15. Thus, the index directly measures the extent of economic integration with the current EU. The Grubel-Lloyd Index (GLI) of Intra-Industry Trade (IIT) is calculated as follows:

$$GLI_i = \frac{\left[(X_i + M_i) - |X_i - M_i|\right]}{(X_i + M_i)} * 100 \qquad (3)$$

X stands for exports to the EU15, *M* for imports from the EU15. The index takes values between 0 and 100. The higher the value, the greater the extent of intra-industry trade the greater the degree of economic integration.

Figures 15, 16 and 17 display the yearly GLI for Poland, the Czech Republic and Hungary, ordered in accordance with national R&D intensities.

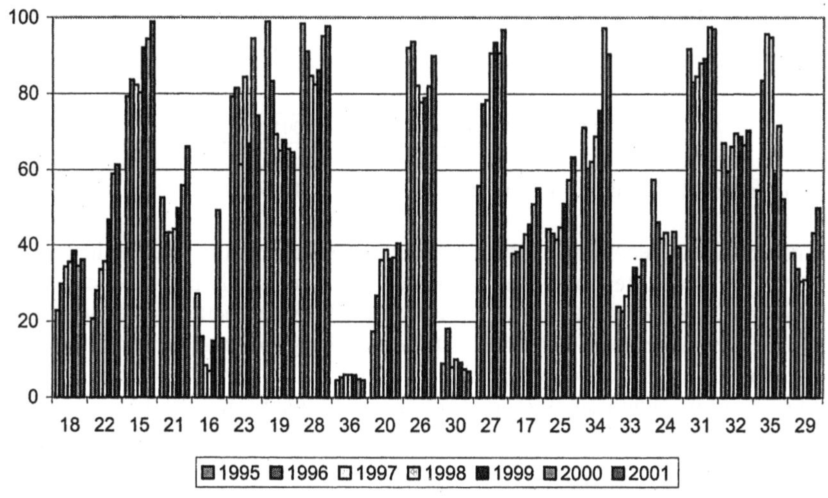

Fig. 15. Grubel-Lloyd Index of IIT in Poland, 1995-2001

Some of Poland's manufacturing branches are highly integrated with the EU15 (GLI above 90), some are hardly at all (GLI below 20 or even 10). High integration can be found at any technological level: low, middle and high. There does not seem to be a correlation between integration and R&D intensity. This finding is in line with the existing empirical literature, which has not been very successful in relating IIT to cross-country differences in endowments and other country characteristics. Generally speaking, Poland's integration with the EU seems to have risen in the second half of the 1990s, although in some product groups there has been a significant decline, e.g. tanning and dressing of leather (19). This might, however, indicate that there is still much potential for gains in foreign trade in these sectors of the Polish economy.

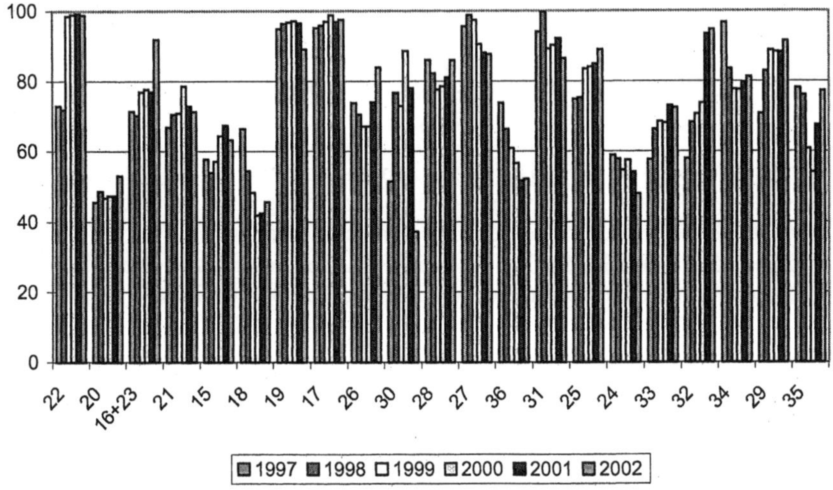

Fig. 16. Grubel-Lloyd index of IIT in the Czech Republic, 1997-2002

Unsurprisingly, economic integration as measured by the GLI is in general higher in the Czech Republic than in Poland. There are hardly any product categories that are integrated less than 50% with the EU15 and certain categories even reach an integration level of almost 100%. Similarly to Poland, high integration can be found in all technology product groups. At the same time integration in middle and high technology sectors tends to be of higher intensity than integration in low technology product groups. This is clearly in line with the findings of the RCAs.

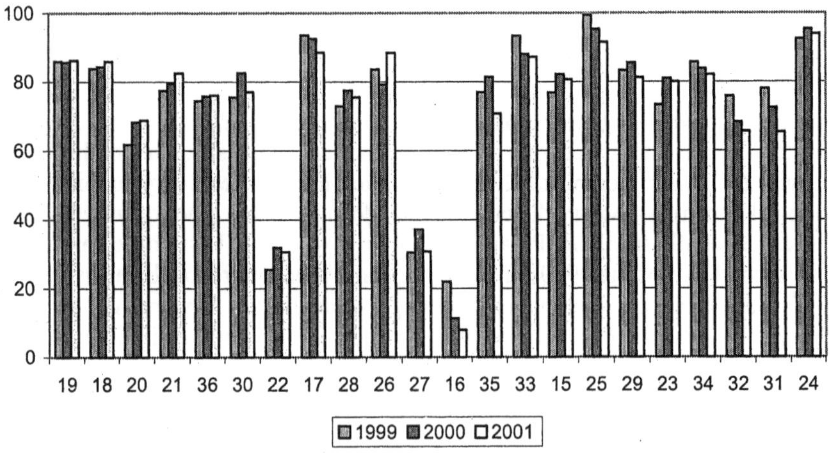

Fig. 17. Grubel-Lloyd Index of IIT in Hungary, 1999-2001

In the case of Hungary, the share of IIT in total EU-trade is highest in high technology sectors, reaching almost 100% in rubber and plastic products (25) and chemicals (24). But it is also quite high in some middle and lower R&D intensive sectors such as leather (18), wearing apparel (18) and textiles (17). The lowest GLs are found in middle technology product groups, e.g. tobacco products (16).

In terms of absolute distribution of GLs between the product groups, the picture for 2001 is quite similar for the Czech Republic and Hungary, and differs from the picture presented for Poland. GLs reach more than 80% in twelve and ten product groups in the Czech Republic and Hungary, respectively, whereas in only six groups in Poland. Moreover, GLs account for less than 40% in merely one product group in the Czech Republic and three in Hungary, while this is the case for six product groups in Poland. Thus in the Czech Republic and Hungary approximately half of the product groups show a rather high economic integration with the EU15, approximately 10% show low economic integration and the remaining approximately 40% of the product groups can be found in between. For Poland this distinction makes up to about 25% for high integration, 25% for low integration and 50% of the product groups are placed in between.

To sum up, the Czech Republic and Hungary are extensively integrated with the EU15. However, for some product groups there is still much potential for increasing economic integration, especially in Hungary and in Poland.

4 Conclusion and Future Research

Based on theoretical considerations this paper empirically analysed the foreign trade structure of three accession countries towards the current EU15 countries, placing an emphasis on the development of export specialization. The outcome of the "Traditional Trade Theory", that accession countries will rather specialize in labour intensive production can, at least for two of the three countries, be rejected. We found that Poland exports rather low and some medium technology (or labour intensive) products, the Czech Republic, on the contrary, shows clear specialization patterns in the field of medium and even high technology, while Hungary mainly specialized in the export of high technology – and also of some very low technology – products in the 1990s. The share of intra-industry trade, as explained by the "New Trade Theory" mainly by differences in demand characteristics, is very high in some product groups in all three countries. However, there are – especially in Hungary and in Poland - also some branches of manufacturing where integration with the current EU-market has not yet proceeded this far. Hungary's and the Czech Republic's specialization in higher technology production questions the assumption of the "New Economic Geography" that mature products - with higher R&D expenditure – will be provided by economies richly endowed with skilled labour and physical capital and less mature products by countries endowed with much unskilled labour. Alternatively it raises the question as to whether the distinction between the EU15, as countries endowed with skilled labour and much capital and the accession countries, as countries endowed with unskilled labour, can still be regarded as an appropriate characterization.

Technology intensity was proxied in this paper by R&D ratios, which were measured as sectoral R&D expenditure as a percentage of sectoral turnover. R&D ratios, as an indicator for technology intensity, are still much lower in the three accession countries considered, than in current EU member states, e.g. Germany. However, we found that the sectoral distribution of R&D expenditure is rather similar.

As regards future research there is a broad range of further interesting issues to deal with. Firstly, the analysis should be expanded to include other accession countries, and in particular certain selected current EU countries (e.g. Portugal or Greece), to be able to compare the developments of structural change - especially foreign trade specialisation – in the course of different enlargement and integration processes within Europe. A comparative analysis of country results should uncover differences and similarities of specialization patterns between selected new and current EU15 members.

Secondly, it would be interesting to examine export and import unit values, in order to reveal specialization patterns. The basic assumption for catching-up should be tested, namely that with rising per capita income there will be high export shares of product groups with a high unit export value. Additionally, the use of alternative variables (e.g. capital stock or total factor productivity) is needed to give better insight into specialisation patterns of accession countries in terms of technology intensity in the Schumpeterian sense. Future research should also include analysis of patents at a disaggregated level to implicate propositions on innovation and structural change. In addition, the impact of FDI flows on RCA dynamics should be analyzed.

Last but not least, it is necessary to use more advanced econometric methods for the analysis. The use of indicators for trade performance is just one of a variety of possible methods for measuring structural change. In future research, convergence indicators – e.g. β-convergence and δ-convergence – should be calculated, as well as other econometric methods (e.g. unit root tests). Finally policy implications should be incorporated, using also the experiences from previous examples of economic integration with the EU.

Annex 1

NACE rev. 1.1. Classification (in parts)

D	Manufacturing
15	Manufacture of food products and beverages
151	Production, processing and preserving of meat and meat products
152	Processing and preserving of fish and fish products
153	Processing and preserving of fruit and vegetables
154	Manufacture of vegetable and animal oils and fats

155	Manufacture of dairy products
156	Manufacture of grain mill products, starches and starch products
157	Manufacture of prepared animal feeds
158	Manufacture of other food products
159	Manufacture of beverages
16	Manufacture of tobacco products
160	Manufacture of tobacco products
17	Manufacture of textiles
171	Preparation of spinning of textile fibres
172	Textile weaving
173	Finishing of textiles
174	Manufacture of made-up textile articles, except apparel
175	Manufacture of carpets and rugs
176	Manufacture of knitted and crocheted fabrics
177	Manufacture of knitted and crocheted articles
18	Manufacture of wearing apparel; dressing and dyeing of fur
181	Manufacture of leather clothes
182	Manufacture of other wearing apparel and accessories
183	Dressing and dyeing of fur; manufacture of articles of fur
19	Tanning and dressing of leather, manufacture of luggage, handbags, saddlery, harness and footwear
191	Tanning and dressing of leather
192	Manufacture of luggage, handbags and the like, saddlery and harness
193	Manufacture of footwear
20	Manufacture of wood and of products of wood and cork, except furniture;manufacture of articles of straw and plaiting materials
201	Sawmilling and planing of wood, impregnation of wood
202	Manufacture of veneer sheets; manufacture of plywood, laminboard, particle board, fibre board and other panels and boards
203	Manufacture of builders carpentry and joinery
204	Manufacture of wooden containers
205	Manufacture of other products of wood; manufacture of articles of cork, straw and plaiting materials
21	Manufacture of pulp, paper and paper products
211	Manufacture of pulp, paper and paperboard
212	Manufacture of articles of paper and paperboard
22	Publishing, printing and reproduction of recorded media
221	Publishing
222	Printing and service activities related to printing
223	Reproduction of recorded media
23	Manufacture of coke, refined petroleum products and nuclear fuel
231	Manufacture of coke oven products
232	Manufacture of refined petroleum products
233	Processing of nuclear fuel
24	Manufacture of chemicals and chemical products
241	Manufacture of basic chemicals

242 Manufacture of pesticides and other agro-chemical products
243 Manufacture of paints, varnishes and similar coatings, printing ink and mastics
244 Manufacture of pharmaceuticals, medicinal chemicals and botanical products
245 Manufacture of soap and detergents, cleaning and polishing preparations, perfumes and toilet preparations
246 Manufacture of other chemical products
247 Manufacture of man-made fibres
25 Manufacture of rubber and plastic products
251 Manufacture of rubber products
252 Manufacture of plastic products
26 Manufacture of other non-metallic mineral products
261 Manufacture of glass and glass products
262 Manufacture of non-refractory ceramic goods other than for construction purposes; manufacture of refractory ceramic products
263 Manufacture of ceramic tiles and flags
264 Manufacture of bricks, tiles and construction products, in baked clay
265 Manufacture of cement, lime and plaster
266 Manufacture of articles of concrete, plaster and cement
267 Cutting, shaping and finishing of ornamental and building stone
268 Manufacture of other non-metallic mineral products
27 Manufacture of basic metals
271 Manufacture of basic iron and steel and of ferro-alloys
272 Manufacture of tubes
273 Other first processing of iron and steel
274 Manufacture of basic precious and non-ferrous metals
275 Casting of metals
28 Manufacture of fabricated metal products, except machinery and equipment
281 Manufacture of structural metal products
282 Manufacture of tanks, reservoirs and containers of metal; manufacture of central heating radiators and boilers
283 Manufacture of steam generators, except central heating hot water boilers
284 Forging, pressing, stamping and roll forming of metal; powder metallurgy
285 Treatment and coating of metals; general mechanical engineering
286 Manufacture of cutlery, tools and general hardware
287 Manufacture of other fabricated metal products
29 Manufacture of machinery and equipment n.e.c.
291 Manufacture of machinery for the production and use of mechanical power, Except aircraft, vehicle and cycle engines
292 Manufacture of other general purpose machinery
293 Manufacture of agriculture and forestry machinery
294 Manufacture of machinetools

	295	Manufacture of other special purpose machinery
	296	Manufacture of weapons and ammunition
	297	Manufacture of domestic appliances n.e.c.
30		Manufacture of office machinery and computers
	300	Manufacture of office machinery and computers
31		Manufacture of electrical machinery and apparatus n.e.c.
	311	Manufacture of electric motors, generators and transformers
	312	Manufacture of electricity distribution and control apparatus
	313	Manufacture of insulated wire and cable
	314	Manufacture of accumulators, primary cells and primary batteries
	315	Manufacture of lighting equipment and electric lamps
	316	Manufacture of electrical equipment n.e.c.
32		Manufacture of radio, television and communication equipment and apparatus
	321	Manufacture of electronic valves and tubes and other electronic components
	322	Manufacture of television and radio transmitters and apparatus for line telephony and line telegraphy
	323	Manufacture of television and radio receivers, sound or video recording or reproducing apparatus and associated goods
33		Manufacture of medical, precision and optical instruments, watches and clocks
	331	Manufacture of medical and surgical equipment and orthopaedic appliances
	332	Manufacture of instruments and appliances for measuring, checking, testing, navigating and other purposes, except industrial process control equipment
	333	Manufacture of industrial process control equipment
	334	Manufacture of optical instruments and photographic equipment
	335	Manufacture of watches and clocks
34		Manufacture of motor vehicles, trailers and semi-trailers
	341	Manufacture of motor vehicles
	342	Manufacture of bodies (coachwork) for motor vehicles; manufacture of trailers and semi-trailers
	343	Manufactures of parts and accessories for motor vehicles and their engines
35		Manufacture of other transport equipment
	351	Building and repairing of ships and boats
	352	Manufacture of railway and tramway locomotives and rolling stock
	353	Manufacture of aircraft and spacecraft
	354	Manufacture of motorcycles and bicycles
	355	Manufacture of other transport equipment n.e.c.
36		Manufacture of furniture, manufacturing n.e.c.
	361	Manufacture of furniture
	362	Manufacture of jewellery and related articles
	363	Manufacture of musical instruments

	364	Manufacture of sports goods
	365	Manufacture of games and toys
	366	Miscellaneous manufacturing n.e.c.
37		Recycling
	371	Recycling of metal waste and scrap
	372	Recycling of non-metal waste and scrap

Annex 2

RCA-Balassa in Poland's exports as compared to EU15, 1995-2001 (NACE rev.1.1, 3-digit-level)

NACE	1995	1996	1997	1998	1999	2000	2001
151	0,70	0,78	0,73	0,78	0,79	0,74	0,76
152	2,19	1,69	1,52	1,74	1,96	1,60	1,42
153	3,05	3,04	3,53	3,20	2,99	2,94	2,96
154	0,35	0,40	0,44	0,27	0,41	0,28	0,33
155	0,21	0,30	0,33	0,19	0,20	0,13	0,27
156	**0,03**	**0,01**	**0,01**	**0,02**	**0,05**	**0,03**	**0,04**
157	0,03	0,07	0,12	0,19	0,27	0,20	0,56
158	0,26	0,35	0,40	0,32	0,29	0,36	0,35
159	0,05	0,06	0,07	0,07	0,07	0,10	0,06
160	**0,04**	**0,01**	**0,00**	**0,00**	**0,01**	**0,04**	**0,01**
171	0,73	0,64	0,79	1,09	1,10	1,21	1,41
172	0,35	0,41	0,43	0,39	0,31	0,33	0,31
174	5,91	6,62	6,20	6,59	6,40	6,42	6,70
175	0,26	0,32	0,44	0,52	0,63	0,70	0,74
176	0,40	0,38	0,31	0,39	0,42	0,49	0,44
177	1,44	1,63	1,56	1,51	1,56	1,41	1,47
181	2,63	2,05	2,10	2,23	2,43	2,02	2,12
182	7,07	6,81	6,15	5,78	5,33	4,33	3,99
183	3,92	4,68	4,28	4,24	4,87	5,58	7,10
191	2,06	1,59	1,78	1,66	1,72	1,77	1,90
192	1,75	1,65	1,08	1,11	0,95	0,74	0,65
193	1,43	1,44	1,15	1,08	1,15	0,92	0,80
201	3,52	2,96	2,92	2,87	2,75	2,49	1,97
202	2,76	2,42	2,40	3,12	3,41	2,85	2,40
203	6,27	6,78	7,22	6,61	6,92	6,10	6,01
204	**27,65**	**20,97**	**16,58**	**15,04**	**14,10**	**11,47**	**9,66**
205	**13,01**	**15,60**	**16,93**	**15,12**	**15,67**	**14,23**	**13,27**
211	0,42	0,46	0,53	0,53	0,63	0,69	0,69

NACE	1995	1996	1997	1998	1999	2000	2001
212	0,81	0,78	0,83	0,73	0,77	0,73	1,27
221	0,14	0,19	0,21	0,28	0,32	0,36	0,38
222	0,29	0,49	0,69	0,52	0,75	0,88	0,75
231	**57,09**	**39,89**	**55,48**	**50,98**	**42,91**	**35,93**	**36,64**
232	0,37	0,28	0,28	0,30	0,28	0,35	0,51
233	0,02	0,02	0,02	0,01	0,01	0,02	0,02
241	0,78	0,78	0,73	0,73	0,58	0,63	0,50
242	0,08	0,06	0,07	0,07	0,09	0,07	0,03
243	0,02	0,03	0,03	0,04	0,05	0,07	0,07
244	0,06	0,08	0,06	0,05	0,04	0,03	0,03
245	0,14	0,18	0,17	0,22	0,29	0,40	0,41
246	0,11	0,13	0,12	0,09	0,11	0,08	0,07
247	0,51	0,43	0,78	0,88	1,02	1,08	1,02
251	0,84	0,99	1,03	1,15	1,32	1,52	1,75
252	0,37	0,47	0,51	0,52	0,68	0,68	0,73
261	1,26	1,37	1,46	1,61	1,73	1,70	1,71
262	1,77	2,50	2,40	2,48	2,75	2,75	2,88
263	**0,01**	**0,01**	**0,01**	**0,01**	**0,02**	**0,02**	**0,02**
264	1,77	2,40	3,20	3,03	2,47	1,95	1,82
265	14,06	12,15	9,59	6,83	4,61	2,39	2,38
266	2,48	2,82	2,83	1,83	2,04	2,23	2,35
267	1,62	1,97	2,03	1,79	1,77	1,39	1,24
268	0,32	0,58	0,66	0,90	0,95	0,93	1,12
271	1,32	0,99	1,14	1,18	1,03	1,13	1,02
272	1,26	1,21	1,14	1,14	1,12	1,12	1,20
273	1,05	1,19	1,22	1,11	1,00	0,81	0,79
274	2,85	2,43	2,39	2,21	2,12	1,82	1,50
281	5,20	6,13	5,66	4,92	4,69	5,35	5,86
282	0,87	0,94	1,10	1,22	1,55	1,86	2,06
283	3,33	3,44	4,93	5,35	7,10	16,87	5,27
286	0,47	0,49	0,50	0,52	0,62	0,69	0,81
287	2,24	2,28	2,37	2,55	2,56	2,51	2,48
291	0,59	0,72	0,60	0,65	0,69	0,86	0,93
292	0,39	0,50	0,56	0,51	0,61	0,59	0,62
293	0,97	1,03	1,05	0,93	0,92	0,87	0,86
294	0,42	0,50	0,53	0,53	0,58	0,61	0,70
295	0,51	0,61	0,66	0,63	0,70	0,65	0,72
296	0,26	0,28	0,16	0,11	0,17	0,09	0,10
297	0,56	0,62	0,67	0,73	0,88	0,87	1,14
300	0,03	0,07	0,03	0,04	0,04	0,03	0,03
311	0,81	1,27	1,64	1,65	1,66	1,42	1,39

NACE	1995	1996	1997	1998	1999	2000	2001
312	0,69	0,81	1,19	1,03	1,13	1,14	1,21
313	3,49	3,26	2,53	3,15	3,18	3,05	3,40
314	0,16	0,86	1,99	2,51	2,33	2,46	2,40
315	2,57	2,91	3,10	3,22	3,26	2,84	2,79
316	0,91	1,32	1,23	1,59	2,15	2,04	2,42
321	0,52	0,65	0,64	0,64	0,61	0,34	0,27
322	0,13	0,16	0,29	0,16	0,15	0,16	0,13
323	0,73	0,93	1,83	2,29	2,37	2,17	2,63
331	0,18	0,16	0,20	0,25	0,32	0,32	0,33
332	0,29	0,32	0,36	0,31	0,34	0,30	0,32
334	0,07	0,07	0,07	0,06	0,06	0,05	0,05
335	0,21	0,87	1,85	1,76	1,42	0,63	0,66
341	0,58	0,66	0,69	0,66	0,65	1,42	1,34
342	1,93	2,23	2,11	2,09	2,19	1,95	1,91
343	0,36	0,42	0,59	0,65	0,82	0,97	1,21
351	12,28	17,20	4,66	2,60	14,08	6,14	7,11
352	0,80	0,86	0,80	0,88	2,02	3,14	3,46
353	0,04	0,05	0,05	0,05	0,05	0,05	0,12
354	0,84	0,90	0,90	0,86	1,06	1,00	0,97
355	4,52	5,32	6,36	4,61	5,37	5,06	5,26
361	6,72	7,25	7,64	7,47	7,87	7,80	8,10
362	0,26	0,29	0,33	0,34	0,25	0,20	0,19
363	1,33	1,37	1,43	1,14	0,90	0,63	0,58
364	0,72	0,75	0,83	0,76	0,69	0,59	0,56
365	0,57	0,55	0,54	0,59	0,59	0,47	0,48
366	1,21	1,42	1,44	1,56	1,63	1,63	1,69

Annex 3

RCA-Balassa in the Czech Republic's exports as compared to EU15, 1997-2001 (NACE rev.1.1, 3-digit-level)

NACE	1997	1998	1999	2000	2001
151	0,20	0,16	0,17	0,17	0,18
152	**0,00**	**0,00**	**0,00**	**0,01**	**0,01**
153	0,17	0,11	0,13	0,13	0,12
154	0,46	0,28	0,22	0,28	0,23
155	0,26	0,25	0,16	0,21	0,20
156	**0,05**	**0,02**	**0,05**	**0,04**	**0,05**
157	**0,02**	**0,02**	**0,02**	**0,02**	**0,02**

NACE	1997	1998	1999	2000	2001
158	0,18	0,17	0,16	0,22	0,26
159	0,45	0,34	0,32	0,42	0,37
160	1,00	0,72	0,40	0,33	0,25
171	1,64	1,52	1,75	2,43	2,63
172	2,24	2,12	2,07	2,26	2,36
174	5,07	4,63	4,78	4,79	4,92
175	0,85	0,87	1,01	1,27	1,34
176	1,11	1,10	1,09	1,05	0,93
177	0,98	0,77	0,79	0,74	0,66
181	1,47	1,18	0,98	0,83	0,61
182	1,64	1,54	1,45	1,37	1,18
183	1,64	1,28	1,48	1,96	1,65
191	0,47	0,29	0,24	0,18	0,14
192	2,04	1,80	1,53	1,43	1,31
193	1,18	1,05	1,04	0,88	0,78
201	3,59	2,97	3,11	2,79	2,43
202	1,76	1,47	1,33	1,22	1,10
203	3,48	3,21	3,45	3,15	4,02
204	**10,95**	**8,13**	**7,81**	**7,06**	**5,83**
205	1,90	1,76	1,93	2,06	1,75
211	0,54	0,51	0,47	0,59	0,49
212	0,48	0,47	0,49	0,54	0,53
221	0,33	0,34	0,38	0,37	0,49
222	1,69	1,31	3,01	3,10	3,16
231	**24,81**	**15,29**	**17,38**	**9,94**	**8,65**
232	0,45	0,45	0,51	0,41	0,36
233	1,41	0,27	0,29	0,33	0,08
241	0,80	0,64	0,52	0,55	0,45
242	0,22	0,15	0,11	0,16	0,14
243	0,26	0,26	0,29	0,27	0,28
244	0,18	0,13	0,11	0,11	0,09
245	0,09	0,19	0,21	0,24	0,16
246	0,14	0,13	0,12	0,10	0,13
247	0,39	0,45	0,54	0,64	0,63
251	1,55	1,82	2,16	2,45	2,38
252	1,20	0,99	1,14	1,23	1,22
261	3,13	3,17	3,17	3,20	2,83
262	3,20	3,37	3,39	3,74	3,59
263	1,18	0,98	1,01	1,04	0,96
264	2,36	2,96	2,55	2,58	2,46

NACE	1997	1998	1999	2000	2001
265	5,16	3,79	3,66	3,17	1,91
266	3,66	2,96	2,84	2,95	2,55
267	1,13	0,98	1,00	0,89	0,77
268	0,92	0,79	1,00	1,09	1,11
271	1,28	1,00	0,97	0,92	0,94
272	1,68	1,78	1,54	1,64	1,44
273	1,81	1,89	1,88	1,62	1,38
274	0,99	0,81	0,82	0,71	0,60
281	**6,51**	**5,65**	**5,48**	**6,07**	**5,42**
282	2,55	2,66	2,59	2,85	2,82
283	2,34	1,57	3,02	3,55	1,72
286	1,44	1,35	1,40	1,66	1,84
287	3,08	3,34	3,44	3,70	3,42
291	1,09	1,21	1,22	1,30	1,57
292	1,47	1,38	1,35	1,40	1,40
293	1,38	1,21	0,84	0,78	0,83
294	2,36	2,21	2,37	2,08	2,14
295	1,50	1,56	1,59	1,78	1,71
296	2,45	2,14	3,65	3,43	2,37
297	0,53	0,51	0,45	0,44	0,51
300	0,12	0,19	0,15	0,19	0,36
311	3,01	2,92	3,04	3,25	3,04
312	3,14	3,11	3,01	3,20	2,84
313	2,74	3,25	4,11	4,07	4,19
314	6,41	4,76	6,94	7,51	9,95
315	0,85	0,87	0,74	0,80	0,84
316	2,13	2,87	3,01	3,18	3,52
321	1,13	1,13	1,13	1,18	1,08
322	0,06	0,05	0,05	0,19	0,75
323	0,54	0,55	0,74	1,29	2,08
331	0,35	0,32	0,35	0,33	0,34
332	0,62	0,64	0,57	0,61	0,64
334	1,22	1,25	1,14	1,23	1,13
335	1,57	1,06	0,64	0,53	0,33
341	0,78	1,00	0,92	0,93	0,85
342	1,91	1,67	1,50	1,46	1,25
343	1,08	1,33	1,63	1,87	2,03
351	1,14	0,84	0,70	0,22	0,34
352	5,47	6,68	7,28	6,12	3,28
353	0,09	0,14	0,14	0,06	0,04

NACE	1997	1998	1999	2000	2001
354	1,48	1,15	0,90	0,94	0,75
355	1,18	1,71	1,97	2,31	2,23
361	3,13	2,96	3,26	3,29	3,41
362	0,18	0,17	0,16	0,10	0,09
363	7,63	6,95	6,15	5,82	5,03
364	3,99	2,98	2,32	2,17	2,11
365	0,98	0,97	0,97	1,04	1,16
366	2,57	2,40	2,17	2,16	1,94

Annex 4

RCA-Balassa in Hungary's exports as compared to EU15, 1999-2001 (NACE rev.1.1, 3-digit-level)

NACE	1999	2000	2001
151	1,4	1,3	1,3
152	**0,0**	**0,0**	**0,0**
153	1,0	0,9	0,8
154	0,2	0,3	0,1
155	0,1	0,1	0,2
156	0,1	0,1	0,3
157	0,5	0,6	0,9
158	0,1	0,1	0,1
159	0,1	0,2	0,2
160	0,1	0,0	0,0
171	0,9	1,2	1,4
172	0,5	0,4	0,4
174	**6,6**	**6,5**	**5,3**
175	0,6	0,6	0,7
176	0,5	0,5	0,5
177	0,7	0,6	0,6
181	**6,4**	**5,4**	**5,2**
182	2,8	2,5	2,5
183	0,3	0,4	0,3
191	0,4	0,4	0,3
192	2,7	2,3	2,0
193	2,0	1,8	1,7
201	0,6	0,6	0,6
202	0,6	0,5	0,5
203	2,8	2,8	2,7

NACE	1999	2000	2001
204	1,9	2,0	1,8
205	1,1	0,9	0,8
211	0,2	0,2	0,3
212	0,5	0,4	0,3
221	**0,0**	**0,0**	**0,0**
222	0,3	0,4	0,4
231	0,0	0,0	0,0
232	0,9	0,6	0,8
233	**0,0**	**0,0**	**0,0**
241	0,3	0,3	0,3
242	0,1	0,2	0,3
243	**0,0**	**0,0**	**0,0**
244	0,2	0,2	0,2
245	0,1	0,1	0,2
246	**0,0**	**0,0**	**0,0**
247	0,2	0,2	0,2
251	0,9	1,0	1,1
252	0,8	0,9	1,0
261	0,5	0,4	0,4
262	2,0	1,7	1,5
263	0,1	0,1	0,1
264	0,5	0,6	0,7
265	0,2	0,2	0,2
266	0,3	0,3	0,3
267	**0,0**	**0,0**	**0,0**
268	0,9	0,9	0,8
271	0,4	0,1	0,1
272	0,1	0,1	0,0
273	0,1	0,1	0,1
274	0,7	0,8	0,8
281	2,5	2,9	3,2
282	2,0	1,4	1,5
283	1,9	3,0	1,2
286	0,3	0,4	0,4
287	0,4	0,5	0,5
291	0,3	0,2	0,3
292	0,4	0,4	0,4
293	1,1	1,3	1,6
294	0,2	0,2	0,3
295	0,3	0,3	0,3

NACE	1999	2000	2001
296	0,2	0,3	0,2
297	1,4	1,4	1,3
300	1,0	0,5	0,7
311	0,9	0,9	0,9
312	1,2	1,3	1,5
313	3,7	3,9	3,4
314	0,0	0,2	1,2
315	5,2	5,7	5,9
316	**5,1**	**7,4**	**13,3**
321	4,3	6,0	2,5
322	0,1	0,3	0,5
323	**6,7**	**7,7**	**9,1**
331	0,2	0,2	0,2
332	0,3	0,3	0,3
334	0,4	0,4	0,4
335	**0,0**	**0,0**	**0,0**
341	1,9	1,7	1,6
342	0,8	0,7	0,9
343	1,2	1,3	1,4
351	0,1	0,1	0,1
352	2,2	2,5	2,5
353	0,0	0,0	0,0
354	0,1	0,1	0,1
355	0,5	0,5	0,6
361	0,7	0,6	0,7
362	0,1	0,1	0,0
363	**0,0**	**0,0**	**0,0**
364	0,5	0,4	0,4
365	0,3	0,2	0,2
366	0,6	0,5	0,5

References

Aiginger, K., "Do Industrial Structures Converge? A survey on the empirical literature on specialisation and concentration of industries", WIFO Working Paper, (116), 1999.

Borbély, D., and K.J. Gern, "Die EU-Osterweiterung – Makroökonomische Aspekte aus Sicht der Beitrittsländer", Die Weltwirtschaft 4, 2003.

Brülhart, M., "Scale Economies, Intra-Industry Trade and Industry Location in the New Trade Theory", Trinity Economic Paper Series, Technical Paper No. 95/4, 1995.

Greenaway, D., Hine, R. C., Milner, Ch., "Vertical and horizontal intra-industry trade: a cross industry analysis for the United Kingdom", The Economic Journal, 1995, 105 (November), pp: 1505-1518.

Heckscher, E., "The Effect of Foreign trade on Distribution of Income." Ekonomisk Tidskrift, pp.497-512, 1919; reprinted in H.S. Ellis and L.A. Metzler (eds.), A. E. A. Readings in the Theory of International Trade, Philadelphia: Blakiston, pp: 272-300. 1949.

Krugman, P., "Increasing Returns and Economic Geography", Journal of Political Economy, 1991, (99), pp: 483-499.

Krugman, P. and Venables, A.J., "Globalization and the Inequality of Nations", Quarterly Journal of Economics, 1995, 60(4), pp: 857-880.

Ohlin, B., Interregional and International Trade. Campbridge, MA: Harvard University Press, 1933.

Puga, D., "Urbanisation patterns: Europe versus Less Developed Countries", Journal of Regional Science, 1998, (38), pp: 231-252.

Ricardo, D., On the Principles of Political Economy and Taxation, London, 1817.

Venables, A.J.,"Equilibrium locations of vertically linked industries", International Economic Review, 1996, Vol. 37, No. 2.

Venables, A. J., "The international division of industries: clustering and comparative advantage in a multi-industry model", CEPR Discussion Paper, 1998, (1961).

Wolfmayr-Schnitzer, Y., "Economic Integration, Specialisation and the Location of Industries. A Survey of the Theoretical Literature", WIFO Working Paper No. 120, 1999.

Comment on: EU Export Specialization Patterns in Selected Accession Countries

Kerstin Schneider

In May 2004 10 new member states joined the EU, enlarging the number of member states from 15 to 25 and raising the population from 375 million people to 450 million. The economic implications of the enlargement will be manifold for the new and also the old members of the EU.[1] Here the focus is on trade of the accession countries with the EU 15 as one of the most viable issues of enlargement. The membership in the EU is only the legal end of the process of integrating the eastern European countries. Clearly, the transition in the new member countries did not start in 2004 but began after the fall of the Iron Curtain and it is still ongoing. Different from earlier enlargements, trade barriers have been significantly lowered in the 1990s, hence the reduction in trade barriers is not likely to play a major role for the development of trade patterns after 2004. Moreover, capital flows and in particular FDI have already played an important role before the accession countries officially became members of the EU, anticipating the official enlargement.

The paper by Dora Borbély looks at the evolution of export patterns in selected accession countries. It is a descriptive study that in the first place aims at understanding the industrial structure and the development of industries of the accession countries. The final goal is to predict how the industrial structure will develop after the EU enlargement to make statements about the future role of the accession countries in the European industrial landscape and the prospects of economic growth. As noted earlier, the evolution of trade flows from the mid 1990s to 2001/02, the time span studied in Borbély, is a result of two processes: first the transition from a communist economy to a market economy and second the integration of these economies in the European economy. The indices looked at in the paper are all worthwhile to be considered, and as the author notes a more sophisticated econometric analysis might be helpful to draw a more complete picture. The main insight of the paper is that Hungary tends to specialize in higher technology intensive industries as compared to Poland and the Czech Republic. But clearly, drawing conclusions for the future development of trade patterns from data for 1995-2001 is challenging.

However, there is an alternative indicator to predict the future industrial structure of countries: FDI. Foreign firms will only invest, if returns from that investment promise to be high in the future. FDI is already a major source of capital for

[1] For a discussion see the EEAG Report on the European Economy 2004. Chapter. 5

the accession countries. Table 1 shows the data on FDI as percent of GDP and GDP growth rates in the Czech Republic, Hungary, Poland.

Table 1. FDI and GDP Growth

	1998	1999	2000	2001	2002
	Czech Republic				
Real GDP growth rate	-1.0	0.5	3.3	3.1	2.0
FDI (percent of GDP)	4.8	9.3	.	8.6	13.4
	Hungary				
Real GDP growth rate	4.9	4.2	5.2	3.9	3.3
FDI (percent of GDP)	.	.	3.5	4.7	1.8
	Poland				
Real GDP growth rate	4.8	4.1	4.0	1.0	1.4
FDI (percent of GDP)	4.0	4.7	5.7	3.1	2.2

Source: European Commission, Enlargement Papers, 2003

Thus, the foreign investment in the accession countries is by no means negligible and with full EU membership FDI into Central Eastern European countries is likely to increase even further. Moreover, as suggested by Tondl and Vuskic (2003), the strong inflow of FDI played an important role for high growth in Eastern European countries. However, besides the effect of aggregated FDI on aggregated growth rates, disaggregated figures on FDI can possibly explain how the potential future international competitiveness of industrial sectors are assessed by foreign investors.

Table 2 summarizes the FDI stocks in the Czech Republic by industry. The first thing to note is that the total stock of FDI has been increasing and has more than doubled from 1997 to 2000. The strongest engagement took place in the tertiary sector, followed by the secondary sector. The primary sector played only a minor role, even though the dynamic in foreign investments is fairly strong even in the primary sector. Within the secondary sector, the focus of Dora Borbély's paper, the industries with the largest FDI stock are petroleum, chemicals and rubber and plastic products, motor vehicles, non-metallic mineral products, and food beverages and tobacco. Looking at relative FDI flows, growing while still relatively small industries, in terms of FDI, are in addition radio, television, office and computing machinery and precision instruments. These findings basically support Borbély's findings and suggest the additional conclusions that while the medium technology industries have the largest stock of FDI, the dynamic is strongest in the high technology industries.

FDI stocks in Hungary are summarized in Table 3. The stock of FDI in the primary sector is negligible and constant, and it is again the tertiary sector that attracts the largest volume of FDI. Within the secondary sector, the industries with the largest stock of FDI are food, beverages and tobacco, electrical machinery and apparatus, and motor vehicles and other transport equipment. However, the stock of FDI is not as strongly growing as in the Czech Republic but fairly constant and in some industries, there is even a decreasing stock of FDI. Examples are chemicals and chemical products and machinery and equipment.

Table 4 supplies the information on the FDI stock for the Polish economy. The first thing to note is that the volume of FDI in Poland is large compared to the other two countries. Thus foreign direct investment in Poland appears to be profitable. The Polish economy has according to Borbély a comparative advantage in low to medium technology sectors. Looking at the secondary industries with the largest investment, three industries stand out with respect to the magnitude of the stock and the dynamic: food, beverages and tobacco, non-metallic mineral products and motor vehicles and other transport equipment. Interesting are the strong FDI activities in food, beverages and tobacco that are not reflected in a comparative advantage according to Figure 12 in Borbély. Similarly, foreign investors appear to expect future profits in the motor vehicle and transport equipment industry with about one tenth of the total FDI stock being in that industry.

Summarizing we state that FDI and comparative advantage draw a similar picture of the industrial structure of the Czech and the Hungarian economy. The evaluation of the Polish economy is somewhat inconclusive.

References

CESifo (2004), EEAG Report on the European Economy.

European Commission (2003), Progress toward meeting economic criteria for accession: the assessment from the 2003 comprehensive monitoring report.

Tondl, Gabriele and Vuksic, Goran (2003), What makes regions in Eastern Europe catching up? The role of foreign investment, human resources and geography, ZEI Working Paper B12.

Table 2. FDI stocks in the host economy, by industry, 1997-2000, Czech Republic (Millions of dollars)

Sector/industry	1997	1998	1999	2000
TOTAL	9 233.7	14 375.1	17 552.1	21 643.7
PRIMARY SECTOR	85.2	149.3	109.2	435.1
Agriculture, hunting, forestry and fishing	5.3	22.7	17.9	34.4
Mining, quarrying and petroleum	79.9	126.6	91.3	400.7
SECONDARY SECTOR	5 127.6	6 579.2	6 786.7	8 256.2
Food, beverages and tobacco	899.8	1 025.3	1 125.6	1 039.4
Textiles and clothing	140.9	232.1	203.6	290.3
Leather	-	3.8	4.1	-1.9
Wood, publishing and printing	417.2	616.4	677.4	669.8
Petroleum, chemicals and rubber and plastic products	674.8	900.6	713.1	1 415.2
Non-metallic mineral products	-	1 370.7	1 467.9	1 268.1
Basic metals and metal products	381.0	487.6	624.2	781.4
Machinery and equipment	139.2	208.5	218.7	372.2
Electrical machinery and apparatus	-	524.7	486.4	533.4
Radio, television, office and computing machinery	53.3	61.4	88.1	179.9
Precision instruments	-	58.3	87.6	158.3
Motor vehicles	774.1	972.3	894.5	1 370.6
Other transport equipment	31.6	37.4	95.0	39.1
Other manufacturing	-	67.1	87.9	124.6
Recycling	-	13.0	12.6	14.1
Unspecified secondary	1 615.7	-	-	1.7
TERTIARY SECTOR	4 020.9	7 646.6	10 656.2	12 952.4
Electricity, gas and water supply	400.3	643.1	1 347.3	1 425.1
Construction	186.2	145.2	176.6	334.5
Trade and repairs	1 116.8	2 490.3	2 770.7	3 254.2
Hotels and restaurants	73.9	10.1	167.0	67.4
Transports, communication	868.2	1 329.6	2 141.9	2 432.6
Financial intermediation	1 047.5	2 121.3	2 648.4	3 182.9
Real estate and business activities	312.0	794.5	1 297.6	1 994.5
Other services	4.4	112.5	106.7	261.2
Unspecified tertiary	11.6	-	-	-

Source: UNCTAD, DITE http://r0.unctad.org/en/subsites/dite/fdistats_files/WID2.htm (Czech National Bank, Statistics Department, Balance of Payments Division (http://www.cnb.cz)).

Note: No data are available prior to 1997.

Table 3. FDI stocks in the host economy, by industry, 1997-2000, Hungary (Billions of forint)

Sector/industry	1997	1998	1999	2000
TOTAL	2 046.2	2 364.4	2 624.5	2 935.5
PRIMARY SECTOR	41.9	33.9	40.6	43.7
Agriculture, hunting, forestry and fishing	19.0	22.4	30.1	32.1
Mining, quarrying and petroleum	22.9	11.5	10.5	11.6
SECONDARY SECTOR	804.7	907.3	981.4	1 080.8
Food, beverages and tobacco	211.5	230.7	229.9	261.8
Textiles, leather and clothing	36.7	41.4	42.8	47.3
Textile and clothing	..	36.0	37.0	40.8
leather	..	5.4	5.8	6.5
Wood	51.4	51.2	53.2	57.2
Wood and wood products	..	10.7	10.5	11.6
Paper and paper-related products	..	40.5	42.7	45.6
Coke, petroleum products and nuclear fuel	-	54.5	50.5	52.5
Chemicals and chemical products	170.3	86.5	96.3	95.7
Rubber and plastics products	-	32.8	44.6	50.6
Non-metallic mineral products	51.1	59.7	66.6	66.9
Basics metal and metal products	59.7	75.2	76.6	66.0
Machinery and equipment	215.3	39.5	45.1	56.8
Electrical machinery and apparatus	-	123.8	154.0	210.8
Motor vehicles and other transport equipment	-	102.9	111.3	104.3
Other manufacturing	8.7	9.1	10.5	10.9
TERTIARY SECTOR	1 199.6	1 423.2	1 602.5	1 811.0
Electricity, gas and water	281.0	349.4	292.1	277.1
Construction	51.0	44.8	39.8	35.9
Wholesale trade	258.5	289.7	318.0	364.2
Hotels and restaurants	50.6	43.2	50.8	54.3
Transport, storage and communications	157.2	167.5	216.5	225.7
Finance	215.9	252.3	273.7	332.8
Real estate, renting and business services	169.2	238.2	353.1	461.5
Education	0.4	0.5	0.6	1.0
Health and social services	2.4	2.4	2.7	2.4
Other services	13.4	35.2	55.2	56.1

Source: UNCTAD, DITE http://r0.unctad.org/en/subsites/dite/fdistats_files/WID2.htm (Hungarian Central Statistical Office, Budapest, unpublished data.)

Notes : Data do not include offshore companies. Paper and paper-related products include publishing and printing. In 1997, chemicals and chemical products include refined petroleum, rubber and plastic products. Machinery and equipment, in 1997, refer to machinery and transport equipment as a whole. Other manufacturing includes recycling. In 2000, finance includes business services; and other services is the sum of electricity, gas and water; hotels and restaurants; education; health and social services; and other services

Table 4. FDI stocks in the host economy, by industry, 1997-2001, Poland (Millions of dollars)

Sector/industry	1997	1998	1999	2000	2001
TOTAL	17 705.4	27 279.6	35 171.0	45 772.0	53 152.2
Estimated FDI of less than $ 1 million	2 882.3	3 371.6	3 741.6	3 620.5	3 681.3
Overall total	20 587.7	30 651.2	38 912.6	49 392.5	56 833.5
PRIMARY SECTOR	31.2	35.9	98.4	73.1	127.4
Agriculture, hunting, forestry and fishing	15.0	24.1	30.1	44.8	40.4
Mining, quarrying and petroleum	16.2	11.8	68.3	28.3	87.0
SECONDARY SECTOR	11 042.0	15 912.1	17 318.4	19 462.9	21 881.7
Food, beverages and tobacco	3 276.9	4 460.7	4 617.4	4 961.9	5 505.7
Textiles, leather and clothing	-	226.1	247.6	271.6	264.6
Wood and furniture	-	634.6	612.2	633.5	1 769.9
Paper, publishing and printing	1 158.4	1 353.9	1 383.8	1 470.3	1 567.3
Chemicals and chemical products	1 087.4	1 272.4	1 304.2	1 285.1	1 304.6
Rubber and plastics products	-	422.7	451.3	591.5	612.0
Non-metallic mineral products	971.4	1 958.5	2 091.9	2 785.7	3 060.0
Basics metal and metal products	375.3	354.2	399.8	403.4	447.7
Machinery and equipment	-	584.8	536.1	317.1	271.7
Electrical machinery and apparatus	664.4	1 016.3	1 269.5	1 575.1	1 683.2
Motor vehicles and other transport equipment	2 510.5	3 627.9	4 404.6	5 167.7	5 395.0
Unspecified secondary	997.7	-	-	-	-
TERTIARY SECTOR	6 632.2	11 331.6	17 754.2	26 236.0	31 143.1
Electricity, gas and water	96.5	241.8	473.0	1 058.6	1 491.8
Construction	554.9	1 685.3	1 930.3	2 490.6	2 764.8
Trade and repairs	1 408.5	2 942.7	3 398.4	3 962.6	6 054.3
Hotels and restaurants	305.5	429.8	423.1	696.8	617.8
Transport, storage and communication	743.5	719.3	1 891.7	5 568.8	5 710.6
Finance	3 130.4	4 802.9	7 862.2	10 392.8	12 251.9
Real estate and business activities	38.3	112.0	190.2	451.4	627.8
Other services	354.6	397.8	1 585.3	1 614.4	1 624.1

Source : UNCTAD, DITE http://r0.unctad.org/en/subsites/dite/fdistats_files/WID2.htm (Polish Agency for Foreign Investment (PAIZ), Research Department, Warsaw (http://www.paiz.gov.pl)).

Notes : Data refer to investments of over $1 million, monitored by PAIZ. The corresponding values in 1994, 1995 and 1996 were respectively $4,320.8 million, $ 6,832.2 million and $ 12,027.7 million.

Sectoral Change and Economic Integration: Theoretical and Empirical Aspects of the Eastern Enlargement of the European Union

Roland Döhrn and Ullrich Heilemann[1]

Contents

1 Introduction 80
2 Theoretical Background and Methods Employed 81
3 Assessing Earlier Estimates and Projections 85
4 Re-estimating the Chenery Hypothesis 90
5 Structural Change and Eastern Enlargement of the EU 92
6 Summary and Conclusions 93
Appendix 94
References 95

[1] This paper is based on a translation of: Döhrn, Heilemann (2003).

1 Introduction

The collapse of the centrally planned systems in Eastern Europe confronted politicians as well as economists with a plethora of questions that had been neglected hitherto. One of the most challenging and, surprisingly, rarely addressed ones was future growth and the structural change connected to it, with Kornai (1990), Hughes/Hare (1991), Klodt (1991) and Inotai (1992) being remarkable exceptions. Structural change must be understood in this context not only in terms of the relation between private and public sector activities, but also as sectoral and regional change. Mostly it was assumed that privatisation, liberalisation and deregulation would lead to an "optimal" allocation of resources with respect to growth. However, this belief soon turned out to be quite unrealistic. Directions, intensity, and speed of structural change are difficult to forecast, as they are influenced by many factors – such as supply and demand, preferences, and technological change – and are closely interlinked as well with economic policy as well as the specific starting conditions of the "new" market economies.

From an analytical point of view, it was quite clear that the past of the transforming economies would provide little information about future developments and structures. Forecasts of structural change were made even more difficult by the speed the economies were integrated into the international markets for goods, services, labour, and capital, which necessarily influenced growth and the composition of production.

Given these difficulties, analyses in the early 1990s concentrated either on the historical integration of the Eastern European countries into the international division of labour (Collins, Rodrik 1991) or used international comparative approaches: To assess future trade and foreign direct investment relation, gravity models were used (Havrylyshyn, Pritschett 1991; Döhrn, Milton 1992; Hamilton, Winters 1992 resp. Döhrn 1996). Concerning sectoral change, well tested hypotheses have been employed assuming a typical and stable relation between income level of an economy and its economic structure such as the three-sector-hypothesis. First proposals in this direction have been made by Winiecki (1988).

In their analyses of sectoral change in Eastern Europe, the authors of this paper made reference to another stage theory (*Stufentheorie*), the so called *Chenery* hypothesis (CH) (Döhrn, Heilemann 1992, 1993a, 1993b, 1996).[2]. This approach played an important role in development theory discussion during the 1960s (Chenery 1960; Chenery, Taylor 1968; Taylor 1966). By comparing countries with different income levels, these authors tried to find "normalities" in their sectoral structures and they based recommendations concerning development strategies on their findings. In the follow up, two interpretations of the CH arose. By some researchers, it was interpreted in a merely descriptive way, using their results as a yardstick in international comparisons. Others understood the structures found as "optimal" with respect to allocation of resources. The second interpreta-

[2] The European Bank for Restructuring and Development employed this approach, too (EBRD 1997: 62-68).

tion, however, means a change in causality. Sectoral structures are no longer seen as a consequence of income growth, but they are considered to be a prerequisite to achieve higher economic growth. This paper, as with our earlier papers as well, will follow the first interpretation of the CH.

In our earlier work cited above, we compared the then observed sectoral structures in the Eastern European economies in transformation to structures found in a sample of industrializing and industrialized economies in the 1980s. From this comparison, the industrial sector appeared to be over-sized, whereas the service sector was considered to be under developed. From this finding, we forecasted that transformation would be accompanied by a considerable structural change. On the other hand, we concluded from our calculations that sectoral change induced by the rise of income levels after the transformation phase would not be too pronounced, even if the intensity of *intra*-sectoral changes should not be underestimated.

As a follow-up to our previous work, this paper pursues three goals. Firstly, it will check, whether our expectations concerning sectoral change actually came true (chapter 3). Secondly, it will evaluate whether the CH is still a meaningful tool to analyse and forecast sectoral change (chapter 4). Finally, the implications of past and future sectoral change in the context of eastern enlargement of the European Union will be addressed (chapter 5). Before discussing these aspects, a short overview of the theories and methods employed will be given (chapter 2). As usual, the paper will be completed by a short summary of our findings (chapter 6).

2 Theoretical Background and Methods Employed

The CH is based on the assumption that sectoral change in an economy is driven by two types of factors. Firstly, so called universal factors, i.e. factors that can be found in a large number of economies and can be determined for example by international cross section analyses. Secondly specific factors, representing national specifics such as geography and climate, endowment with natural resources, exchange rates, policies pursued or the cultural and legal framework of economic activites (Chenery, Taylor 1968: 391ff.). Empirical analyses aim at finding out these universal factors.

Following Chenery's proposal, these factors are detected by estimating sectoral growth functions as a rule. They can be understood as a reduced form of a relatively simple model in which – elastic factor supplies assumed – the domestic production of a sector is driven by domestic final demand, intermediate demand and exports. In such a model, a sector's share in aggregate domestic demand is determined by and large by two factors. Income per capita, which is considered to be exogenous in this context, is used as an indicator of the stage of development of an economy and the preferences linked to it. Population is also an indictor of what extent economies of scale can be realised. As a control variable, furthermore the sector specific endowment with natural resources can be included in the growth function. Chenery used the latter in a qualitative way only. Thus, the approach used can be written as:

$$V_{ij} = V_{ij} (Y_j, N_j, R_{ij}) \tag{1}$$

with V_{ij}: Value added in sector i in country j;
Y_j: income per capita in country j;
N_j: population in country j;
R_{ij}: resources for sector i in country j.

It should be noted that this approach describes an equilibrium only and gives no mention of the time needed to form the sectoral structures that are adequate to the income levels given.

Typically, (1) is specified as follows (Fels et al. 1971; Görgens 1975): Assuming constant elasticities, all variables are transformed to their logarithms and instead of sectoral value added, the share of a sector in total valued added (V_{ij}/V_j) is examined. The latter assumption avoids all problems arising from the necessity to convert sectoral data available in national currencies as a rule into a single currency. However, this advantage is won by being faced with all econometric problems arising from estimating share equations (Ronning 1992). To determine the influence of per capita income, an approach allowing for variable elasticities is used; the variable enters the equation as well linear as well as in a logarithmic transformation[3]. Sector specific natural resources for the agricultural sector are approximated by the area of arable land available per capita (AF). Resources of the mining sector are measured by exports of mining products per capita (RB). Furthermore, the investment quota (IQ) defined as the share of gross fixed capital formation in GDP, is included in the equation to test the influence of capital formation on sectoral structures. In summary, the following equation is estimated:

$$\log(V_{ij}/V_j) = \log \alpha_{i0} + \alpha_{i1} * \log Y_j + \alpha_{i2} * Y_j + \alpha_{i3} * \log N_j + \alpha_{i4} * AF_j + \alpha_{i5} * RB_j + \alpha_{i6} * IQ_j + u_{ij}. \tag{2}$$

The index i associated with the parameters stands for the different sectors.

As mentioned above, the CH is used subsequently in a descriptive way only. However, in the relevant literature the validity of the approach is criticised (Steiner 1981). In particular, the reservations are based on the selection of sectors and countries the empirical work is based on. *Chenery* (1960) as well as *Fels et al.* (1971) and *Görgens* (1975) analyse a large number of countries and sectors and gain results that are satisfactionary in a statistical sense. The explanatory power of the approach very much relies on the differences in the state of development, and hence in per capita income, of the economies considered, as experience shows that only a high variance in the data ensures a good statistical explanation (Meißner, Fassing 1989: 106). If the relation is tested for different income groups, the results for the different categories differ too much to allow speaking of a "normal" sectoral structure (Görgens 1975: 264 ff.). All in all, a statistical test of the CH renders the better results, the higher the differences in income levels of the economies

[3] In a log-linear function $y = \alpha_1 * \log x + \alpha_2 * x$ the elasticity of y with respect to x is $\alpha_1 + \alpha_1 * x$.

considered are and the higher is the level of aggregation on the sectoral level (Meißner, Fassing 1989: 107).

The judgement of sectoral change in the transformation economies therefore seems to depend highly on choosing the "right" reference group of countries. Following the terminology of the World Bank, the Eastern European economies are "middle income countries of the upper income category". Therefore the reference group here is chosen mainly from countries having the same or a higher income. Highly industrialized, but very small countries (e.g., Luxembourg, Singapore and S.A.R. Hong Kong) are excluded as well as economies highly dependent on the exports of raw materials such as the OPEC members. In addition, some countries are included that are in a geographic situation comparable to one of the transformation economies, namely some Mediterranean countries and Mexico. All in all, our reference group consists of 30 economies (table 1). Concerning the transformation countries we have restricted our analysis to Poland and Hungary as well as the Czech and Slovak Republics.

Concerning sectoral aggregation, six industries are considered: agriculture, mining and energy, manufacturing, construction, market oriented services and government services. We refrained from going deeper on account of the methodological reservations mentioned, but also because of statistical problems, as the definition of sectors varies greatly between the different countries. Nevertheless, earlier work based on a larger number of sectors showed a quite good fit for manufacturing industries, whereas the results for the sevice sector were not very convincing (Döhrn, Heilemann 1996: 415).

The parameters of equation (2) can be estimated from cross section as well as from panel data. As the variance in the data between countries is markedly higher than the variance over time, a cross section analysis seems to be the appropriate method for this kind of anlysis. The estimates presented here are based on the arithmetic average of all data in our observation in the period 1988 - 2000[4]. All data are taken from statistics of the United Nations, the OECD and EUROSTAT, supplemented by national data. In some cases, estimates were made to replace missing data. In a few cases, our observations begin later than 1988 or ended earlier than 2000.

[4] In other words, we determine between groups estimates. In a random-effects panel model, the estimate can be written as the weighted arithmetic mean of the between groups and the within groups estimates with the cross section variances and the variances over time serving as weights (Hsiao 1986: 36). Here, our estimates come close to the results of a random effects panel model.

Table 1. Comparison of sectoral growth functions 1978-88 and 1988-2000 Cross section regression, average of the respective time period

Sector	Agriculture		Energy & Energie		Manufacturing		Construction		Private Services	
	1978-88[1]	1988-2000[2]	1978-88[1]	1988-2000[2]	1978-88[1]	1988-2000[2]	1978-88[1]	1988-2000[2]	1978-88[1]	1988-2000[2]
Constant	9.000	9.977	3.865	3.260	-0.147	3.445	-0.077	-0.800	2.336	2.565
	(11.3)	(9.9)	(8.7)	(5.6)	(0.2)	(4.1)	(0.2)	(1.1)	(7.3)	(6.8)
Per-capita income,	-0.587	-0.625	-0.290	-0.212	0.365	0.029	0.095	0.072	0.084	0.093
log	(10.9)	(10.4)	(5.5)	(3.2)	(4.7)	(0.4)	(4.3)	(2.0)	(4.1)	(4.0)
Per-capita income	-	-	-	-	-0.0518	-0.0032	-	-	-	-
	-	-	-	-	(3.6)	(0.3)	-	-	-	-
Population, log	-0.171	-0.237	-	-	0.090	0.005	-	-	0.062	0.028
	(3.0)	(3.9)	-	-	(3.0)	(0.1)	-	-	(2.8)	(1.2)
Agricultural	0.065	-0.009	-	-	-0.053	-0.083	-	-	-	-
Ressources-log	(0.9)	(0.1)	-	-	(1.5)	(2.0)	-	-	-	-
Exports of Primary-	-0.045	-0.083	0,000416[a]	0,000402[a]	-0.080	-0.069	-0.052	-0.048	-	-
products per capita, log	(1.1)	(1.7)	(6.1)	(4.1)	(3.9)	(2.4)	(3.6)	(1.8)	-	-
Investment rate, log	-	-	-	-	-	-	0.415	0.669	-	-
	-	-	-	-	-	-	(3.2)	(3.6)	-	-
$R^2(R^2_{adj})$	0.822	0.842	0.621	0.401	0.585	0.282	0.434	0.338	0.370	0.324
F	36.0	39.6	26.0	10.7	9.0	3.3	9.0	5.9	10.0	7.9

Own calculations. –[1]31 Countries see *Döhrn, Heilemann* (1996). –[2]30 Countries. – [a]linear.

3 Assessing Earlier Estimates and Projections

Our estimates of the CH made more than ten years ago showed for the most part a good statistical fit. The adjusted coefficient of determination of our sectoral growth functions was well above 0.6; only for market oriented services and the construction sector was the fit worse (table 2). Per capita income was positively correlated with the share of the sector in aggregate value added in four cases. Not very surprisingly considering the three sector hypothesis, the share of the agricultural sector had declined as income rose, whereas the share of the manufacturing sector rose in low income regions and shrank when per capita income reached a certain level. From our estimates, the share of manufacturing reached its largest value at a per capita income of 7,100 US$ (at prices and exchange rates of 1987). Concerning population, a negative correlation was found in agriculture and government services, hinting at economies of scale in these sectors. In manufacturing and market oriented services, on the other hand, a positive correlation was found. The size of capital formation, as measured by the investment quota, showed a positive influence in the equation for the construction sector only. In other sectors, no correlation with this supply side variable could be found, what may be explained by the fact that we did not use a dynamic specification. As expected, a coincidence between the endowment with natural resources and the size of the mining and energy sector was found, whereas the correlation with the share of manufacturing was negative, which may reflect that many countries with rich natural resources suffered from the so-called Dutch disease. The large and highly significant constant in the service sector, finally, hints at the fact that in the early phase of industrialisation services make an important share of total production (Gershuny 1978), which contradicts a simple interpretation of the Three-Sector-Hypothesis.

Based on these results, we tried in a first step to estimate the need of restructuring in the economies in transformation. For this purpose the sectoral structure of their economies existing in 1988 was compared to a hypothetical structure derived from the regressions. By this standard, we found that the manufacturing sector and the construction sector were clearly over-sized; some reasons for that can be found in the analysis by Lipton and Sachs (1990). On the other hand, the service sector turned out to be smaller than in developed market economies, which holds for market oriented services and government services as well. In another paper we analysed the manufacturing sector more and detail finding that in particular the production of investment goods and intermediate goods was over-sized, whereas the share of producers of consumer goods more or less was the same as in market economies (Döhrn/Heilemann 1996). Summing up, a significant change in the composition of aggregate production could be expected during the transformation process.

Table 2. Sectoral Growth Functions, Cross country regressions on 23 countries, Average of 1988 to 2000

			Manufacturing				
	Agriculture	Mining & Energy	34 Countries	without GR	Construction	Private Services	Public Services
Constant	7.774	3.370	3.266	2.778	1.678	2.107	3.740
	(7.2)	(5.3)	(5.5)	(6.1)	(3.5)	(4.6)	(5.9)
Per capita income,	-0.606	-0.214	0.110	0.170	0.075	0.188	-0.218
log	(8.2)	(3.1)	(1.5)	(3.0)	(1.9)	(3.2)	(2.8)
Per capita income	-	-	-0.00839	-0.015	-	-0.010000	0.028669
	-	-	(1.2)	(2.7)	-	(1.8)	(3.8)
Population, log	-0.062	-	-	-	0.0492	-	-
	(0.9)	-	-	-	(1.5)	-	-
Agricultural	-	-	-0.041	-0.047	-	-	-
Ressources, log	-	-	(1.2)	(1.8)	-	-	-
Exports of Primary	-	0,000386[a]	-0.069	-0.067	-0.034	-	-
Products per capita, log	-	(4.0)	(3.0)	(3.9)	(1.2)	-	-
Investment rate, log	-	-	0.438	0.373	0.672	-	-0.415
	-	-	(2.8)	(3.2)	(3.9)	-	(2.7)
R^2_{adj}	0.664	0.347	0.461	0.634	0.358	0.375	0.485
F	33.6	9.8	6.6	12.1	5.6	10.9	11.3

Own calculations. 30 countries (Table 1) plus Czech Republic, Slovak Republic, Poland and Hungary. – [a]linear

In a second step, we used our regression to forecast future sectoral structures. For this purpose, assumptions about the exogenous variables had to be made. Of particular relevance was the assumption about per capita. It was lead by the idea that the economies in transformation should be able to double per capita income within a span of ten years. However, there was much uncertainty about per capita income in the starting year of our analysis. At this time the economies in transformation have mostly followed a strategy of an under-valued currency. Calculating comparable income figures leads to substantial differences whether taking market exchange rates or purchasing power parities (PPP). Therefore, we developed two scenarios. In the first we based our estimates of future structure on per capita incomes expressed in US Dollars, in the second we used PPPs (Döhrn, Heilemann 1993b). In the latter we expressed the expectation that exchange rates will come close to PPPs in the long run, which is plausible for theoretical and empirical reasons as well.

Table 3. Sectoral Growth Functions, Cross country on 34 countries, Average of 1988 to 2000, Version I: Dummy-variable for Transition Countries

			Manufacturing				
Sector	Agriculture	Mining & Energy	34 Countries	Without GR	Construction	Private Services	Public Services
Constant	9.018	3.265	3.320	2.820	1.457	2.084	3.793
	(8.7)	(4.8)	(5.6)	(6.1)	(2.8)	(4.5)	(5.9)
Per capita income,	-0.675	-0.204	0.103	0.164	0.087	0.192	-0.230
log	(9.7)	(2.8)	(1.4)	(2.9)	(2.2)	(3.2)	(3.0)
Per capita income			-0.00663	-0.01385		-0.0107	0.0307
			(0.9)	(2.4)		(1.8)	(3.9)
Population, log	-0.115				0.0574		
	(1.8)				(1.7)		
Agricultural			-0.050	-0.052			
Ressources, log			(1.4)	(1.9)			
Exports of Primary		0,000387[a]	-0.071	-0.069	-0.035		
Products per capita, log		(3.9)	(3.1)	(3.9)	(1.2)		
Investment rate, log			0.414	0.360	0.656		-0.422
			(2.6)	(3.0)	(3.9)		(2.7)
Dummyvariable	-0.739	0.127	0.108	0.064	0.126	-0.038	0.105
Transition Countries	(3.1)	(0.5)	(1.1)	(0.8)	(1.1)	(0.5)	(1.0)
R^2_{adj}	0.735	0.258	0.463	0.630	0.363	0.359	0.485
F	31.5	4.7	5.8		4.8	7.2	8.8

Own calculations – [a]linear

To what extent our forecasts on structural change came true is difficult to assess for various reasons. Firstly, it has already been said that the forecasts are based on the idea that per capita income will double within ten years (i.e., between 1988 and 1998). Whether this actually is the case is hard to determine, as per capita incomes observed in 1998 are influenced by exchange rate developments as well as by various changes in the base year of price indices used for calculating PPPs. Furthermore, the Czech Republic and the Slovak Republic only exist since 1993. Data for 1988 refer to Czechoslovakia. However, per capita income for 1988 actually lays within the range marked by our earlier estimates based on US Dollar exchange rates on the one hand and those based on PPPs on the other (table 3). By and large, our assumptions on per capita income were fulfilled.

Secondly, the comparison of our projections with the existing sectoral structures is spoiled by the fact that the definition of sectors is not fully comparable. In the 1995 System of National Accounts (SNA), the service sector is divided according to functional aspects, whereas it is no longer relevant whether a service is provided by the market sector or by the state. To allow at least some comparisons between the 1998 figures and the situation in the late eighties, the education and the health sector were considered as part of the state sector, ignoring the fact that an increasing part of production in these fields is provided by private enterprises, so that the share of government services is systematically over-estimated in 1998.

Table 4. Per Capita Income in CEEC Countries, in US-Dollar

	1988	1998	
		Projection	Actual
Poland			
In constant prices and exchange rates[1]	1 790	3 580	3 879
In PPP	5 400	10 800	6 740
Hungary			
In constant prices and exchange rates[1]	2 590	5 180	6 168
In PPP	6 000	12 000	10 479[a]
CSFR			
In constant prices and exchange rates[1]	3 450	6 900	
In PPP	8 300	16 600	
Czech Republic			
In constant prices and exchange rates[1]			5 469
In PPP			12 289[a]
Slovak Republic			
In constant prices and exchange rates[1]			3 568
In PPP			9 811[a]

Own calculation based on IMF and Worldbank data. – [1]1988 and Projection 1998: Pricebasis 1987; Actual 1998: Pricebasis 1995. - [a]1999.

Taking into account these caveats, the comparison of projected and existing sectoral yields that our forecasts more or less point in the right direction (table 4).

The contribution of manufacturing to aggregate production was reduced by the extent expected. On the other hand, the share of services increased. That the share of market oriented services grew less than projected most probably reflects the changes in the definition of sectors mentioned.

Table 5. Sectoral Economic Structure in CEEC countries, in % of GDP

		Industry					
	Agricul-ture	Total	Mining and Energy	Manu-facturing	Con-struction	Market Based Services	Public Services
				1988, actual values			
CSFR	6.3	57.5				36.2	
Poland	13.1	52.4				34.4	
Hungary	14.4	38.4	8	23.5	6.9	23.3	9.4
				1988, hypothetical values			
				Version A			
CSFR	9	33	7	21	6	37	11
Poland	11	33	7	19	6	37	9
Hungary	12	31	6	20	6	36	11
				Version B			
CSFR	5	33	5	22	6	40	13
Poland	6	36	5	24	6	41	11
Hungary	7	33	4	23	6	38	12
				1998, Projection			
				Version A			
CSFR	6	35	5	23	7	40	12
Poland	8	35	6	23	6	40	10
Hungary	8	34	4	23	7	38	12
				Version B			
CSFR	4	29	4	19	6	43	14
Poland	4	34	4	24	6	43	12
Hungary	5	31	3	22	6	40	14
				1998, observed values			
Slovak Rep.	4.2	31.9	4.1	21.4	6.4	39.7	14.9
Czech Rep.	3.9	36.8	5.3	25.1	6.4	39.2	13.5
Poland	4.2	31.8	5.4	18.8	7.6	36.3	15.3
Hungary	4.9	28.9	3.7	21.2	4.0	37.3	17.0

Own calculations, Döhrn, Heilemann (1993b).

With respect to its "forecast accuracy" the CH turned out to be a valuable approach. This at least holds true as long as highly aggregated sectors are considered. On a more detailed level, structural change is increasingly coined by national specifics, in the case of the Central European countries also by the decisions of multinational companies. The composition of the manufacturing sector differs substantially between the countries considered (table 5).

4 Re-estimating the Chenery Hypothesis

However, to analyse the explanatory power of the CH in detail, it must be asked whether the econometric structures of the sectoral growth functions used for the projections are sufficiently stable over time. Therefore we re-estimated the functions that had been specified for the 1978-1988 period using data for the 1988-2000 period. In doing so, some empirical problems arose. Yugoslavia had to excluded from our new sample, and unified Germany took the place of Western Germany. Furthermore, the change in the definition of sectors must be mentioned again. Concerning exogenous variables, we tried to be compatible with our earlier estimates to the greatest extent possible. In particular, we used per capita income in prices and exchange rates of 1987.

By and large, the coefficients estimated for our reference period were the same as those found in our earlier studies (table 2). The most significant difference is associated with the population variable which turned out to be statistically insignificant in all sectors except agriculture. However, the fit of the functions was worse in the 1988-2000 period as a rule, especially concerning manufacturing and state services.

This was reason enough to re-specify the sectoral growth functions. As we also wanted to test the extent to which sectoral structures in the economies in transition still differ from those in established market economies, the first were included in the sample here. This required a change in the base year of our income comparisons. Subsequently, 1995 prices and exchange rates were used in our calculations.

The re-specification and the broadening of our sample resulted in a better fit of the functions estimated for manufacturing and state services. On the other hand, the explanatory power of our regression for the agricultural was inferior to the earlier work (table 6). In the manufacturing sector, it turned out that our results were heavily influenced by the data on Greece, where the share of industry is extraordinary small in relation to its per capita income in an international comparison. Considering Greece to be an outlier and excluding it from our sample led to a better fit and resulted in coefficients that were quite different from those in the function including Greece.

Compared to our estimates for the 1980s, some striking differences appear. No influence of the size of population is found anymore in the manufacturing sector nor in services. This may be interpreted as a result of the globalisation of production with national economies of scale losing importance compared to enterprise specific factors. On the other hand, the investment quota shows a positive correlation with the share of manufacturing and a negative one with the share of government services.

Table 6. Structure of Manufacturing in Selected Transition Countries, 1995 and 1998, in %

	1995			1998		
Manufacture of...	Czech Rep.	Hungary	Slovak Rep.	Czech Rep.	Hungary	Slovak Rep.
Food Products and Tobacco Product	14.7	18.5	13.8	15.6	14.8	13.4
Textiles	5.4	7.1	6.1	5.4	6.4	5.9
Leather	1.3	1.7	1.6	0.9	1.3	0.9
Wood	3.0	2.6	3.4	3.6	1.9	3.0
Pulp, Paper and Printing	5.6	5.8	8.7	5.8	5.3	7.3
Coke, Refined Petroleum Products and Nuclear Fuel	3.6	8.4	8.4	1.3	7.9	5.9
Chemicals and Chemical Products	6.5	11.6	8.9	6.2	9.7	7.6
Rubber and Plastic Products	2.0	3.7	4.2	4.2	3.9	3.5
Other Non-Metallic Mineral Products	6.6	4.9	5.2	7.5	4.5	6.0
Basic Metals and Fabricated Metal Products	20.4	10.8	16.0	16.9	8.9	16.5
Machinery	13.4	7.1	9.9	10.5	6.6	8.8
Electrical and Optical Instruments	7.0	9.7	6.2	9.4	15.7	9.0
Motor Vehicles, Ships and Aircraft	6.1	5.6	4.6	8.5	10.9	8.2
Other Products	4.3	2.6	3.1	4.2	2.2	4.1
Total	100.0	100.0	100.0	100.0	100.0	100.0

Own calculations based on OECD data.

In the 1980s, approaches using variable elasticities with respect to per capita income were only superior in the case of manufacturing. They showed that the industry sector reached its maximum at a per capita income of 7,100 US$. Now in the sectoral growth functions for market oriented services and government services, the fit was also improved by use of the flexible elasticity approach. According to the new regression, the share of manufacturing rises to a per capita income of 10,600 US$ (in 1995 prices and exchange rates). Moreover, when taking into account inflation this means that the maximum is reached at a higher income level.

The share of private services decreases when income exceeds 16,950 US$. Given the small number of cases in this income group, the result should not be overstressed. The share of government services first declines with income rising, reaching a minimum at 5,400 US$. After this point, the share rises. This may reflect high income elasticities of the demand for education and health services. As already mentioned, however, nothing is said as to whether these services are actually provided by the state or by the private sector in the individual countries.

An interesting feature of our analysis is that the share of the manufacturing sector seems to be somewhat higher in the 1990s than in the 1980s, but the curve is quite flat when plotted against per capita income (Chart). This could be interpreted as a "structural convergence" between different economies (i.e., sectoral structures vary less between incomes groups than they did ten years earlier). This result seems quite plausible against the background of increasing globalisation of production. However, a more in-depth analysis is required which goes beyond the focus of our study.

In a next step, we tested whether sectoral structures in transforming economies still must be considered as special cases, or whether they have become more or less the same as those in well-established market economies in the meantime. This was done by including a dummy variable in our sectoral growth functions, taking the value 1 in the case the economy in question is a transforming economy, while being represented by 0 in all other cases. In five out of six sectors the variable does not show a significant influence in our regressions, and the coefficients of other variables do not change much[5]. Obviously, the adjustment process in the Eastern European countries went into the direction we forecasted in our earlier studies, resulting in structures that resemble those in the remaining economies in our sample. The only exception is the agricultural sector, whose share seems to be significantly smaller in the transforming economies than in the reference group.

5 Structural Change and Eastern Enlargement of the EU

Our analysis shows that the four countries considered here have undergone an enormous structural change since the early 1990s. Today, as they have become members of the European Union, their sectoral structures do not differ too much from those in established market economies of a comparable size and income level. With respect to the consequences of Eastern enlargement this is good news, as there seems to be no need of further adaptations that could be a burden on the EU as a whole. However, this result only holds true for the broad categories considered and surely not for all sectors and regions.

Past as well as future structural change will not go unnoticed without corresponding consequences for Western European countries. Fears were occasionally expressed that low labour costs in Eastern Europe could lead to a displacement of production in the industry sector in particular. In terms of our approach here, this

[5] The results of these regressions are available upon request.

would translate into an "over-industrialisation" of the economies in transition. Hitherto, we could not find an incidence of such effects on the sectoral level we analysed. However, this does not exclude them for some sectors. Moreover, one should not forget that our analyses end in 2000. Many papers on the consequences of eastern enlargement focus on the agricultural sector. Concerning this sector, our results surprisingly suggest that its share in GDP is even somewhat smaller than the reference value recovered in the international comparison. We also found hints that an enormous adjustment will still be required in agriculture at least in some countries In particular the sector's share in Poland comprises about 20 % of total employment - above all self-employed – which is much higher than its GDP share.

The share of the public sector is somewhat larger than in our reference group, even if the differences are not significant in a statistical sense. One could argue that the heritage of the central planning era could be embellished within these figures. However, we found no proof of this claim. On the contrary, public sectors share in total employment was between 5.5 % and 7.5 % in the four economies in transition, which was somewhat below the share in EU employment. As already mentioned, international comparisons in this field are somewhat spoiled by differences in the way education and healthcare sectors are treated in the statistics.

6 Summary and Conclusions

The paper presented has two goals. Firstly, we want to test whether the Chenery-Hypothesis offers a sound basis for the explanation and projection of structural change. A comparison or sectoral forecasts we made in the early 1990s and recent observation made evident that the hypothesis serves as a useful approach to analyse structural change. Discrepancies lie within the typical error margins. This view is supported by the fact that re-estimation of the equations used in our earlier studies led to similar results. However, income lost some of its explanatory power with respect to sectoral discrepancies, leading to the question of whether "structural convergence" can be observed across countries and different levels of development. Answering this question as well as finding driving forces behind this, however, is beyond the scope of this paper.

From a policy point of view, our analysis underpins the speed at which structural change took place in Eastern Europe. Whether this was the same in other regions (e.g., in South-East Asia) remains open for discussion. Furthermore we did not analyse the macro-economic environment under which this change was achieved as well as the costs it caused in terms of unemployment for instance. It seems clear that under market economy conditions given similar preferences and production technologies, sectoral structures seem to converge quite soon, at least at the aggregation level considered here. As already said, income has lost parts of its power to explain differences across countries. New research in this field should ask whether this is merely a transitory effect or whether liberalisation und deregulation have given rise to international factors of structural change at the detriment of nation-specific factors. Concerning EU membership, it seems plausible that this impact on intra-sectoral change will be larger than on inter-sectoral change, which should make it easier to handle.

Appendix

Table 7. Per Capita Income, Population and Economic Structure, Average of 1988-2000

			in % of GDP					
	Per Capita Income in $[1]	Population in 1000	Agriculture	Mining and Energy	Manufacturing	Construction	Private Services	Public Services
			Asian- Pacific- Countries					
Indonesia	850	189 862	18.5	11.8	22.7	6.3	31.1	9.5
Philippines	1 090	67 706	20.8	3.6	23.6	5.6	32.2	14.1
Thailand	2 440	58 280	13.9	4.1	26.3	6.7	38.0	11.0
Malaysia	3 800	19 870	13.6	10.3	26.8	5.1	36.5	10.3
Korea	7 530	44 429	6.6	2.9	29.8	10.4	36.5	14.1
Taiwan	14 050	21 813	3.0	2.4	27.8	4.8	51.3	10.2
New Zealand	15 930	3 574	7.4	4.1	18.0	3.8	46.6	16.6
Japan	39 080	125 123	2.2	3.0	26.1	10.1	36.9	26.2
			Mediterranean Countries, Mexico					
Egypt	1 010	55 961	17.7	8.1	18.0	5.3	32.4	18.4
Morocco	1 350	25 763	16.8	9.8	17.6	4.8	25.6	19.6
Tunisia	1 990	8 699	13.7	7.3	18.0	4.5	25.8	21.8
Turkey	2 100	59 940	16.0	3.9	22.0	6.6	39.6	12.0
Mexico	2 760	88 240	6.0	2.9	19.1	4.0	46.2	15.2
Greece	10 470	10 346	7.7	2.5	10.9	6.2	46.0	18.1
Portugal	15 680	9 925	4.6	6.0	21.1	5.7	43.1	16.5
Spain	17 600	39 222	3.9	7.2	16.7	8.1	48.4	14.5
Italy	18 370	57 111	3.1	2.5	20.8	5.1	45.3	17.7
			Central- and Northern Europe, North America					
Ireland	17 660	3 594	6.1	2.2	26.0	5.0	33.2	17.1
Great Britain	18 570	58 306	1.3	6.3	18.6	5.3	47.9	15.7
Canada	19 970	28 806	2.4	6.8	16.0	5.3	37.4	20.9
Belgium	23 710	10 080	1.6	7.0	16.6	5.2	52.1	13.0
France	25 970	58 918	2.9	2.3	17.2	4.8	44.1	21.3
Finland	26 060	5 066	4.4	2.4	20.9	5.0	36.4	20.0
Netherlands	26 330	15 298	3.4	6.2	15.8	5.1	48.8	15.2
USA	27 700	259 119	1.7	4.1	15.9	4.1	45.1	21.4
Austria	29 060	7 918	2.6	3.1	19.4	7.2	42.3	19.6
Sweden	29 130	8 709	2.2	4.3	18.9	5.8	40.0	24.4
Germany	29 140	80 755	1.2	2.5	22.0	5.7	42.3	19.9
Norway	32 770	4 324	2.4	15.3	11.3	3.6	42.8	16.1
Denmark	33 880	5 207	3.2	2.9	15.1	4.3	40.2	23.4
				CEEC				
Slovak Rep.	3 150	5 347	4.6	6.3	22.1	6.2	39.4	13.4
Poland	3 180	38 422	5.2	6.4	20.7	7.0	33.2	16.2
Czech Rep.	5 330	10 325	4.6	6.9	25.2	7.4	36.3	13.0
Hungary	5 680	10 262	5.0	3.5	20.7	4.0	37.5	17.2

Own calculations. – [1]in prices and exchange rates of 1995.

References

Chenery, H.B. (1960), Patterns of Industial Growth, *American Economic Review* 50: 624-654.

Chenery, H.B. and Taylor, L. (1968), Development Patterns: Among Countries and Over Time, *Review of Economics and Statistics* 50: 391-416.

Collins, S. and D. Rodrik (1991); Eastern Europe and the Soviet Union in te World Economy. *Policy Analyses in International Economics* 32. Washington D.C.

Döhrn, R. (1996), EU-Enlargement and Transformation in Eastern Europe – Consequences for Foreign Direct Investment in Europe. *Konjunkturpolitik* 42: 113-132.

Döhrn, R. und U. Heilemann (1992), Zur allokativen Dimension: Sektorale Entwicklungstendenzen für Ungarn, Polen und die CSFR. *Beihefte der Konjunkturpolitik* 40: 51-69.

Döhrn, R. and U. Heilemann (1993a), Structural Change in Eastern Europe. In: L. Waverman and B. Heitger (Eds.), German Unification and the World Economy. London und New York, Routledge: 83-112.

Döhrn, R. und U. Heilemann (1993b), Sektorale Entwicklungsperspektiven in Osteuropa und ihre Konsequenzen für die deutsche Wirtschaft. *RUFIS-Veröffentlichung* 3/1993. Bochum.

Döhrn, R. and U. Heilemann (1996), The Chenery Hypothesis and Structural Change in Eastern Europe. *Economics of Transition* 4: 411-425.

Döhrn, R. and U. Heilemann (2003), Strukturwandel und Integration: Theoretische und empirische Aspekte der Ostererweiterung. In: D. Cassel und P.J.J. Welfens (eds.), regionale Integration und Osterweiterung der Europäischen Union. Schriften zu Ordnungsfragen der Wirtschaft. Stuttgart: Lucius&Lucius: 375-392

Döhrn, R. and A. R. Milton ((1992), Zur künftigen Einbindung der osteuropäischen Reformländer in die Weltwirtschaft. *RWI-Mitteilungen* 53: 19-40

EUROSTAT (Hrsg.) (versch. Jahre) Volkswirtschaftliche Gesamtrechnungen ESVG. Detaillierte Tabellen nach Produktbereichen. Europäische Gemeinschaften, Luxemburg.

Fels et al. (1971), Der Zusammenhang zwischen Produktionsstruktur und Entwicklungsniveau. *Weltwirtschaftliches Archiv* 106 : 240-278.

Gershuny, J. (1978), After Industrial Society? The Emerging Self-Service Economy. London: Basingstoke.

Görgens, E. (1975), Wandlungen der industriellen Produktionsstruktur im Wirtschaftlichen Wandel. Bern und Stuttgart: Paul Haupt.

Hamilton, C. and A. Winters (1992), Opening Up Trade with eastern Europe. *Economic Policy* 14: 78-116

Havrylishyn, O and L. Pritchett (1991), European Trade Patterns after the Transition. *World Bank Working Papers* WPS 748. World Bank, Washington D.C,

Heller, W. (1933), Die Zukunft der Eingliederung Ungarns in die Weltwirtschaft *Weltwirtschaftliches Archiv* 37: 79-112.

Hughes, G. and P. Hare (1991), Competitiveness and industrial restructuring in Czechoslovakia, Hungary and Poland. *European Economy* Special edition 2/1991. EU-Kommission, Brüssel: 83-??.

Hsiao, C. (1986), Analysis of panel data. Cambridge: Cambridge University Press.

Inotai, A. (1992) Die Lage und Entwicklung der Wirtschaftssektoren in den ostmitteleuropäischen Ländern. Budapest, mimeo.

Klodt, H (1991), Comparative Advantage and Prospective Structural Change in Eastern Europe. *Kiel Working Paper* 477. Institut für Weltwirtschaft, Kiel.

Kornai, J. (1990), The Road to a Free Economy. Shifting From a Socialist System. The Example of Hungary. New York: W. W. Norton.

Lipton, D. and J. Sachs (1990), Creating a Market Economy in Eastern Europe: The Case of Poland, *Brookings Papers on Economic Activity* 1990 (1): 75-147.

Meißner, W. und G. Fassing (1989). Wirtschaftsstruktur und Strukturpolitik. München: Vahlen.

OECD (ed.) (versch. Jahre), National Accounts of OECD Countries. Detailed Tables. Volume II. OECD, Paris.

Ronning, G (1992), Share Equations in Econometrics: A Story of Repression, Frustration and Dead Ends. *Statistische Hefte* 33: 307-??

Steiner, M. (1981), Zur Aussagekraft von Normalstrukturmodellen, *Empirica* 8: 106-127

United Nations (ed.) (versch. Jahre), National Accounts. Statistical aggregates and detailed tables. United Nations, New York.

Winiecki, J. (1988), The Distorted World of Soviet Type Economies. London and New York: Routledge.

Comment on: Sectoral Change and Economic Integration: Theoretical and Empirical Aspects of the Eastern Enlargement of the European Union

Paul J.J. Welfens

The real sphere of economic adjustment dynamics in transition countries are complex, and the particularly important link between structural change and growth – and vice versa – has rarely been analyzed consistently. Moreover, convincing empirical evidence is at a premium. Only in the field of trade dynamics gravity modelling has shed light on changes in export and imports of transition countries. Fortunately Döhrn and Heilemann in a series of innovative papers based on the Chenery model (which had its major focus on structural change in developing countries) have conducted pioneering research in the field of structural change and growth in EU accession countries.

In their most recent contribution the authors have argued that the radical switch to a market economy implies that historical structures inherited in formerly socialist command economies can tell us little about future economic dynamics. This is an adequate perspective, although one might have to consider path dependencies in some sectors in some countries as well. Chenery basically has suggested that the composition of output and per capita income – plus some other economic variables – are linked which then leads to a kind of normality pattern in terms of structural dynamics and the level of economic development in market economies. Normality patterns represent a potentially useful benchmark. This is the way that Chenery is interpreted by the authors, the alternative perspective to interprete existing patterns as an optimum to which economic policymakers in other countries should strive is not considered as adequate. Taking a look at sectoral patterns of market economies in Western countries, the authors' previous studies had concluded that the industrial sector in eastern Europe was oversized, while the services sector looked underdeveloped so that a trajectory of rising per capita income in EU accession countries should go along with strong structural change. After presenting a brief summary of the theory and basic methods, the new paper by Döhrn and Heilemann checks the implicit forecast of previous own approaches and raises the topic whether the Chenery hypothesis (sectoral output in country j is a function of per capita output, the population N and availability of resources R_{ij} useful for sector i) remains a valid perspective for analyzing and forecasting structural change. Interestingly, this approach is then linked to key issues of the EU eastern enlargement issues.

Taking a look at their previous studies they recall the important finding that the share of industrial output in GDP will rise parallel to a certain level of per capita

GDP – beyond this point ($ 7100: at prices and exchange rates of 1987) the share of industry is declining. As regards the population variable they found a negative link between per capita income and government services which suggests economies of scale. Or, one should add as an alternative an income elasticity of demand for such services which is in the range between zero and unity.

The new paper replaces the previous estimation period 1978-88 by the period 1988-2000. Population is no longer a significant variable except in agriculture. This might be explained by the fact that all countries considered have become more open and more integrated through trade than previously so that the size of the domestic market – as proxied by N – became less relevant for industry and services. Using flexible elasticities improved the regression fit. The maximum point for the output share of industry (expressed in 1995 prices and exchange rates) is estimated to be $17,000. Interestingly, as regards government services there is a transitory minimum at $5,400. Beyond this income level the demand for government services seems to increase. If this perspective is correct the EU accession countries will be characterized for many years by a reindustrialization following the early transition period of a sharp industrial contraction. This obviously implies that the new international division of labour in EU 25 will be shaped for many years by relocation of industry to eastern European accession countries. In the medium term firms from western European high wage economies have an incentive to relocate industrial production of standardized (non-high technology) goods to low cost – and low tax – countries in EU accession countries. However, one should not overlook that a similar logic applies to the long run industrial development in eastern Europe. As real wages and relative wage costs both will rise in the accession countries in the medium term, there will be a strong incentive for a second round of industrial relocation, namely towards non-EU countries in eastern Europe and the former CIS, assuming that partnership agreements with the EU have stabilized these countries politically and thus reduced the risk premium for investors. Döhrn and Heilemann are not much concerned about EU eastern enlargement as they find that patterns observed in eastern Europe do not differ much from western European countries with low per capita income levels.

The transitory minimum in government services output is also interesting since it suggests that sustained medium term growth in Eastern Europe could go along with a gradual long term rise of government activity. This in turn could mitigate some of the present conflicts between EU-15 countries which emphasize the need to generate adequate corporate tax revenues in order to finance government expenditures while most EU accession countries mainly discuss reducing already low corporate tax rates. At the bottom line, the contribution is quite welcome to the broader discussion about EU dynamics and the links between growth and structural change. One may wonder how the long term development towards a digital market economy (Audretsch/ Welfens, 2002; Welfens, 2002; Barfield/ Heiduk/ Welfens, 2003; Van Ark/ Piatkowski, 2004) will affect structural change in western Europe and eastern Europe.

References

VAN ARK, B.; PIATKOWSKI, M. (2004). Productivity, Innovation and ICT in Old and New Europe. International Economics and Economic Policy, Vol. 1, Issue 2+3, pp: 215-246.

AURDRETSCH, D.B.; WELFENS, P.J.J.; (eds., 2002), The New Economy and Economic Growth in Europe and the USA, Heidelberg, New York 2003.

BARFIELD, C.; HEIDUK, G.; WELFENS, P.J.J. (eds., 2003), Internet, Economic Growth and Globalization, Perspectives on the Digital Economy in Europe, Japan and the U.S., Heidelberg, New York, 2003.

WELFENS, P.J.J. (2002), Intereconomics.net, Macroeconomics, Deregulation, and Innovation, Heidelberg, New York, 2002.

Structural Change and Economic Dynamics in Transition Economies

Albrecht Kauffmann

Contents

1 Introduction 102
2 Historical Perspective of the Theory of Structural Change 103
3 Selected Statistical Aspects of Structural Change 105
4 Growth and Structural Change 108
4.1 Standard Approaches 108
4.2 Towards Theories of Structural Adjustment 109
4.3 Two-Sector Approaches and Three-Sector Models for Closed Economies 110
4.4 Structural Change in Open Economies and Convergence Issues 111
5 Perspectives 112
References 113

1 Introduction

The collapse of the socialist central planning system in the former Soviet Union and the eastern European partner countries in the Council of Mutual Economic Assistance (CMEA) has brought enormous changes in terms of the politico-economic system – the switch to a democracy – and in terms of economic activities. After a sharp initial transformational crisis economic growth increased in most transition countries in the second half of the 1990s. A structural change which is line with shifts in technologies and consumer preferences is a key element of the transition to a market economy. Moreover, structural change along the logic of comparative advantage and in the context of adequate innovation and imitation policies is important for nurturing eastern European economic growth as well as economic catching-up.

The structure of output has strongly changed in post-socialist transformation economies where an explanation could focus on several impulses:

- The former socialist system had a strong bias in favour of industry – in the Soviet Union also in favour of the military sector – and discriminated services for two reasons: the socialist ideology considered non-industrial services not as value-added which brought insufficient allocation of input factors for the services sector; there was also a low degree of outsourcing of firms eager to control the value-added chain in order to achieve production targets in an economic system where planned inputs to be obtained from external suppliers were notoriously unreliable.
- Economic opening up brought enormous changes in the tradables sector as relative prices – in a newly designed competitive market system – adjusted to the world market. Following the logic of the Heckscher-Ohlin trade model, countries in eastern Europe should have specialized according to relative factor endowments (the latter, however, is partly endogenous as foreign direct investment and a new postsocialist institutional framework for domestic investors change the prospects for capital accumulation); given both relative labor abundance and low wages, the share of labor-intensive production thus should increase in Eastern Europe in the medium run. Such a factor proportion perspective does not rule out that over the long run other impulses become relatively decisive; in particular high inflows of foreign direct investment could stimulate a switch to a more capital intensive production.
- A medium term rise of per capita income brings changes in the demand structure, and at the same time there are Schumpeterian supply-side effects in some sectors due to the parallel development of per capita levels and technology levels. With supply side shifts and changes on the demand side in the nontradables sector and continuing shifts in international relative prices of tradables, structural adjustment will occur. This adjustment process involves a reallocation of resources across sectors, and this goes along with certain adjustment costs.

Structure is defined here on the basis of defining homogeneous non-overlapping subcategories X_i of the variable X, whereby $\sum X_i$ (for i=1 to n) adds up to X. One can thus define shares $x_i =: X_i/X$ so that $\sum x_i = 1$ (for i=1 to n). Over time subcategories X_i cannot only grow with different speed (for $i \neq j$) but there could be qualitative changes which suggest the need to change the definition of subcategories or change the number of subcategories considered. For example, it could be useful to consider additional categories so that i runs from to $n+m$; or to redefine categories i=1 to n. Structural analysis in Economics means considering such categories as output, employment or investment (or capital input or land input) across sectors. While the sectoral structure of an economy is constant in the steady state, the transition process to the steady state normally goes along with different growth rates of output – or employment or capital input – across sectors (the case that transition to the new steady state goes along with no sector change is a special case). In principle both impulses from markets such as changing relative output prices or factor prices and political impulses (e.g., in the form of innovation policy, industrial policy or education policy) as well as other impulses, say from demographical shifts, can affect structural change.

The well-known 3 sector hypothesis and other more advanced approaches can to some extent be applied in Eastern Europe. However, the transition phenomenon raises special problems. Economic opening up in a period of globalization and growing information also implies special aspects. Section 2 considers the problem of defining sectors and adopts a historical perspective of the analysis of structural change. Section 3 looks at structural change and section 4 gives an overview about main alternative approaches to explaining structural change. Finally, section 5 draws some policy conclusions.

2 Historical Perspective of the Theory of Structural Change

After the Industrial Revolution, the 3-sector hypothesis has become popular arguing that relatively high technological progress in one sector and cross-sectoral factor mobility lead to changes in the sectoral shares of agriculture, industry and services. The Industrial Revolution was fuelled by excess labor in the previously dominating agricultural sector and as rising labor input plus industrial capital accumulation raised the share of industry the industrial sector become dominant in terms of output and employment at the start of the 20th century in the US and Western Europe (except for Spain and Portugal which were late industrializers). With industrial firms starting to outsource services considered to be relatively labor intensive, there began another structural shift in the sense that the services sector became the dominant sector in terms of the employment share and with a delay also in the share of output. However, industry has remained the dominant driver of the business cycle in most OECD countries.

In a historical perspective, one should point out that sectors were defined by the French physiocrats of the 18th century by emphasizing the role of land in value-added. Economic value-added was considered possible only on the basis of agricultural land. It could be owned, it could be used or the respective individual had no link to land. Accordingly, the physiocrats distinguished between three different groups in society: Classe des propriétaires (owners), classe productive (farmers) and classe stérile (infertile group). Moreover, the distinction was made that products could be split into consumer goods as well as immaterial goods and services. The physiocrats (e.g. Quesnay, 1694-1774) focused on tangible goods from areable land only. Adam Smith adopted a wider perspective as he argued that craftsmen and construction workers which transformed raw material also represented value-added. However, Smith still considered personal services unproductive and thus part of the classe stérile.

MARX to some extent followed the physiocratic and classical ideas of emphasizing the production of tangible goods and that one input factor was quite crucial: While capital accumulation was considered by MARX, the real hero of production was labor. Services which were not input in industry were not considered to be value-added. The Marxist ideological heritage largely explains why socialist command economies neglected personal services. The whole service sector remained underdeveloped in Eastern Europe in the socialist post-1945 era. Disregarding the Tchechoslovakia one may add that at the same time there was overemphasis on industry due to the late-industrializer phenomenon. Eastern European countries and Russia had not been latecomers in industrialization, and Lenin and Stalin pushed for the state-driven, rapid industrialization of Russia and Eastern European countries once they had a communist government.

Alan G.B. Fisher (1933, 1935a, b, 1939) suggested a three-stage approach to economic development which widened the classical model by taking into account the role of immaterial services as value-added. In the early 20th century, services had obviously grown in economic importance, and a large and growing number of jobs was in the service sector. Fisher emphasized the role of education, science and technological progress as the drivers of growth and productivity. Each stage of economic development was shaped by the dominance of value-added of one sector, bringing with it the distinction between primary, secondary and tertiary. He considered shifts in demand patterns to be a major source of structural change, referring to Engel (1857; 1895). Clark (1940) emphasized in his discussions on structural change that the primary sector was characterized by the use of natural resources and falling scale economies. By contrast, industry was shaped by rising scale economies and the opportunity to transport goods across space. The tertiary sector was defined as a residual sector which was considered heterogeneous (e.g., with some services activities standing for rising marginal costs while trade and transport were characterized by rising productivities over time). Often services are an input for industry; part of the services is, however, a kind of final product offered to households.

A major step towards a more theoretical approach came only with the analysis of Fourastie (1949) whose main focus was on the role of sectoral technological progress assumed to relatively high in industry and rather low in the services sector where labor productivity would grow only slowly; agriculture has a medium rate of technological progress. In addition, he takes into account the role of income elasticities: The demand for primary goods would reach saturation rather quickly while saturation for industrial goods comes only at relatively high per capita income levels, followed even later by saturation levels for services. Thus the interplay of supply forces and demand side dynamics drives structural change in a dynamic way. The latter reflects temporary tensions between the supply side and the demand side. Medium term technological progress and early saturation levels in agriculture imply an excess supply of workers in the countryside who then move towards the industrial sector. Due to the high rate of technological progress, industry will at some point generate – at a certain income level – an excess supply of labor as well. This excess supply can move towards the services sector which can absorb large numbers of additional workers since the income elasticity of services is rather high. As regards drawing demarcation lines across sectors, this has been quite difficult. If one wants to make the relevant distinctions only on the basis of the relative dominance of one input factor (Wolfe, 1955), it is quite difficult to get clear categories. Finally, one should note that the sectoral assignment of mining is controversial, as Clark (1940) and Chenery/ Taylor (1968) have suggested that there are many similarities with agriculture while Kuznets (1971) and Fuchs (1968) argued that mining – in addition to transport and communications – should be considered part of industry. For decades, services were considered to be hardly tradable but Bhagwati (1984) has pointed out that the traditional definition of services which assumes that the service provider and the service user have to physically meet at a specific location at the same time is not adequate as technological progress has made service providers or service users mobile in many cases; the latter implies an increase of competition which in turn could contribute to productivity growth.

As regards socialist command economies in eastern Europe, it is obvious that they achieved considerable economic growth in the first decades. However, central planners gave very limited attention to shifts in private demand patterns and income elasticities, respectively. This in turn stimulated the expansion of the socialist shadow economy, contributing thereby to an undermining in the stability and productivity of the official socialist system. Distorted output patterns and the distortions stemming from the socialist shadow economy thus stand as impediments at the beginning of the process of transformation and market-oriented structural change.

3 Selected Statistical Aspects of Structural Change

The SNA approach of the UN is based on the International Standard of Industrial Classification of All Economic Activities (ISIC). NACE is the sectoral classification approach of the EU which largely follows the UN. Tab. 1 indicates the categories of ISIC (Rev. 3) and NACE (Rev. 1). Definition is a matter of usefulness for research so that a pragmatic approach is adequate. The UN defines three sectors (A, I, S) as broad aggregates; more narrowly defined than industry is the subaggregate Manufacturing Industry. Such figures are published by the World Bank for most countries. If one is to follow a more pragmatic distinction of primary, secondary and tertiary sectors (P-S-T; with mining as a part of the primary sector) one would have to look into national statistics and calculate the respective sectoral indicators. As regards the split between industry and services, it is clear that there is only a soft dividing line.

Table 1. Categories of the ISIC Rev. 3 Standard (or NACE Rev. 1, respectively)

Category	Contains Divisions	Description
A	1–2	Agriculture, hunting and forestry
B	5	Fishing
C	10–14	Mining and quarrying
D	15–37	Manufacturing
E	40–41	Electricity, gas and water supply
F	45	Construction
G	50–52	Wholesale and retail trade; repair of motor vehicles, motorcycles and personal and household goods
H	55	Hotels and restaurants
I	60–64	Transport, storage and communication
J	65–67	Financial intermediation
K	70–74	Real estate, renting and business activities
L	75	Public administration and defence; compulsory social security
M	80	Education
N	85	Health and social work
O	90–93	Other community, social and personal service activities
P	95	Activities of households
Q	99	Extra-territorial organizations and bodies

Table 2. Definition of Broad Economic Sectors by means of ISIC Rev. 3 bzw. NACE Rev. 1 Categories

Sector	Contains categories
Agriculture	A, B
Manufacturing	D
Industry	C-F
Services	G-Q

Table 3. Definition of Broad Economic Sectors by Means of ISIC Rev. 3 Categories (A-I-S vs. P-S-T Scheme)

A-I-S		P-S-T	
Sectors	Categories	Sectors	Categories
Agriculture	A, B	Primary	A-C
Industry	C-F	Secondary	D-F
Services	G-Q	Tertiary	G-Q

Table 4. Composition of Output in the EU-15, Norway, Japan, US, and Eastern Europe, 1993 and 2002 (Value Added at Basic Prices as Percent of GNP)

	1993			2002		
	A	I	S	A	I	S
Austria	2.6	28.7	57.9	2.0	28.8	58.7
Belgium	1.8	26.0	62.2	1.2	24.0	64.1
Denmark	3.1	21.9	62.0	2.2	22.7	60.6
Finland	4.4	27.2	55.8	3.0	28.4	55.7
France	2.8	24.7	62.5	2.4	22.3	64.9
Germany	1.2	31.2	57.8	1.0	26.7	62.3
Greece	9.0	23.1	58.4	6.4	19.6	61.6
Ireland	7.6	31.7	52.1	3.1*	37.8*	48.8*
Italy	3.1	28.4	59.0	2.4	25.5	61.5
Luxembourg	1.1	23.5	64.7	0.6	17.8	70.8
Netherlands	3.3	26.1	62.0	2.4	22.9	63.2
Norway	2.7	29.5	55.0	1.6	33.8	52.9
Portugal	5.4	26.1	56.6	3.2*	25.9*	57.4*
Spain	4.6	28.8	59.1	3.1	27.2	60.0
Sweden	2.3	24.8	58.4	1.6	24.7	61.3
United Kingdom	1.6	28.0	59.9	0.9	23.4	64.4
Japan	2.0	36.2	61.7	1.4*	30.6*	68.1*
United States	1.7	23.9	67.3	1.5*	21.6*	70.3*
Armenia	49.3	25.8	20.8	23.6	33.2	33.4
Azerbaijan	27.3	32.1	35.6	14.2	47.8	29.4
Belarus	17.2	36.0	40.6	9.4	31.9	45.0
Bulgaria	9.9	32.7	45.3	11.0	24.5	51.0
Croatia	11.7	30.3	42.6	6.9	24.3	50.4
Czech Republic	4.9	37.6	46.1	3.4	35.6	51.0
Estonia	10.2	28.2	51.3	4.8	26.1	56.7
Hungary	5.8	28.0	51.3	3.7	26.6	54.9
Kazakhstan	16.4	37.5	39.9	8.0	35.8	49.0
Kyrgyz Republic	39.1	30.5	25.7	35.6	24.2	32.4
Latvia	10.7	31.8	48.3	4.2	22.0	62.8
Lithuania	13.9	38.4	40.5	6.3	27.7	54.8
Moldova	31.2	42.2	22.5	21.0	21.5	44.6
Poland	6.6	40.0	53.4	2.8	26.6	58.0
Romania	21.0	39.0	32.7	11.7	34.1	43.7
Russian Federation	7.6	40.5	42.8	5.2	30.5	54.8
Slovak Republic	4.3	32.1	63.6	4.2	29.2	66.7
Slovenia	4.5	33.4	48.1	2.7	31.3	52.5
Turkmenistan	11.5	67.4	21.0	26.8*	47.1*	19.0*
Ukraine	21.5	37.5	40.4	13.4	33.5	40.8
Uzbekistan	27.6	31.2	31.8	30.6	19.0	38.7

*2001

Source: WDI 2004, own computations.

Figures about the composition of output for Western countries, Eastern Europe and Japan show that there is an ongoing rise in the share of the services sector in the long run. In terms of employment, the services sector is dominant in OECD countries.

4 Growth and Structural Change

4.1 Standard Approaches

An important approach of structural change is based on Chenery (1960), Chenery/ Taylor (1968), Chenery/ Syrquin (1975; 1986): It is argued that economic development in each country is shaped by universal sectors relevant for all countries and by some sector-specific impulses. Universal factors are:

- similarity of production functions, factor substitution and commonly-used knowledge;
- similarity of demand with respect to private good and public goods, respectively;
- common access to export markets and import markets as well as capital markets;
- the general link between rising per capita income and capital accumulation (including human capital accumulation).

The basic Chenery hypothesis says that those factors shape economic dynamics across countries. The sectoral structure thus is shaped by the dynamics of universal factors influencing the respective country and sector. Chenery's arguments are less clear when it comes to country-specific factors such as climate, geography, culture, economic policy. Chenery's empirical approach puts the focus for the variable $\ln x_i$ (x is the share of output of sector i) on the following equation:

$$\ln x_i = \alpha_i + \beta_{i1} \ln y + \beta_{i2} \ln N + \vec{\gamma}_i \vec{z} + u \tag{1}$$

where u is a random variable (white noise) and $\vec{z}$ is a vector other than per capita income y (or population N). While the above equation explains sectoral growth patterns over time it is not so clear how a "normal structure" – used as a benchmark for other countries – really looks (for a critical view on Chenery see Görgens, 1975, pp. 41-45; Steiner, 1981). Döhrn/ Heilemann (1991; 1992; 1993a; b; 1996) have used the Chenery model to analyze the pattern of sectoral dynamics in socialist transition countries. It is also noteworthy that Raiser et al. (2003) and World Bank (2004, ch. CII) suggest sectoral employment dynamics in transition countries where Western market economies are used as a benchmark.

4.2 Towards Theories of Structural Adjustment

Before one can analyze the dynamics of structural adjustment in market economies, one should identify and describe key elements ("stylized facts"):

- (I) the relative price of services is rising in the long run;
- (II) the share of employment in the services sector is rising;
- (III) the share of nominal value-added in overall GDP is rising;
- (IV) the share of the real value of the services sector is ambiguous which follows from (I) and (III).

If one identifies services and nontradables, one may argue that the rise of the relative price of services simply is the well-known Balassa-Samuelson effect (Balassa, 1964; Samuelson, 1964); the price ratio tradables to nontradables is often defined as the internal real exchange rate which can be shown to have a close link to the real foreign exchange rate (e.g. Hinkle/ Montiel, 1999). As regards post-socialist transition countries the change of the relative price of nontradables is important, not in the least because workers in the services sector can benefit from rising relative wages. As regards resource-rich countries with a strong industrial sector (e.g., Russia) one has to take into account the experiences of other resource rich OECD countries showing particular patterns of output and trade dynamics. There is a potentially serious long run problem that expansion of the natural resources sector could undermine the expansion of industrial sectors or services sectors with large opportunities for long term productivity growth and profits. High medium-term windfall profits in the natural resources sector can lead to a bias in sector development (Dutch Disease) in favour of the energy sector which is less innovative than many sectors in both manufacturing industry and the services sector (e.g. Corden/ Neary, 1982; Van Wijnbergen, 1984; Welfens/ Kauffmann, 2005).

As regards theoretical analysis of structural change one has to consider both supply-side dynamics and demand patterns. Basically, modelling will aim at presenting an approach which should allow to answer such questions as:

1. What is the impact of differences in the elasticities on both the demand side and the supply side?
2. Can the aggregate economy grow at a constant rate if the sectoral composition of output is changing?
3. What is the impact of a large natural resources sector (or agricultural sector) on output and trade dynamics?
4. How can internationally available knowledge be tapped in an efficient way such that new sectors become competitive in world markets – or that the competitiveness of the tradables sector is enhanced?
5. Can the services sector create enough new jobs in countries with a shrinking industry?
6. What determines the scope and speed of privatization of state-owned firms?

4.3 Two-Sector Approaches and Three-Sector Models for Closed Economies

A standard model for explaining structural change is Baumol (1967) who considers a model with industry and services. Both sectors produce with labor as inputs, only the supply-side dynamics are modelled. If technological progress affects only industry there will be – assuming equality of wages across sectors (and that wage growth is determined by productivity growth of industry) – factor reallocation in favour of an expanding services sector provided that the structure of output is exogenous. The relative price of the services sector will increase, and the overall economic growth rate will converge to the growth rate of the services output: zero. Several authors have enriched the Baumol model, including Gundlach (1994) and Quibria/ Harrigan (1996) who consider sector demand functions in addition to the supply side. With a CES utility function the latter can explain the stylized facts mentioned above.

An interesting model of structural change is Rowthorn/ Ramaswamy (1997) which is only labor as a production factor. In this three sector model the authors assume that demand is characterized by low income elasticity and a low price elasticity. Productivity is assumed to be identical across sectors in t=0. Moreover, the sectoral rates of productivity growth are assumed to be constant. The growth rate of productivity in industry is assumed to be identical to that in agriculture, while the growth rate of productivity in the services sector is below that of the other two sectors. The consequences in the model are as follows: There is a relocation of labor from the agricultural sector to the services sector and manufacturing industry; the output share of industry will shrink over time. As the demand side is not modelled adequately, we basically have a modification of Baumol's 2-sector model.

Raiser et al. (2003) reconsider the Rowthorne-Ramaswamy model by assuming different initial sectoral productivity levels and other changes at the beginning of the period. Based on simulations it is shown that national chances in initial conditions and changes in output growth rates amounts to changes in the parameters of the Chenery approach to sectoral growth functions. Moreover, the authors consider how a narrowing of the international technology gap on the one hand and a rise of the output share of the services sector on the other will affect employment dynamics. The demand side in various sectors is based on Stone-Geary-utility functions $u(c_i)$ which assume sector-specific minimal consumption levels $\bar{c}_i$; that is the sectoral utility functions are given by:

$$u(c_i) = \frac{(\prod_i (c_i - \bar{c}_i)^{\beta_i})^{1-\Theta}}{1-\Theta}, \quad \sum_i \beta_i = 1 \tag{2}$$

If such a utility function is integrated into the well-known Ramsey-Cass-Koopmans growth model, one can derive conditions for a generalized balanced growth path: all aggregate variables will grow at constant and identical rates while the sectorally disaggregated variables will witness changes in their relative shares.

For such approaches, one may point to the models of Echevarria (1997), Kongsamut et al. (1997) and Meckl (1999) who use advanced three sector models. DE Groot (1998) presents a growth model with several sectors which uses a modified CES growth function with specific minimum consumption levels. Moreover, endogenous growth is considered where sector-internal "learning by watching" effects of taken into account. In this fairly general model one may derive some of the older models as a special case by choosing certain parameter values adequately. The model shows that there could be continuous structural change even in a closed economy. The relevance of this approach is mainly with respect to some of the world's relatively large economies such as in the US and Japan (or Germany) which were characterized by a relatively low degree of economic openness.

4.4 Structural Change in Open Economies and Convergence Issues

A standard approach to structural change in a two-sector model – with agriculture and industry – was developed by Matsuyama (1992). This model uses labor as input and a Stone-Geary preference function to explain the share of industry in a closed and an open economy (a small open economy). It is shown that under autarchy an exogenous rise of labor productivity in agriculture leads to a shift of labor from agriculture to industry which results in higher output growth for the overall economy. By contrast, the case of a small open economy – acting within a free trade approach – will be shaped by an expansion of the agricultural sector (provided that there is a comparative advantage in this sector). This expansion is due a shift of input factors in favour of agriculture. At the bottom line output growth is falling unless there are sufficient international productivity spillovers. Note that the case of a closed economy obviously is consistent with the early growth – and industrialization – in the Soviet Union (Gerschenkron, 1962). Moreover, the case of an open economy obviously is relevant for the sudden post-Soviet external liberalization in the new Russia after 1992. Mutatis mutandis one also could argue that the Dutch Disease problem can be explained in such a model.

One also should note the recent model of Gries/ Jungblut (1997a, 1997b) and Gries/ Wigger (1993) which present a three sector endogenous growth model which leads only to partial international convergence of per capita income levels. The three sectors considered here are a traditional sector, a modern industrial sector and an innovation sector (R&D). The R&D sector offers knowledge on the basis of imported technology intensive products. Such products are used as inputs in both the traditional and the modern sector. The traditional sector also employs labor, the R&D sector employs human capital only while the modern sector uses both sectors. Consumer preferences are described by a Cobb-Douglas function. There will be long term catching-up only if the output growth of the R&D sector is higher than that of innovations in the world economy. Output growth of the R&D sector depends on inputs for the R&D sector and on the amount of imported technology intensive goods. If there is economic catching-up it will be shaped by a logistical function. Overtaking the foreign country is impossible on the basis of imitation only. If the knowledge generated in the R&D sector is affecting the traditional sector and the modern sector with different speed there will be adjustment impulses in the sense that there will be changes in the share of the respective sectors.

5 Perspectives

Structural change is clearly a crucial element of post-socialist transformation. The switch to a market economy brings about changes in technology which comes both through the import of technology-intensive goods, foreign direct investment – associated with technology transfer – and new innovation efforts in privatized firms.

While the Chenery model seems to be quite useful for explaining structural change in eastern European EU accession countries it is rather unlikely to be very useful for analyzing the more complex case of the former Soviet Union and the CIS, respectively (an exception are the Baltic Republics). The CIS countries and the new Russia suffer in a specific way from the disintegration of the former Soviet Union as well as the Council of Mutual Economic Assistance. Moreover, there is a lack of reliable institutions in the political and economic system so that investment patterns are likely to differ from the case of EU accession countries which faced strong incentives to adjust institutions towards those typically found in West European countries. This observation does, of course, not rule out that several transition countries have adopted new institutions for a market economy based on own ideas (e.g., one may mention reforms in the social security system which favour private savings and the expansion of the capital market). As regards methodological and statistical issues one should note that there is a lack of adequate price indices for the various sectors in the CIS countries so that real output of the respective sectors is difficult to assess over time.

Economic policymakers in eastern Europe will have to carefully find a balance between a strict general competition policy and incentives for certain sectors. Ideally, there should be a venture capital market and stock markets which mainly finance dynamic firms and innovators. However, in the presence of national or international technology spillovers and in sectors with positive external effects of innovation government will have to consider various alternatives for internalizing such external effects. Incentives for accelerated or broader imitation could be as important as a rise of the budget for R&D policies. Given well-organized industrial lobbies one cannot rule out that they will capture government R&D funds so that innovation policy will not play a really strong role in some of the accession countries in eastern Europe.

There is no doubt that understanding structural change in post-socialist countries is crucial not only for investors but also for international organizations aiming to support the transition process (e.g., the EBRD, the EU or the World Bank). The speed of structural adjustment is crucial for improving growth, employment and the terms of trade. More theoretical and empirical research needs to be done.

References

Balassa, B. (1964): The purchasing power parity doctrine: a reappraisal. – *The Journal of Political Economy 72*, 584–96.

Bhagwati, J. N. (1984): Splintering and disembodiment of services and developing nations. – *The World Economy 7*, 133–144.

Chenery, H. B. (1960): Patterns of industrial growth. – *The American Economic Review 50*, 624–654.

Chenery, H. B., Syrquin, M. (1975): *Patterns of Development, 1950–1970*. London: Oxford University Press.

Chenery, H. B., Syrquin, M. (1986): Typical patterns of transformation. – Chenery, H. B., Robinson, S., Syrquin, M. (eds.): *Industrialization and Growth: A Comparative Study*. New York *et al.*: Oxford University Press, 37–83.

Chenery, H. B., Taylor, L. (1968): Development patterns: among countries and over time. – *The Review of Economics and Statistics 50*, 391–416.

Chenery, H. B., Robinson, S., Syrquin, M. (1986): *Industrialization and Growth: A Comparative Study*. New York *et al.*: Oxford University Press.

Clark, C. G. (1940): *The Conditions of Economic Progress*. Dritte Auflage. London: Macmillan.

Clark, C. G. (1942): *The Economics of 1960*. London: Macmillan. Cook, M., Healey, N. M. (1995): *Growth and Structural Change*. Houndmills *et al.*: Macmillan.

Corden, W. M., Neary, J. P. (1982): Booming sector and de-industrialisation in a small open economy. – *The Economic Journal 92*, 825–848.

Döhrn, R., Heilemann, U. (1991): *Sectoral Change in Eastern Europe – the Chenery Hypothesis Reconsidered*. RWI-Papiere, Nr. 25: Rheinisch-Westfälisches Institut für Wirtschaftsforschung.

Döhrn, R., Heilemann, U. (1992): Zur allokativen Dimension: Sektorale Entwicklungsperspektiven für Ungarn, Polen und die CSFR. – *Beihefte der Konjunkturpolitik 40*, 51–69.

Döhrn, R., Heilemann, U. (1993a): *Sektorale Entwicklungsperspektiven in Osteuropa und ihre Konsequenzen für die deutsche Wirtschaft*. RUFIS Veröffentlichungen Nr. 3/1993: Ruhr-Forschungsinstitut für Innovations- und Strukturpolitik e.V..

Döhrn, R., Heilemann, U. (1993b): Structural change in Eastern Europe. – Waverman, L., Heitger, B. (eds.): *German Unification and the International Economy*. London, New York: Routledge, 83–112.

Döhrn, R., Heilemann, U. (1996): The Chenery hypothesis and structural change in Eastern Europe. – *Economics of Transition 4*, 411–425.

Echevarria, C. (1997): Changes in sectoral composition associated with economic growth. – *International Economic Review 38*, 431–452.

Engel, E. (1895): *Die Lebenskosten belgischer Arbeiter-Familien früher und jetzt*. Dresden: C. Heinrich.

Fisher, A. G. B. (1933): Capital and the growth of knowledge. – *The Economic Journal 43*, 379–389.

Fisher, A. G. B. (1935a): *The Clash of Progress and Security*. London: Macmillan.

Fisher, A. G. B. (1935b): The economic implications of material progress. – *International Labour Review 11*, 5–18.

Fisher, A. G. B. (1939): Production, primary, secondary and tertiary. – *Economic Record 15*, 24–38.
Fourastié, J. (1949): *Le grand espoir du XXe siècle*. Dritte Auflage. Paris: Gallimard.
Fourastié, J. (1954): *Die große Hoffnung des zwanzigsten Jahrhunderts*. Köln-Deutz: Bund-Verlag.
Fuchs, V. R. (1968): *The Service Economy*. New York, N.Y.: National Bureau of Economic Research.
Geary, R. C. (1951): A note on ‚A Constant Utility Index of the Cost of Living. – *Review of Economic Studies 18*, 65–66.
Gerschenkron, A. (1962): *Economic Backwardness in Historical Perspective: A Book of Essays*. Cambridge, Massachusetts: Belknap Press.
Görgens, E. (1975): *Wandlungen der industriellen Produktionsstruktur im wirtschaftlichen Wachstum*. Bern: Paul Haupt.
Gries, T., Jungblut, S. (1997a): Catching up and structural change. – *Economia Internazionale 50*, 561–582.
Gries, T., Jungblut, S. (1997b): Catching up of economies in transformation. – Welfens, P. J. J., Wolf, H. C. (eds.): *Banking, International Capital Flows and Growth in Europe: Financial Markets, Savings and Monetary Integration in a World with Uncertain Convergence*. Berlin, Heidelberg: Springer, 297–313.
Gries, T., Wigger, B. (1993): The dynamics of upgrading or how to catch-up. – *Economia Internazionale 46*, 377–387.
Groot, H. L. F. de (1998): *The Determination and Development of Sectoral Structure*. CentER Paper No. 125: Tilburg University, Center for Economic Research.
Gundlach, E. (1994): Demand Bias as an explanation for structural change. – *Kyklos 47*, 249–267.
Hinkle, L. E., Montiel, P. J. (eds.) (1999): *Exchange Rate Misalignment: Concepts and Measurement for Developing Countries*. New York: Oxford University Press.
Kongsamut, P. P., Rebelo, S. T., Xie, D. (1997): *Beyond Balanced Growth*. CEPR Discussion Paper 1693: Centre for Economic Policy Research, London.
Kuznets, S. (1971): *Economic Growth of Nations: Total Output and Production Structure*. Cambridge, Mass.: Belknap Press of Harvard University Press.
Matsuyama, K. (1992): Agricultural productivity, comparative advantage and economic growth. – *Journal of Economic Theory 58*, 317–334.
Meckl, J. (1999): *Structural Change and Generalized Balanced Growth*. Diskussionsbeiträge Serie I, Nr. 298: Universität Konstanz, Rechts-, Wirtschafts- und Verwaltungswissenschaftliche Sektion, Fachbereich Wirtschaftswissenschaften.
Quibria, M. G., Harrigan, F. (1996): Demand bias and structural change. – *Kyklos 49*, 205–213.
Raiser, M., Schaffer, M., Schuchhardt, J. (2003): *Benchmarking Structural Change in Transition*. EBRD Working Paper No. 79: European Bank for Reconstruction and Development.
Rowthorn, R., Ramaswamy, R. (1997): *Deindustrialization: Causes and Implications*. WP/97/42: International Monetary Fund.
Samuelson, P. A. (1964): Theoretical notes on trade problems. – *Review of Economics and Statistics 46*, 145–64.
Smith, A. (1776): *An Inquiry into the Nature and Causes of the Wealth of Nations*. Vol. 1. Reprint 1976. London: Oxford University Press.
Steiner, M. (1981): Zur Aussagekraft von Normalstrukturmodellen. – *Empirica 8*, 111–127.

Stone, R. (1954): Linear expenditure systems and demand analysis: an application to the pattern of British demand. – *Economic Journal 64*, 511–527.

Syrquin, M., Chenery, H. B. (1989): Three Decades of Industrialization. – *The World Bank Economic Review 3*, 145–181.

Welfens, P. J. J. (1993), Market-oriented Systemic Transformations in Eastern Europe, New York: Springer.

Welfens, P. J. J., Kauffmann, A. (2005): Structural change, natural resources sector expansion and growth in Russia. – Graham, E. M., Oding, N. Yu., Welfens, P. J. J. (eds.): *Internationalization and Economic Policy Reforms in Transition Countries.* Heidelberg: Springer (forthcoming), 5–50.

Wijnbergen, S. van (1984): The 'Dutch Disease': A Disease after All?. – *The Economic Journal 94*, 41–55.

Wolfe, M. (1955): The concept of economic sectors. – *The Quarterly Journal of Economics 69*, 402–420.

World Bank (2004): *From Transition to Development: A Country Economic Memorandum for the Russian Federation.* Moscow: World Bank, Russia Country Department.

Comment on: Structural Change and Economic Dynamics in Transition Economies

Christopher Schumann

The paper "Structural Change and Economic Dynamics in Transition Economies" by Albrecht Kauffmann deals with the question as to which approaches are suitable in analyzing the changes that the post-socialist economies in Eastern Europe have undergone in the past decade. It consists of three parts. In the first part, the author gives an overview of the theoretical discussion on structural changes in a historical perspective. Different approaches that were developed in the 19th and 20th century are characterized and compared. The second part describes statistical categories that can be used to distinguish different sectors and branches which is a necessary to analyze structural changes. First statements on the structural change in the transition economies are made on the basis of a table illustrating the composition of output using the traditional three sector division. In the last part of the paper, rather modern approaches to the analysis of structural change are portrayed, and it is then discussed which is the most suitable for the case of transition economies.

The author states that in socialist economies, there was a strong bias in the economic structure towards industrial production. This was partly ideologically driven since the service sector was not considered valuable. Indeed, table 4 undermines this statement – the industrial sectors were rather extensive in the beginning if the 1990s in comparison to those in Western economies. But this does not necessarily point towards a distortion; the question is whether the observed structure reflect the relative advantages of the respective countries. The observation that there was a strong decline in the relative share of the industries in the output supports the statement of an inflated second sector. On the other hand, however, especially resource-rich and labor-abundant countries like Russia may have an international comparative advantage in this field.

This also poses the question as to which role the openness of the countries play with respect to structural change. In the socialist era, the countries of Eastern Europe were rather closed. Meanwhile, they take part in international trade and contribute to the international specialization of production processes. The author points out that there are positive factors of openness for the transition countries: there are gains from trade, international productivity spill-overs, foreign direct investments and technological transfers. On the other hand, there is a lack of reliable institutions in the political and economic system in several of the countries. It is quite clear that the transition countries that have now joined the EU have profited from the openness of the economies. But it is questionable that openness leads to an adjustment to "typical Western structures". There is a strong diversity within the countries under consideration, and especially Russia cannot be considered a monolith. The country is rather big and has huge regional diversities with respect to the production patterns.

Finally, the question must be posed as to which role human capital in these countries plays. All structural changes can only take place if there is labor available that is complementary to the new needs. In other words, the shifts in the sectoral composition must also be reflected in the labor market data. There might be limitation to the shifts because of a lack of labor force with the corresponding skills and knowledge. Many important factors crucial for the analysis of structural change are discussed in the models mentioned in the paper. It might be fruitful to include shifts in human capital in more detail than in the framework.

Patterns of Industrial Specialization and Concentration in CEECs: Theoretical Explanations and their Empirical Relevance

Antje Hildebrandt and Julia Wörz[1]

Contents

1 Introduction 120
2 Evolution of Geographical Concentration in Central and Eastern European Countries 121
2.1 Measuring Geographical Concentration 121
2.2 The Evolution of Concentration based on Output Data 124
2.3 The Evolution of Concentration based on Employment Data 126
2.4 A CEEC-EU Comparison 128
3 Driving Factors behind Concentration and Specialization Patterns 129
4 Explaining Concentration inside CEECs 132
5 Developments in Individual Industries 138
6 Conclusions 141
Appendix 143
References 145

[1] The authors would like to thank Jarko Fidrmuc, Helene Midelfart-Knarvik, Peter Neary, Doris Ritzberger-Grünwald, and Robert Stehrer for their helpful suggestions and comments. We are thankful for comments we received from participants of the wiiw Seminar in International Economics held in Vienna on January 8, 2004 and from participants at the EIIW Workshop held in Wuppertal on January 12-13, 2004. This research was commissioned by the Foreign Research Division of the Oesterreichische Nationalbank.

1 Introduction

The process of European integration certainly had a strong impact on the industrial landscape in Europe. The single market program brought about an increased mobility of production factors inside the EU-15. On the one hand, this allowed for a more efficient allocation of resources, on the other hand it also allowed for a more equal distribution of key resources across Europe by facilitating the exchange of knowledge and ideas with a positive influence on the diffusion of new technologies. With respect to Eastern Europe, the Europe Agreements have set the basis for a similar development by substantially reducing trade barriers and transport costs between East and West. All this has shaped the distribution of industrial activity in Europe.

In the early 1990s, Central and Eastern European countries rapidly re-oriented their external relations towards Western Europe. Consequently, one would expect them to join into a pan-European pattern of specialization according to comparative advantage. In this paper we analyze the changes in industrial specialization and concentration patterns between Central and Eastern European countries (CEECs) that took place during the transition period. We will restrict our attention to the industrial sector, and here to manufacturing in particular, as this sector experienced a radical opening-up to international competitors through trade and investment flows experiencing a far greater amount of structural change than all other sectors of the economy.

There exists already a relatively large body of literature dealing with the location of industry. In general, this literature analyzes regional specialization patterns, often at a rather detailed level of regional disaggregation. Numerous studies for the US (e.g. Ellison and Glaeser, 1997, Hanson, 2002) and the EU (e.g. Amiti 1999, Brühlhart 1998, Haaland et al., 1999) exist, whose results seem to depend crucially on the time period covered. Due to an obvious lack of data until very recently, Central and Eastern Europe has been left out of most European studies. We try to fill this gap by analyzing a relatively new and comprehensive set of industry specific time series at the national level. Thus, our breakdown is by industries rather than by regions. Existing studies for Western Europe at the industry level make clear that developments seem to have been quite diverse over the past few decades, with alternating periods of increasing specialization/concentration and diversification. In this paper, we want to give an overview of patterns and driving forces behind the location of industry in Eastern Europe and see how these developments fit with those in Western Europe over the past. Our results should also help to assess the likely impact of further integration on future developments.

Clearly, the history of industrial specialization patterns in Eastern Europe has been subject to very specific conditions, thus leading to a distinct industrial structure up until the start of the transition. The fall of the Iron Curtain implied the collapse of the Council of Mutual Economic Assistance (CMEA) which was formally dissolved in 1991. Under CMEA system, industrial specialization patterns were more or less predetermined and sustained through the accordance of central plans of all involved countries under Soviet hegemony. The rapid re-orientation towards

Western European trading partners that was observed immediately after 1991 resulted on the one hand from the strong interest to reduce economic dependence on the former Soviet Union and on the other hand from the desire to catch up with the economically far more advanced Western European countries (Richter, 1997 and 2001). Given these motivations, it does not seem surprising that CEECs first engaged in contracts with partners in Western Europe and the European Union before concluding agreements between each other. Thus, the far reaching bilateral Europe Agreements[2] between individual CEECs and each member of the European Union as well as the Union itself were signed in the first half of the 1990s and predate the CEFTA agreement from 1992, which is a pure free trade agreement, again on a bilateral basis. This makes clear that during the nineties no integration process inside CEECs could be observed, on the contrary. Each country was pursuing a policy of integration with the Western world while being reluctant towards their former communist partners. As an example, roughly 90% of industrial goods can be traded freely inside CEFTA since 1997. Also since 1998, CEECs industrial exports to the EU are free from tariffs.[3] Thus, when speaking about the impact of integration on industry location in the Eastern European context, this has to be seen as a bilateral East-West integration rather than a regional Eastern European integration process.

With this paper we want to shed some light on the empirical evidence concerning industrial re-location patterns in CEECs during their transition phase. Section 2 describes the patterns of industrial specialization in EU acceding countries and compares these developments to those in the EU-15. Section 3 explains how the variables that are used in the analytical part are derived. In section 4, industrial concentration inside the region is explained using a panel of thirteen industries and eight years. Finally, section 5 looks at the factors that drive specialization inside individual industries using again a panel data set of ten countries and eight years for each industry. Section 6 concludes.

2 Evolution of Geographical Concentration in Central and Eastern European Countries

2.1 Measuring Geographical Concentration

Our database contains data for ten CEECs (Bulgaria, Czech Republic, Estonia, Hungary, Latvia, Lithuania, Poland, Romania, Slovak Republic and Slovenia) from 1993 to 2000. This period allows us to analyze the impact stemming from

---

[2] The Europe Agreements are not restricted to economic issues and include among others political, financial, cultural cooperation as well as general regulations, movement of workers, etc.

[3] The asymmetric nature of the Europe Agreements implied that EU exports to CEECs were tariffed up to 2000.

[4] wiiw Industrial Database Eastern Europe, July 2003.

the transitional change and from the stronger trade integration of the CEECs with the European Union. Our starting point – 1993 – has the clear advantage that the data are not blurred by the transformational recession, which was largely over in most transition countries by 1993. From the wiiw Industrial Database[4] we use output, employment, wages, exports and imports (total and to the EU), and FDI inward stocks for thirteen manufacturing industries. Industries are classified according to NACE, rev.1 subsections DA to DN.[5] All values are in Euro, converted at current exchange rates. The database contains 1040 observations across three dimensions: industries, countries, and years. The measures of the degree of geographical concentration are based on output data at current prices[6] as well as on employment data.

Until the start of the transition process in the late 1980s, production and employment patterns in CEECs strongly deviated from those of Western European economies. In the late 1980s, they were basically dominated by the manufacturing sector in general and heavy industry in particular. Transition set in motion a process of catching-up of CEECs towards current EU Member States that triggered per-capita income and structural convergence.

On a broader level, the sectoral allocation of production and labor resources among the three main sectors (agriculture, industry and services) has become more similar to the sectoral allocation prevailing in EU countries. Generally, CEECs have seen the shares of value added and of employment in agriculture[7] and in the industry sector[8,9] decline, whereas they have seen the service sector gain in importance. These fundamental structural changes can be traced – among other factors – to the stronger integration with the EU that has taken place. Trade integration and an increased inflow of FDI have changed the competitive environment of CEECs firms and have modified the patterns of geographic concentration.

In the period under review, the structure of manufacturing changed broadly in CEECs. In 1993, the three largest countries in terms of output – Poland, the Czech Republic, and Romania – accounted for as much as 67% of manufacturing production in the region. By 2000 Romania had fallen behind and Hungary had advanced to the third rank, with the share of the three largest countries having increased to 72%. Poland, Romania and the Czech Republic also ranked first to third in 1993 in

[5] In some countries, the manufacturing of coke, refined petroleum products and nuclear fuel and manufacturing n.e.c. were not reported separately. Thus, we aggregated these industries in all countries.

[6] There are various other ways to measure the size of an industry (for instance employment or value-added data). Apart from the fact that value-added data are not available for all CEECs, production output data are less affected by structural shifts from outsourcing to other sectors than value-added data (Midelfart-Knarvik, 2002).

[7] Remarkable exceptions are Bulgaria and Romania where the share of labor force in agriculture has increased.

[8] The industry sector comprises manufacturing industry, mining, water and electricity supply and construction.

[9] Today, the contribution of the manufacturing sector to GDP in CEECs is only slightly larger than the average in the current EU member states.

terms of employment. At the time, 68% of all manufacturing employees of the region worked in these three countries; their share was virtually unchanged in 2000.

How has the degree of geographical concentration changed in Central and Eastern Europe? Let us first explain our measure of concentration in more detail. To start with, the issue of specialization versus concentration should be set out clearly. While the two concepts are strongly linked – both describe convergence or divergence of industrial structure, in terms of output, employment, trade patterns and the like -, they do not describe exactly the same developments. Specialization is measured across countries and relates to increasing differences in industrial structure between individual countries. Concentration is measured with respect to individual industries and refers to the question whether certain industries locate only in certain regions or countries as opposed to a pattern where output is homogeneously dispersed across all countries. The two often coincide such that increasing specialization is observed together with increasing concentration. However, if countries differ in size, they need not coincide. If one country was twice the economic size of its trading partner, one industry could be completely concentrated in this country, while the country itself would remain unspecialized.

This leads us to our measure of concentration. In the literature on geographical concentration, a variety of approaches to measure the degree of concentration can be found. We decided to use a measure of concentration in accordance with Haaland et al. (1999) which is a modified form of the Hoover-Balassa-Index. They make the distinction between absolute and relative concentration (or specialization) measures. Absolute concentration measures the spread of industrial activities across countries. An industry is said to be absolutely concentrated if its output is generated in only one or a few countries. Relative concentration measures the difference of an industry's spread of production to the average spread of production. Thus, an industry is relatively concentrated if its output is more concentrated than total manufacturing (or economy wide) output in the area. Consequently, high relative concentration implies also a high degree of country specialization. The above example of high concentration without specialization is only possible when using the concept of absolute concentration. Again, relative country size matters crucially. If all countries are of equal size, the two measures are identical. Analyzing both concentration indices, relative and absolute, has the advantage of providing a comprehensive picture of the localization of industries in the CEECs. While the measure of relative concentration allows us to draw conclusions on the ongoing specialization process in CEECs, absolute concentration can be seen as being important in a broader pan-European perspective.

The absolute concentration index $\left(CIP_i^A\right)$ is defined as:

$$CIP_i^A = \sqrt{\frac{1}{c}\sum_j\left(\frac{X_{ij}}{\sum_j X_{ij}}\right)^2} \qquad (1)$$

The value of production is denoted by X_{ij},[10] the index i refers to industries and j to countries. Total industry i production in the CEECs is depicted by $\sum_j X_{ij}$ and the share of production in industry i carried out in country j by $\frac{X_{ij}}{\sum_j X_{ij}}$. The term c indicates the number of countries in our sample.

The relative concentration index CIP_i^R adjusts for country size and is defined as:

$$CIP_i^R = \sqrt{\frac{1}{c}\sum_j\left(\frac{X_{ij}}{\sum_j X_{ij}} - \frac{\sum_i X_{ij}}{\sum_i\sum_j X_{ij}}\right)^2}, \tag{2}$$

where $\frac{\sum_i X_{ij}}{\sum_i\sum_j X_{ij}}$ reflects country j's share in total manufacturing production of all ten countries.

2.2 The Evolution of Concentration based on Output Data

Comparing the beginning and the end of our time series (1993 and 2000), we observe an increase of absolute concentration in terms of production in all industries, except for the textile industry (see fig. 1). However, the intensity of changes varies strongly across industries.

The ranking of individual industries (see table 1 in the Appendix) indicates that the production of electrical and optical equipment underwent the most striking change. Whereas in 1993 this industry was one of the least concentrated industries, it ranked among the most concentrated ones in 2000. This significant shift is attributable to the fact that this industry became strongly concentrated in Hungary in the period under review (within our sample, the latter accounted for more than 40% of production activity in this industry in 2000[11]). Furthermore, the manufacturing of nonmetallic mineral products and the production of pulp, paper and paper products experienced a considerable increase in their degree of concentration. Both industries are concentrated predominantly in the Czech Republic and in Poland, the two largest countries in terms of production in our sample. The pulp, paper and paper products industry also gained importance in the Baltic States. In absolute terms, the manufacturing of textiles and textile products became less

[10] For the concentration indices based on employment data X_{ij} refers to number of people employed in sector i in country j. Absolute concentration is denoted by CIE_i^A, relative concentration by CIE_i^R, respectively.

[11] The four largest companies of the Hungarian electrical and optical equipment sector are IBM Storage Products Kft., Philips Group, GE Lightening Tungsram Rt. and Flextronics International Kft.

concentrated. This can be explained by the fact that this labor-intensive industry became less important in several countries, including Hungary, Poland and the Czech Republic, as a result of which production became more dispersed across countries.

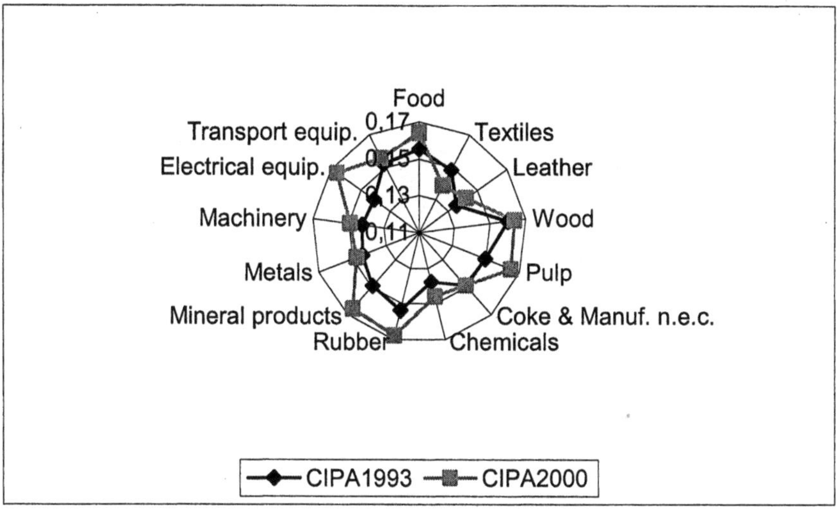

Fig. 1. Evolution of absolute concentration (production) in CEECs

Similar to the developments in absolute concentration, the geographical concentration of production also increased in relative terms which – according to our measure of relative concentration – implies that the CEECs became more specialized.[12] Again, there is one exception: Concentration decreased in the chemical industry, causing the latter to rank last in 2000 (see table 6 in the Appendix). This reflects a general decline of the chemical industry, which led to a more dispersed production structure. Again, the manufacturing of electrical and optical equipment experienced the largest increase in the degree of concentration, reflecting Hungary's stronger specialization in this field (in 2000 the electrical and optical equipment industry accounted for almost 30% of Hungarian manufacturing). In addition, the concentration level of the wood and wood product industry increased significantly, given that the Baltic States, especially Latvia, specialized more strongly in this industry. Mirroring the development of absolute concentration, the

[12] At first sight, this observation of increasing specialization stands in contrast to the observation of increasing intra industry trade between CEECs and EU-15 during the same period (Fidrmuc and Djablik, 2003). Increasing intra industry trade clearly implies decreasing specialization. This apparent discrepancy may be explained on the one hand by the fact that we look at intra-CEEC patterns of specialization, while Fidrmuc and Djablik analyze trade between EU-15 and CEECs. On the other hand, the level of disaggregation used in the two analyses is different. We use manufacturing data for only 13 industries whereas the study mentioned above uses data on a much more disaggregated level.

production of mineral products became more strongly concentrated also in relative terms.

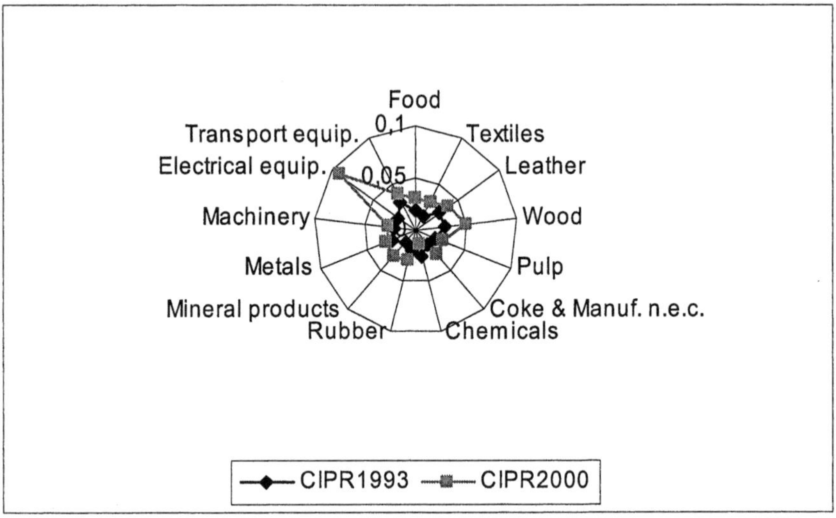

Fig. 2. Evolution of relative concentration (production) in CEECs

2.3 The Evolution of Concentration based on Employment Data

Employment data also show concentration of labor force to have increased in general. Particularly employment concentrated in the leather and leather product industry both in absolute and relative terms (see also tables 7 and 8 in the Appendix). Romania and Poland, the two largest countries[13], are the dominant employers; some smaller countries, e.g. Bulgaria, have increased the share of employees in this sector. In 2000, the transport industry was the industry with the highest degree of employment concentration in absolute terms (because a mere three countries – Poland, Romania and the Czech Republic – account for the bulk of employees in this industry).

[13] Based on employment data.

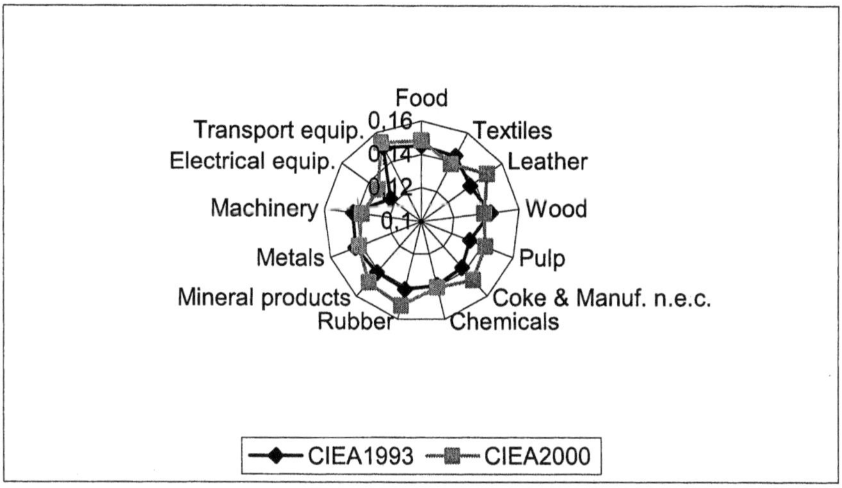

Fig. 3. Evolution of absolute concentration (employment) in CEECs

In terms of relative concentration, the industry of coke, refined petroleum and manufacturing n.e.c. underwent the strongest decrease of concentration of the labor force in contrast to its increasing concentration in absolute terms. The decrease in the relative concentration level reflects the fact that the largest country, Poland, became the main employer in this industry (in our sample, more than 36% of all people working in this industry were employed in Poland in 2000) whereas smaller countries such as Bulgaria and Slovakia employed relatively less people in this industry in the year 2000 than in 1993. In addition, the degree of concentration also dropped in the field of people employed in the food production, in the manufacturing of machinery and equipment n.e.c. and in the chemical industry.

The leather industry, by contrast, recorded the strongest increase in the degree of concentration of labor force; in 2000, employment was most concentrated in this industry in relative terms. This can be traced to an increase of employment in this industry in the Bulgarian and Romanian economy whereas the leather industry lost in importance as a place of employment in all other sample countries.

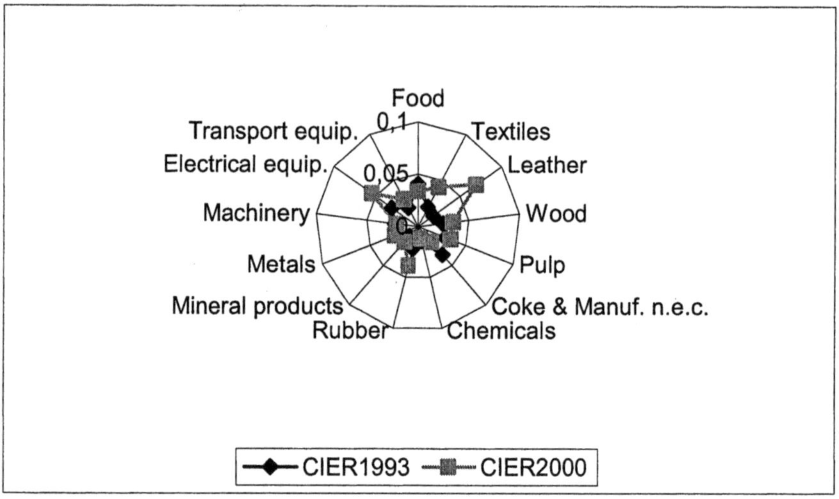

Fig. 4. Evolution of relative concentration (employment) in CEECs

2.4 A CEEC-EU Comparison

The analysis of the afore-described structural changes raises the question whether the development in the CEECs corresponds to production and employment patterns in the EU Member States.

We calculated corresponding geographical concentration indices, both in relative and absolute terms for the 15 EU countries for the years 1985, 1993 and 2000. The time period allows us to draw some conclusions on the extent to which stronger economic integration has influenced geographic concentration in the EU.

From 1985 to 1993, which can be considered the "pre-single market period", geographic concentration with regard to employment data increased in all industries (in absolute terms) and in 11 (out of 13) industries (in relative terms). In 1985 the three most concentrated industries (in absolute terms) were the following industries: the manufacturing of leather and leather products, the machinery industry and the manufacturing of electrical and optical equipment. A slightly different picture emerges with regard to relative concentration. Here the textile industry replaces the electrical industry in the group of the three most concentrated industries. The least concentrated industries in absolute terms were coke and refined petroleum products, food products and wood, and in relative terms chemicals, rubber and plastic products and basic and fabricated metals.

The period from 1993 to 2000, which can be named "single market period" and which corresponds to our observation period for the Central and Eastern European sample, was marked by a general decrease of concentration. Based on employment data, concentration decreased in absolute terms within all 13 industries and in relative terms within seven industries. The ranking of industries according to their degree of concentration changed as well. Most strikingly, the production of transport equipments ranks both in absolute and in relative terms among the most concentrated industries. Notably, this industry became widespread especially in Germany. The manufacturing of leather and leather products is in both cases the most concentrated industry, which is due to the fact that Italy is strongly specialized in this industry.

The evolution of concentration is less clear cut with regard to indices based on production data. Over the period 1985 to 1993, concentration increased in only five (measured in absolute terms) and in nine (measured in relative terms) industries. From 1993 to 2000 there was a decrease in concentration within ten (measured in absolute terms) and an increase within nine (measured in relative terms) industries. The ranking of the most and least concentrated industries is almost equal to the concentration ranking based on employment data.

What are the most striking similarities and differences between the evolution of geographical concentration in the CEECs and in the EU, and what conclusions can be drawn?

Overall, Central and Eastern Europe has experienced a substantial amount of structural change since the start of the transition process, which has led to greater similarities both among the individual countries in the region and vis-à-vis the current EU Member States. Convergence results from the relative decline of initially important labor-intensive and low value-added activities. From 1993 to 2000 the concentration of the manufacturing industries in the CEECs increased both to higher levels and by a higher percentage than in the EU during the "pre-single market period".

However, the ranking of industry types according to the degree of concentration in CEECs deviates to a large extent from the structure which can be found in the current EU countries. Furthermore, in the EU the correlation between concentration indices based on employment and on production data is very high, whereas this correlation is very low in CEECs. This can possibly be ascribed to the time lag between the adjustment of output and employment and relates to the prevalent lower level of productivity in Central and Eastern Europe compared to the EU countries.[14] Initially low levels of productivity allowed for rapid catching-up. This productivity boost implied increased concentration in output levels that were not accompanied by increased employment in the same industries.

3 Driving Factors behind Concentration and Specialization Patterns

From the theoretical literature we can identify a range of factors behind empirically observed patterns of industrial concentration. In the following, we will use proxies for individual factors in order to assess their importance in determining the

[14] In 2001, labour productivity for the manufacturing industry (converted with 1996 purchasing power parities for gross fixed capital formation) ranged between 10% (Bulgaria) to 41% (Hungary) of the productivity level reached in Austria (wiiw 2003).

structure of industrial production in CEECs.[15] As our observation period corresponds more or less to the transformation phase of these countries we expect different factors to play an important role in shaping the industrial landscape as compared to Western Europe. For instance, traditional Ricardian and Heckscher-Ohlin factors are expected to still play a relatively strong role. In the following we discuss each variable and its calculation in turn.

Comparative advantages are at the heart of traditional Ricardian trade theory. *Technological differences* are captured by differences in productivity levels, more specifically we will use labor productivity given our lack of good capital stock data. Large differences in technology levels between countries are expected to have a positive influence on concentration of an industry after adjusting for country size (i.e. relative concentration). The variable is calculated as labor productivity in relation to the average labor productivity in each industry, adjusting for the country's overall productivity level.

In a Heckscher-Ohlin model, relative cost differences arise from differences in the *endowment structure* between trading partners. Greater differences will again induce a higher degree of relative concentration. As we are only interested in whether industries are concentrated or not, all that matters is whether an industry is intensive in the use of a certain factor or not.[16] Thus, we only look at deviations in factor use from the mean regardless of the direction. We include the following factors in our analysis: labor, human capital and foreign owned physical capital. Domestic physical capital is then implicitly captured by assuming that output is produced using only these four factors. With this, we assert a qualitative distinction between foreign owned and domestically owned physical capital. *Labor intensity* is measured as absolute deviations in employment per unit of output from the sample mean. When explaining absolute concentration we refine this measure and use the industry average employment level in relation to output. *Human capital intensity* is proxied for by deviations from the average labor compensation. If an industry's wage level lies above the average wage level of the region, it is said to be relatively human capital intensive, assuming that wages reflect qualification and education of employees. We further include a measure of *foreign capital intensity* for the following reason: Economic development in all transition economies was naturally heavily influenced by privatization in those countries. Although privatization and FDI are distinct issues the two are closely related, especially in our sample countries. Privatization has dominated FDI inflows to a large extent (Kalotay and Hunya, 2000). However, privatization policies have been very distinct in individual CEECs. While Hungary pursued a policy of early privatization via the capital market, thus attracting large FDI inflows into all sectors, the voucher privatization in Romania and Bulgaria implied that foreign capi-

[15] Our analysis is similar to the one in Haaland et al. (1999) but in contrast to their paper, which analyses structural developments in incumbent member states of the EU, our paper puts the regional focus entirely on the Eastern European countries (including Bulgaria and Romania).

[16] This together with the relative endowments of a country (abundancy or scarecity of the specific factor) determines specialization patterns in the Heckscher Ohlin model.

tal was kept out of the country for a relatively long time period. Poland started to privatize state owned firms at a later time point and so FDI inflows occurred at a later stage. Consequently, the timing and industrial spread of privatization-induced foreign capital inflows into individual CEECs differed according to different FDI policies. Thus, FDI inflows can be seen as exogenous in this analysis. We measure FDI intensity as deviations of FDI inward stock over output from the mean; in the regressions for absolute concentration we use the average FDI stock.

In contrast to traditional trade theories, new trade theory adopts entirely different assumptions, allowing for increasing returns to scale, preference for variety and imperfect competition (Krugman 1980, Helpman 1981, Ethier 1982). Industries with strong increasing returns to scale in production can realize efficiency gains if they concentrate in certain locations. *Scale economies* can explain both, absolute and relative concentration patterns. With the data we have at hand, we are unable to measure scale economies directly. To our knowledge, no recent study exists that has estimated scale economies for the industries we are looking at. Thus, we take scale elasticities from Forslid et al. (2002, Table 5, p.104), which are themselves based on estimates of scale economies by Pratten (1988). According to these figures, the transport industry realizes the greatest economies of scale in production, followed by chemicals, machinery (including electronics) and metals. The smallest efficiency gains from a larger scale of production are found to prevail in the textiles, leather and food industry.

The effect of *expenditure* patterns on concentration has been acknowledged by all of the theories outlined here: traditional and new trade theories as well as economic geography. Traditional trade theory predicts net imports of a good towards which home demand is biased. According to new trade theory, a home market bias for a specific product will induce concentration of production of this good in the home country. Finally, new economic geography models state that a larger demand for a certain product implies stronger backward linkages and thus induces an industry to concentrate absolutely. Thus, the location of demand (for an industry's output, regardless whether it is used as an intermediate elsewhere or for final consumption) matters for the concentration of industries and we expect a positive impact from a higher concentration of demand or expenditure on output concentration. The expenditure variable is calculated as output plus imports minus exports, the variable is constructed analogously to the concentration measure.

Traditional and new trade theories imply a negative relationship between *trade costs* and concentration. The more expensive it is to move goods around, the less likely they will be produced in only one or a few locations. New economic geography models stress the existence of a non-linear, inverse U-shaped relationship between trade costs and location decisions in industries with increasing returns to scale. At high levels of trade costs, production will be dispersed in order to serve all markets at low costs. Falling transport costs first induce a concentration of production, as this allows to exploit scale economies while it is still possible to serve all markets at reduced costs. Consequently, firms realize higher efficiency levels. However, increasing concentration also produces agglomeration costs (rising wages in the center, congestion, etc.). With further decreasing transport costs it becomes profitable to shift production to the periphery again, taking advantage of low wage costs while transport costs do not play a role at all any more. Transport costs are again taken from Forslid et al. (2002) and measured as the percentage of trade costs to Western Europe in producer prices, averaged by each industry over the region. We assume that we are still in the part of the curve where lower transport costs lead to an increase in concentration of industrial activity, as predicted also by traditional and new trade theory.[17] The empirical evidence confirmed this choice, as a linear specification of the transport cost variable gave a better fit of the regression than specifying a quadratic term.

Economic geography models put heavy emphasis on the role of forward (i.e. with intermediate input producers) and backward (i.e. with consumers) *linkages*. The strength of forward linkages in an industry is captured by the share of inputs in total costs that originate in the same industry. Again, we use estimates from Forslid et al. (2002), based on data from Central and Eastern European input-output matrices. From this data, textiles, chemicals, metals and the wood industry emerge as having strong intra-industry linkages. The expected sign of this variable is again positive, stronger forward linkages inside the same industry should ceteris paribus lead to more concentration in an industry. Thus, we would expect these industries to be more clustered than for instance the food, transport or leather industry, which show weak intra-industry forward linkages. Backward linkages measure the extent to which closeness to one's customers (who can be either purchasers of intermediate goods or final good consumers) creates positive spillovers and enhances efficiency. This effect can be proxied by the demand in the region for output of the respective industry and is so captured by our expenditure variable.

4 Explaining Concentration inside CEECs

All the above measures are calculated as averages across all ten countries for each industry, leaving a panel of thirteen industries over eight years. We estimated a random effects model, using an instrumental variables estimator proposed by Hausman and Taylor (1981). We chose this estimator because it allows us to make best use of our knowledge of individual (i.e. industry) specific fixed effects (like scale economies, trade costs, forward linkages) that is lost in a fixed effects regression, as the fixed effects estimator removes all individual specific time-invariant effects. A random effects model however would lead to inconsistent estimates in the presence of those fixed effects. In contrast to traditional instrumental variables estimation procedures, the Hausman-Taylor estimator assumes that a subset of the explanatory variables in the model are correlated with the individual-level random effects μ_i (i.e. the error component that varies across individuals but

[17] Thus, the transport cost variable does not allow us to distinguish between different theories. The purpose of the analysis is however to investigate the determinants of industrial location in CEECs rather than scrutinizing different theories.

not over time) but none of the explanatory variables is correlated with the idiosyncratic error component.

The estimator requires to discriminate between exogenous and endogenous (i.e. correlated with μ_i) as well as time-varying and time-invariant right hand side variables. We identified labor intensity, wages and expenditure levels as endogenous, time-varying regressors and forward linkages as a time-invariant endogenous variable. Applying more or less the same model as Haaland et al. (1999) to Central and Eastern European data yields the following results, which are given in table 1. We find that relative concentration patterns are determined by comparative advantages (differences in technology), expenditure patterns, and the location of FDI. In line with the observations in the descriptive part, differences between relative concentration in employment and output can be identified. These differences in concentration between output and employment data by themselves hint towards different developments in productivity levels between individual industries in Central and Eastern Europe as mentioned previously. This has not been observed between individual industries in the Western European data and is as such an interesting observation. However, the differences in underlying factors driving these concentration patterns suggest that different mechanisms are at play in shaping the industrial landscape with respect to output and with respect to the allocation of the labor force.

Output patterns are more strongly influenced by expenditure patterns than employment. The coefficient on our variable for expenditure is more than twice as high and significant at a much higher level in the output equation as compared to the employment equation. Thus, the location of demand matters which also implies a role for backward linkages. Also the FDI variable turns out to be more significant in the output equation as compared to the employment equation, although the coefficient is of the same magnitude in both regressions. Consequently, FDI intensive industries tend to be clustered in few locations. The observation that FDI intensity spurs output (but not employment) concentration gives further some indirect evidence for the productivity enhancing impact of FDI. Industries with a high share of FDI produce more output in the same location with a less than proportional increase in labor.

Certain industries could be identified in driving the overall results. The strong increase in output concentration was heavily influenced by developments in the electrical equipment industry. Since 1997, strong increases in output levels in this industry could be observed. The fact that employment has not increased to the same extent suggests especially strong improvements in labor productivity inside the electrical equipment industry in CEECs. As will be discussed below, high FDI inflows especially in Hungary play an important role in this context. Apart from the electronics industry since 1997, we also controlled for the general trend of increasing concentration, given our descriptive results. Although this is already captured by the time dimension in our panel specification, we further included a quadratic time trend, which improved the fit of the regression to a great extent. One may also assign an economic meaning to this exogenous time trend: It can control for changes in relative factor endowments that are endogenous to relative concentration. For instance, a sufficiently high degree of factor mobility would enable skilled and unskilled workers to relocate according to where they were most demanded. This actually describes exactly the picture drawn by new economic geography models and would thus suggest that such models are relevant in explaining industry location in CEECs. However, there are few other hints for the importance of these factors in the data. Apart from the expenditure variable, the variables designed to capture explicitly new economic geography explanations – scale economies, trade costs and input-output linkages – remain insignificant.

A puzzle is presented by the negative coefficient on the human capital intensity measure. By construction both, the dependent variable and the endowment variables, measure deviations from the average. Thus, we clearly expect industries to cluster or concentrate which are especially intensive in the use of human capital (or use relatively little human capital). In either case, the sign of the endowment variable should be positive. The negative coefficient on the human capital variable implies that industries with an average use of human capital, measured by labor compensation, concentrate in a few countries only. This result could also reflect the fact that differences in human capital intensity, as measured here, are in general rather small across industries. The reason might lie in a tradition of strong central wage bargaining, a heritage from the communist past, that ruled out large differences in labor compensation for individual activities.

Similar to concentration of industrial output, also employment concentrates in those industries where productivity levels are relatively high controlling for the average productivity level in each country. FDI levels play again an important role for relative employment levels, as do – to a lesser extent than for output levels – expenditure levels. Concentration in employment also shows a time trend, but much weaker than in output levels. A pronounced increase in relative concentration can only be observed very recently and was influenced strongly by developments in the leather industry. The leather industry, which is a typical labor intensive industry, has especially high employment shares in a few small countries, most notably so in Latvia. This is controlled for by a dummy variable for this industry that takes the value one from 1998 onwards.

Again, the typical new economic geography variables remain insignificant and apart from FDI stocks, relative factor endowments also cannot explain employment patterns across industries. Thus, employment is distributed according to comparative advantages and concentrates in relative terms in industries where productivity levels differ most strongly from the average. Industries which produce at similar productivity levels in different countries will be more dispersed across the region. This observation refers to both, output and employment levels.

Table 1. Regressions Results for Relative Concentration Indices

	Output	Employment
FDI	0.0686	0.0682
	0.002	*0.014*
Technological differences	0.0279	0.0371
	0.000	*0.000*
Labour intensity	-4.01E-05	-1.26E-06
	0.430	*0.986*
Human capital intensity	-5.45E-05	-5.05E-05
	0.045	*0.132*
Expenditure	0.2652	0.1254
	0.000	*0.055*
Scale economies	-0.0214	-0.0062
	0.198	*0.876*
Trade costs	-7.99E-05	2.04E-04
	0.319	*0.349*
Linkages	0.0014	-0.0304
	0.960	*0.580*
$Trend^2$	0.0001	
	0.003	
Dummy 2000		0.0033
		0.048
Industry Dummy*	1.78E-06	0.0254
	0.000	*0.000*
Constant	0.0161	0.0190
	0.059	*0.227*
Wald-chi^2	724.33	150.59
Prob >chi^2	0.00	0.00
Number of observations	104	104

* In the first regression fort eh electronics industry, in the second regression for the leather industry.
p-values in italics.

In contrast to the study by Haaland et al. (1999), we include the same exogenous variables in our model for relative and absolute concentration. Although technological differences and differences in endowment structures cannot explain absolute concentration patterns, we view these characteristics as industry specific fixed effects. Given our knowledge of these industry characteristics – such as labor intensity of an industry, human capital intensity, etc. – we would like to include them in our regressions. The regression results for absolute concentration are given in table 2.

First of all, whereas technological differences and FDI determine relative concentration patterns, absolute concentration is driven by differences in human capital. The more human capital intensive industries have experienced a stronger trend towards high concentration than industries whose use of human capital deviates less from the average. The results suggest again pronounced differences between absolute concentration in output and in employment. Output concentration is driven primarily by absolute expenditure, i.e. the home market effect matters as might backward linkages. Scale economies, inputs from the same industry (forward linkages) and transport costs do not turn out to be significantly related to concentration. Again, electrical equipment accounts to a large extent for increases in output concentration due to the fact that this industry has become very concentrated in Hungary. Because Hungary is among the larger economies in the region, relative and absolute concentration have both increased significantly.

From our descriptive analysis we know that concentration of employment has in general risen, with some exceptions (wood, textiles, machinery, metals). Not surprisingly, this results from increased concentration in labor intensive industries, notably so in the leather industry. Our observation that formerly strongly concentrated industries were the ones who experienced decreases in concentration levels turns out to be a significant trend as indicated by the significant coefficient on the dummy variable for 1993 in the second column of table 2. It is interesting to note that the location of demand (i.e. whether demand for a certain industry's output is concentrated in one or a few countries) has no influence on employment patterns, while trade costs show up with a weakly significant positive sign.

Table 2. Regressions Results for Absolute Concentration Indices

	Output	Employment
FDI	-0.0056	-0.0093
	0.543	*0.159*
Productivity	-0.2329	0.0473
	0.063	*0.593*
Labour intensity	5.02E-07	9.39E-05
	0.992	*0.001*
Human capital intensity	7.78E-05	3.22E-05
	0.003	*0.015*
Expenditure	0.3797	0.0411
	0.000	*0.320*
Scale economies	0.0261	0.0383
	0.409	*0.114*
Trade costs	0.0003	0.0003
	0.142	*0.047*
Linkages	0.0417	-0.0299
	0.428	*0.349*
Trend	-0.0008	
	0.250	
Dummy1993		-0.0026
		0.014
Industry Dummy*	0.0093	0.0049
	0.000	*0.010*
Constant	0.0646	0.1186
	0.000	*0.000*
Wald-chi2	127.49	53.06
Prob >chi2	0.00	0.00
Number of observations	104	104

* In the first regression for the electronics industry, in the second regression for the leather industry.
p-values in italics.

5 Developments in Individual Industries

Let us now turn to developments in individual industries. By calculating our concentration indices all country-specific information is lost through averaging. To avoid this it seems appropriate to take a closer look at specialization patterns of individual countries with respect to individual industries. Thus, for each industry we now use a panel of all ten countries from 1993-2000.[18] The dependent variable we look at is each country's share of output in the respective industry's total output in CEECs. We control for country size by including total manufacturing output on the right hand side. Because of severe endogeneity problems we did not use a measure reflecting labor abundance of each country.

Human capital is captured by the wage differential in the respective industry to the average wage level in each country. Under the assumption that qualified labor receives a higher wage than unskilled labor, those industries which require a higher share of skilled workers in production (i.e. human capital intensive industries) should show a higher wage level than those with a less skilled (average) labor force. Consequently we expect a positive coefficient on this variable for human capital intensive industries (i.e. Electronics, chemicals, etc.) as these industries would locate where human capital is abundant.

Technological differences are expressed through industry and country specific productivity levels. FDI also enters in the same way. We further included the share of exports to the EU over total exports as well as the import share from the EU to account for the amount of trade re-orientation. As outlined before, transition from communist to market economies implied a rapid and substantial re-orientation of trade flows, away from Eastern European partners and CIS countries towards EU-15. This is likely to have had an impact also on location decisions of firms, albeit a different one in different industries. Table 3 presents the results obtained from a two-way error component, fixed effects regression for those industries, where we observed the greatest changes in absolute or relative concentration measures in section 2. Table 4 reports the results for all remaining industries. The results are well in line with our descriptive results: Country size does not matter for those industries with a high degree of relative concentration, such as electronics, wood, transport and leather. The first striking observation from both tables reveals that differences in productivity levels are the most important determinant for the location of industries across countries. The variable for technological differences is always highly significant, with the exception of the food industry.

[18] The analysis here does not tell us, which countries are specialized in which industries, although it is based on this data. For a description of individual country patterns see Wörz (2004).

Table 3. Regression Results for Individual Industries (I)

	Wood industry	Pulp and paper industry	Coke and petroleum	Rubber and Plastic Industry	Mineral products	Electronics
FDI	0.0001	-0.0003	0.0001	0.0003	0.0003	0.0004
	0.510	*0.208*	*0.134*	*0.170*	*0.000*	*0.002*
Technological differences	1.4244	1.3392	0.4859	1.5024	0.7207	1.7903
	0.002	*0.000*	*0.000*	*0.000*	*0.000*	*0.000*
Human capital intensity	1.8368	0.0580	0.2672	-0.6783	0.6818	-0.6724
	0.027	*0.803*	*0.275*	*0.257*	*0.039*	*0.223*
Size	3.80E-07	9.33E-07	6.06E-07	1.03E-06	3.60E-07	2.46E-07
	0.238	*0.000*	*0.001*	*0.001*	*0.004*	*0.395*
EU Exports	0.7447	-0.9382	0.0971	-0.2721	0.0095	0.8800
	0.009	*0.000*	*0.179*	*0.482*	*0.971*	*0.005*
EU Imports	-0.9166	0.3661	-0.1747	-0.4321	-0.2741	-0.6022
	0.004	*0.267*	*0.178*	*0.198*	*0.221*	*0.066*
Constant	-5.3850	-4.8781	-4.4336	-5.0096	-4.3909	-4.5327
	0.000	*0.000*	*0.000*	*0.000*	*0.000*	*0.000*
R^2	0.584	0.604	0.628	0.803	0.687	0.813
Number of observations	80	80	80	79	80	80

Year dummies are included.
* countrydummy for Latvia is included.
** country dummies for Estonia, Latvia and Poland are included.
*** country dummies for Estonia and Latvia are included.
p-values in italics.

When looking at those industries that experienced the strongest increases in concentration (or decrease in the case of chemicals), we find a rather diverse picture. It is surprising to note that relative human capital levels have no significant impact on specialization in the electronic industry, while they show a positive effect on specialization tendencies in the wood and mineral products industries. FDI plays a strong role in only two industries: electronics and mineral products which have both become more concentrated in absolute terms. Not surprisingly, this increase in concentration in the electronics industry has come along with a re-orientation of exports towards EU-15. Export orientation to the EU turns out to be highly significant in three out of the six industries. It increases concentration tendencies in the electronics and the wood industry, while the correlation is negative for the paper and printing industry. The share of EU-imports is hardly ever significant, and if it is its sign is opposed to that of EU-exports. This hints towards inter-industry trade, where inputs are sourced from different countries than those where output is sold to. This observation may reveal a successful price competition of CEECs in those industries that turn out to be highly concentrated. It is conceivable that inputs are purchased from other Eastern European partners or also from (Central or East) Asia at relatively low costs due to lower wages, while final products are sold into the EU-15 market, where higher prices can be achieved.

Table 4. Regression Results for Individual Industries (II)

	Food and beverages	Textile industry	Leather industry	Machinery	Transport equipment
FDI	4.48E-05	-5.47E-04	6.30E-03	2.80E-04	1.48E-04
	0.174	*0.212*	*0.085*	*0.097*	*0.098*
Technological differences	0.0457	2.7136	2.7764	1.5095	0.6926
	0.587	*0.000*	*0.000*	*0.000*	*0.000*
Human capital intensity	-0.4249	1.0287	-0.2006	-0.2237	1.2886
	0.16	*0.080*	*0.824*	*0.412*	*0.010*
Size	2.11E-07	5.92E-07	-1.16E-07	8.39E-07	6.32E-08
	0.102	*0.001*	*0.572*	*0.000*	*0.824*
EU Exports	-0.4619	-0.2887	-0.2948	0.2198	-0.1172
	0.020	*0.406*	*0.149*	*0.132*	*0.327*
EU Imports	0.0113	0.3125	0.2684	-0.2884	-0.2547
	0.907	*0.391*	*0.191*	*0.028*	*0.201*
Constant	-2.6179	-5.4225	-3.8522	-4.3637	-5.0504
	0.000	*0.000*	*0.000*	*0.000*	*0.000*
R^2	0.204	0.584	0.675	0.735	0.699
Number of observations	80	80	80	80	80

Year dummies are included.
p-values in italics.

As for those industries which experienced more modest changes in their concentration patterns (table 4), FDI induced concentration in the leather, machinery and transport industry. However, the coefficients are only weakly significant. Human capital plays a significant role in textiles and transport equipment and EU export orientation is never significant (with the exception of the food industry). This is an interesting observation in contrast to table 3: Exports to the EU turned out to be a determining factor in many of those industries that experienced strong increases in concentration. Trade re-orientation towards Western Europe has increased concentration, which implies that integration into those markets has a strong impact on industrial re-structuring in CEECs.

Thus, there are differences across industries with respect to the factors that determine industrial location patterns. Apart from the general importance of having an appropriate technology level, expressed here by productivity levels, some industries locate where they find high human capital levels, while others are attracted by high FDI stocks. Export orientation towards the EU always accompanies high concentration levels. Thus, the amount of trade re-orientation towards the West clearly had a significant impact on the location of industry in Eastern Europe.

6 Conclusions

Central and Eastern European countries have experienced a massive reallocation of production and the labor force during transition, which strongly affected the patterns of regional concentration of manufacturing firms. Industrial activity has become increasingly concentrated between 1993 and 2000, both in terms of production and employment. In contrast to this, the EU-15 exhibited a de-concentration of industrial activity over the same period. Still, this has been preceded by a rise in concentration in the pre-single market period from 1985-1992, albeit to a lesser degree than observed for CEECs. This suggests that economic integration initially induces a more efficient allocation of resources with an increase in concentration as predicted by traditional trade theories. However, ongoing economic integration will bring about higher factor mobility (especially for capital) and technology spillovers, thus eroding traditional Ricardian or Heckscher-Ohlin factors. This leads to a stronger role for intra-industry trade with a consequent decline in concentration patterns and less pronounced specialization of individual countries. The deepening of integration among EU-15 and CEECs (and consequently also among individual CEECs) through the latter's accession to the common market thus leads us to expect a turning point in the concentration trends observed up to date. In the medium term, concentration of industrial activity inside CEECs is expected to decrease rather than increase further, along with an increased role for intra-industry trade. This view is based on the expectations that technology spillovers between Western and Eastern Europe are going to gain in scale and scope. Further, investment ratios (and especially foreign investment) are already higher in the new member states than in incumbent members. FDI has been identified as one of the important determinants in shaping the industrial landscape in CEECs.

In order to identify the driving forces behind the patterns of concentration in the CEECs, we referred to traditional and new trade theory as well as to the new economic geography models. Our data set comprises output and employment data for ten Central and Eastern European countries and thirteen industries over the period from 1993 to 2000. We used panel estimation techniques to explain the location of manufacturing activities in the CEECs according to two different measures of geographical concentration (relative and absolute concentration) as well as two measures of the size of an industry (production and employment).

Our results for relative concentration showed that relative concentration is strongly influenced by comparative advantages, the location of demand and of FDI. However, we identified some differences between the relative concentration of output and employment: While the former is more strongly affected by expenditure patterns, the latter is driven by technological differences. We found that variables reflecting new economic geography models had very little impact on the evolution of concentration patterns in the CEECs. Further, the electronic industry, being probably the most typical high skill, high tech industry in this classification, accounts to a large extent for the strong increase in output concentration, while a typical labor intensive, low tech industry (namely leather) influenced strongly concentration in the location of the labor force.

In contrast to the determinants of relative concentration, our results provided support that absolute concentration was crucially driven by differences in human capital. Differences can again be found between the results of absolute concentration of output and of employment. Once again, the absolute concentration of production was mainly influenced by absolute expenditure. As it was already the case for relative concentration, scale economies, forward linkages and transport costs had no significant impact on absolute concentration either.

In a further step we investigated the location of industries across CEECs by closely looking at specialization patterns inside individual industries. In doing so, we try to explain the location of industries across countries. Our results suggest that differences in productivity levels – and thus traditional Ricardian factors - are the determining factor for a country's share of output in the respective industry's total output, whereas the influence of FDI was only important for two industries. The same applied to export orientation towards the EU, which plays a role in just a few industries. Thus, while FDI had a significant impact on relative concentration in production, its influence was confined to two industries, electronics and minerals. The concentration of the electronics industry in Hungary was certainly policy driven to a great extent. FDI was attracted to Hungary by distinct policies and a general attitude towards an early and comprehensive capital market liberalization. The concentration of the mineral industry in Poland is more likely to be connected to the general importance of the construction industry in this country.

The paper examined trends in industrial concentration patterns inside Central and Eastern Europe. Given the process of further and also deeper integration of these countries with their Western European counterparts, it seems appropriate to shift attention towards the enlarged European Union. Thus, future research should analyze concentration and specialization patterns in the EU-25 rather than for EU-15 and CEEC separately. Our study here may serve as a reference by giving a detailed picture of the developments in Eastern Europe prior to accession. However, in the future a more comprehensive perspective is called for.

Appendix

Table 5. Ranking of Absolute Concentration Indices (production) for the years 1993 and 2000

Industry name	1993		2000	
	Rank	CIP_i^A	Rank	CIP_i^A
Wood and wood products	1.	0.1599	6.	0.1636
Food, beverages, tobacco	2.	0.1553	5.	0.1643
Rubber and plastic products	3.	0.1535	1.	0.1678
Transport equipment	4.	0.1523	7.	0.1558
Pulp, paper and paper products	5.	0.1495	4.	0.1650
Mineral products (non-metallic)	6.	0.1491	3.	0.1659
Coke, petroleum, manuf. n.e.c.	7.	0.1485	9.	0.1489
Textiles and textiles products	8.	0.1483	13.	0.1386
Basic and fabricated metals	9.	0.1442	10.	0.1476
Machinery and equipment n.e.c.	10.	0.1423	8.	0.1491
Electrical and optical equipment	11.	0.1408	2.	0.1664
Chemicals and chemical products	12.	0.1378	11.	0.1460
Leather and leather products	13.	0.1356	12.	0.1422

Table 6. Ranking of Relative Concentration Indices (production) for the years 1993 and 2000

Industry name	1993		2000	
	Rank	CIP_i^R	Rank	CIP_i^R
Transport equipment	1.	0.0315	4.	0.0376
Wood and wood products	2.	0.0298	2.	0.0506
Leather and leather products	3.	0.0290	3.	0.0407
Chemicals and chemical products	4.	0.0246	13.	0.0129
Basic and fabricated metals	5.	0.0244	8.	0.0302
Machinery and equipment n.e.c.	6.	0.0222	12.	0.0275
Pulp, paper and paper products	7.	0.0206	10.	0.0296
Electrical and optical equipment	8.	0.0202	1.	0.0931
Food, beverages, tobacco	9.	0.0198	9.	0.0298
Rubber and plastic products	10.	0.0185	11.	0.0284
Coke, petroleum, manuf. n.e.c.	11.	0.0182	7.	0.0307
Mineral products (non-metallic)	12.	0.0156	5.	0.0329
Textiles and textiles products	13.	0.0151	6.	0.0310

Table 7. Ranking of Absolute Concentration Indices (employment) for the years 1993 and 2000

Industry name	1993		2000	
	Rank	CIE_i^A	Rank	CIE_i^A
Transport equipment	1.	0.1500	1.	0.1532
Food, beverages, tobacco	2.	0.1453	5.	0.1483
Textiles and textiles products	3.	0.1441	11.	0.1385
Basic and fabricated metals	4.	0.1435	8.	0.1413
Machinery and equipment n.e.c.	5.	0.1426	12.	0.1371
Wood and wood products	6.	0.1426	10.	0.1388
Rubber and plastic products	7.	0.1416	2.	0.1517
Mineral products (non-metallic)	8.	0.1410	4.	0.1486
Chemicals and chemical products	9.	0.1391	9.	0.1405
Coke, petroleum, manuf. n.e.c.	10.	0.1371	6.	0.1471
Leather and leather products	11.	0.1362	3.	0.1489
Pulp, paper and paper products	12.	0.1317	7.	0.1418
Electrical and optical equipment	13.	0.1232	13.	0.1326

Table 8. Ranking of Relative Concentration Indices (employment) for the years 1993 and 2000

Industry name	1993		2000	
	Rank	CIE_i^R	Rank	CIE_i^R
Food, beverages, tobacco	1.	0.0407	7.	0.0334
Coke, petroleum, manuf. n.e.c.	2.	0.0360	12.	0.0195
Electrical and optical equipment	3.	0.0308	2.	0.0549
Pulp, paper and paper products	4.	0.0286	6.	0.0342
Wood and wood products	5.	0.0246	5.	0.0348
Machinery and equipment n.e.c.	6.	0.0225	10.	0.0212
Rubber and plastic products	7.	0.0217	4.	0.0388
Basic and fabricated metals	8.	0.0216	9.	0.0237
Textiles and textiles products	9.	0.0210	3.	0.0431
Transport equipment	10.	0.0205	8.	0.0294
Leather and leather products	11.	0.0183	1.	0.0695
Chemicals and chemical products	12.	0.0140	13.	0.0120
Mineral products (non-metallic)	13.	0.0124	11.	0.0197

References

Aiginger, K. (1999), Do Industrial Structures Converge? A Survey on the Empirical Literature on Specialization and Concentration of Industries, WIFO Working Paper 116, Austrian Institute of Economic Research (WIFO), Vienna.

Amiti, M. (1999), Specialization Patterns in Europe, *Weltwirtschaftliches Archiv* 135(4), 573-593.

Brühlhart, M. (1998), Trading Places: Industrial Specialization in the European Union, *Journal of Common Market Studies* 36(3), 319-346.

Carlin, W. and M.A. Landesmann (1997), From Theory into Practice? Corporate Restructuring and Economic Dynamism in Transition Economies, wiiw Research Report No. 240, Vienna.

Combes, P.-P. and H. Overman, The Spatial Distribution of Economic Activities in the EU, CEPR Discussion Paper 3999, Centre for Economic Policy Research, London.

Ethier, W. J. (1982); National and International Returns to Scale in the Modern Theory of International Trade, *American Economic Review* 72, 389-405.

Ellison, G. and E. Glaeser (1997); Geographic Concentration in US manufacturing industries: A Dartboard Approach, *Journal of Political Economy*, 105, 889-927.

Fidrmuc, J. and M. Djablik (2003), Intra industry trade between the EU and the acceding countries: the importance of foreign direct investment on trade structure, East-West-Conference Volume, forthcoming.

Forslid, R., J.I. Haaland, K.H. Midelfart-Knarvik, and O. Mestad (2002), Integration and Transition: Scenarios for the Location of Production and Trade in Europe, *Economics of Transition* 10(1), 93-117.

Fujita, M., P. Krugman, and A.J. Venables (1999), *The spatial Economy: Cities, Regions and International Trade*, MIT Press, Cambridge Massachusetts.

Gugler, K. and M. Pfaffermayr (2000), Convergence in Structure and Productivity in European Manufacturing, WIFO Working Paper 127, WIFO, Vienna.

Haaland, J.I., Kind, H.J., Midelfart-Knarvik, K.H. and J. Torstensson (1999), What Determines the Economic Geography of Europe?, CEPR Discussion Paper 2072, Centre for Economic Policy Research, London.

Hanson, G. (2002); Market Potential, Increasing Returns, and Geographic Concentration, processed University of Michigan, November. Revised version of NBER Working Paper 6249, February 1998.

Hausman, J.A. and W.E. Taylor (1981), Panel Data and Unobservable Individual Effects, *Econometrica* 49(6), 1377-1398.

Helpman, E. (1981); International Trade in the Presence of Product Differentiation; Economies of Scale and Monopolistic Competition – a Chamberlin-Heckscher-Ohlin approach, *Journal of International Economics* 11, 305-340.

Kalotay, K. and G. Hunya (2000), Privatization and FDI in Central and Eastern Europe, *Transnational Corporations* 9(1), 39-66.

Krugman, P. (1980); Scale Economies, Product Differentiation, and the Pattern of Trade, *American Economic Review* 70(5), 950-959.

Midelfart-Knarvik, K., Henry G. Overman, Steven R. Redding and Anthony J. Venables (2002), The Location of European Industry, *European Economy*, 2, 216-273.

Posner, M.V. (1961), International Trade and Technical Change, Oxford Economic Papers, 13, 323-41.

Pratten, C. (1988), A Survey of the Economies of Scale, Commission of the European Communities: Research on the "cost of non-Europe", vol. 2. Studies on the Economies of Integration, European Commission, Brussels.

Puga, D. and A.J. Venables (1996), The Spread of Industry: spatial Agglomeration and economic development, Journal of the Japanese and International Economies10(4), 440-64.

Richter, S. (2001), Transition and regional economic cooperation in Central Europe, wiiw mimeo, Vienna.

Richter, S. (1997), European Integration: The CEFTA and the Europe Agreements, wiiw Research Report No. 237, Vienna.

wiiw (2003), *Competitiveness of Central and Eastern European Industries – now and in an Enlarged EU*, A study commissioned by Bank Austria Creditanstalt, Economic Department, Vienna.

Wolfmayr-Schnitzer, Y. (1999), Economic Integration, Specialization and the Location of Industries: A Survey of the Theoretical Literature, WIFO Working Paper 120, Austrian Institute of Economic Research (WIFO), Vienna.

Wörz, J. (2004); Specialization patterns in CEEC manufacturing output, wiiw Monthly Report 2/04, 6-13.

Comment on: Patterns of Industrial Specialization and Concentration in CEECs: Theoretical Explanations and their Empirical Relevance

Simon Görtz

In 1989 the Iron Curtain in Europe lifted. This was the starting point for the EU enlargement to the east, but not the beginning of economic development in the Central and East European countries (CEEC). To understand the patterns of industrial specialisation and concentration in the CEEC, we should not forget its history. Most of the 10 states, nowadays members of the EU, had a vital industrial sector in regard to the Council for Mutual Economic Assistance (Comecon). The Soviet Union usually provided raw materials and the CEEC provided finished equipment and machinery. Although the Soviet Union was the leading country, most of the CEEC had a higher level of welfare. This reflected the situation before World War II as the Soviet Union was mainly determined by agriculture, while the industrialisation of the CEEC had taken place at the beginning of the 20th century.

Without empirical data it is difficult to determine the drivers for the industrial specialisation in these countries after World War II, but it is easy to show that most of the industrial locations were planned by the central administrations. In the system of Comecon, which mirrored the member countries' planned economies; central decisions did not take into consideration the influences of market forces or private initiative. Although the planned nature of the Comecon members' economies often hindered progress and economic development, one of the Comecon's goals was the economic integration of its members. Therefore, progress in integration and specialisation had to depend upon conscious acts of policy; but those acts were more political than in similar processes in Western market economies.

For example, Eisenhüttenstadt was founded in 1950 in the GDR. The city and its industry, the production of steel, were located at a riverside near to Frankfurt where the railway from Berlin to Warsaw crosses the Oder River. There was neither iron-ore nor coal nor chalk nearby, the region was scarcely populated, but it was far away from the Iron Curtain. The location of this important industrial complex was a strategic decision rather than an economical one, motivated by geographic and military aspects.

Applying pure trade theory to the CEEC' economies before the fall of the Iron Curtain is difficult. An approach based on economic geography might be more helpful: The patterns of industrial localisation are path dependent and that localisation is initialised by accident and individual decisions. In the system of Comecon, however, plans formed the paths. After the end of Comecon, the planned economy came to an end. Moreover, the young free countries had to overcome a regression due to the competition in the world market; most of the heavy industries were in trouble because their productivity was too low and the investment in new technology too expensive. Obviously, the paths determining the industrial location changed dramatically, but they did not completely disappear. After the end of planned economy in the CEEC and the beginning of a market oriented economy, only competitive industries could survive in the world market. Competitiveness might result from skilled workers, innovative products and production technology, as well as by low transportation and location costs. The governments of the CEEC can influence the last two factors. For example, Estonia introduced a flat tax rate for industrial firms in order to reduce location costs. Transportation costs in the CEEC are very low as most of the railways are still state-owned and the governments take the investments in new highways. The skilled work force remained, however, as a main determinant of the industrial localisation. In socialistic countries, capital in a western sense did not exit. Only with the privatisation of the state-owned industries, the constitution of capital begun. Now the new owners had to get money from the capital market on their own risk.

The shift from planned economy towards market economy allows asking which are the drivers of industrial concentration. Hildebrandt and Wörz found empirical evidence that the patterns of industrial specialisation and concentration are mainly driven by FDI and differences in human capital. Therefore, one might argue that paths of industrial localisation initialised during the Comecon period continue through the transition period. Especially paths, characterised by a critical mass of skilled workers, are still determining the industrial specialisation and concentration. FDI helps constituting capital in a Western sense. Therefore, industries supported by FDI maintain their locations.

The Absence of Technology Spillovers from Foreign Direct Investment in Transition Economies

Jutta Günther

Contents

1 Introduction 150
2 Channels of Technology Spillovers – the View of Contemporary Economic Literature 152
3 Spillover Channels – Towards a Consistent Theoretical Framework 153
3.1 Spillovers as External Effects 153
3.2 Spillovers through Cooperation 154
3.3 Special Case: Competition Effects 155
4 Results of Econometric Studies on Technology Spillovers in Transition Economies 156
5 Obstacles to Technology Spillovers on the Enterprise Level 159
6 Conclusions 161
Appendix 162
References 164

1 Introduction

The worldwide increase of foreign direct investment (FDI) in the past decades has given rise to numerous studies investigating the economic effects of FDI on the host economies. One frequently analyzed issue is that of technology transfer via foreign subsidiaries. Apart from the direct transfer of modern equipment and know-how from the parent company to the foreign subsidiary, especially the trickle down or spillover effects from foreign subsidiaries in favor of domestic firms caught researchers' attention. These spillover effects are expected to positively contribute to domestic firm's productivity. Consequently, spillover effects are of interest particularly for countries or regions in the process of catching up economically.

Existing empirical studies on technology spillovers usually apply an econometric approach in which labor (or total factor) productivity is regressed on a number of independent variables. To measure spillovers, single variables are included in order to serve as proxy for the presence of foreign firms, usually the share of employment or sales in foreign subsidiaries in total industry employment or sales.[1] A large number of econometric spillover studies exists for developing countries, the results of which, however, differ considerably.[2] Recently, econometric spillover research has also been carried out for developed countries, especially EU member countries with structurally weak regions, not very surprisingly also with different outcomes.[3] Blomström/ Kokko (1998), in their summarizing study about multinational enterprises and spillovers, conclude that the occurrence of spillovers depends largely on the country and sector observed. In particular, the positive effects of foreign investment are likely to increase with the level of local capability and competition.

With the political changes in Eastern Europe and the beginning of transition, FDI for the first time grew strongly in these economies, as well. Especially the

[1] Econometric research of that type was pioneered by Caves (1974) and Globerman (1979) using cross sectional industry level data for Australia and Canada respectively. They found a positive impact of foreign investors on local firms.

[2] Prominent examples for spillover studies on developing countries are works by Blomström (1986), Blomström/ Wolff (1994), Kokko (1994), and Kokko (1996), who found a positive impact on productivity in the Mexican industry for the early 1970s. Aitken/Harrison (1999) in contrast found a negative impact of foreign investors on productivity in Venezuela for 1976-1989. For the Indonesian manufacturing industry, Blomström/Sjöholm (1999), Sjöholm (1999a), and Sjöholm (1999b) in turn found a positive impact on local companies (for various time periods between 1980 and 1991). For the Uruguayan manufacturing industry, Kokko et al. (1996) and Kokko et al. (2001) could not find a statistically significant impact of foreign subsidiaries on productivity. Kathuria (2000) and Kugler (2001) did not find statistically significant evidence for spillovers in India and Columbia, either.

[3] See for example: Girma (2003) and Driffield/Love (2002) for the UK, Ruane/Ugur (2001) for Ireland, Barrios/Strobl (2002) for Spain, etc.

candidate countries for EU enlargement – the most advanced and stable transition economies – received considerable amounts of FDI (see Figure 1).

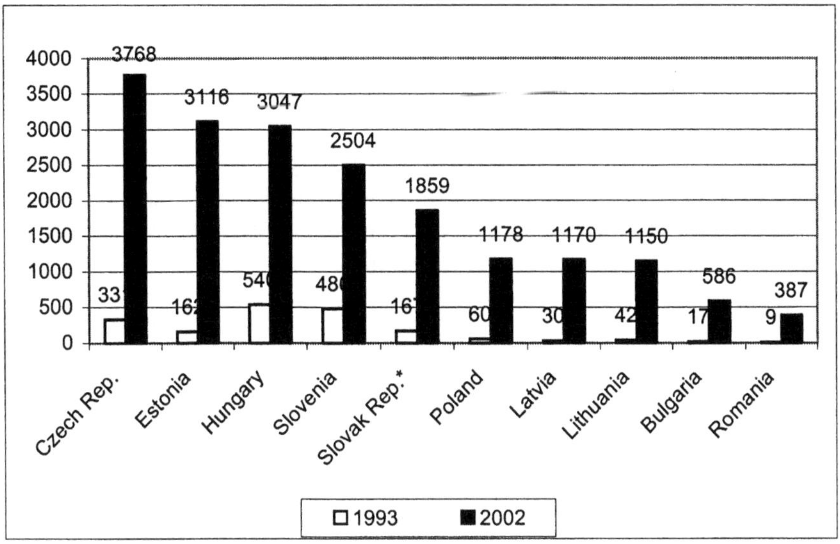

Fig. 1. FDI stock per head in CEEC 2002 (US $)

Data source: WIIW (The Vienna Institute for International Economic Studies)/WIFO (Austrian Institute for Economic Research): WIIW-WIFO Database on FDI.
*1994 instead of 1993

From the outset, foreign direct investment has been regarded as an important source of technology transfer in transition economies. As a consequence, the question of technology spillovers also caught the attention of researchers for this group of countries (e. g. Konigs, 2001; Bosco, 2001; Kinoshita, 2000; Smarzynska, 2002; Zukowska-Gagelmann, 2001). Thus far, however, econometric spillover studies on transition economies have hardly provided evidence for positive spillover effects on domestic firms. Some investigations even point out a negative impact on domestic enterprises. Explanations for the current lack of spillovers are provided only sparingly. Furthermore, there seems to be no consistent theoretical framework about technology spillover mechanisms. Empirical studies – be it on developing, developed, or transition economies – either take for granted that foreign subsidiaries somehow generate trickle down effects or they mention more or less exemplarily different channels for spillovers.

Therefore, this paper will first develop a consistent and comprehensive theoretical framework explaining how technology spills over from foreign subsidiaries to domestic firms. This is followed by a presentation of the results of existing econometric spillover studies for transition economies. Finally, possible explanations for the obvious lack of technology spillovers will be deduced from an empirical qualitative study that takes an enterprise perspective.

2 Channels of Technology Spillovers – the View of Contemporary Economic Literature

Economic literature dealing with technology spillovers from FDI consists for the most part of econometric studies on particular countries and/or industries. The empirical studies are based on different perceptions of how technology spillovers occur, and they normally mention different channels of how technology spillovers are realized.

For example, Blomström/ Sjöholm (1999, 916) state that "spillovers from FDI may occur from increased competition and labor turnover, or through demonstration". Dunning (1993, 446ff) explains that spillovers derive from upstream and downstream linkages, i. e. linkages with suppliers or customers, from labor turnover, or form foreign firm's membership in trade associations, research consortia, etc. Konings (2001, 621) refers to labor turnover, imitation, and other channels. Kinoshita (2000) with reference to Kokko (1992) and Kinoshita (1999) distinguishes between four spillover channels: demonstration-imitation effects, competition effects, foreign-linkage effects, and training effects. Görg/ Greenaway (2002, 2ff) differentiate between imitation, acquisition of human capital, competition, and export spillovers. The latter means that domestic firms learn how to penetrate foreign markets from observing foreign subsidiaries. Djankov/ Hoekman (2000, 52) state that "knowledge will move from firm to firm through demonstration effects, labor turnover, or reverse-engineering." Lutz/ Talavera (2003, 5) write: "The channels of these effects [spillover effects] are technology transfer effect, competition effect, backward and forward linkage effect, training effect, and demonstration effect". Other studies distinguish between vertical spillovers (along the value added chain, i.e. towards suppliers or customers) and horizontal spillovers (towards competitors) (OECD, 2002, 98f; Damijan/ Knell/ Majcen/ Rojec, 2003).

This is, of course, not a complete list of perceptions about spillover mechanisms. It could rather be continued for a number of further studies, but this would not provide any new information. What stands out when looking at the above quotations is that nearly all authors mention labor mobility and demonstration as practical spillover mechanisms. Some studies also refer to supplier and customer relations as a crucial spillover mechanism, although it remains unclear whether supplier and customer relations only support demonstration effects or whether they are regarded as a further independent form of a spillover channel. To sum up, the perceptions of how technology spills over from foreign investment enterprises to domestic firms are manifold and anything but consistent. The literature provides a number of ideas, which needs to be reconsidered and put together systematically towards a comprehensive theoretical framework of technology spillovers.

3 Spillover Channels – Towards a Consistent Theoretical Framework

The following considerations are based on a definition of technology spillovers as the non-market transfer of soft technology (knowledge) or hard technology (tangible assets) from foreign subsidiaries to domestic companies.

Due to their non-market character, spillovers are often simply equated with positive external effects (Grossman/ Helpman, 1997, 15f; UNCTAD, 1999, 203). But the concept of external effects does not go far enough for a comprehensive coverage of spillover channels. As described in more detail below, a non-market technology transfer from foreign subsidiaries to domestic companies can also take place outside externalities, i.e. intentionally and voluntarily.[4]

3.1 Spillovers as External Effects

Technology spillovers in the sense of external effects typically appear anonymously and without any return through the technology-taking company. What comes to mind first of all when talking about spillovers in the sense of external effects is imitation. Technological knowledge can nevertheless also be transferred tacitly when workers switch from a foreign subsidiary to a domestic firm. Thus, it makes sense to distinguish demonstration effects (imitation) and labor mobility as practical mechanisms of so-called "externality spillovers".

Demonstration (imitation)
The demonstration of technology through foreign subsidiaries may lead to reverse engineering (Mohnen, 1996, 41) or learning-by-watching (Burger, 1998, 56). Reverse engineering means the inspection of a product and copying of a product technology, while domestic firms are learning by watching when they observe foreign investor's actions, e. g. in the field of marketing or logistics, and imitate certain practices or techniques. Imitation can take place without any relation between the two sides, but it is more likely to occur in the context of business relations between foreign and domestic firms.

Labor mobility
Labor mobility constitutes another practical channel of technology spillovers in the sense of external effects. Foreign subsidiaries often invest in education and training of their local staff.[5] Thus, employees of foreign subsidiaries acquire general and specific qualifications through education and training programs or just by learning on the job. When qualified employees go to domestic employers or open

---

[4] The concept presented here is a revised version of the theoretical framework developed in Günther (2003).

[5] There is plenty of empirical evidence that foreign subsidiaries invest in their local employees. See e. g. Behrman/Wallender, 1976; Dunning, 1993, 372ff; Estrin/Hughes/Todd, 1997; Gerschenberg, 1987; Hill, 1982; Reuber/Crookell/Emerson/Gallais-Hamonno, 1973.

their own businesses, they transfer technological knowledge which can be of use to the existing or newly founded domestic enterprise. Since the domestic firm does not have to reimburse the foreign subsidiary for its human capital investments, this channel of technology spillovers corresponds to the principles of positive external effects.

3.2 Spillovers through Cooperation

As mentioned above, spillovers in the sense of a non-market transfer of technology are not necessarily restricted to externalities. Foreign subsidiaries can also intentionally transfer hard or soft technology to domestic companies without asking a price to be paid in direct return, although they implicitly or explicitly expect future advantages for themselves. It can, for example, be in the foreign firm's interest to enable a domestic company to produce certain products and become a future supplier. Channels of this second type of technology spillovers, which are based on cooperation and a direct link between the two sides, will be looked at below.

Supplier support
In the literature, supplier contacts (backward linkages) are very often mentioned as a crucial technology spillover mechanism (e. g. Dunning, 1993, 446ff). However, supplier contacts as such do not automatically constitute an independent spillover channel. They may result in learning-by-watching but this has already been covered above. Backward linkages only constitute an independent spillover channel if foreign firms voluntarily transfer hard or soft technology to domestic enterprises in order to enable them to deliver adequate supplier products in the future. The foreign subsidiary's motive for such technological support is to circumvent transaction costs related to the otherwise costly search for adequate suppliers.

Customer support
On the other hand, spillovers can occur in the context of foreign subsidiaries' contact with domestic firms as customers. But here again, customer contact as such does not yet constitute a spillover channel. Only if the foreign subsidiary voluntarily transfers extra technology to a domestic customer firm will technology spillover occur. The reason for such voluntary technology transfer may be the attempt to bind an existing domestic customer, i.e. for marketing-strategic reasons.[6]

Both, supplier and customer support, require direct cooperation between the two sides, and the transfer of technology is anything but anonymous. Thus, they do not represent external effects but still meet the crucial criterion for technology spillovers, namely the non-market character of technology transfer.

6 Compared to supplier support, this spillover mechanism plays a less important role in the empirical literature. But Blomström (1991) and Blomström/Kokko (1996), however, provide evidence for the growing importance of customer support, especially with respect to the sale of computer-based production goods.

Other forms of enterprise cooperation

Besides cooperation in the context of business (supplier or customer) relations, foreign subsidiaries might transfer soft or hard technology to domestic firms in the context of other cooperation activities, for example joint research & development or innovation projects (Dunning, 1993, 470f). Thus, the fifth spillover channel – called "other forms of enterprise cooperation" – covers all remaining forms of cooperation between independent foreign and domestic companies outside business contacts. Technology spillovers within such cooperation or networking activities occur when foreign subsidiaries regard it as efficient (also for themselves) to transfer technology to the domestic cooperation partner, who in turn does not have to pay for it.

3.3 Special Case: Competition Effects

As outlined above, several authors also regard competition effects from FDI as an independent channel for spillovers (e. g. Görg/ Greenaway, 2002; Kinoshita, 2002; Lutz/ Talavera, 2003) and of course, foreign investment companies are likely to increase competition in the host economy. Yet competition effects themselves are not a channel for a non-market transfer of technology from a foreign to a domestic firm. Competition by foreign investors may (especially on a horizontal level) stimulate domestic firms to modernize in order to keep pace, but competition does not induce a technology transfer from foreign to domestic firms. Finally, it depends on the definition of spillovers whether competition effects count as an independent spillover mechanism. For technology spillovers as defined above, competition effects do not represent a further and independent spillover channel.

To sum up, technology spillovers in the sense of a non-market transfer of technology from foreign to domestic firms are realized through demonstration, labor mobility, supplier support, customer support, or other forms of enterprise cooperation. Strictly speaking, each of these five spillover channels can exist without foreign subsidiaries "next door". In other words, the demonstration of (new) technology does not stop at national borders. Similarly, supplier or customer support can take place across countries, and any other form of enterprise cooperation can take place independent of where the partners are located. Last but not least, international labor mobility is nothing impossible although there are still many restrictions especially with respect to labor mobility between Central-East European countries and the European Union. Still, it is reasonable to assume that spatial proximity strongly supports spillover effects since it reduces transaction costs (costs for searching, observing etc.) and facilitates demonstration effects. Finally, this is why industry clusters exist at all.

4 Results of Econometric Studies on Technology Spillovers in Transition Economies

As mentioned above, there has been a growing number of econometric investigations into the existence of technology spillovers for transition economies. The studies use company level data and usually focus on productivity measures (labor productivity or total factor productivity) as proxies for measures of technology spillovers. Several transition countries have already been covered (see Table 1). Overall, there is no clear cut evidence for the existence of technology spillovers from FDI. The majority of analyses rather point to the fact that there are no positive productivity effects on domestic firms. The relevant spillover studies on Central European transition countries[7] will briefly be presented in the following.

Bosco (2001, 43), in her empirical investigation of Hungary, concludes that "the evidence for technology spillovers is weak and does not allow clear cut conclusions. [Only] foreign presence in high-technology industries does seem to have a positive effect on both local and foreign firms". Damijan et al (2003) differentiate between horizontal (intra-industry) and vertical (inter-industry) spillovers and analyze 10 transition economies. Positive horizontal spillovers to domestic firms are only found in the Czech Republic, Poland, Romania, and Slovakia, and positive vertical spillovers only in the Czech Republic, Poland, and Slovenia. Djankov/Hoekman (2000, 49) investigate spillover effects in the Czech Republic and find that there are even "negative spillover effects on firms that do not have foreign partnerships". The findings of Kinoshita (2000) for the Czech Republic correspond to these results. In his spillover study on Poland, Bulgaria, and Romania Konings (2001, 619) discovers "... no evidence of positive spillovers to domestic firms on average. [But] ... there are [even] negative spillovers to domestic firms in Bulgaria and Romania". Jensen (2002, 29) provides evidence for the "... absence of horizontal spillovers from multinational to domestic firms" in the Polish food industry. Schoors/ van der Tol (2002) investigate spillovers from foreign subsidiaries to domestic firms in the Hungarian economy based on company level data from Amadeus data bank (Bureau van Dijck)[8]. Their study provides evidence for positive spillover effects both within sectors and between sectors. Smarzynska's (2002) results for technology spillovers in Lithuania are mixed. She presents evidence for "... productivity spillovers from FDI taking place through contacts between foreign affiliates and their local suppliers in upstream sectors but there is no indication of spillovers occurring within the same industry". Smarzynska/ Spatareanu (2003) investigate whether the existence of spillovers is affected by the foreign ownership share. Their analysis, based on unbalanced panel data (from Amadeus data base) of Romanian firms, indicates positive spillovers within sec-

7 The literature review covers the new EU member countries of Central Europe as well as Bulgaria and Romania.

8 Amadeus is a commercial data base which provides company data for several European countries. The information mainly comes from balance sheets so that the vast majority of firms in the database are big enterprises. Small firms are strongly underrepresented. For further information on the database see: www. bvdep.com.

tors, but only for fully foreign owned subsidiaries whereas joint ventures (mixed foreign/domestic firms) produce no positive horizontal spillovers. Zukowska-Gagelmann (2001), in her comprehensive study on productivity spillovers from FDI in the Polish manufacturing industry, concludes that there are negative productivity spillovers, especially on private firms in highly competitive sectors.

Overall, the majority of econometric spillover studies provides no evidence for a positive impact on domestic firms' productivity. Two explanations are usually provided for the lack of technology spillovers in transition economies, if the studies deal with such explanations at all. First, an insufficient absorption capacity of the domestic sector and second, a crowd out effect caused by foreign subsidiaries. A lack of absorption capacity means that domestic firms are unable to assimilate and implement the external technology "offered" by foreign subsidiaries. In other words, the technology gap between foreign and domestic firms is too large, as put forward by Konings (2001, 632) for instance. In the case of crowd out effects, the competition caused by foreign firms is so strong that domestic firms lose market shares. As a result, they produce less, increase their cost – especially when fixed costs are high – and finally end up having lower productivity if they survive at all (Bosco, 2001, 50).[9] These explanations are logical and obvious, but they are limited insofar as they take only a global (macro) perspective.

Company level insights are necessary to broaden the view and to allow for a deeper understanding of what is immediately going on between foreign and domestic firms. An empirical qualitative study that takes an enterprise perspective and is based on a theoretical framework as suggested in this paper has been carried out on the example of Hungarian industry (Günther, 2002; Günther, 2003). The field study investigates the behavior of foreign and domestic firms with respect to the different technology spillover mechanisms. The results largely correspond to the findings of econometric research that has found no evidence of technology spillovers thus far. Insights gained from the enterprise level study will be introduced in the following.

[9] The argument of a crowding out effect had first been put forward by Aitken/Harrison (1999), who investigated technology spillovers in Venezuela and found a negative effect of foreign subsidiaries on domestic firms.

Table 1. Results of econometric spillover studies of transition economies

Author(s)	Country of investigation	Time period	Branch(es)	Results[a]		
Bosco (2001)	Hungary	1993-1997	all branches (NACE 1-93)	-		
Damijan et al (2003)	Bulgaria (BG), Latvia (LV), Poland (PL), Lithuania (LT), Romania (RO), Hungary (HU), Czech Rep. (CZ), Slovakia (SK), Estonia (EE), Slovenia (SI)	1995-1999 for all countries except Estonia (1994-1998) and Slovenia (1994-1999)	manufacturing industry		verti-cal spill-overs	Hori-zontal spill-overs
				BG:	-	-
				LV:	-	-
				PL:	+	+
				LT-	-	-
				RO:	-	+
				HU:	-	-
				CZ:	+	+
				SK:	-	+
				EE:	-	-
				SI:	+	-
Djankov/ Hoekman (2000)	Czech Republic	1992-1996	manufacturing industry, retail services, finan-cial services	-		
Jensen (2002)	Poland	1993-2000	food industry	-		
Kinoshita (2000)	Czech Republic	1995-1998	manufactur-ing industry	-		
Konings (2001)	Bulgaria Poland Romania	1993-1997 1994-1997 1993-1997	all branches (manufacturing and non-manufacturing firms)	- - -		
Schoors/ van der Tol (2002)	Hungary	1997-1998	all branches (NACE 1-74)	+		
Smarzynska/ Spatareanu (2003)	Romania	1998-2000	all branches (NACE 1-99)	+ only for 100% for-eign subsidiaries, - for joint ventures		
Smarzynska (2002)	Lithuania	1996-2000	manufacturing industry (NACE 15-36)	+ for upstream sec-tors, - within same sector		
Zukowska-Gagelmann (2001)	Poland	1993-97	manufacturing industry	-		

Source: author's presentation.
[a] + = positive effects on domestic firms; - = no positive or (even) negative effects on domestic firms

5 Obstacles to Technology Spillovers on the Enterprise Level

The following considerations are based on an explorative field study carried out through qualitative interviews with leading representatives of foreign and domestic firms as well as business associations and policy makers in Hungary in the year 2000.[10] The qualitative findings cannot be generalized in the sense of statistical representativeness since it is not the intention of qualitative research to collect numerical data on standardized variables. Instead, qualitative studies usually explore complex and non-measurable phenomena, here the functioning of spillover mechanisms from foreign to domestic firms. The findings on the Hungarian industry can be generalized in the sense that it is reasonable to assume a comparable behavior of firms operating in a similar environment. In other words, the patterns of firm's behavior may be similar in other former socialist countries that have experienced comparable economic development since the beginning of transition. In this respect, the qualitative findings contribute to a better understanding of the absence of technology spillovers in transition economies in general.

Technology-Spillovers via *demonstration* are difficult to investigate empirically. Learning-by-watching mostly takes place without being noticed, neither through the learning company nor through the foreign firm demonstrating technology. If at all, demonstration effects were important in the early stage of transition "when more and more foreign investors came and domestic firms copied one or another directly observable practice, especially in marketing and logistics. However, many observable techniques require investments which domestic companies are hardly able to finance" (expert group: domestic companies). With respect to "reverse engineering", no evidence could be found that it was relevant at any time during transition. "In the service sector, companies adopted many new services which were unknown before and possibly copied from foreign companies but not necessarily from those within Hungary. In industry, the copying of products is insignificant and often impossible from a legal perspective" (expert group: domestic companies). A sophisticated intellectual property right scheme that meets the standards of the European Union's patent office limits the scope for copying new products in Hungarian industry (Hungarian Patent Office, 1999; Smid, 1998).

With respect to *labor mobility*, expert interviews show that the majority of foreign investors in the Hungarian industry invests in professional training of their local work force. Nevertheless, it can be concluded that it is utterly unattractive for employees to switch from foreign to domestic employers because the latter usually cannot pay an income or additional benefits as high as foreign investors.

[10] A total of 40 expert interviews have been carried out. The evaluation of the interview material (verbal data) took place through "reductive procedures" according to Lamnek (1995, 36ff) and Meuser/Nagel (1991). Summarized expert quotations are put in inverted commas in this paper. The relevant expert group is declared in parentheses. Names of companies or persons cannot be given for reasons of data protection. For a detailed description of the research concept see Günther (2003, 55ff).

"Sometimes labor turnover from a foreign subsidiary to domestic companies takes place but rather occasionally than generally. It is too expensive for Hungarian owned firms to attract employees from multinational companies, especially those with an academic degree and leading position" (expert group: policy makers). The opportunities for qualified persons to open a small or medium sized company in Hungary are not very attractive, either, due to credit market failure. Private banks hardly offer finance schemes for small and medium sized companies, and there is only limited support for company start ups on the part of the state.

Considering *supplier support*, one has to recognize first of all that foreign subsidiaries receive most of their input (raw material and intermediate products) from abroad or from other foreign firms within the host economy.[11] Especially the big foreign investment companies usually bring in their suppliers from abroad, who establish subsidiaries close to their customers in Hungary. That contributes to the domestic value added but does not help existing Hungarian suppliers to modernize technologically. Supplier contacts are a necessary but not a sufficient condition for technology spillovers to take place in the above described sense. But still, it is reasonable to assume that the scope for spillovers via supplier contact is higher the more domestic suppliers are involved. But so far, the proportion of domestic suppliers is low. According to the qualitative interviews, supplier support through foreign firms is offered very rarely and only to the already advanced and competitive domestic suppliers. "Supplier support is not the main task of foreign investors in Hungary. It can be efficient but the domestic supplier must fulfill minimum quality standards and production capacities. This is often not the case with Hungarian suppliers. The technological backwardness of domestic suppliers is usually too large" (expert group: foreign investment companies).

Customer support does not play an important role because foreign investors in Hungary mainly produce for export[12], for other foreign investment enterprises within Hungary, or for the local or regional consumer markets. "The Hungarian market is too small for foreign investment companies. They rely on export, especially to the EU. Customer support in order to gain customers in Hungary or in order to compete with other firms is of no importance" (expert group: business associations). No further survey material exists on customer contacts as a spillover mechanism, probably another indication for its insignificance in transition economies.

The question remains, however, whether there are spillover effects via *other forms of enterprise cooperation*. This has also been the subject of the qualitative study focusing on activities within business associations, joint research & development or innovation projects, etc. It shows that business associations are either dominated by foreign investment companies (e. g. foreign chambers of commerce

[11] An enterprise survey carried out by the Economic Research Institute of the Hungarian Chamber of Commerce and Industry (MKIK-GVI) in the year 2000 among all 100% foreign owned firms in central Hungary points in the same direction. Foreign investment firms buy, on average, 43% of their industrial supplier products within Hungary, but one third of this comes from other foreign investment firms settled in Hungary.

[12] Foreign investment enterprises accounted for 89% of Hungarian exports in the manufacturing industry in 1999 (Hunya, 2002, 10).

and industry, Joint-Venture-Association) or do not engage in activities that are suitable to increase cooperative links between foreign owned and domestic companies (e. g., Hungarian Chambers of Commerce and Industry, industry associations). Joint research & development projects of foreign and domestic companies hardly exist in Hungary because of the technological backwardness of domestic firms and the embeddedness of foreign subsidiaries in the global research & development strategy of the multinational concern.

6 Conclusions

Overall, the empirical-qualitative study does not provide evidence for the existence of technology spillovers from foreign to domestic companies thus far. As the qualitative results hold true for the Hungarian industry, it is reasonable to assume that the patterns of enterprise behavior also apply to other advanced transition economies of the region. Thus, the findings constitute company level explanations for the obvious lack of technology spillovers in transition economies.

This does not mean, however, that foreign subsidiaries do not have any effects on economic development at all. Foreign subsidiaries certainly contribute to the overall modernization process of transition economies. The establishing of modern production plants alone is a significant contribution to technological catching up. So far, however, foreign subsidiaries have built "modern islands" cooperating mainly among themselves, if at all. Foreign and domestic companies have no significant contact and build virtually separate spheres within the host economy.

Multinational companies are, of course, no development agencies for economies in the process of catching up. Still, Central European transition countries have to take into account that an increasing gap between modern equipped foreign owned companies and technologically backward domestic firms leads to the already visible dual structure of the economy. If that process continues, innovation stimulating spillovers between the two sides will become more and more difficult. From the author's perspective, a first step against the increasing duality should be stronger support for small and medium sized enterprises so that they can become equal partners to all companies in the relevant host economy. Furthermore, the capability to carry out innovation activities – an important prerequisite for competitiveness on the world market – requires a development strategy that in the long run supports the establishment of firms in the sense of parent companies.

Appendix

List of expert interviews

	Number of interviews
Expert group 1: Foreign investment enterprises	
AUDI Hungaria Motor Kft.	2
General Electric Lighting Tungsram Rt.	1
Henkel Magyarország Kft.	1
TEMIC Telefunken microelectronic Hungary Kft.	1
Reemtsma Debrecen Tobacco Factory Kft.	1
Zeuna Stärker Magyarország Kft.	1
Expert group 2: Policy makers	
Economic policy	
Hungarian Ministry of Economic Affairs, Department: supplier program	2
Hungarian Ministry of Economic Affairs, Department: regional development	1
Hungarian Foundation for Enterprise Development (MVA)	2
Investment and Trade Development Agency (ITD)	1
Technology policy	
Hungarian Ministry of Education and Technology, Department: R&D-strategy	1
Hungarian Ministry of Education and Technology, Depatrment: Technology Foresight Program	1
Institute for International Technology (NETI), Department: International Technology-transfer	1
Expert group 3: Business associations	
Industry associations	
Association of Hungarian Automobile Industry (MGSZ)	1
Association of Hungarian Automobile Supplier Industry (MAJOSZ)	1
Association of the Hungarian Chemical Industry	1
Association of the Hungarian Electrical Industry	1

Chambers of Commerce and Industry	
Hungarian Chamber of Commerce and Industry (MKIK)	1
Budapest Chamber of Commerce and Industry (BKIK)	1
Further interest associations	
German-Hungarian Chamber of Commerce and Industry (DUIHK)	1
American Chamber of Commerce and Industry (AmCham)	1
Austrian Chamber of Commerce	1
Joint-Venture-Association (JVA)	2
Hungarian Association of International Companies (HAIC)	1
Association of Hungarian Employers and Industrialists (MGYOSZ)	1
Expert group 4: Representatives of domestic companies	
Videoton Holding Rt.	2
Videoton Precíziós Kft.	1
Hungarian Foundation for Enterprise Development (MVA), Department: Domestic supplier industry	1
Budapest Agency for Enterprise Support	2
Expert group 5: Science	
Hungarian Academy of Sciences, Institute for World Economics	1
Economic Research Institute of the Hungarian Chamber of Commerce and Industry (MKIK-GVI)	1
GKI Economic Research Co.	1
Kopint Datorg - Economic Research Institute	1
Eco Stat (Research Institute of the Central Statistical Office)	1

References

Aitken, Brian/Harrison, Ann E. (1999): Do Domestic Firms Benefit from Direct Foreign Investment? Evidence from Venezuela. In: American Economic Review, Vol. 89, pp. 605-618.

Barrios, Salvador/Strobl, Eric (2002): Foreign Direct Investment and Productivity Spillovers: Evidence from the Spanish Experience. In: Weltwirtschaftliches Archiv, Vol. 138, No. 3, pp. 459-481.

Behrmann, Jack N./Wallender, Harvey W. (1976): Transfers of Manufacturing Technology within Multinational Enterprises. Cambridge: Ballinger.

Blomström, Magnus (1986): Foreign Investment and Productivity Efficiency: The Case of Mexico. In: Journal of Industrial Economics, Vol. 35, pp. 97-112.

Blomström, Magnus (1991): Host Country Benefits of Foreign Investment. In: McFetridge, D. G. (ed.): Foreign Investment, Technology and Economic Growth. Toronto, London: Toronto University Press, pp. 93-108.

Blomström, Magnus/Kokko, Ari (1996): Multinational Corporations and Spillovers, CEPR Diskussionspapier Nr. 1365. London: Centre for Economic Policy Research.

Blomström, Magnus/Sjöholm, Fredrik (1999): Technology Transfer and Spillovers: Does Local Participation with Multinationals Matter? In: European Economic Review, Vol. 43, pp. 915-923.

Blomström, Magnus/Wolff, Edward N. (1994): Multinational Corporations and Productive Convergence in Mexico. In: Baumol, William J. et al. (eds.): Convergence of Productivity: Cross National Studies and Historical Evidence. Oxford: Oxford University Press, pp. 263-283.

Bosco, Maria Giovanna (2001): Does FDI contribute to technological spillovers and growth? A panel data analysis of Hungarian firms. In: Transnational Corporations, Vol. 10, No. 1, pp. 43-68.

Burger, Bettina (1998): Ausländische Direktinvestitionen, technologische Spillover-Effekte und industrielle Entwicklung, dargestellt am Beispiel Mexiko. Baden-Baden: Nomos-Verlag.

Damijan, Joze P./Knell, Mark/Majcen, Boris/Rojec, Matija (2003): Technology Transfer through FDI in Top-10 Transition Countries: How important are Direct Effects, Horizontal and Vertical Spillovers?, William Davidson Working Paper No. 549.

Djankov, Simeon/Hoekman, Bernard (2000): Foreign Investment and Productivity Growth in Czech Enterprises. In: The World Bank Economic Review, Vol. 14, No. 1, pp. 49-64.

Driffield, Nigel/Love James H. (2002): Who learns from whom? Spillovers, competition effects & technology sourcing by foreign affiliates in the UK. Birmingham: Aston Business School Research Paper No. 0215.

Dunning, John H. (1993): Multinational Enterprises and the Global Economy. Reading: Addison-Wesley.

Estrin, Saul/Hughes, K./Todd, S. (1997): Foreign Direct Investment in Central and Eastern Europe. Multinationals in Transition. London, Washington: The Royal Institute of International Affairs.

Gerschenberg, Irving (1987): The Training and Spread of Managerial Know-how. A Comparative Analysis of Multinational and Other Firms in Kenya. In: World Development, Vol. 15, pp. 931-939.

Girma, Sourafel (2003): Absorptive capacity and productivity spillovers from FDI: a threshold regression analysis. European Economy Group (EEP) Working Paper No. 25/2003.

Globerman, Steven/Ries, J./Vertinsky, I. (1994): The economic performance of foreign affiliates in Canada. In: Canadian Journal of Economics, Vol. 27.

Görg, Holger/Greenaway, David (2002): Much ado about nothing? Do domestic firms really benefit from foreign investment? CEPR Discussion Paper No. 3485, London: Centre for Economic Policy Research.

Grossman, Gene M./Helpman, Elhanan (1997): Innovation and Growth in the Global Economy. Cambridge: MIT Press.

Günther, Jutta (2002): FDI as a Multiplier of Modern Technology in Hungarian Industry. In: Intereconomics. Review of European Economic Policy, Vol. 37, No. 5, pp. 263-269.

Günther, Jutta (2003): Das Zustandekommen von Technologie-Spillovers durch ausländische Direktinvestitionen. Eine empirische Untersuchung am Beispiel der ungarischen Industrie. Baden-Baden: Nomos-Verlagsgesellschaft.

Hill, Hal (1982): Vertical Inter-Firm Linkages in LDCs: A Note on the Philippines. In: Oxford Bulletin of Economics and Statistics, Bd. 44, S. 261-271.

Hungarian Patent Office (1999): Summary of Industrial Property Protection in Hungary. Budapest: Hungarian Patent Office.

Hunya, Gabor (2002): Recent Impacts of Foreign Direct Investment on Growth an Restructuring in Central European Transition Economies. WIIW Research Report No. 284. Vienna: The Vienna Institute for International Economic Studies (WIIW).

Jensen, Camilla (2002): Spillovers in the Polish Food Industry. Exploring the role of local externalities and global networks. Working paper presented at the 3rd CEES Workshop on Transition and Enterprise Restructuring, Copenhagen Business School, 15-17 August, 2002.

Kathuria, Vinish (2000): Productivity Spillovers from Technology Transfer to Indian Manufacturing Firms. In: Journal of International Development, Vol. 12, pp. 343-369.

Kinoshita, Yuko (2000): R&D and technology spillovers via FDI: innovation and absorptive capacity. William Davidson Institute Working Paper No. 349. Ann Arbor.

Kokko, Ari (1994): Technology, Market Characteristics, and Spillovers. In: Journal of Development Economics, Vol. 43, pp. 279-293.

Kokko, Ari (1996): Productivity Spillovers from Competition between Local Firms and Foreign Affiliates. In: Journal of International Development, Vol. 8, pp. 517-530.

Kokko, Ari/Tansini, Ruben/Zejan, Mario C. (1996): Local Technological Capability and Productivity Spillovers from FDI in the Uruguayan Manufacturing Sector. In: Journal of Development Studies, Vol. 32, pp. 602-611.

Kokko, Ari/Tansini, Ruben/Zejan, Mario C. (2001): Trade Regimes and Spillover Effects of FDI: Evidence from Uruguay. In: Weltwirtschaftliches Archiv, Vol. 137, pp. 124-149.

Konings, Jozef (2001): The Effects of Foreign Direct Investment on Domestic Firms. Evidence from Firm-level Panel Data in Emerging Economies. In: Economics of Transition, Vol. 9, No. 3, pp. 619-633.

Kugler, Maurice (2001): The Diffusion of Externalities from Foreign Direct Investment: The Sectoral Pattern of Technological Spillovers, mimeo, University of Southampton.

Lamnek, Siegfried (1995): Qualitative Sozialforschung. Band 2: Methoden und Techniken. Weinheim: Psychologie Verlags Union.

Lutz, Stefan H./Talavera, Oleksandr (2003): Do Ukrainian Firms Benefit from FDI? ZEW Discussion Paper No. 03-05. Mannheim: Centre for European Economic Research.

Meuser, Michael/Nagel, Ulrike (1991): ExpertInneninterviews – vielfach erprobt, wenig bedacht. Ein Beitrag zur qualitativen Methodendiskussion. In: Garz, D. & Kraimer, K. (Hg.): Qualitativ-empirische Sozialforschung, pp. 441-468. Opladen: Westdeutscher Verlag.

Mohnen, Pierre (1996): R&D Externalities and Productivity Growth. In: STI-Review: Science, Technology, Industry, No. 18, pp. 39-66.

OECD (2002): Foreign Direct Investment for Development. Maximising Benefits, Minimising Costs. Paris: OECD.

Reuber, Grant L./Crookell, H./Emerson, M./Gallais-Hamonno, G. (1973): Private Foreign Investment in Development. Oxford: Clarendon Press.

Ruane, Frances/Ugur, Ali (2002): Foreign Direct Investment and Productivity Spillovers in the Irish Manufacturing Industry: Evidence from Firm Level Panel Data. Trinity Economic Paper No. 2002/6. Dublin: Trinity College.

Schoors, Koen/van der Tol, Bartoldus (2002): Foreign direct investment spillovers within and between sectors: evidence from Hungarian data. Ghent University Working Paper No. 2002/157.

Sjöholm, Fredrik (1999a): Technology Gap, Competition and Spillovers from Direct Foreign Investment: Evidence from Establishment Data. In: Journal of Development Studies, Vol. 36, pp. 53-73.

Sjöholm, Fredrik (1999b): Productivity Growth in Indonesia: The Role of Regional Characteristics and Direct Foreign Investment. In: Economic Development and Cultural Change, Vol. 47, pp. 559-584.

Smarzynska, Beata K. (2002): Does Foreign Direct Investment Increase the Productivity of Domestic Firms? In Search of Spillovers through Backward Linkages. World Bank Policy Research Paper No. 2923. Washington: World Bank.

Smarzynska, Beata K./Spatareanu, Mariana (2003): To share or not to share: Does local participation matter for spillovers from foreign direct investment. World Bank Policy Research Working Paper No. 3118, Washington: World Bank.

Smid, Siemon (1998): Intellectual Property Law Uniformity in the CEECs and the EU: Conformity Issues and an Overview. In: Altvater, Elmar (ed.): Intellectual Property Rights in Central and Eastern Europe. The Creation of Favourable Legal and Market Preconditions. Berlin: IOS Press, pp. 72-81.

UNCTAD (1999): World Investment Report 1999. Foreign Direct Investment and the Challenge of Development. New York: UNCTAD.

Zukowska-Gagelmann, Katarzyna (2001): Productivity Spillovers from Foreign Direct Investment. The Case of Poland. Frankfurt/Main: Peter Lang Verlag.

Comment on: The Absence of Technology Spillovers from Foreign Direct Investment in Transition Economies

Federico Foders

Jutta Günther's paper addresses a controversial topic: while the theories of foreign direct investment (FDI) and endogenous growth draw heavily on technology spillovers and other externalities, empirical country studies have been largely unable to detect them. In fact, the few successful attempts at measuring spillovers from FDI in selected countries and industries only indicate that the evidence is, at best, mixed. Günther's interpretation of the ongoing debate is that it lacks a common framework and that it has been unable to supply a plausible explanation for the failure of research to provide clear-cut results.

In the paper, a framework is developed to help understand how and through which channels spillovers may occur in association with FDI. Then, econometric studies dealing with the experience of the Central and Eastern European Countries (CEECs) are summarised and, finally, reference is made to the results of a qualitative study of Hungary Günther carried out as part of her dissertation to complete the survey of evidence for the presence or absence of technology spillovers from FDI in transition countries. The starting point of the paper is the definition of technology spillovers as a non-market means of transfering technology from foreign to local firms. Invoking a behavioural criterion, she defines two kinds of spillovers: unintentional spillovers (in the sense of textbook externalities) and intentional spillovers. In doing so, she adds a new dimension to spillovers by creating the category of an intentional, but still non-market, transfer of technology. Despite the extension of the traditional definition of spillovers, which could be taken as an opportunity to increase the probability of finding evidence of spillovers, Günther subscribes to the absence-of-spillover hypothesis, especially in relation to the transition economies.

Despite this, the paper lacks a discussion of the consequences of the absence-of-spillover hypothesis – in case one would be willing to adhere to it – for local and foreign firms as well as for European integration. From the viewpoint of local firms, the hypothesis raises a number of questions. Even if a domestic firm should decide to continue serving the local market (for example in the CEECs), it would be somewhat naïve to assume that it would not be affected at all by the growing internationalisation of business. In the wake of trade liberalisation (free trade agreements with the EU) and mounting capital inflows in many CEECs during the 1990s, local firms have since been exposed to increased competition from both foreign low cost and foreign high tech suppliers. In other words, strong forces have been operating in the world economy, driving local firms to adopt new technologies and organisational innovations that help them re-position themselves in the new global environment. The questions raised by the above-mentioned hypothesis are: why should local firms in the CEECs be isolated from those forces? What determines the low exposure of local firms to state-of-the-art technology and/or their low absorptive capacity? What specific barriers to firm-to-firm spillovers exist in the CEECs?

From the viewpoint of foreign firms, the hypothesised absence of spillovers could imply that either: (i) the technological gap between local and foreign firms is too large to be bridged at the firm level through spillovers or (ii) foreign firms operating in an environment characterised by a relatively weak protection of intellectual property rights (IPRs) might switch to internal forms of organisation to protect their knowledge advantage over local firms and thus *deliberately* avoid spillovers. Both aspects have not yet been thoroughly scrutinised in the relevant literature.

What about European integration? Given that the Copenhagen criteria for EU membership require *inter alia* the ability of local firms to "demonstrate… the capacity to cope with competitive pressure and market forces within the EU" (Foders, Piazolo and Schweickert 2002, p. 43), does the absence of technology spillovers imply that local firms might *not* yet be ready for accession and that the candidate countries should therefore postpone it until a critical mass of local firms have successfully adopted new technologies? Or should the absence of spillovers in the candidate countries be taken only as a rough indication that the R&D activity of local firms is insufficient and that local firms lack incentives for investment in R&D?

As regards the incentives for innovation, there is suspicion in a number of sources that the protection of IPRs is still inadequate and that there is infringement of IPRs on a commercial scale in many CEECs despite the fact that some countries of the region, notably the group of candidate countries, have already joined the World Trade Organization and signed the Trade-Related Intellectual Property Rights agreement and have also transposed the relevant parts of the *aquis communautaire* into national law as part of the requirements for membership in the EU. One of the ways in which IPRs are being infringed upon is by product piracy in the sense of counterfeiting or exact copying of products. Counterfeit products are being both manufactured illegally in some CEECs and imported or smuggled from third countries. Products affected range from music, software and automotive parts to garments, cosmetics and foodstuffs (UNECE 1998).[1]

Qualitative evidence in favour (or against) the conjecture of weak IPR protection in the CEECs can be obtained from an index published by the Fraser Institute, Vancouver, as part of its overall Index of Economic Freedom. A glance at table 1 shows that on average, the 13 CEECs listed are still at quite a distance from the

[1] Media reports asserting this abound (for a recent example, see Die Welt 2004). For an economic analysis of the issues involved see Grossmann and Lai (2002).

average level of IPR protection in the EU (15) countries and far away from the level of IPR protection in the U.K., the best performer among the EU countries. This notwithstanding, Slovenia and Hungary seem to be doing well already and two other countries (the Czech Republic and Estonia) seem to be on the right track; all four perform better than Greece. Moreover, the 8 candidate countries for EU accession all show index values that are well above those of other transition countries. Interestingly, the index value of Greece, the worst performer among the EU countries, is below the average index value of the candidate countries.

The relatively weak protection of IPRs in the CEECs could contribute to explaining at least to some extent both the reluctance of foreign firms to transfer technologies to domestic firms and the relatively low level of R&D activity of domestic firms in the CEECs. On the same token, it could also serve as a tentative explanation for the absence of technology spillovers from FDI in transition countries as established in the quantitative and qualitative studies quoted in Günther's paper.

Table 1. Protection of Intellectual Property Rights in the CEECs, 1995 and 2001 (index[a])

Country	1995	2001
Czech Republic	4.5	5.7
Estonia	n.a.	5.7
Hungary	4,9	6.0
Latvia	n.a.	3.7
Lithuania	n.a.	3.7
Poland	3.6	3.9
Slovak Republic	4.0	4.4
Slovenia	n.a.	6.3
Average of CEECs (8)	–	4.9
Bulgaria	n.a.	3.1
Croatia	n.a.	3.3
Romania	n.a.	2.7
Russia	1.6	2.4
Ukraine	1.2	1.9
Average of CEECs (13)	–	4.1
Greece	5.4	4.7
United Kingdom	7.1.	9.0
Average of EU (15)	6.8	7.5

[a]Index values run from 0 (lowest) to 10 (highest); the index of protection of intellectual property rights is one of the components of the index of economic freedom constructed by Gwartney and Lawson (2003); n.a.: not available

Source: Gwartney and Lawson (2003).

References

Die Welt (2004), "Produkt-Piraten ärgern Industrie. Plagiate überschwemmen den Markt. Schäden in Millionenhöhe. Beiersdorf, Oetker und Unilever stark betroffen", 14 April.

Foders, Federico, Daniel Piazolo and Rainer Schweickert (2002), "Ready to Join the EU? On the Status of Reform in the Candidate Countries", World Economics, 3(4), pp. 43-71.

Grossmann, Gene M. and Edwin L.-C. Lai (2002), International Protection of Intellectual Property Rights. CESifo Working Papers 790, Munich, October.

Gwartney, James and Robert Lawson (2003), Economic Freedom of the World. 2003 Annual Report. The Fraser Institute, Vancouver (B.C.).

United Nations Economic Commission for Europe (UNECE) (1998), All Europe Affected by Counterfeiting and Piracy. Press Release, Geneva, 22 October.

Innovations, Technological Specialization and Economic Convergence in the EU

Andre Jungmittag[1]

Contents

1 Introduction 172
2 Innovations, Specialization and Growth: Theoretical Issues 173
3 Methodology and Data Issues 175
3.1 The Empirical Model 175
3.2 Data Issues 178
4 Empirical Results 180
4.1 Estimation Results 180
4.2 Results of the Growth Decompositions 186
4.3 Results of the Convergence Decompositions 190
5 Summary and Conclusions 196
References 197

[1] A previous version of the paper was prepared while the author was a Visiting Fellow at the Directorate General for Economic and Financial Affairs, EU Commission. I gratefully acknowledge the stimulating research atmosphere at DG ECFIN and would like to thank Werner Röger and Klaus Wälde for helpful comments. Furthermore, I would like to thank Jürgen Wolters, FU Berlin, for further helpful comments at the workshop for the special issue 2+3 of *International Economics and Economic Policy* in Brussels, February 6-8, 2004.

1 Introduction

Although the growth enhancing effects of technological change and innovations had been known for some time, it took several decades to attract the interest of researchers to study technical change. This lack of interest may be explained in part by complex procedures ruling science and technology and the unknown mechanisms translating innovations into broad-based economic effects.

Besides the general innovativeness of a country, its technological specialization might also affect its economic performance. Based on new growth theory, we can differentiate between two kinds of specialization: Smithian specialization and Ricardian specialization (Dowrick, 1997; Dalum/ Laursen/ Verspagen, 1999). Smithian specialization leads to 'learning-by-doing' effects and increasing returns to scale, independent of the technological areas in which countries are specialised. Ricardian specialization, on the other hand, concerns the qualitative character of a country's technological specialization, because countries specialised in technological areas with opportunities for higher rates of productivity growth might be in a better position to achieve fast overall growth. Furthermore, technologically backward countries can catch up by imitating technologies from other countries. This paper aims at assessing empirically in a consistent manner the impact of these three facets of technological progress on economic growth and convergence of output per worker within the EU.

To this end, I estimate different versions of a growth model that captures innovations, technology diffusion and the different kinds of technological specialization in an augmented technical progress function. The model is based on panel data for 14 EU countries from 1969 to 1998 and allows also for unobserved country effects. Patents granted at the US Patent and Trademark Office are used as an indicator for commercially relevant innovations and to calculate measures of Smithian and Ricardian technological specialization. The superior models, i.e. the models with the most appropriate indicators of technological specialization, are then used to assess the effects of innovations, technology diffusion and technological specialization as well as the impact of the usual production factors on long-term economic growth of the EU countries. Furthermore, a simple transformation of the empirical growth model enables us to calculate the partial contributions of these factors to β- and σ-convergence of output per worker within the EU.

The paper proceeds in four parts. Section 2 deals with some theoretical issues concerning the links between innovations, technological specialization and economic growth. A description of the methodology applied in the empirical analysis follows in section 3. In this context, some data issues especially with regard to the calculation of patent stocks and specialization measures are also considered. Section 4 contains the empirical results and finally, in section 5 some conclusions are presented.

2 Innovations, Specialization and Growth: Theoretical Issues

In spite of their dissimilarities in the theoretical foundation and the concrete design, the numerous approaches in neoclassical growth theory, evolutionary economics and a central branch of new growth theory show the common quintessence that technical progress and innovations are important driving forces of economic growth (Aghion/ Howitt, 1998). However, with regard to technological specialization the conclusions are not unambiguous. One branch of new growth theory, following Romer (1986) and Lucas (1988), emphasizes the importance of 'learning-by-doing' effects and increasing returns to scale, independent of the technological areas, in which countries are specialised. From this viewpoint, Smithian specialization matters to growth. Another branch of new growth theory, following Romer (1990) and Grossman/ Helpman (1991), concludes on the basis of so-called 'R&D-models of growth' that the qualitative character of a country's specialization is decisive, because countries specialised in technological areas with opportunities for higher rates of productivity growth might be in a better position to achieve fast overall growth. From this viewpoint Ricardian specialization matters to growth, because positive spillovers emerge mainly in R&D-intensive technologies and industries.

Both viewpoints of specialization can also be found in evolutionary economics. One branch, based on the variation-selection principle, emphasizes the importance of Smithian specialization by concluding that specialization advantages emerge "regardless of the particular sectors in which individual countries concentrate their efforts; in other words, for advanced countries being specialized appears to be even more important than choosing the 'right' fields" (Archibugi/ Pianta, 1992). The other branch, inspired by the post-Keynesian tradition, takes a neo-Schumpeterian view and argues that Ricardian specialization matters to growth because of differential income elasticities between activities (e.g. Dalum/ Laursen/ Verspagen, 1999). This view adds a demand-side related argument to the supply-side related argument of new growth theory.

Neoclassical growth theory, on the other hand, first of all emphasizes that decreasing marginal productivity of capital drives convergence of per capita incomes and labour productivities. This might be the reason why in cross-country growth analyses usually identical exogenous rates of technical change are assumed. A classical example for this approach is the influential analysis in Mankiw/ Romer/ Weil (1992) which has been reproduced – in spite of all criticism – many times. As a consequence, differences in growth rates of per capita income or labor productivity stem mainly from differences in capital accumulation, because differences in national innovation capabilities are assumed away in explaining both relative output levels and growth rates, and therefore economic convergence. To the extent that these capabilities, i.e. the adoption and accumulation of technologies, are important for convergence, a large part of the empirical literature to date is misguided (Bernard/ Jones, 1996).

Following Bernard/Jones (1996), I will elaborate this argument within the context of the Solow growth model. The aggregate production function of a country n is given by

$$Y_n = K_n^{\alpha_n}\left(A_n L_n\right)^{1-\alpha_n} \Rightarrow \frac{Y_n}{L_n} = A_n^{1-\alpha_n}\left(\frac{K_n}{L_n}\right)^{\alpha_n}, \tag{1}$$

where Y_n represents the output, A_n the level of labour-augmenting technical progress, K_n the capital employed and L_n the amount of labour. The partial production elasticity α_n as well as A_n are allowed to vary across countries. For the sake of simplicity, I assume that these variations are caused by differences in aggregate innovation capabilities and perhaps different technological specializations.

As usual, net capital accumulation is a constant fraction of output, i.e.

$$\dot{K}_n = s_n Y_n - \delta_n K_n, \tag{2}$$

while convergence of national innovation capabilities as a catching-up process requires that the accumulation of labor-augmenting technology be faster, the larger the gap towards the technologically leading country is. Hence, a simple assumption for the growth rate of technology is

$$g_{A_n} = \frac{\dot{A}_n}{A_n} = \xi_n \frac{A_w}{A_n}, \tag{3}$$

where ξ_n represents the ability of a country to reduce the technological gap. Furthermore, it is assumed that the level of technology in the leading country A_w grows exogenously at a rate $g \equiv \xi_w$. Solving this differential equation yields the steady state technology ratios

$$\frac{A_n}{A_w} = \frac{\xi_n}{\xi_w}. \tag{4}$$

In this framework, steady state growth rates of output per capita and capital per capita for each country as usual equal the growth of the labor-augmenting technology in the technologically leading country:

$$g_{\left(\frac{Y_n}{L_n}\right)} = g_{\left(\frac{K_n}{L_n}\right)} = g_{A_n} = g, \tag{5}$$

but the relative steady state levels of output per capita depend not only on saving rates s_n, depreciation rates δ_n and population growth rates p_n, but also on the abilities of countries to reduce the technological gap towards the leading country and on the aggregate partial production elasticities, namely

$$\frac{(Y_n L_n)^*}{(Y_w L_w)^*} = \frac{\xi_n}{\xi_w} \frac{(s_n p_n + g + \delta_n)^{\frac{\alpha_n}{1-\alpha_n}}}{(s_w p_w + g + \delta_w)^{\frac{\alpha_w}{1-\alpha_w}}}. \tag{6}$$

Thus, in a world with technologies varying across countries, convergence of per capita incomes and labor productivities will only occur if there is a converging development of national innovation capabilities. Otherwise, countries will only converge to their own steady states.

3 Methodology and Data Issues

For the empirical analysis, the approach developed by de la Fuente (2002) for the analysis of convergence between the Spanish regions has been taken up and modified as well as augmented. This modification allows us to assess the effects of innovations, technological specialization and technology diffusion as well as the impact of the usual production factors labour and capital on economic growth and convergence within the EU. Furthermore, data issues are discussed in this section.

3.1 The Empirical Model

The starting point for the derivation of the empirical model is an augmented Cobb-Douglas production function

$$Y_{nt} = A_{nt} K_{nt}^{\alpha} L_{nt}^{\beta} P_{nt}^{\gamma} S_{nt}^{\delta}, \tag{7}$$

where P_{nt} represents the patent stock and S_{nt} the technological specialization of EU-country n in the period t.[2] The interplay of A_{nt}, P_{nt} and S_{nt} could be interpreted as a technical progress function: A_{nt} measures the level of – at the moment still – exogenous technical progress, which will be partly endogenized in the further course of specification of the empirical model, while P_{nt}^{γ} and S_{nt}^{δ} reflect the degree of efficiency due to the stock of results of R&D activities (innovations) and technological specialization. In logarithmic form the production function can be written as

---

[2] The following presentation leans on de la Fuente (2002), but the Cobb-Douglas production function is – additionally to the approach presented in de la Fuente (2002) – extended to include the patent stock and a measure of technological specialisation. Furthermore de la Fuente (2002) assumes labour-augmenting Harrod-neutral technical progress, while I assume Hicks-neutral technical Progress for the sake of a slightly simpler parametrisation of the underlying model. However, in the case of a Cobb-Douglas production function and also for the empirical model derived from it, the different kinds of technical progress have no impact on the parameters to be estimated.

$$y_{nt} = a_{nt} + \alpha k_{nt} + \beta l_{nt} + \gamma p_{nt} + \delta s_{nt}, \tag{8}$$

where lower case letters denote logarithms. Taking first differences gives growth rates as

$$\Delta y_{nt} = \Delta a_{nt} + \alpha \Delta k_{nt} + \beta \Delta l_{nt} + \gamma \Delta p_{nt} + \delta \Delta s_{nt}, \tag{9}$$

where Δ is the difference operator.

For the log level of – at the moment still – exogenous technical progress a_{nt} it is assumed that it consists of an index of transferable technical knowledge b_{nt} and of a temporally fixed country-specific effect r_n, which takes into account e.g. different geographic conditions or endowments of natural resources. Hence

$$a_{nt} = b_{nt} + r_n. \tag{10}$$

Next, the transferable part of technical knowledge is endogenized as a function of the patent stock, technological specialization and the technological gap between the respective country and the EU average. To this end, it is written as

$$b_{nt} = b_t + \tilde{b}_{nt}, \tag{11}$$

where $b_t = (1/N)\sum_{n=1}^{N} b_{nt}$ is the EU average of b_{nt} and $\tilde{b}_{nt} = b_{nt} - b_t$ the technological distance between EU country *n* and the EU average. Let the average (log) level of transferable technical knowledge b_t continue being exogenous and it depends on e.g. the technological gap between the EU and other technologically leading countries. For its change, i.e. the average rate of technical progress, it is assumed that it can be approximated for the considered period of time by a constant *g* and a trend *t*, therefore

$$\Delta b_t = g + ct. \tag{12}$$

The change of the technological distance between EU country *n* and the EU average depends, on the one hand, on the difference between its log patent stock and the EU average at the end of the previous period ($\tilde{p}_{nt-1} = p_{nt-1} - p_{t-1}$ with $p_{t-1} = (1/N)\sum_{n=1}^{N} p_{nt-1}$) as well as on its relative specialization with regard to the EU average at the end of the previous period ($\tilde{s}_{nt-1} = s_{nt-1} - s_{t-1}$ with $s_{t-1} = (1/N)\sum_{n=1}^{N} s_{nt-1}$), and, on the other hand, on its technological distance $\tilde{b}_{nt-1}$ to the EU average in the previous period. Adding furthermore an identically independently distributed error term u_{nt} gives

$$\Delta \tilde{b}_{nt} = \varepsilon \tilde{p}_{nt-1} + \zeta \tilde{s}_{nt-1} - \eta \tilde{b}_{nt-1} + u_{nt}. \tag{13}$$

If technologies actually diffuse from one EU country to another, it can be expected that the coefficient η is negative, i.e. ceteris paribus the rate of technical progress is higher the more technologically backward a country is.

In order to obtain a feasible empirical model, $\tilde{b}_{nt-1}$ has to be depicted by observable variables. Substituting to this end (10) into (8), taking into account the time lag and solving for b_{nt-1} gives

$$b_{nt-1} = y_{nt-1} - \alpha k_{nt-1} - \beta l_{nt-1} - \gamma p_{nt-1} - \delta s_{nt-1} - r_n. \tag{14}$$

Analogously, we get for the EU average

$$b_{t-1} = y_{t-1} - \alpha k_{t-1} - \beta l_{t-1} - \gamma p_{t-1} - \delta s_{t-1} - r. \tag{15}$$

Subtracting (15) from (14) yields

$$\tilde{b}_{nt-1} = b_{nt-1} - b_{t-1} = \tilde{y}_{nt-1} - \alpha \tilde{k}_{nt-1} - \beta \tilde{l}_{nt-1} - \gamma \tilde{p}_{nt-1} - \delta \tilde{s}_{nt-1} - \tilde{r}_n, \tag{16}$$

where variables marked with tildes represent deviations from the EU average, so is $\tilde{r}_n = r_n - r$ with $r = (1/N)\sum_{n=1}^{N} r_n$, too.

Substituting (12), (13) and (16) into (9) gives the feasible empirical model

$$\begin{aligned} \Delta y_{nt} &= g + \eta \tilde{r}_v + ct + \alpha \Delta k_{nt} + \beta \Delta l_{nt} + \gamma \Delta p_{nt} + \delta \Delta s_{nt} + \varepsilon \tilde{p}_{nt-1} + \zeta \tilde{s}_{nt-1} \\ &\quad - \eta \left(\tilde{y}_{nt-1} - \alpha \tilde{k}_{nt-1} - \beta \tilde{l}_{nt-1} - \gamma \tilde{p}_{nt-1} - \delta \tilde{s}_{nt-1} - \sum_{n=1; n \neq v}^{N} \theta_n DC_n \right) \\ &\quad + u_{nt}, \end{aligned} \tag{17}$$

where the index v denotes a reference country and the coefficient of the n-th country dummy DC_n is $\theta_n = \tilde{r}_n - \tilde{r}_v$. Austria is used as reference country in all estimations because it is relatively close to the hypothetical EU average country. The model can be estimated by nonlinear least squares.

The estimation results from the empirical model can be used, on the one hand, in the line of the usual growth accounting to put down the long-term economic growth of the individual EU countries to its different sources: capital, labour, innovations, specialization and transferable technical knowledge. On the other hand, due to relative simple transformations of the empirical model, the measures of σ- and β-convergence of labour productivities within the EU can be decomposed into additive components, which capture the contributions of the just mentioned sources. For that I again fall back on a methodology proposed by de la Fuente (2002), which he labels as "partial convergence analysis" (cf. Jungmittag, 2004, and Jungmittag, 2004a).

3.2 Data Issues

Before the results of the econometric estimations will be presented, some issues with regard to data used should be discussed. The output data are real GDP in 1990 PPP-US-$, which are taken from the data base of the Groningen Growth and Development Centre. Domestic civil employment numbers are from the AMECO data base of the DG ECFIN of the European Commission. This source also contains real net capital stocks with 1995 as the base year in million Euro (for the members of the European Monetary Union) or in national currencies (for the other EU countries). These data were converted into 1990 PPP-US-$ to achieve comparability with the GDP data. Furthermore, for these variables the unique level shift in 1991 due to German unification was eliminated from the time series for Germany.

The patent stocks of the EU countries were calculated from the patents granted to these countries at the US Patent and Trademark Office. With regard to the calculation of patent stocks from patents granted, two opposite opinions predominate in the literature. In the one vein of the literature, the view is taken that the economically relevant life time of a patent is much longer than its legal life. Thus Anderson/ Walsh (1998), Cantwell/ Anderson (1996) and Cantwell/ Piscitello (2000) calculate patent stocks by accumulating patents over a thirty-year period and assume thereby a linear depreciation function as in vintage capital models, i.e. the current number of patents is weighted with 1, those of the previous periods with factors from 29/30 to 1/30. They justify their assumption with the hint that new technical knowledge is partly embodied in new equipment or devices, which have an average life span of 30 years. Zachariadis (2000), who calculates patent stocks using the perpetual inventory method with a depreciation rate of 7 per cent, argues similarly by pointing out that his rate would correspond with this century's average annual rate of technological obsolescence estimated by Caballero/ Jaffe (1993).

In the other vein of the literature, the opinion is held that the economically relevant life span of a patent is much shorter than its legally possible life. As evidence for it, among other things, the analysis of Mansfield/Schwartz/Wagner (1981) is quoted, which shows that 60 per cent of all patents are invented at most 4 years ago. Therefore many authors use a depreciation rate of 15 per cent in their calculations of patent stocks by means of the perpetual inventory method, which implies a average life of $6.\overline{6}$ years (e.g. Chen/ Ho/ Ik et al., 2002; Gambardella/ Torrisi, 2000; Hall/ Jaffe/ Trajtenberg, 2001 and Lach, 1995). Other authors use even higher depreciation rates of 20 per cent (e.g. Agrawal/ Henderson, 2001 and Henderson/Cockburn, 1996) or 30 per cent (e.g. Blundell/ Griffith/ Van Reenen, 1998; Cockburn/ Griliches, 1988 and Dushnitsky/ Lenox, 2002).

I also assume a depreciation rate $\mu = 0.15$ for the calculation of patent stocks, but the problem of calculating a initial stock is avoided by following the suggestion of Heeley/ Khorana/ Matusik (2000) to confine the depreciation of the patent stock to a period lasting only several years.[3] Here, a six year period is used, such that the patent stock P_{nt} is given by

$$P_{nt} = \sum_{\tau=t-5}^{t} (1-\mu)^{(t-\tau)} P_{n\tau}^{gr}, \qquad (18)$$

where P_{nt}^{gr} is the number of US patents granted to EU country n in year t.

Table 1. Concordance between ISIC2 and SIC for the R&D-intensive industries

ISIC2	Description	SIC (USPTO sequence number)
	Leading-edge technology	
3522	Drugs and medicines	14
3825	Office and computing machinery	27
3832	Radio, TV and communication equipment	42+43
3845 (and partly 3829)	Aircraft, guided missiles and space vehicles	47, 54
	High-level technology	
351+352 (without 3522)	Chemicals ex. drugs	6-9, 11-13
382 (without 3825)	Non-electrical machinery (ex. office and computing machinery)	23-26, 29-32
383 (without 3832)	Electrical machinery (ex. radio, TV, communication equipment)	35+36, 38-40
3843	Motor vehicles	46
3841+3842+3844+3849	Other transport equipment	49-53
385	Professional goods	55

These patent stocks are also used to calculate measures of specialization. For these calculations, I differentiate – as already mentioned – between Ricardian specialization, which concerns the qualitative character of a country's technological specialization, and Smithian specialization, which leads to 'learning-by-doing' effects and increasing returns to scale, independent of the technological areas, in which countries are specialised.

As measures of Ricardian specialization, the patent stock share in the area of the entire R&D-intensive technology as well as those in the areas of leading-edge and high-level technology were used. The assignment of industries to these areas

[3] Assuming that the number of annual patents granted evolved in the past with the same average rate g like in the observation period, an initial stock may be calculated as $P_{n0} = P_{n0}^{gr}\left[(1+g)/(\mu+g)\right]$, but for several EU countries the number of patents granted is zero in the first available year 1963, especially when patents granted in the area of leading-edge or high-level technology are considered.

is based on the high-technology list developed at the Fraunhofer Institute for Systems and Innovation Research, which is displayed in Table 1 (cf. Grupp/ Jungmittag/ Legler et al., 2000). In order to use this list based on ISIC2 for a classification of US patents, I developed a concordance to the US classification (SIC from 1972) to which each US patent is originally assigned. Furthermore, it can be shown easily that the log patent share of a technological area adjusted to the EU average equals the national log relative patent share $\log RPS_{mn}$ adjusted to the EU average log relative patent share $\frac{1}{N}\sum_{n=1}^{N}(\log RPS_{mn})$ (cf. Jungmittag, 2004).

For the analysis of the impact of Smithian specialization, standardized diversity indices

$$D_n = \left(1 - \sum_{m=1}^{M} \sigma_{mn}^2\right) / \left(1 - 1/M\right)$$

were calculated, where σ_{mn} is the patent share of sector m in the EU country n. Here, $M = 42$ sectors according to the SIC classification were included.

GDP data are available for 14 EU countries (excluding Luxemburg) and because taking into account a six year period for the calculation of patent stocks, patent stock data are available from 1968 to 1998. Since a further year is needed for taking first differences, a total of 420 observations is used for the empirical analysis.

Since some rather strong restrictions are introduced in the course of the specification of the empirical model, I also undertake some "pre-testing" to check whether the data are consistent with these restrictions and whether the model as a whole is balanced.[4] Some of these results can be found in Jungmittag (2004a).

4 Empirical Results

4.1 Estimation Results

In the first step, the empirical model considering technological specialization in the entire R&D-intensive area was estimated in three variants (Table 2). In the first variant (model 1), no restrictions were imposed on the model. The estimates of the production elasticities of the factors capital and labour (α and β) show the usual magnitude. At the same time, the null hypothesis of a F-test that their sum equals 1 cannot be rejected on the usual levels of significance. Furthermore, there is a significant positive growth effect of an increase of the patent stock. The estimate of this elasticity γ is rather similar to those of other analyses (e.g. Jungmittag/ Blind/ Grupp, 1999 and Jungmittag/ Welfens, 2002). However, the relative level

[4] The pre-testing analysis was suggested by Jürgen Wolters (FU Berlin) who argued that the time series dimension dominates the cross section dimension in the model used so that it is appropriate to apply this concept coming from time series analysis.

of the patent stock (ε) has no significant impact on economic growth. For the Ricardian specialization in the entire R&D-intensive area, the effects are inverted. The change of specialization (δ) has no significant effect on growth, while the relative level of specialization (ζ) shows a highly significant positive impact. The coefficient that captures technology diffusion (η) is at a significance level below 1 per cent different from zero and indicates a moderate rate of diffusion (6.3 per cent per year). Moreover, a *F*-test shows that the country-specific fixed effects arc different from zero.

In model 2, the non-rejected null hypothesis that the sum of the production elasticities of the factors capital and labour equals 1 is taken into account explicitly. This hardly has any effect on the other parameters of the model. Additionally, the non-significant variables are removed in model 3. This leads to a slight increase of the estimate of the coefficient of the level effect of technological specialization, while the estimate of the rate of technology diffusion decreases slightly.

Table 2. Estimation results considering specialization in R&D-intensive technology

	Model 1		Model 2		Model 3	
	Coefficient	*t*-value	Coefficient	*t*-value	Coefficient	*t*-value
$g+\eta\tilde{r}_v$	0.0502	3.08[a)]	0.0449	3.18	0.0469	3.45
c	-0.0004	-2.48	-0.0004	-2.60	-0.0004	-2.71
α	0.3068	2.47	0.3751	5.54	0.3662	5.48
β	0.6191	9.14	[0.6249]		[0.6338]	
γ	0.0371	2.52	0.0349	2.50	0.0358	2.54
δ	0.0057	0.23	0.0082	0.33		
ε	0.0075	1.27	0.0076	1.30		
ζ	0.0399	2.07	0.0401	2.07	0.0448	2.49
η	0.0632	2.86	0.0576	2.71	0.0512	2.37
$R^2_{adj.}$	0.3778		0.3786		0.3769	
$\alpha+\beta=1$	0.4292[b)]	0.51[c)]				
$\theta_n=0$	4.5575[b)]	0.00[c)]	3.9335[b)]	0.00[c)]	3.1155[b)]	0.00[c)]

[a)] White's heteroskedasticity-consistent estimators of the various matrix are used to calculate *t*-statistics.
[b)] *F*-value
[c)] Level of significance

Table 3. Estimation results considering specialization in leading-edge technology

	Model 4		Model 5		Model 6	
	Coefficient	*t*-value	Coefficient	*t*-value	Coefficient	*t*-value
$g+\eta\tilde{r}_v$	0.0425	2.70[a]	0.0402	2.86	0.0427	3.17
c	-0.0003	-1.96	-0.0003	-2.19	-0.0003	-2.28
α	0.3770	3.01	0.4074	5.90	0.4097	5.90
β	0.5906	8.51	[0.5926]		[0.5903]	
γ	0.0353	2.46	0.0345	2.51	0.0339	2.47
δ	-0.0077	-1.07	0.0075	-1.06		
ε	0.0039	0.61	0.0038	0.59		
ζ	0.0103	1.54	0.0105	1.61	0.0133	2.35
η	0.0619	2.65	0.0595	2.66	0.0604	2.71
$R^2_{adj.}$	0.3820		0.3834		0.3838	
$\alpha+\beta=1$	0.0814[b]	0.78[c]				
$\theta_n=0$	4.4531[b]	0.00[c]	4.1842[b]	0.00[c]	4.3280[b]	0.00[c]

[a] White's heteroskedasticity-consistent estimators of the various matrix are used to calculate *t*-statistics.
[b] *F*-value
[c] Level of significance

In the second step, technological specialization in the area of leading-edge technology is taken into account instead of specialization in the area of the entire R&D-intensive technology (Table 3). In this case, an increase in the patent stock also has a positive effect on economic growth in the most general specification (model 4). However, the null hypothesis that the relative level of specialization has no impact on growth cannot be rejected at a significance level of 10 per cent. Furthermore, the influence of the relative level of the patent stock and of the change of technological specialization is again not different from zero at the usual levels of significance. The null hypothesis, that the sum of the production elasticities of capital and labour is zero, cannot be rejected either. The opposite holds for the null hypothesis with regard to fixed country-effects.

Explicitly taking into account the restriction concerning the production elasticities of capital and labour again hardly changes the estimation results (model 5). However, if the clearly non-significant variables are removed from the model, the positive impact of the relative level of specialization in the area of leading-edge technology is statistically highly significant (model 6), while the estimates of the other coefficients remain largely unchanged. Particularly as well by taking into account this kind of specialization, the rate of technology diffusion is around 6 per cent per year.

Table 4. Estimation results considering specialization in high-level technology

	Model 7		Model 8		Model 9	
	Coefficient	*t*-value	Coefficient	*t*-value	Coefficient	*t*-value
$g+\eta\tilde{r}_v$	0.0452	2.74[a)]	0.0395	2.78	0.0416	3.00
c	-0.0004	-2.34	-0.0003	-2.41	-0.0004	-2.51
α	0.3214	2.51	0.3900	5.55	0.3843	5.34
β	0.6061	8.64	[0.6100]		[0.6157]	
γ	0.0352	2.37	0.0331	2.34	0.0321	2.24
δ	0.0030	0.13	0.0043	0.18		
ε	0.0103	1.71	0.0104	1.73		
ζ	0.0015	0.09	0.0012	0.08		
η	0.0586	2.56	0.0520	2.37	0.0408	1.83
$R^2_{adj.}$	0.3670		0.3679		0.3638	
$\alpha+\beta=1$	0.3920[b)]	0.53[c)]				
$\theta_n=0$	3.6893[b)]	0.00[c)]	3.2210[b)]	0.00[c)]	1.8804[b)]	0.03[c)]

[a)] White's heteroskedasticity-consistent estimators of the various matrix are used to calculate *t*-statistics.
[b)] *F*-value
[c)] Level of significance

When specialization in the area of high-level technology is included, the relative level of the patent stock is also initially in the most general specification beside the rate of change of the patent stock – at a significance level of 10 per cent – different from zero (model 7 in Table 4). On the other hand, the two specialization variables do not show any significance. Restricting the sum of the production elasticities of capital and labour to zero again hardly affects the other parameters (model 8). However, if the non-significant variables are removed from the model, the relative level of the patent stock also loses significance, so that we come to a model which includes – besides capital, labour and exogenous technical progress – only the change of the patent stock. In this specification, the estimate of the rate of technology diffusion also is distinctly lower (4 per cent).

In the last step, the standardized diversity index as a measure of absolute Smithian specialization is included in the model (Table 5). The two coefficients for the change (δ) and the relative level (ζ) of this measure of specialization show in the most general specification (model 10) a negative value which implies that a low specialization of this kind has a negative effect on economic growth. But they are only slightly above a significance level of 10 per cent different from zero (12.65 per cent for δ and 10.51 per cent for ζ). At the same time, the level effect of the patent stock is at a significance level of 5.64 per cent different from zero for the first time. However, since countries with a relative large patent stock often show a low degree of Smithian specialization, a certain degree of intercorrelations among these variables can be expected. This suspicion is confirmed when at a time one of these three variables is eliminated from the model. Then the two others clearly lose significance. Therefore, it can be assumed that the impact of a low Smithian specialization is not robust, so that we finally end up again with a model without specialization variables (model 12 = model 9).

Table 5. Estimation results considering Smithian technological specialization

	Model 10		Model 11		Model 12	
	Coefficient	t-value	Coefficient	t-value	Coefficient	t-value
$g+\eta\tilde{r}_v$	0.0427	2.56[a)]	0.0395	2.76		
c	-0.0004	-2.11	-0.0003	-2.33	see model 9	
α	0.3757	2.89	0.4142	5.66		
β	0.5830	7.97	[0.5858]			
γ	0.0341	2.35	0.0330	2.39		
δ	-0.2470	-1.48	-0.2537	-1.53		
ε	0.0114	1.90	0.0114	1.91		
ζ	-0.1865	-1.59	-0.1896	-1.62		
η	0.0542	2.44	0.0510	2.35		
$R^2_{adj.}$	0.3746		0.3759			
$\alpha+\beta=1$	0.1298[b)]	0.72[c)]				
$\theta_n=0$	3.3289[b)]	0.00[c)]	2.9945[b)]	0.00[c)]		

[a)] White's heteroskedasticity-consistent estimators of the various matrix are used to calculate *t*-statistics.
[b)] *F*-value
[c)] Level of significance

The country-specific fixed effects are in all models highly significantly different from zero. This result shows that there are long-term productivity differentials between the EU countries which cannot be explained by the variables in the models. The normalized country-specific effects, i.e. their average is exactly one after adding the fixed effect for Austria, are displayed in Figure 1. In the model without specialization variables (model 9), Ireland shows the largest positive difference in long-term productivity relative to the EU average with 18.7 per cent, followed by Belgium, Spain and France. At the lower end Germany, Sweden, Great Britain and particularly Greece with -39.6 per cent can be found. The standard deviation of the unexplained long-term productivity differentials is 14.6 per cent. It decreases to 13.6 per cent, when the specialization in the area of entire R&D-intensive technology is included in the model (model 3). At the upper end the same countries as before are located in a slightly changed order, while at the lower end Sweden is replaced by the Netherlands in the group of the last four countries. If specialization in the area of leading-edge technology is taken into account (model 6), the standard deviation increases distinctly to 16.3 per cent, with mainly a rise in the range while those countries with unexplained small below-average productivity differentials approach the average. In the group of the four countries with the largest positive unexplained productivity differentials, Finland replaces France, while there is only an internal change of ranks within the group of the last four countries with the largest negative unexplained productivity differentials. Altogether, however, the ranking of unexplained long-term productivity differentials is rather stable. Of course this result also shows that a certain scope for the further search for the determinants of long-term productivity differentials within the EU remains.

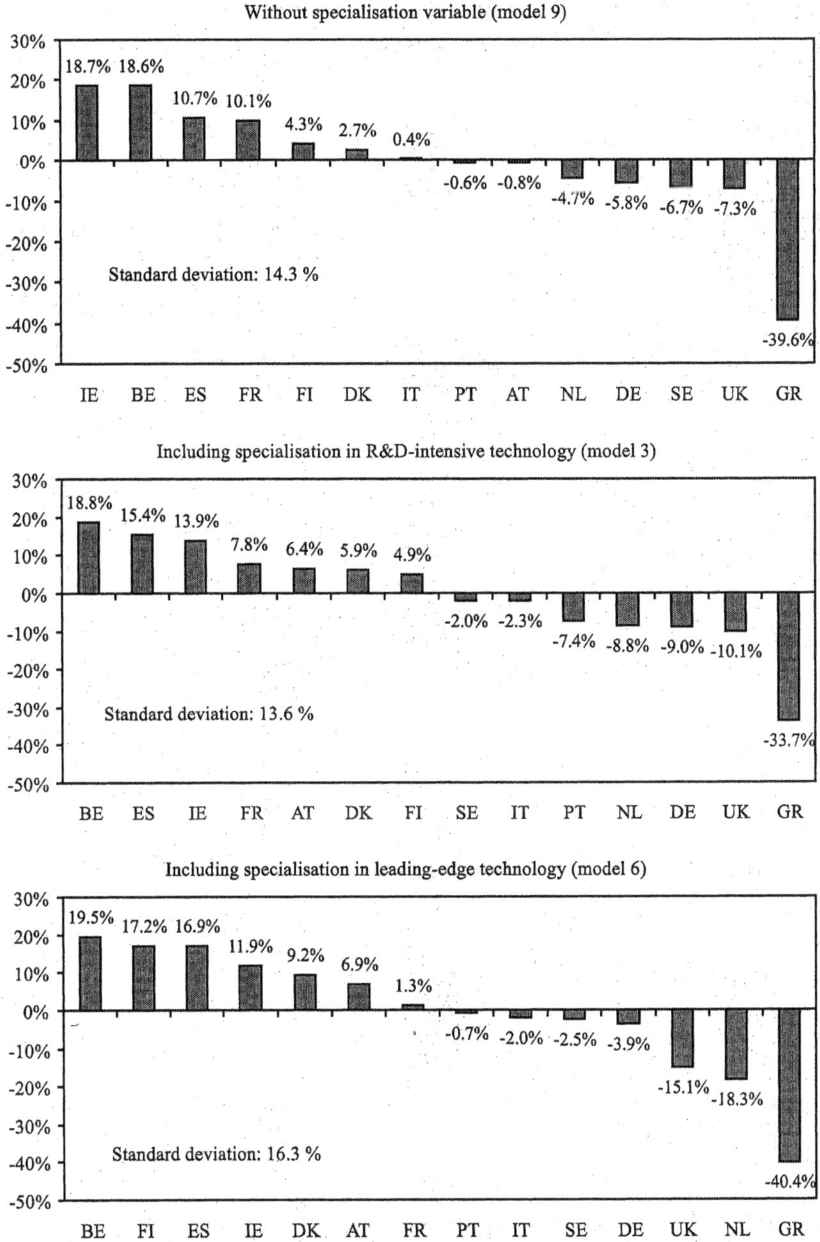

Fig. 1. Unexplained long-term productivity differences within the EU

4.2 Results of the Growth Decompositions

Based on the models capturing specialization either in the area of the entire R&D-intensive technology (model 3) or in the area of leading-edge technology (model 6), the average annual GDP growth of EU countries from 1969 to 1998 can be decomposed into its various components. In the period under consideration, Ireland shows the highest average annual growth with 4.63 per cent, followed by the four other initially lagging countries Portugal, Spain, Greece and Finland, whose growth rates were between 3.60 and 3.09 per cent (Table 6). Austria, the Netherlands, France, Belgium and Italy form the medium group with growth rates above 2.5 per cent. Denmark, Great Britain, Germany and Sweden with growth rates between 2.26 and 2.00 per cent are to be found in the last group.

Table 6. Decomposition of average annual growth of GDP from 1969 to 1998 considering specialization in R&D-intensive technology

Country	$\overline{\Delta y_n}$	Percentage contribution to average annual growth				
	(%)	$\hat{g}+\hat{c}\overline{t}-\hat{\eta}(\cdot)$	$\hat{\alpha}\overline{\Delta k_n}$	$(1-\hat{\alpha})\overline{\Delta l_n}$	$\hat{\gamma}\overline{\Delta p_n}$	$\hat{\zeta}\overline{\tilde{s}_n^{R\&D}}$
IE	4.63	46.0	31.5	15.7	5.9	0.9
PT	3.60	34.3	41.0	14.1	2.0	8.7
ES	3.32	53.7	43.1	6.2	5.2	-8.2
GR	3.13	33.3	51.0	15.6	3.1	-3.0
FI	3.09	57.6	31.5	4.8	11.0	-4.9
AT	2.93	49.1	42.3	15.8	4.0	-11.1
NL	2.78	23.3	36.0	28.0	2.9	9.8
FR	2.63	41.8	39.9	10.8	3.7	3.7
BE	2.62	49.1	38.8	7.2	5.1	-0.3
IT	2.54	40.6	43.7	4.0	5.3	6.5
DK	2.26	51.0	33.8	14.7	5.9	-5.4
UK	2.21	53.9	33.0	8.6	0.5	4.0
DE	2.19	29.2	45.8	10.3	4.3	10.4
SE	2.00	65.7	35.8	6.6	3.3	-11.5

Within the group with high average annual GDP growth, Finland, Spain and Ireland saw relatively high growth contributions from transferable technical knowledge (between 57.6 and 46.0 per cent), measured by the term $\hat{g}+\hat{c}\overline{t}-\hat{\eta}(\cdot)$. In contrast, this contribution is comparatively small for Greece and Portugal with 33.3 and 34.3 per cent. At the same time, the growth contribution of capital is relatively small for Ireland and Finland at 31.5 per cent, mediocre for Portugal and Spain, and very high for Greece with 51.0 per cent. Moreover, Ireland, Greece and Portugal show a comparatively high contribution of labour to GDP growth (between 15.7 and 14.1 percent), while this contribution is rather small in the case of Spain and Finland (6.2 and 4.8 per cent). In this group, Finland profits above all from the growth of its patent stock, followed by Ireland and Spain with a clear margin. In comparison, the contributions of this component as expected are very small in the case of Greece and Portugal. The relative level of specialization in the area of the entire R&D-intensive technology shows a slightly negative impact for Greece, Finland and Spain, while it is negligible or slightly positive in the case of Ireland and Portugal.

Within the second group, above all the Netherlands are striking, for which a very small relative contribution of transferable technical knowledge (23.3 per cent) can be observed at the same time as a very large relative contribution of labour growth (28.0 per cent) to GDP growth. This development is accompanied by moderate contributions of capital and the patent stock (36.0 and 2.9 per cent) as well as a distinct contribution of the relative technological specialization to GDP growth. In comparison, the contributions of transferable technical knowledge are clearly higher for the other countries of this group, with values between 49.1 (Austria and Belgium) and 40.6 per cent (France). The same also holds to a lesser degree for the contributions of capital and patent stocks. With regard to the contributions of technological specialization, however, no clear-cut picture evolves. France and Italy profit slightly from their relative specialization in the area of R&D-intensive technology (3.7 and 6.5 per cent), while this contribution is negligible for Belgium and clearly negative for Austria (-11,1 per cent).

Within the last group of EU countries with relatively low GDP growth, three countries show either high or very high relative contributions of transferable technical knowledge to growth (Denmark and Great Britain with 51.0 and 53.9 per cent as well as Sweden with 65.7 per cent). At the same time, these countries experienced relatively small contributions of capital growth to GDP growth. Moreover, Denmark realized a distinct contribution of employment growth to GDP growth, while the contribution of this component is moderate in the case of Great Britain and Sweden. The growth of the patent stock is a contributing factor in two of these three countries (Denmark and Sweden), with 5.9 and 3.3 per cent on average to economic growth; in the case of Great Britain this influence is negligible. Finally, Great Britain profits comparatively moderately from its relative specialization in the area of the entire R&D-intensive technology, while this contribution is clearly negative for Denmark and Sweden which bring up the rear within the EU with -11.5 per cent.

Germany takes a special position within this group, but partly also within the EU as a whole. Its relative contribution of transferable technical knowledge only amounts to 29.2 per cent. This value is only undercut by the Netherlands. At the same time it shows the highest relative contribution of specialization in the area of the entire R&D-intensive technology to growthwith 10.4 per cent. The picture is completed by relatively high contributions of capital and labour (45.8 and 10.3 per cent) as well as by an average contribution of patent stock growth.

Table 7. Decomposition of average annual growth of GDP from 1969 to 1998 considering specialization in leading-edge technology

Country	$\overline{\Delta y_n}$	Percentage contribution to average annual growth				
	(%)	$\hat{g}+\hat{c}\overline{t}-\hat{\eta}(\cdot)$	$\hat{\alpha}\overline{\Delta k_n}$	$(1-\hat{\alpha})\overline{\Delta l_n}$	$\hat{\gamma}\overline{\Delta p_n}$	$\hat{\zeta}\overline{\tilde{s}_n^{R\&D}}$
IE	4.63	44.6	35.2	14.6	5.6	0.0
PT	3.60	38.8	45.8	13.1	1.8	0.5
ES	3.32	55.9	48.2	5.7	4.9	-14.8
GR	3.13	20.2	57.0	14.5	2.9	5.4
FI	3.09	80.7	35.2	4.5	10.4	-30.7
AT	2.93	47.8	47.3	14.7	3.7	-13.6
NL	2.78	-4.8	40.2	26.0	2.8	35.7
FR	2.63	21.2	44.6	10.1	3.5	20.6
BE	2.62	48.0	43.4	6.7	4.9	-2.9
IT	2.54	37.8	48.8	3.7	5.0	4.8
DK	2.26	54.3	37.7	13.6	5.6	-11.3
UK	2.21	33.3	36.8	8.0	0.5	21.3
DE	2.19	34.7	51.2	9.6	4.1	0.5
SE	2.00	58.2	40.0	6.2	3.1	-7.5

When the growth decomposition is based on the model capturing specialization in the area of leading-edge technology, all countries – of course without changing the ranking – have slightly higher contributions of capital to GDP growth and the contributions of labour and patent stocks are a little bit smaller (Table 7). However, there are distinct shiftings of the contributions of transferable technical knowledge and of the relative level of technological specialization. Within the group of heavily growing, initially lagging countries more than 80 per cent of Finland's average annual GDP growth can be ascribed to transferable technical knowledge, while with -30.7 per cent it experienced a high negative contribution of its relative specialization in the area of leading-edge technology. Spain also experienced a negative contribution of its specialization (-14.8 per cent) and at the same time a high positive contribution of transferable technical knowledge. The contributions of the latter component are more moderate for Ireland and Portugal (44.6 and 36.8 per cent), for which, furthermore, the effects of their relative specialization in the area of leading-edge technology are negligible. The case of Greece is different. It experienced only a small relative contribution of transferable technical knowledge (with 20.2 per cent the penultimate position within the EU) and a moderate contribution of its technological specialization (5.4 per cent).[5]

Within the second group, especially the Netherlands and in a less pronounced form also France are striking, because they have either no or only a small contribution of transferable technical knowledge and, at the same time, either a very or strongly distinct contribution of their relative specialization in the area of leading-

[5] With regard to the interpretation of Greece's technological specialisation, a certain degree of caution is required due to its small patent stocks, especially in the area of leading-edge technology.

edge technology. In comparison, the contribution of transferable technical knowledge is much higher in the case of Italy, with at the same time a moderate contribution of its specialization to GDP growth. Finally, a very high share of growth can be ascribed to transferable technical knowledge in the case of Austria and Belgium, while their specializations in the area of leading-edge technology contributed either strongly or slightly negatively to their growth performance.

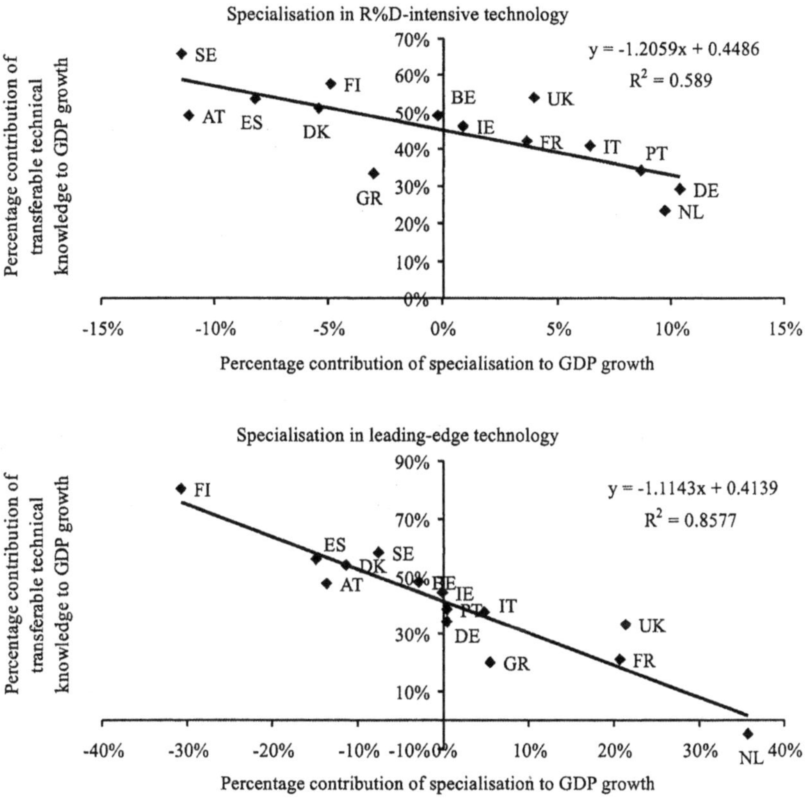

Fig. 2. Correlations between contributions of transferable technical knowledge and technological specialization to GDP growth

Among the four countries of the last group with relatively low average annual growth rates, a very large part of growth can be attributed to transferable technical knowledge in the case of Denmark and Sweden (54.3 and 58.2 per cent). Moreover, both countries experienced losses of growth by -11.3 and -7.5 per cent respectively due to their specialization. In contrast, Great Britain and Germany profit only to a modest extent from transferable technical knowledge with 33.3 and 34.7 per cent. They differ, however, to a large extent with regard to the contribution of their relative technological specialization to growth, which is negligible in the case of Germany, while Great Britain comes second within the EU with 21.3 per cent.

In summary, it may be noticed that on the one hand, growth of capital stocks and transferable technical knowledge provided the most important contributions to long-term GDP growth in the EU during the period from 1969 to 1998. However, the contributions of the other components (changes in employment and patent stocks as well as the relative levels of technological specialization) cannot be neglected. On the other hand, a glance at the decomposition results already shows the opposite tendency of the contributions of transferable technical knowledge and technological specialization to GDP growth. This impression is confirmed, when both components are plotted against each other in a scatter diagram (Figure 2). Considering specialization in the area of the entire R&D-intensive technology, the R^2 is 0.589 and we have a highly significant negative relationship at a level of one per cent. If alternatively specialization in the area of leading-edge technology is considered, the R^2 increases to 0.858. This result indicates that some of the countries negatively specialized in the entire R&D-intensive technology or – even more pronounced – in leading-edge technology managed in the past to achieve high relative contributions to growth due to technology transfer and imitation. Therefore, it can be assumed that especially for those countries which catched-up strongly within the EU, increases of efficiency enabled by technology transfer and imitation are an important preliminary stage to an own innovation capability in the R&D-intensive area.

4.3 Results of the Convergence Decompositions

The starting point of the decomposition of σ- and β-convergence is the calculation of the labour productivities in the initial year of the observation period 1968 and of their average annual changes until 1998 as well as the decomposition of the latter into the components of the empirical model. The results of this exercise on the basis of the model with specialization in the entire R&D-intensive technology are displayed in Table 8. With regard to the initial level of labour productivity in 1968, Germany was clearly in the first place with a value of about 34 per cent above the (hypothetical) EU average. France (21.77 per cent) and Belgium (21.31 per cent) followed with a clear margin. An additional six countries also show an above-average initial level (from the Netherlands with 19.75 per cent to Austria with 1.59 per cent). Finland, Ireland and the three South European countries were clearly below the average, with Portugal (-54.72 per cent) far behind.

Table 8. Decomposition of relative labour productivity growth from 1969 to 1998 considering specialization in R&D-intensive technology

Country	q_{n1968}	$\overline{\Delta q_n}$	$\hat{\alpha}\overline{\Delta\tilde{k}_n}$	$-\hat{\alpha}\overline{\Delta\tilde{l}_n}$	$\hat{\gamma}\overline{\Delta\tilde{p}_n}$	$\hat{\zeta}\overline{\tilde{s}_n^{R\&D}}$	$-\hat{\eta}(\cdot)$
				(per cent)			
DE	33.91	-0.48	-0.11	0.07	-0.04	0.23	-0.63
FR	21.77	-0.14	-0.06	0.03	-0.03	0.10	-0.17
BE	21.31	0.00	-0.10	0.09	0.00	-0.01	0.01
NL	19.75	-0.76	-0.11	-0.25	-0.05	0.27	-0.62
DK	17.76	-0.57	-0.35	0.01	0.00	-0.12	-0.11
IT	16.36	0.06	0.00	0.14	0.00	0.16	-0.24
SE	14.23	-0.53	-0.40	0.12	-0.06	-0.23	0.04
UK	9.83	-0.41	-0.38	0.09	-0.12	0.09	-0.08
AT	1.59	-0.11	0.13	-0.07	-0.01	-0.33	0.17
FI	-15.69	0.55	-0.14	0.11	0.21	-0.15	0.51
ES	-20.03	0.68	0.32	0.08	0.04	-0.27	0.51
IE	-28.74	1.17	0.35	-0.22	0.14	0.04	0.86
GR	-37.34	0.05	0.49	-0.09	-0.03	-0.09	-0.23
PT	-54.72	0.48	0.36	-0.10	-0.06	0.31	-0.04

If average annual changes of relative labour productivity are considered, countries being initially positioned above-average – with the exception of Belgium and Italy – show negative values, while initially backward countries show positive rates of change, which were highest for Ireland (1.17 per cent) and lowest for Greece (0.05 per cent). Thus, a broad majority of the EU countries show a more or less distinct tendency towards the average of log labour productivities.[6]

With the exception of Austria, the contributions of changes of the capital stock are negative for all countries with initially above-average labour productivities, which partly explains the tendency of labour productivities towards the EU average. These were most pronounced for Sweden, Great Britain and Denmark. On the other hand, four of the five initially lagging countries (except Finland) show a clearly positive contribution of relative capital stock growth. In contrast, the impact of changes in relative employment is rather heterogeneous. Among the initially above-average countries they contribute to an approach towards the average in the case of the Netherlands and Austria. The results are similar with an opposite sign for the initially backward countries. In the case of Finland and Spain changes of relative employment support the tendency towards the average, while they act as a brake in the case of Ireland, Greece and Portugal.

For six of the nine initially above-average countries, changes of relative patent stocks contribute to the tendency towards the EU average labour productivity, while their contributions are negligible in the case of Belgium, Denmark and Italy. Among the initially backward countries, Finland and Ireland – as well as to a modest extent Spain – profit from an improvement of their relative positions with

[6] However, it cannot be excluded that there is not only a tendency towards the average, but that in the long-term some initially backward countries will top the average, while some initially leading countries will fall back below the average.

regard to patent stocks. In contrast, for Greece and Portugal, this component counteracts the slight (Greece) or stronger (Portugal) tendency towards the EU average of labour productivities.

The impact of relative technological specialization varies rather considerably. Among the countries with initially above-average labour productivity, it alleviates the decrease in relative levels of labour productivity in the case of the Netherlands and Germany as well as – to a smaller extent – also in the case of Italy, France and Great Britain, while it supports this process in the other four countries. The picture is similarly heterogeneous for the initially lagging countries. The influence of technology diffusion is generally a mirror image of the impact of technological specialization, so that among the initially advanced countries it provides the highest contribution to the approach towards the average in the case of Germany and the Netherlands. Among the initially backward countries, Ireland, Finland and Spain profit from very high contributions of technology diffusion to the growth of their relative levels of labour productivity. On the other hand, a negative contribution in the case of Greece takes prime responsibility for its small tendency towards the average.

Table 9. Decomposition of relative labour productivity growth from 1969 to 1998 considering specialization in leading-edge technology

Country	q_{n1968}	$\overline{\Delta q_n}$	$\hat{\alpha}\overline{\Delta\tilde{k}_n}$	$-\hat{\alpha}\overline{\Delta\tilde{l}_n}$	$\hat{\gamma}\overline{\Delta\tilde{p}_n}$	$\hat{\zeta}\overline{\tilde{s}_n^{R\&D}}$	$-\hat{\eta}(\cdot)$
				(per cent)			
DE	33.91	-0.48	-0.12	0.07	-0.03	0.01	-0.41
FR	21.77	-0.14	-0.07	0.04	-0.03	0.54	-0.61
BE	21.31	0.00	-0.11	0.10	0.00	-0.08	0.09
NL	19.75	-0.76	-0.13	-0.28	-0.05	0.99	-1.30
DK	17.76	-0.57	-0.39	0.01	0.00	-0.25	0.06
IT	16.36	0.06	0.00	0.15	0.00	0.12	-0.21
SE	14.23	-0.53	-0.44	0.13	-0.06	-0.15	-0.01
UK	9.83	-0.41	-0.43	0.10	-0.11	0.47	-0.43
AT	1.59	-0.11	0.15	-0.08	-0.01	-0.40	0.23
FI	-15.69	0.55	-0.15	0.12	0.20	-0.95	1.33
ES	-20.03	0.68	0.36	0.09	0.04	-0.49	0.69
IE	-28.74	1.17	0.39	-0.25	0.14	0.00	0.89
GR	-37.34	0.05	0.55	-0.10	-0.03	0.17	-0.54
PT	-54.72	0.48	0.40	-0.11	-0.06	0.02	0.23

Alternatively taking into consideration specialization in the area of leading-edge technology leads mainly to a shift of the contributions of technological specialization and technology diffusion to the changes of relative labour productivity, without changing their total contribution to a greater extent (Table 9). Among the countries with above-average initial levels, the comparatively highly positive specialization in the area of leading-edge technology reduces the tendency towards the EU average in the case of the Netherlands, France and Great Britain. Technology diffusion works against this, such that the sum of both effects is positive only for Great Britain. Compared to specialization in the area of the entire R&D-

intensive technology, the positive contributions of technological specialization decrease particularly in the case of Germany and to a lesser extent for Italy, while the amount of negative contributions increase in the case of Belgium, Denmark and Austria. Only for Sweden is the amount of the negative contribution a little bit lower. The changes in contributions of technology diffusion are almost a mirror image of the changes in contributions of specialization. For Denmark, the Netherlands and Sweden, the sum of these components is now slightly higher, so that the tendency towards the average diminishes a bit.

Table 10. Decomposition of σ-convergence of labour productivities within the EU considering technological specialization

	Standard deviation of relative labour productivities						
		R&D-intensive			Leading-edge		
	1968	1998	%Δ	% total	1998	%Δ	% total
Actual	0.266	0.176	-33.7		0.176	-33.7	
Without level shift DE 1991	0.266	0.185	-30.5	100	0.185	-30.5	100
Growth due only change in:							
capital	0.266	0.207	-22.2	72.8	0.202	-24.3	79.8
labour	0.266	0.283	6.1	-20.0	0.285	6.9	-22.7
capital/labour	0.266	0.221	-17.1	56.1	0.217	-18.7	61.4
patents	0.266	0.260	-2.3	7.7	0.260	-2.2	7.4
specialization	0.266	0.278	4.4	-14.5	0.336	26.2	-86.2
technology diffusion	0.266	0.227	-14.7	48.4	0.247	-7.2	23.7

Among the five countries with labour productivities below the EU average in 1968, the trade-off between growth contributions of technological specialization and technology diffusion increases in favour of the latter in the case of Finland and Spain and to a lesser extent in the case of Portugal. The opposite occurs in the case of Greece, where the contribution of technology diffusion to relative growth decreases further, while the contribution of specialization moves into the positive zone.[7] Due to its negligible contributions of the specialization in the entire R&D-intensive technology as well as in leading-edge technology, there hardly is any change in the high contribution of technology diffusion to growth for Ireland.

Based on these figures, the decomposition of σ- and β-convergence within the EU can be carried out. With regard to σ-convergence, the standard deviation of the relative labour productivities of the 14 considered EU countries was 0.266 in 1968 (Table 10). Until 1998 it actually decreased by 33.7 per cent to 0.176, while a decrease of 30.5 per cent to 0.185 has to be assumed when the unique level shift due to German unification is eliminated. Since this was done with the data of the em-

[7] As already mentioned in footnote 3, a certain degree of caution is required with regard to the interpretation of Greece's technological specialisation because of its small patent stocks, especially in the area of leading-edge technology.

pirical model, this adjusted measure of σ-convergence is also the basis of the decomposition.

Obviously the development of capital stocks provided the largest contribution to σ-convergence in the thirty-year period until 1998. If growth in this period had been caused only by changes in capital stocks, the standard deviation would have decreased by 22.2 per cent to 0.207 based on the empirical model considering specialization in the area of the entire R&D-intensive technology, that is 72.8 per cent of the total decline. When the model considering specialization in the area of leading-edge technology is used, the share in the total decline is even slightly higher at 79.8 per cent. On the other hand, the standard deviation would have increased by 6.1 and 6.9 per cent respectively if growth had been caused only by changes of employment. Altogether, capital deepening would have contributed 56.1 per cent (taking into account specialization in the area of the entire R&D-intensive technology) and 61.4 per cent (taking into account specialization in the area of leading-edge technology) to the total decline of the standard deviation of relative labour productivities respectively.

If growth of labour productivities had been caused solely by changes of patent stocks, the decline of the standard deviation would have been rather small with 7.7 and 7.4 per cent respectively of the total decline. The effect of specialization in the area of the entire R&D-intensive technology is moderately negative – the standard deviation would have increased by 4.4 per cent – and the effect of specialization in leading-edge technology is strongly negative – the standard deviation would have been increased by 26.2 per cent. Finally, technology diffusion provides an important contribution to the reduction of the standard deviation. Its sole consideration on the basis of the model with specialization in the area of the entire R&D-intensive technology would have reduced the standard deviation by 14.7 per cent, which is a contribution of 48.4 per cent to total σ -convergence. When the model with specialization in the area of leading-edge technology is used, the hypothetical reduction is only 7.2 per cent, thus 23.7 per cent of total σ -convergence.

The estimate of β is 0.0151, which implies a rate of absolute β-convergence λ= 0.0201 within the EU from 1969 to 1998, since $\lambda = (-1/T)[\ln(1-\beta T)]$ (Table 11). This value tallies with the ubiquitous 2 per cent which is ascertained in various cross-section studies of convergence (e.g. Barro/Sala-i-Martin, 1991 and Sala-i-Martin, 1996). The contribution of the factor capital to the estimate of β amounts to 55.3 per cent on the basis of the model with technological specialization in the entire R&D-intensive area and to 61.9 per cent on the basis of the model with specialization in leading-edge technology. Changes of employment, on the other hand, slowed down β-convergence slightly, such that the contribution of capital deepening was between 43.7 and 48.9 per cent, depending on the model used.

Table 11. Decomposition of β-convergence of labour productivities within the EU considering technological specialization

	Absolute β-convergence					
	R&D-intensive			Leading-edge		
	$\hat{\beta}$	t-value	%	$\hat{\beta}$	t-value	%
Total	-0.0151	-3.34[a)]	100	-0.0151	-3.34	100
Contribution of change in:						
capital	-0.0083	-5.10	55.3	-0.0093	-5.10	61.9
labour	0.0018	1.74	-11.6	0.0020	1.74	-13.0
capital/labour	-0.0066	-3.83	43.7	-0.0074	-3.83	48.9
patents	-0.0009	-0.97	6.1	-0.0009	-0.97	5.8
specialization	0.0006	0.23	-4.1	0.0051	1.25	-33.9
technology diffusion	-0.0082	-1.67	54.3	-0.0119	-1.82	79.2
	Conditional β-convergence (GR, PT vs. rest of the EU)					
	R&D-intensive			Leading-edge		
	$\hat{\beta}$	t-value	%	$\hat{\beta}$	t-value	%
Total	-0.0258	-6.46	100	-0.0258	-6.46	100
Contribution of change in:						
capital	-0.0073	-2.53	28.3	-0.0082	-2.53	31.7
labour	0.0015	0.65	-5.8	0.0017	0.65	-6.5
capital/labour	-0.0058	-2.01	22.5	-0.0065	-2.01	25.2
patents	-0.0032	-3.26	12.3	-0.0030	-3.26	11.6
specialization	0.0041	1.45	-15.8	0.0134	1.80	-51.7
technology diffusion	-0.0209	-10.01	81.0	-0.0297	-4.73	114.9

a) White's heteroskedasticity-consistent estimators of the variance matrix are used to calculate *t*-statistics.

The contributions of patent stocks and technological specialization are not significantly different from zero, but the magnitude of the estimate for the contribution of specialization in the area of leading-edge technology points to a considerable convergence impeding effect. The contribution of technology diffusion is almost as large as the contribution of capital in the model with specialization in the area of the entire R&D-intensive technology, and it is even higher in the model with specialization in the area of leading-edge technology. Therefore, convergence of capital stocks per person employed and technology diffusion are the important driving forces of absolute β-convergence.

Since Greece and Portugal still have a special position within the EU, it was assumed by introducing a dummy variable for these two countries that they and the rest of the EU would converge to different steady states. This dummy variable is highly significant and the estimate of β rises to 0.0258, which implies a conditional convergence rate of 4.96 per cent (the lower panel of Table 11). In the case of such a conditional convergence, the contribution of capital reduces distinctly to either 28.3 per cent (when specialization in the area of the entire R&D-intensive technology is considered) or 31.7 per cent (when specialization in the area of leading-edge technology is considered). Altogether, capital deepening is then responsible for only one-fifth to one-quarter of the total estimate of the convergence parameter.

The contribution of the development of patent stocks is now highly significantly different from zero and constitutes about 12 per cent of the total estimate of β, independent of the specification of the empirical model. With regard to technological specialization, at least specialization in the area of leading-edge technology is now at a level of 10 per cent significantly different from zero. At this magnitude, it prevents a 51.7 per cent higher estimate of β. Thus the different degrees of relative specialization in the area of leading-edge technology are an important obstacle for conditional β-convergence within the EU. On the other hand, with contributions of either 81 or 115 per cent, technology diffusion is to a even larger extent the driving force of convergence of labour productivities in this specification of the convergence regressions, however, towards two different steady states.

5 Summary and Conclusions

The empirical analysis of the impact of innovations, technological specialization and technology diffusion on economic growth and convergence of the EU countries from 1969 to 1998 provided some clear-cut results. Innovations measured by the growth rates of the patent stocks of the EU countries foster economic growth. With regard to specialization, there is only little empirical evidence that technological Smithian specialization is conducive to economic growth within the EU. In contrast, the level of relative technological specialization in the area of R&D-intensive industries and especially in the area of leading-edge industries contributes significantly to economic growth within the EU. Moreover, the estimations suggest a moderate rate of technology diffusion, depending on the specification of the empirical model between 5 and 6 per cent per year.

The growth decomposition showed that besides capital accumulation, technology diffusion is a driving force for growth of catching-up countries within the EU, while it is the level of relative Ricardian technological specialization for initially leading EU countries. Furthermore, the decomposition of measures of σ- and β-convergence reveals that technology diffusion is also a main driving force – at least as important as capital accumulation – of the convergence of labour productivities within the EU, while different levels of relative Ricardian technological specialization slow down convergence. The relative growth of the patent stock, however, only contributes significantly to β-convergence if conditional convergence (Greece and Portugal against the rest of the world) is considered.

In accordance with Dalum/ Villumsen (1996), it can be concluded on the basis of the empirical results, that a sole specialization in leading-edge technology is probably no panacea for a "paradise on earth". However, it is also obvious from the empirical results that processes of structural change towards R&D-intensive

industries should be supported by policy, because countries which were successful in this process also experienced higher growth opportunities in the recent past. Furthermore, national as well as EU policy should support cross-border technology diffusion and knowledge spillovers. Especially with regard to the catching-up but still backward countries within the EU, it might be necessary to promote these countries through a selective EU research and technology policy, so that they succeed in setting up efficient national innovation systems and, at the same time, participate in a gradually emerging European innovation system.

References

Aghion P, Howitt P (1998) Endogenous growth theory. Cambridge (MA) London.
Agrawal A, Henderson R (2001) Putting patents in context: exploring knowledge transfer from MIT. Working paper Queen's University and MIT Sloan School.
Anderson B, Walsh V (1998) Co-evolution of technological systems, blurring of industry boundaries and broadening of competencies in the chemical industry. Paper presented at 1998 DRUID Summer Conference, 9-11 June, Bornholm.
Archibugi D, Pianta M (1992) The technological specialisation of advanced countries, A report to the EEC on international science and technology activities. Dordrecht/ Boston/ London.
Barro RJ, Sala-i-Martin X (1991) Convergence across states and regions. Brookings Papers on Economic Activity: 107-182.
Bernard AB, Jones CI (1996) Technology and convergence. The Economic Journal 106: 1037-1044.
Blundell R, Griffith R, Van Renen J (1998) Market share, market value and innovation in a panel of British manufacturing firms. Working paper University College London and Institute for Fiscal Studies.
Caballero R, Jaffe A (1993) How high are the giant's shoulders. NBER Working paper No. 4370.
Cantwell JA, Anderson B (1996) A statistical analysis of corporate technological leadership historically. Economics of Innovation and New Technology 4: 211-234.
Cantwell JA, Piscitello L (2000) Accumulating technological competence - Its changing impact on corporate diversification and internationalisation. Working paper University of Reading.
Chen SS, Ho KW, Ik KH et al. (2002) How does strategic competition affect firm values? A study of new product announcements. Financial Management: 5-22.
Cockburn I, Griliches Z (1988) Industry effects and appropriability measures in the stock market's valuation of R&D and patents. American Economic Review 78: 419-423.
Dalum B, Laursen K, Verspagen B (1999) Does specialization matter for growth. Industrial and Corporate Change 8: 267-288.
Dalum B, Villumsen G (1996) Are OECD export specialisation patterns 'sticky'? Relations to the convergence-divergence debate. DRUID Working paper No. 96-3, Aalborg University.
de la Fuente A. (2002) On the sources of convergence: A close look at the Spanish regions. European Economic Review 46: 569-599.

Dowrick S (1997) Innovation and growth: Implications of the new theory and evidence. In: Fagerberg J, Lundberg L, Hansson P et al. (eds) Technology and international trade. Cheltenham.

Dushnitsky G, Lenox MJ (2002) Corporate venture capital and incumbent firm innovation rates. Working paper Stern School of Business, NY University.

Gambardella A, Torrisi S (2000) The economic value of knowledge and inter-firm technological linkages: An investigation of science-based firms. Paper prepared for the Dynacom TSER project (Contract No. SOE1-CT97-1078).

Grossman G, Helpman E (1991), Innovation and Growth in a Global Economy. Cambridge (MA).

Grupp H, Jungmittag A, Legler H et al. (2000) Hochtechnologie 2000 – Neudefinition der Hochtechnologie für die Berichterstattung zur technologischen Leistungsfähigkeit Deutschlands. Karlsruhe/Hannover.

Hall BH, Jaffe A, Trajtenberg M (2001) Market value and patent citations: A first look. Working paper Department of Economics, UC Berkeley.

Heeley MB, Khorana A, Matusik SF (2000) Underpricing and the long-run financial performance of IPOs: Information asymmetry and firm incentive capability. In: Reynolds D (ed.) Frontiers of entrepreneurship research – Proceedings of the 19th annual entrepreneurship research conference 1999, Babson College.

Henderson R, Cockburn I (1996) Scale, scope and spillovers: The determinants of research productivity in drug discovery. Rand Journal of Economics 27: 32-59.

Jungmittag A (2004) Innovations, technological specialisation and economic growth in the EU. Economic Papers No. 199, European Commission, Directorate-General for Economic and Financial Affairs, Brussels.

Jungmittag A (2004a) Innovations, technological specialisation and economic growth in the EU, in: International Economics and Economic Policy 1, 247-273.

Jungmittag A, Blind K, Grupp H (1999) Innovation, standardisation and the long-term production function - A cointegration analysis for Germany, 1960-1996. Zeitschrift für Wirtschafts- und Sozialwissenschaften 119: 205-222.

Jungmittag A, Welfens PJJ (2002) Telecommunications, innovations and the long-term production function: Theoretical aspects and a cointegration analysis for West Germany 1960 – 1990. In: Audretsch D, Welfens PJJ (eds), The new economy and economic growth in Europe and the US. Berlin et al., 99-127.

Lach S (1995) Patents and productivity growth at the industry level: A first look. Economics Letters 49: 101-108.

Lucas RE (1988) On the mechanics of economic development. Journal of Monetary Economics 22: 3-42.

Mankiw NG, Romer D, Weil DN (1992) A contribution to the empirics of economic growth. The Quarterly Journal of Economics 107: 407-438.

Mansfield E, Schwartz M, Wagner S (1981) Imitation costs and patents: An empirical study. The Economic Journal 91: 907-918.

Romer PM (1986) Increasing returns and long-run growth. Journal of Political Economy 94: 1002-1037.

Romer PM (1990) Endogenous technological change. Journal of Political Economy 98: S71-S102.

Sala-i-Martin X (1996) Regional cohesion: Evidence and theories of regional growth and convergence. European Economic Review 40: 1325-1352.

Zachariadis M (2000) R&D-induced growth? Evidence from the U.S. manufacturing sector. Working paper Department of Economics, LSU, Baton Rouge, LA.

Comment on: Innovations, Technological Specialization and Economic Convergence in the EU

Andreas Pyka

The question of prevailing convergence or divergence processes plays an important role in both the theoretical as well as political discussion of development within the European Union. Theoretically, most neoclassically motivated models assume convergence processes to be basically due to decreasing returns of capital and freely available technological spillovers. Accordingly, the traditional approach to growth suggests that poorer economies grow faster than richer ones and that they finally converge to the same long-run steady-state. Many evolutionary economics settings instead also discuss the possibility of divergence processes caused by path dependencies and local effects of innovation. The contribution of André Jungmittag offers important and innovative insights into this discussion by combining the arguments of different strands of the literature in a sophisticated and well elaborated empirical analysis.

By differing between Smithian specialization inspired mainly by learning-by-doing effects and increasing returns to scale as well as Ricardian specialization inspired by qualitative differences between different technologies and their respective technological opportunities, Jungmittag is able to work out the relevance of the arguments emphasized by neoclassically motivated new growth theory and the recent development approaches in an evolutionary economics fashion. In particular, the growth processes of 14 European nations over a time span of 30 years are analyzed in a growth decomposition analysis for the whole sample and for each country separately. Additionally, the growth rates are decomposed according to their contribution to sigma- and beta-convergence.

Jungmittag's rich empirical picture clearly shows that technological factors, such as specialization in high technologies or the diffusion of technological know-how do matter for an understanding of the underlying patterns of economic development. The image of the empirical analysis shows Europe as a compilation of rather heterogeneous economies with different growth strategies, different dynamics and different sensitivities with respect to assumed growth factors. In a way, the results offered by André Jungmittag can be interpreted as a first bridgeover between the only quantitative oriented literature on economic growth on the one hand, and the qualitative factors emphasizing literature on National Innovation Systems (e.g. Lundvall, 1992, Nelson, 1993) on the other. Moreover, one critical remark has to be made in this respect. As the results are so extensive, their understanding could be improved considerably by devoting more space to interpretation as well as more descriptive information. For example, including information on historical developments would be extremely helpful for the explanation of some of the striking results (e.g., concerning Finland or Portugal, where a time span of 30 years obviously covers not only very different macroeconomic patterns but also extremely different political frameworks and institutional settings).

One of the major results of this contribution points to the importance of technological specialization in the area of leading-edge industries for spurring economic growth within the EU. From my point of view, this hints directly at a necessary extension of empirical analysis, focussing on European regions instead of national states. Theoretically, the aforementioned convergence processes are more likely to happen in regions inside a national economy, because there it is more likely that similar behavioural and technological parameters can be observed. In accordance with recent literature on regional growth and development, however, convergence on a regional level is even less visible than compared to the national level. In other words, whereas the growth rates of European nations are getting closer (keeping in mind Jungmittag's results emphasizing rather heterogeneous determinants), there is nothing similar going on at the regional level (e.g., Cappelen, Fagerberg and Verspagen 1999).

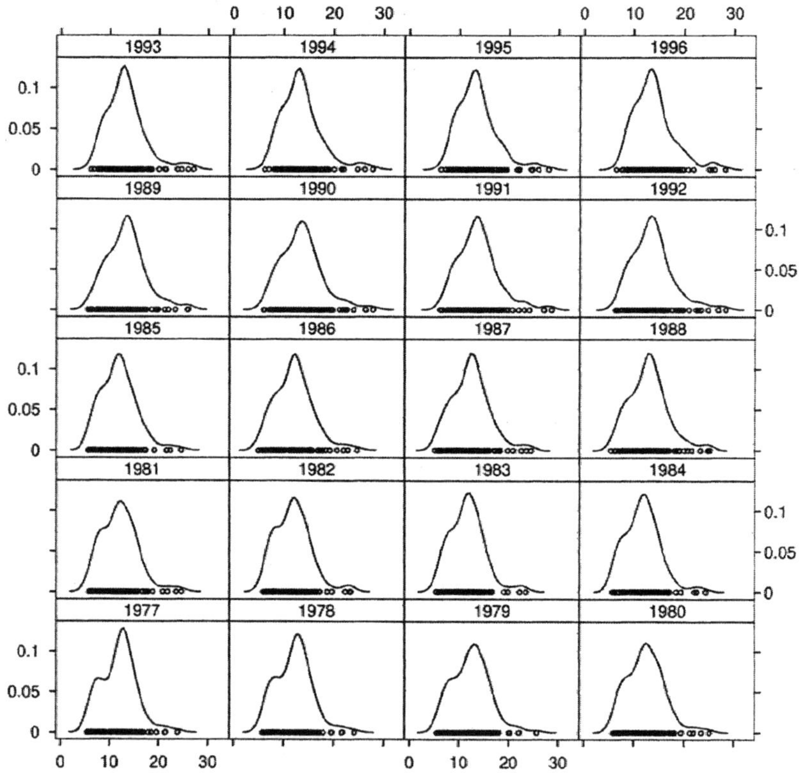

Fig. 1. Kernel density plots for the regional distribution of GDP/capita within the European Union from 1977 to 1996 (NUTS-2 level, source: Eurostat)

Figure 1 shows the development of GDP per capita for European regions on a Nuts-2 level for a time span of almost 20 years using kernel density plots. What clearly can be observed is that no convergence at all has taken place between the European regions. Instead, we clearly see the persistence of an almost twin-peaks-like structure; even a third peak on the right side describing the development of the richest regions emerges after 1985. Cappelen, Fagerberg and Verspagen (1999) speak of different European growth clubs in this respect.

As a potential theoretical approach for the explanation of these heterogeneous growth processes, I would like to suggest a method only recently applied to a rather similar macro-economic phenomenon (Cantner, Ebersberger, Krüger, Pyka, 2004). A new stylised fact of economic growth is the bimodal shape of the distribution of per capita income or the twin-peaked nature of that distribution (e.g. Quah, 1997). Drawing on the Summers/Hestons Penn World Table (1991), for example, kernel density distributions of world income can be constructed which are able to detect the aforementioned twin-peaked structure and show that world income distribution starting with a unimodal structure in 1960 evolves subsequently to a bimodal or twin-peak structure. These empirical results can be explained theoretically by a synergetic model based on the master equation approach (Pyka, Krüger, Cantner 2003). Our recent paper (Cantner, Ebersberger, Krüger, Pyka, 2004) attempts to extend the discussion by taking a reverse approach, i.e. to find empirical evidence for the working mechanism of the theoretical model. In our paper, we empirically determine the transition rates used in the synergetic approach by alternatively applying NLS to chosen functional forms and genetic programming in order to determine the functional forms and the parameters simultaneously. Using the so determined transition rates in the synergetic model leads in both cases to the emergence of the bimodal distribution.

An empirical specification of the basic transition rates of this model for the growth processes of European regions, which include the effects of technological infrastructure, the diffusion of new technological knowledge as well as technological obsolescence, could very likely lead to important new insights into different sources of economic growth as well as their relative weights. Thus, our theoretical understanding of the scattered impacts of these different sources of growth – improved upon in Jungmittag's contribution – could also be systematically improved.

References

Cantner, U. , Ebersberger, B. , Krüger, J. and Pyka, A. (2004), Empirically Based Simulation: The Case of Twin Peaks in National Income, Revue Economique, N° 5, forthcoming.

Cappelen, A., Fagerberg, J. and Verspagen, B 1999. Lack of regional convergence, in Fagerberg, J., Guerrieri, P., Verspagen, B. (eds.), The Economic Challenge for Europe. Adapting to Innovation Based Growth, Edward Elgar, Cheltenham., pp. 130-148.

Lundvall, B.-Å. (ed.), 1992. National Systems of Innovation: Towards a Theory of Innovation and Interactive Learning. Pinter, London.

Nelson, R.R. (ed.), 1993. National Innovation Systems: A Comparative Analysis. Oxford University Press, Oxford.

Pyka, A., Krüger, J. and Cantner, U. (2003), Twin Peaks – What the Knowledge-Based Approach can say about the Dynamics of the World Income Distribution, in: Paolo Saviotti (ed..), Applied Evolutionary Economics, Edward Elgar, Cheltenham, 235-259.

Quah, D. (1997), Empirics for growth and distribution: stratification, polarization and convergence clubs, Journal of Economic Growth, Vol. 2, 27-59.

Summers, R., Heston, A. (1991), The Penn World Table (Mark 5): An Expanded Set of International Comparisons 1950-1988, Quarterly Journal of Economics 106, 1991, 327-368.

Equilibrium Exchange Rates in the Transition: The Tradable Price-Based Real Appreciation and Estimation Uncertainty

Balázs Égert and Kirsten Lommatzsch[1]

Contents

1 Introduction 206
2 Theoretical Motivation 207
3 Some Stylized Facts and the Role of Foreign Capital 211
4 Reduced-Form Equation 216
5 Data and Econometric Issues 217
5.1 Data 217
5.2 Testing Procedure 220
6 Results 222
6.1 Time Series 222
6.2 Panels 229
6.3 Real Misalignments 231
7 Conclusions 236
References 237

[1] We would like to thank Jesús Crespo-Cuaresma, Jarko Fidrmuc, Thomas Reininger and Doris Ritzberger-Grünwald for valuable comments and suggestions. The paper has also benefited from discussion from participant at the following workshops: Second Workshop on Macroeconomic Policy Research organized by the National Bank of Hungary (2003), Workshop on Empirical Economic Research at the Institute of Econometrics and Statistics of the Freie Univeristät Berlin (2003), seminar at MODEM, University of Paris X-Nanterre, the 57th International Atlantic Economic Conference (Lisbon, 2004), BOFIT Workshop 2004, and an internal seminar at the European Department of the IMF (2004). We are also grateful to Jakub Borowski, Anna Czogala and Bostjan Jazbec for providing us with data for Poland and Slovenia. All remaining errors are ours.

1 Introduction

The upcoming enlargement of the European Union catapulted the issue of equilibrium exchange rates for CEE acceding countries into the limelight of policy discussion. In contrast with Denmark and the UK, the new Member States do not have an opt-out clause from the obligation to adopt the euro at some point in the future. Sooner or later, it will therefore be necessary to assess what exchange rate might be best suited for entry to ERM -II and for the irrevocable conversion rate.

In accordance with the Maastricht Treaty, important prerequisites for participation in monetary union are low inflation and a stable exchange rate for at least two years before examination of convergence. A considerably undervalued exchange rate parity could, however, make it very difficult to attain low inflation. At the same time, fixing the exchange rate at an overvalued level against the euro would most probably require adjustment mechanisms that harm growth and thus real convergence. The irrevocable conversion rate should therefore trigger neither inflation caused by too large an undervaluation, nor an immediate loss of competitiveness caused by overvaluation. This is all the more important since with fully liberalized capital accounts as a background, financial markets may be eager to test the chosen parity especially in the presence of policy mixes in the acceding countries that are perceived as unsustainable. This may induce exchange rate fluctuations incompatible with the criterion on exchange rate stability.

However, assessing equilibrium real exchange rates is no easy task. As argued earlier,[2] a systematic analysis that includes all the alternative theoretical and statistical approaches is necessary for us to judge equilibrium real exchange rates confidently. But there are virtually no such studies for acceding countries[3]. One exception is Csajbók (2003), who, in the spirit of Detken et al. (2002), makes use of different approaches to the equilibrium real exchange rate such as the Natural Rate of Exchange (NATREX), the Behavioral Equilibrium Exchange Rate (BEER) and different versions of the Fundamental Equilibrium Exchange Rate (FEER) to derive a range of real misalignments[4] (defined as the difference between the equilibrium and the observed real exchange rates) for the case of Hungary. Although Csajbók (2003) employs all important theoretical approaches, the empirical investigation is rather limited.

This can only mark the beginning of a systematic assessment. Indeed, in this paper, an attempt is made to contribute to the systematic evaluation of equilibrium rates in acceding countries. For five acceding countries from Central and Eastern Europe, notably the Czech Republic, Hungary, Poland, Slovakia and Slovenia, reduced-form estimations of the real exchange rate are performed. Emphasis is laid more on the comparison of the results of different estimation methods than on different theoretical approaches. A number of time series and panel cointegration

[2] Égert (2003a).

[3] However, it should be noted that this is also the case for other developed and developing countries.

[4] The term real misalignment is defined in the literature as the difference between the observed and the equilibrium real exchange rate.

methods are employed, which leaves us with a score of estimates. This enables us to examine the uncertainty surrounding estimates of equilibrium exchange rates and the size of the real misalignment.

Our approach to the real exchange rate is in line with BEER, as in MacDonald (1997) and Clark and MacDonald (1998), i.e. the choice of the variables included in the reduced-form equation is in principle based on a number of standard models of the real exchange rate (see MacDonald, 1997; Clark and MacDonald 1998).

However, in the case of transition economies, special attention should be devoted to the appreciation of the real exchange rate that most of these countries witnessed in the aftermath of their economic transformation from plan to market. The traditional view is that the Balassa-Samuelson (B-S) effect, based on market service inflation fueled by productivity increases in the open sector, is capable of explaining this. Recent research, however, attributed a strikingly low relevance to the B-S effect. Indeed, a sustainable appreciation of the real exchange rate can also result from changes in regulated prices, and most importantly, from the appreciation of the tradable prices-based real exchange rate.[5] Taking account of tradable prices appears to be crucial, given that in a number of transition economies the real exchange rate deflated by means of tradable prices (proxied with the producer price index) appreciated nearly as much as the real exchange rate based on overall inflation (proxied with the consumer price index).[6] In this paper, a theoretical model is introduced that provides an explanation for this phenomenon.

The rest of the paper is organized as follows: Section 2 presents the theoretical framework for the appreciation of the real exchange rate based on the price of tradable goods. Section 3 offers some stylized facts on real exchange rates in transition economies. In section 4, the reduced-form equation is discussed. Section 5 describes the dataset and the econometric techniques. Section 6 then interprets the estimation results followed by the presentation of the derived real misalignment. Finally, section 7 concludes.

2 Theoretical Motivation

Let us consider a two-country, two-good framework where the external equilibrium is defined as a balanced trade account without taking account of capital

5 For an overview, see Égert (2003a).

6 Two things merit mention here. First, the nature of the appreciation of the real exchange rate of the transition economies appears different from that observed in Southern Europe. The size of the real appreciation of the CPI-deflated real exchange rate was much lower in Greece, Portugal and Spain. In addition, in some cases, the tradable price-based real exchange rate did not appreciate at all. Second, the long-term appreciation of the tradable price-deflated real exchange rate in transition economies does not result from nominal exchange rate persistence as put forward in the literature. Engel (1993) and Duval (2001) argue, for instance, that fluctuations in the nominal exchange rate affect both the relative prices of tradable and non-tradable goods, and this is why the real exchange rate of the open sector and that of the whole economy are strongly correlated.

flows. The traditional elasticities approach focuses on modeling the effects of real exchange rate variation on the trade balance. This paper introduces technology change and studies its the effects on the trade balance and the real exchange rate.

The supply sides of the home and foreign economies can be described as functions of capital, labor and total factor productivity, which in turn depends on technology T. The level of technology is initially higher in the foreign than in the domestic economy. This implies higher GDP per capita in the foreign country. Each country produces one good and consumes both. The two goods are at least imperfect substitutes, so that purchasing power parity (PPP) does not hold and demand for the respective good depends primarily on its price. Let us now assume that while $T^* > T$ (the asterisk denotes the foreign economy), technology changes faster in the domestic economy ($dT > dT^*$). Hence, GDP growth is higher in the domestic economy due to technological catching-up.

Demand for the domestic good depends on technology. With increasing technological content, demand for the domestic good increases both in the domestic and the foreign economy. This can be motivated by utility functions where both goods are included in each economy, and where the utility of consuming the domestic good is a positive function of technology: The higher the technological content, the higher the utility. In addition, it is assumed that in the home country, demand for the foreign good is negatively linked to the technological content of the domestic good. It does not affect the demand for the foreign good in the foreign economy, though.

Prices are assumed to be fixed in the respective currency, so that the relative price of the domestic and foreign goods is given by:

$$Q = \frac{P^* \cdot E}{P} \tag{1}$$

Where Q and E denote the real and nominal exchange rates, defined as units of domestic currency per one unit of foreign currency. P represents prices and the asterisk stands for the foreign economy. Based on these assumptions, one can derive the impact of changes of technology on the nominal and thus the real exchange rate.

The equilibrium condition we posit is that the trade account is balanced:

$$TB = 0 = P \cdot X - P^* \cdot E \cdot M \tag{2}$$

where X and M are exports from and imports to the home economy, respectively. Equation (2) can be rewritten as follows:

$$P \cdot X = P^* \cdot E \cdot M \tag{3}$$

Changes in the trade balance occur if any of its determinants changes:

$$\frac{dP}{P} + \frac{dX}{X} = \frac{dP^*}{P^*} + \frac{dE}{E} + \frac{dM}{M} \tag{4}$$

Using circumflexes for growth rates, equation (4) would look like this:

$$\hat{p} + \hat{x} = \hat{p}^* + \hat{e} + \hat{m} \tag{5}$$

As both domestic and foreign prices are assumed to be fixed, a change in the trade balance can be linked to a change in either the nominal exchange rate or determinants of imports and exports, which reduces equation (5) to:

$$\hat{x} = \hat{e} + \hat{m} \tag{6}$$

Exports of the home economy depend positively on foreign income and the technological content of the domestic good whereas it is negatively linked to the price of the domestic good relative to that of to foreign good, i.e. the nominal exchange rate:

$$X = f(\overset{+}{Y}^*, \overset{+}{T}, \overset{-}{\frac{P}{E}}) \tag{7}$$

How a change in the nominal exchange rate, technology and foreign demand influences exports can be shown using the total differential of the export function (7):

$$dX = \frac{\partial X}{\partial Y^*} dY^* + \frac{\partial X}{\partial T} dT + \frac{\partial X}{\partial \frac{P}{E}} \left(-\frac{P}{E^2} \right) dE \tag{8}$$

Dividing equation (8) by X and rearranging terms,[7] a change in exports is given as:

$$\hat{x} = \varepsilon^x_{Y*} \cdot \hat{y}^* + \varepsilon^x_T \cdot \hat{t} + \varepsilon^x_E \cdot \hat{e} \tag{9}$$

where $\varepsilon^x_{Y*}, \varepsilon^x_T$ and ε^x_E denote the elasticity of demand for exports to changes in the three variables. In a similar manner, one can establish the elasticities of import demand to changes in domestic income, technology and the price of the foreign good. Imports are a positive function of domestic income and depend negatively on the technological content of domestic goods and the price of the foreign good expressed in domestic currency units:

$$M = f(\overset{+}{Y}, \overset{-}{T}, \overset{-}{(P^* E)}) \tag{10}$$

[7] $$\frac{dX}{X} = \frac{\partial X}{\partial Y^*} \cdot \frac{dY^*}{X} \cdot \frac{Y^*}{Y^*} + \frac{\partial X}{\partial T} \cdot \frac{dT}{X} \cdot \frac{T}{T} + \frac{\partial X}{\partial (P/E)} \cdot \left(-\frac{P}{E^2} \right) \cdot \frac{dE}{X} \cdot \frac{E}{E} \tag{9'}$$

$$\frac{dX}{X} = \frac{\partial X}{\partial Y^*} \cdot \frac{Y^*}{X} \cdot \frac{dY^*}{Y^*} + \frac{\partial X}{\partial T} \cdot \frac{T}{X} \cdot \frac{dT}{T} + \frac{\partial X}{\partial (P/E)} \cdot \left(-\frac{P}{E^2} \right) \cdot \frac{E}{X} \cdot \frac{dE}{E} \tag{9''}$$

Totally differentiating equation (10) and then dividing the obtained equation by M and rearranging terms yields:[8]

$$\hat{m} = \varepsilon_Y^m \cdot \hat{t} + \varepsilon_T^m \cdot \hat{t} + \varepsilon_E^m \cdot \hat{e} \tag{11}$$

The substitution of equations (9) and (11) into equation (6) gives:

$$\varepsilon_{Y*}^x \cdot \hat{y}* + \varepsilon_T^x \cdot \hat{t} + \varepsilon_E^x \cdot \hat{e} = \hat{e} + \varepsilon_Y^m \cdot \hat{t} + \varepsilon_T^m \cdot \hat{t} + \varepsilon_E^m \cdot \hat{e} \tag{12}$$

Assuming zero growth in the foreign economy ($dY = 0$), the influence of a change in technology on a change in the nominal exchange rate can be written as follows:

$$\frac{\hat{e}}{\hat{t}} = \frac{\varepsilon_T^x - \varepsilon_T^m - \varepsilon_Y^m}{1 + \varepsilon_E^m - \varepsilon_E^x} \tag{13}$$

The elasticity of imports to the nominal exchange rate is negative whereas the elasticity of exports to the nominal exchange rate is positive. Therefore, both elasticities diminish the denominator $(1+\varepsilon_E^m - \varepsilon_E^x)$. The denominator will become negative if the sum of the absolute values of ε_E^m and ε_E^x is larger than 1 ($|\varepsilon_E^m| + |\varepsilon_E^x| > 1$). This appears to be a reasonable assumption because it is a restatement of the Marshall-Lerner condition.[9] Hence, if $|\varepsilon_E^m| + |\varepsilon_E^x| > 1$, the effect of the change in technology on the nominal exchange rate depends on the numerator The first term in the numerator, (ε_T^x), which represents the elasticity of exports to changes in technology, is positive. The second term, (ε_T^m), the elasticity of imports to changes in technology, is negative. The last term, (ε_Y^m), the elasticity of imports to domestic output, is positive. For the numerator to become positive, the combined effect of the export and import elasticities to technological change has to exceed the import elasticity to domestic output:

$$\varepsilon_T^x - \varepsilon_T^m > \varepsilon_Y^m \tag{14}$$

If the denominator is negative and the numerator is positive, a change in the domestic technology brings about a decrease in the nominal exchange rate, i.e. a real appreciation, given that prices are fixed in the respective currency. Let us consider the decomposition of the real exchange rate:

---

8 $$\frac{dM}{M} = \frac{\partial M}{\partial Y} \cdot \frac{\partial Y}{\partial T} \cdot \frac{dT}{M} \cdot \frac{T}{T} + \frac{\partial M}{\partial T} \cdot \frac{dT}{M} \cdot \frac{T}{T} + \frac{\partial M}{\partial P*E} \cdot P* \cdot \frac{dE}{M} \cdot \frac{E}{E} \tag{11'}$$

$$\frac{dM}{M} = \frac{\partial M}{\partial Y} \cdot \frac{\partial Y}{\partial T} \cdot \frac{T}{M} \cdot \frac{dT}{T} + \frac{\partial M}{\partial T} \cdot \frac{T}{M} \cdot \frac{dT}{T} + \frac{\partial M}{\partial P*E} \cdot P* \cdot \frac{E}{M} \cdot \frac{dE}{E} \tag{11''}$$

9 Aglietta et al. (1999) and Aglietta et al. (2003) provide empirical evidence in favor of the fact that the Marshall-Lerner condition is verified in the transition countries of Central and Eastern Europe.

$$Q = E\frac{P^T *}{P^T} - ((1-\alpha)\frac{P^{NT}}{P^T} - (1-\alpha *)\frac{P^{NT} *}{P^T *}) \tag{15}$$

where Q and E are the real and nominal exchange rates expressed as domestic currency units to one unit of foreign currency (decrease = appreciation, increase = depreciation), and P^T, P^{NT} and α denote tradable and nontradable prices, and the share of tradable goods in the consumer price index. Thus, the real appreciation (Q decreases) would occur through an appreciation of the real exchange rate of the tradable sector ($E\frac{P^{T*}}{P^T}$) with a decrease in E. Under the equilibrium condition of TB = 0, such an appreciation could be viewed as an equilibrium phenomenon similar to the B-S effect, which also leads to an equilibrium appreciation.

The level of and changes in technology (T and *dt*) can be approximated by the level of and changes. Hence, the testable relationship of our model is as follows:

$$Q = f(\overset{-}{PROD}) \tag{16}$$

where PROD is the productivity in the tradable sector in the home economy relative to that in the foreign economy. The expected sign is negative, implying that an increase (decrease) in the productivity variable causes the real exchange rate to appreciate (depreciate).

3 Some Stylized Facts and the Role of Foreign Capital

The model developed above shows that in addition to productivity-induced market-based service price inflation along the lines of the B-S model, successful catching-up may also entail real appreciation based on an improvement of supply capacities and of the quality of tradable goods. Several transition economies in Central and Eastern Europe have indeed recorded an appreciation of the real exchange rate measured in terms of tradable prices.[10]

According to most models of open economies, an appreciation of the tradable price-deflated real exchange rate is followed by a loss of competitiveness and entails a worsening of the trade balance and thus the current account. Although most of the transition countries have been running large current account deficits, there have been episodes of improvements in the trade balance and the current account in spite of the real appreciation of the exchange rate. Export revenues measured in foreign currency have indeed experienced tremendous growth and have risen nearly as much as imports.

[10] Tradable prices are proxied by the Producer Price Index (PPI). See Égert (2003a) for graphs. It should be noted that whereas the PPI-deflated real exchange rate appreciated steadily in the Czech Republic, Poland and Slovakia, it did not appreciate much in Slovenia and it did so only at a later stage of the transition period in Hungary.

At the beginning of the transition process, the countries produced goods of lower quality and lower technological content, in particular when compared with more developed countries.[11] The liberalization of foreign trade necessitated a substantial nominal and real devaluation of the currencies, because exports broke down after the dissolution of the Council for Mutual Economic Assistance (CMEA) and imports surged due to pent-up demand for foreign goods. Uncertainties surrounding demand for foreign currency coupled with fast trade liberalization led policymakers to prefer a devaluation larger than external imbalances would have required, as argued in Rosati (1996). For instance, the devaluation of the Polish zloty against the U.S. dollar in early 1990 resulted in an exchange rate that was roughly 20% weaker than the then prevailing black market rate (Rosati, 1994).

These devaluations may have led to or may have amplified initial undervaluation, also detected in Halpern and Wyplosz (1997) and Krajnyák and Zettelmeyer (1998) by means of panel estimations. It could therefore be argued that part of the real appreciation over the last ten years or so reflects adjustment towards equilibrium. However, this explanation appears insufficient. If the initial devaluation had been too large, the correction towards the pretransition levels should have occurred within the next few years. Instead, real appreciation in both CPI and PPI terms proved to be a rather steady process. Chart 1 shows the development of the real exchange rate vis-à-vis Germany since 1985. Notwithstanding the fact that prices and exchange rates in the 1980s basically reflected the intentions of the planning authorities, important insights can be gained about the process of real appreciation since the start of the transition.

Real devaluation was the sharpest in the Czech Republic (Czechoslovakia prior to 1993), where market-based information or world market-relative prices played a rather limited role in determining the planned price and exchange rate system, and where the uncertainties as regards the markets' assessment of competitiveness were the highest. Note that the devaluation was the lowest in Hungary, where some market-oriented reforms were introduced from the late 1960s. Furthermore, because price liberalization for items included in the CPI basket started in the mid-1980s, the CPI-deflated real exchange rate started appreciating earlier than the real exchange rate based on PPI.

[11] For recent empirical evidence, see e.g. Dulleck et al. (2003).

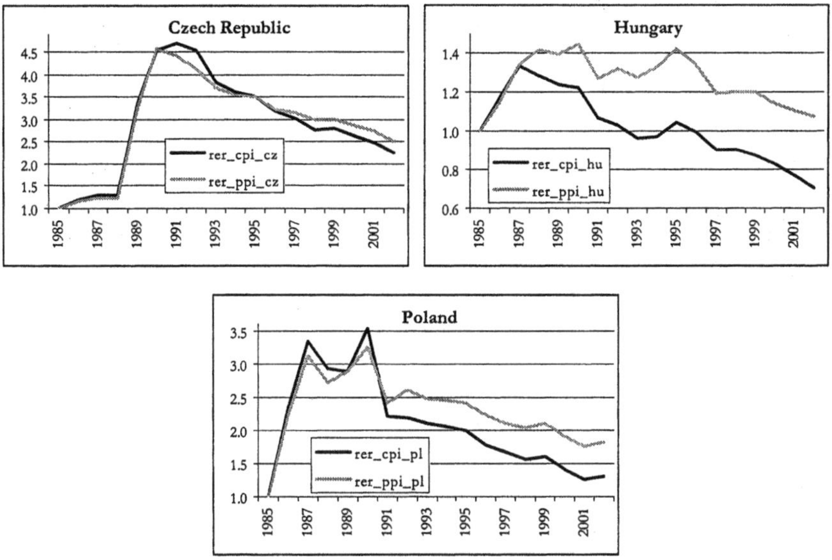

Fig. 1. Real exchange rates vis-à-vis the DEM since the late-1980s (1985=100)

Note: Prior to 1993, the nominal exchange rate used for the Czech Republic is the one that prevailed for Czechoslovakia. A decrease (increase) in the real exchange rate denotes an appreciation (depreciation)

Yearly average figures. Data for Slovakia and Slovenia are not available for the period under consideration.

Source: IMF IFS Statistics, OECD Main Economic Indicators and Czech National Bank.

Therefore, the huge initial devaluation may have been necessary because domestic supply lacked competitiveness in domestic and foreign markets. In all three countries the devaluation proved to be rather lasting possibly because the currencies were strongly overvalued when entering transition from plan to market and thus facing the challenge of market forces.

The real exchange rate may appreciate if domestic supply capacities and product quality increase, i.e. during the transition and catching-up process. The transition from plan to market entails a change in incentive structures and a reallocation of existing resources. And this already improves supply. However, a sustained catching-up process requires investments in human as well as fixed capital, and quality improvements are needed in capital stock, technology, managerial and organizational skills and in infrastructure.

In this regard, foreign capital and in particular foreign direct investment (FDI) can play a very beneficial role. In the transition countries, FDI gave rise to very rapid changes in the composition of GDP and especially of manufactured goods. A marked shift occurred from predominantly low quality, low value added, and labor and raw material intensive goods towards products of increasingly higher quality and higher value added that triggered increased foreign demand for these products. This may have at the same time supported simultaneous economy-wide quality improvement of goods and services, even if changes in the domestically orientated goods and services may have occurred more slowly. Hence, both exported goods and those sold primarily in domestic markets have changed markedly in quality. It should, however, be underlined that exported goods can differ to a large extent from those sold in the domestic market, with regard to both quality and technological content.

Rapid improvement in quality then raised prices, which through the replacement of low-quality goods for high-quality goods in the price basket led to a rise in the price level. In principle, such changes in the price level should not be reflected in inflation rates and thus the real appreciation of the currency. Nevertheless, adjusting inappropriately for quality improvements may result in higher inflation of tradable goods and the subsequent appreciation of the PPI-based real exchange rate.

Prices may also increase and thus the real exchange rate may appreciate when quality improvements go in tandem with a better reputation. The outset of transition was characterized by a strong bias towards imported foreign goods. With an ameliorating quality and better marketing of domestically manufactured goods and with a higher capacity of countries to produce goods of the more preferred foreign brands,[12] the bias towards imported goods may become weaker. In other words, domestic and foreign demand for goods produced domestically increases.

While exported goods enter the trade balance directly and increase export revenues, the higher quality of domestic goods sold in domestic markets reduces the income elasticity of import demand[13] and thus impacts on the trade balance indirectly. In this context, higher prices are an accompanying phenomenon of the growth in non-price competitiveness. Changes in non-price competitiveness of goods produced in the home country and improving supply capacities could indeed reverse the strong initial devaluation and lead to a steady appreciation of the real exchange rate measured in PPI and CPI terms.

Chart 2 below shows that the five selected transition countries have witnessed, over the period from 1995 to 2002, a strong increase in export revenues expressed in Deutsche mark at current prices. More specifically, Hungary and Poland featured the highest increases, whereas export growth proved slowest in Slovenia despite the fact that the real exchange rate appreciated least in this country.[14]

The transition countries' export performance indeed seems to be closely related to privatization strategies and to attitudes towards FDI inflows. Foreign direct investment has had particularly beneficial effects on exports, which became the en-

[12] This means that consumers would buy goods of well-know foreign brands they prefer vis-à-vis the domestic brands. Goods of the well-known foreign brands are produced in the country rather than imported.

[13] At the same income level, import demand will be lower because residents will consume more domestically produced goods instead of imported goods.

[14] Growth in export revenue is also pronounced in 1993 and 1994. However, real appreciation is less marked.

gine of economic growth.[15] FDI helped economic restructuring by financing fixed capital investment and by implementing state-of-the-art technology and Western-style organizational structures and schemes. But most importantly, FDI in manufacturing often aimed at export sectors and hence created new export capacities. Foreign involvement made access to foreign markets easier. However, because countries adopted different strategies towards privatization and capital inflows, the extent to which they benefited from FDI differs strongly. Privatization in Hungary relied heavily on sales to foreign investors whereas in the Czech Republic foreign capital started to pour in on a wider scale only after reforms accelerated in 1997. Political instability in Slovakia prevented direct investment inflows until 1998 and Slovenia hesitated to open up its economy to foreign investment until quite recently.[16]

For this reason, the observed appreciation of the real exchange rate based on tradable prices could reflect improving supply capacities. Changes in supply capacities and thus real appreciation may have been faster in countries where foreign investors contributed more to economic restructuring.

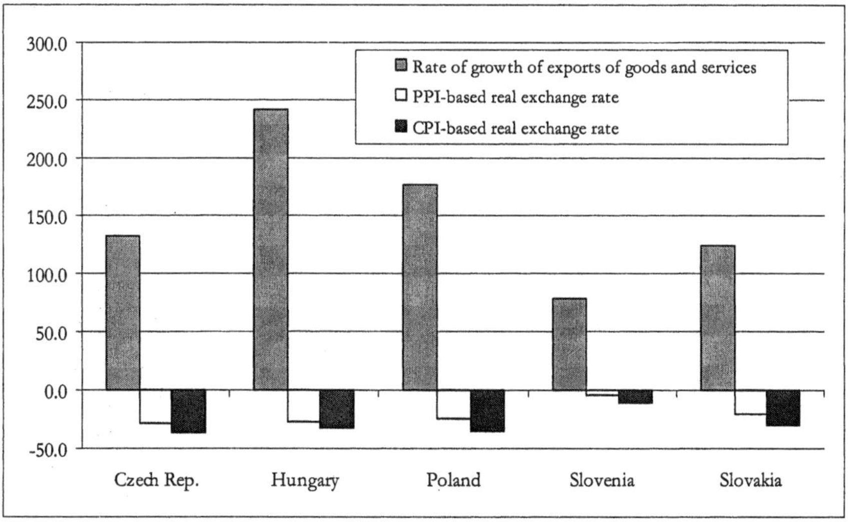

Fig. 2. Real Exchange Rates and Export Revenues, Changes from 1995 to 2002

[15] See e.g. Darvas and Sass (2001), Sgard (2001), Campos and Coricelli (2002) and Benacek et al. (2003).

[16] Note, however, that exports and imports to GDP were much higher in Slovenia at the beginning of the 1990s. This higher basis effect could explain lower export growth.

4 Reduced-Form Equation

Equation (12) shown in section 2 can be completed with variables suggested by standard models.[17] This gives the following reduced-form equation of the real exchange rate:

$$Q = f(\overset{-}{PROD}, \overset{-}{REG}, \overset{-}{RIR}, \overset{+}{FDEBT}, \overset{+}{OPEN}, \overset{+/-}{TOT}, \overset{+/-}{GOV},) \tag{12'}$$

The real exchange rate (Q) is computed both on the basis of the CPI and PPI indexes. A decrease (increase) denotes an appreciation (depreciation) of the real exchange rate

Labor productivity in industry (PROD) is expected to be negatively related to the real exchange rate, i.e. an increase (decrease) in productivity should lead to an appreciation (depreciation) of the real exchange rate. Labor productivity primarily stands for higher supply capacities that can lead to an appreciation through the channel of higher quality and changes in preferences in line with increasing technological content of and thus demand for the domestic good in the domestic and foreign economies. The sector that is likely to benefit the most from technological catching-up and produces most exported goods is industry. However, changes in technology and preferences may not only be limited to domestic tradables, but may span all goods and services in the economy as a whole. In this case, higher supply capacities will be reflected in higher real GDP *(GDP)*. Therefore, real GDP will be used as a fourth proxy for productivity. However, labor productivity in industry also captures the traditional B-S effect that operates through service prices. But, as summarized in Égert (2003), this effect is rather limited due to the small share of nontradables in the acceding countries' CPI basket.

The *differential in regulated prices vis-à-vis Germany (REG)* is also included. In transition economies, regulated prices rose the fastest among the components of the CPI over the last ten years or so. On the one hand, regulated prices constitute a cost-push factor, which may erode competitiveness if it raises the price of traded goods. On the other hand, however, only part of the regulated prices directly affect traded goods costs, so a correction of the real exchange rate may not be needed to maintain external balance. Furthermore, a rise in regulated prices lowers disposable income and should thus reduce imports. In sum, an increase (decline) in regulated prices is expected to bring about an appreciation (depreciation) of the real exchange rate.

The real interest rate differential (RIR) indeed reflects imbalances between investment and savings and is expected to be negatively connected to the real exchange rate, implying that an increase leads to the real appreciation of the currency.

Foreign debt as percentage of GDP (FDEBT) should lead to a depreciation of the real exchange rate due to the higher interest payments to the rest of the world.

Openness (OPEN) is traditionally viewed as an indicator of trade liberalization. Increasing openness indicates a higher degree of trade liberalization. Because it

[17] See e.g. MacDonald (1997) and Clark and MacDonald (1998).

comes through the abolishment of trade barriers and thus allows foreign products to enter the country more freely, an increase in openness is expected to worsen the trade balance. Hence, a rise in openness is expected to yield a depreciation of the real exchange rate. However, openness can also stand for higher exports resulting from increasing supply capacities and can thus be negatively connected with the real exchange rate. Nonetheless, we think that this effect should be captured by the productivity variables. Thus, the expected sign of the openness variables is positive.

The *terms of trade (TOT),* determined as export prices over import prices, do not have an obvious sign. If exports and imports have low price elasticities, like primary or very differentiated goods, an increase in the terms of trade would imply an increase in export revenues and hence an amelioration of the trade balance, which could result in an appreciation of the nominal and thus the real exchange rate. But increasing export revenues would also lead to higher income, and because higher income could imply more consumption of nontradables, a demand side-driven increase in the relative price of nontradables is also likely to make the real exchange rate appreciate. By contrast, in the event that exports are price sensitive, an increase in the terms of trade would not necessarily yield an improved trade balance. As a result, a combination of price elasticities of domestic supply and foreign demand might or might not lead to an increase in trade when export prices increase. So whether an increase in the terms of trade will bring about real appreciation or depreciation remains uncertain.

The expected sign of *government debt to GDP (GOV)* is not clear-cut. If an increase in the public debt is due to increasing public spending on nontradable goods, it is expected to lead to an appreciation of the real exchange rate through the relative price channel. However, if government spending falls more heavily on tradable goods, no appreciation occurs. Moreover, in the event that public debt is on an unsustainable path, the real exchange rate may depreciate mainly because of the depreciation of the nominal exchange rate. The depreciation related to government debt may dominate the appreciation in the long run and if government debt exceeds a given threshold, even in the medium-term.

5 Data and Econometric Issues

5.1 Data

The dataset used in the paper consists of quarterly time series for the Czech Republic, Hungary, Poland, Slovakia and Slovenia. The period spans from 1993:Q1 to 2002:Q4. The dataset also includes Croatia, Estonia, Latvia and Lithuania, which are used for the panel estimations. The period runs from 1995:Q1 to 2002:Q4 for Croatia and from 1994:Q1 to 2002:Q4 for the Baltic countries.

Average labor productivity is computed as labor productivity in the home country relative to labor productivity in Germany. Three measures are used. PROD1 is calculated using industrial production over industrial employment obtained from the Main Economic Indicators of the OECD or the International Financial Statistics of the IMF. PROD2 is based on similar data but drawn from the WIIW. Finally, PROD3 is obtained as value added over sectoral employment in industry obtained from national accounts. Although representing the same series, PROD1 and PROD2 may differ even markedly in some countries. Value added in industry and industrial production based measures turn out to exhibit significantly different developments; however without obvious causes or regularities across the countries. Note also that PROD1 starts only in 1995 for Estonia and no data for PROD2 is available for the Baltic States. Furthermore, real GDP in the domestic and the reference economies is also used as a proxy for productivity.

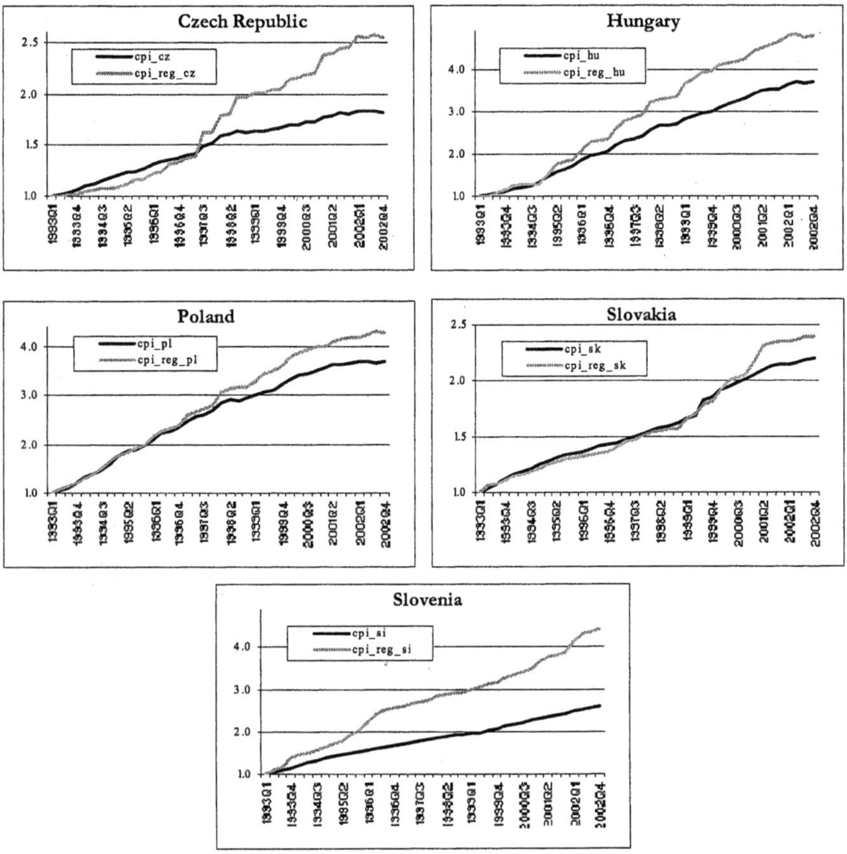

Fig. 3. Consumer price index and its regulated price comp

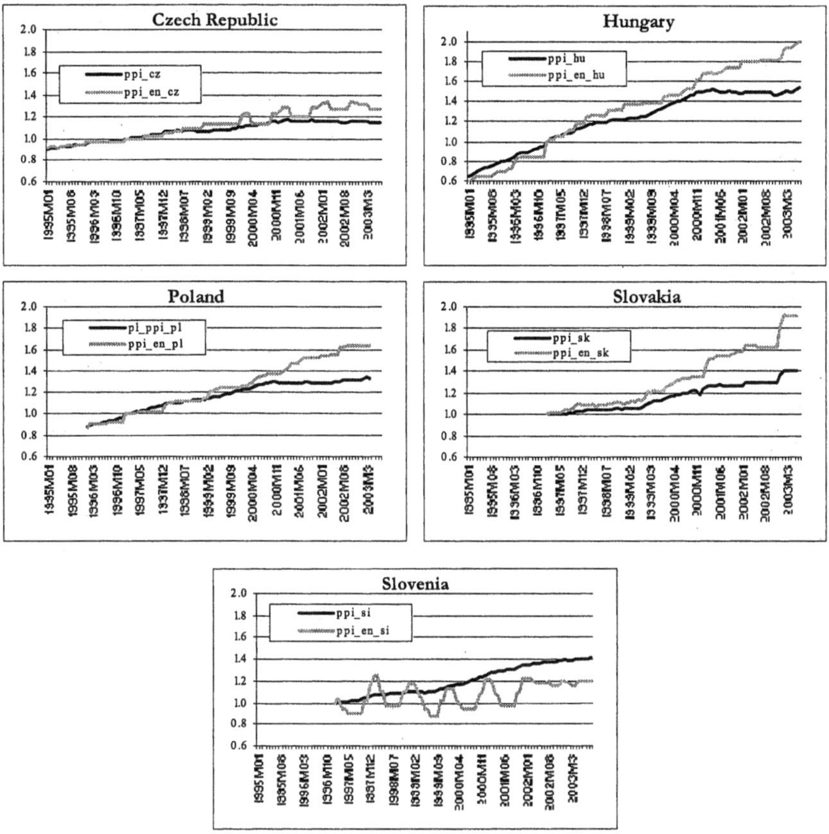

Fig. 4. Producer price index and its regulated price component (1997=100)

Note: ppi_en= PPI of energy and water supply

The *differential of regulated prices* in the home country and those in Germany are mainly based on regulated prices provided by national sources. Thus, series come from the respective national banks for the Czech Republic, Hungary and Poland. Regulated prices for Germany are obtained from the Federal Statistical Office of Germany. The series for Estonia corresponds to that used in Égert (2003b). For the cases of Slovenia, Slovakia, Croatia and Latvia, regulated prices are proxied by rents. In Lithuania, the price series on fuel and electricity serve as a proxy. Regulated prices are expected to impact not only on the CPI-deflated real exchange rate, but also on the real exchange rate based on PPI. The reason for this is that producer price indexes in the countries under investigation contain prices of domestic energy and water suppliers, which are partly regulated. Also, cost pressure related to increased (regulated) input prices are likely to impact on producer prices.

The other variables used in the paper are (a) the *real interest differential* towards Germany computed as the one-year treasury bill yield in period t divided by the CPI or the PPI, both of which are year-on-year figures from year t-1 to year t (b) *gross foreign debt* as a percentage of GDP; (c) *government debt* as a percentage of GDP (calculated as the cumulated government deficit over GDP); (d) *openness* computed as nominal exports and imports of goods and services expressed in terms of nominal GDP; (e) the *terms of trade* obtained as export prices over import prices. Data on terms of trade are available only for the Czech Republic, Hungary and Poland.

The source of these data is NewCronos (Eurostat), Main Economic Indicators (OECD), International Financial Statistics (IMF) and the monthly database of the WIIW. Note that all series are seasonally adjusted if needed. Regulated prices are an exception, because their frequent and perhaps erratic adjustments are not primarily related to seasonal factors. Furthermore, the series are taken in natural logarithms and are normalized to 1994 except for the real interest differential.

5.2 Testing Procedure

It is professional wisdom that a large number of macroeconomic time series are integrated of order 1. This is tested for by employing conventional Augmented Dickey Fuller (ADF) and Phillips-Perron (PP) tests. If the series turn out to be I(1) processes, the appropriate estimation technique to use is the cointegration approach. In this paper, we use four different types of cointegration techniques:

The Engle and Granger (EG) technique, dynamic ordinary least squares (DOLS) popularized by Stock and Watson (1993), the autoregressive distributed lag (ARDL) approach of Pesaran et al. (2001) and the maximum likelihood estimator of Johansen. The EG approach to cointegration is based on the following static equation:

$$Y_t = \beta_0 + \sum_{i=1}^{n} \beta_i X_{i,t} + \varepsilon_t \tag{17}$$

Equation (1) does not account for the endogeneity of the regressors and serial correlation in the residuals. This is corrected for using DOLS that includes leads and lags of the regressors in first differences:

$$Y_t = \beta_0 + \sum_{i=1}^{n} \beta_n X_{i,t} + \sum_{i=1}^{n} \sum_{j=-k_1}^{k_2} \gamma_{i,j} \Delta X_{i,t-j} + \varepsilon_t \tag{18}$$

with k1 and k2 denoting respectively leads and lags. The error correction form of the ARDL model is given in equation (19) where the dependent variable in first differences is regressed on the lagged values of the dependent and independent variables in levels and first differences:

$$\Delta Y_t = \beta_0 + \rho(Y_{t-1} + \sum_{i=1}^{n} \beta_n X_{i,t-1}) + \sum_{j=1}^{l_1} \eta_j \Delta Y_{t-j} + \sum_{i=1}^{n} \sum_{j=0}^{l_2} \gamma_{i,j} \Delta X_{i,t-j} + \varepsilon_t \tag{19}$$

where l1 and l2 are the maximum lags. In the EG and DOLS approaches, whether or not Y and X are cointegrated is examined by testing for unit root in the residuals and applying critical values tabulated in MacKinnon (1996). In contrast to this, Pesaran et al. (2001) employ a bounds testing approach. Using conventional F-tests, the null of $H_0 : \rho = \beta_1 = ... = \beta_n = 0$ is tested against the alternative hypothesis of $H_1 : \rho \neq 0, \beta_1 \neq 0, ..., \beta_n \neq 0$. Pesaran et al. (2001) tabulate two sets of critical values, one for the case when all variables are I(1), i.e. upper bound critical values and another one when all variables are I(0), i.e. lower bound critical values. Critical values are provided for five different models, of which model (3) with unrestricted intercept and no trend will be used in the paper. If the test statistic is higher than the upper bound critical value, the null of no cointegration is rejected in favor of the presence of cointegration. On the other hand, an F-statistic lower than the lower bound critical value implies the absence of cointegration. In the event that the calculated F-statistic lies between the two critical values, there is no clear indication of the absence or existence of a cointegrating relationship.

Nonetheless, in the presence of more than one cointegration relationship, the aforesaid single-equation approaches may not be able to identify the additional cointegrating relationships. Therefore, the Johansen cointegration technique is used for testing for the number of cointegrating vectors in a VAR framework. In the event that only one long-term relationship is found using the trace statistics, the maximum likelihood estimates are used as a robustness check in the following form:

$$Y_t = (m_0 + m_1 t + (1 + \alpha\beta')Y_{t-1}) - \sum_{i=1}^{p-1} \Phi_i \Delta Y_{t-i} + \varepsilon_t \tag{20}$$

where Y represents the vector including the dependent and the independent variables.

We first conduct a general-to-specific model selection strategy that involves top-down and bottom-up F presearch coupled with a sample split analysis so as to identify blocks of statistically significant variables.[18] Departing from all variables described in section 4, the general-to-specific approach to model selection is performed. The residuals of the models chosen are subsequently checked for stationarity in line with the EG approach, and the selected models are taken as an input

[18] In the top-down procedure, F-tests are carried out on blocks of regressors, which are organized in an increasing order in terms of their t^2-values until the null hypothesis is rejected. In the bottom-up procedure, F-tests are performed for regressors put in a decreasing order in terms of their t^2-values until the null is not rejected. The sample-split analysis analyzes the significance of the variables in two subsamples. The model is considered robust if significance is also conserved in the two subsamples. This model selection was conducted using PcGets.

for the estimation of the DOLS and ARDL. Leads and lags are determined on the basis of the Schwarz, Akaike and Hannan-Quinn information criteria.

The VAR-based Johansen approach is used to verify the number of cointegration relationship that might link the variables. The detection of a single long-term relationship that turns out to be stable over time then validates results of the single-equation methods. The Johansen technique involves the verification of the roots of the VAR model (to ensure stationarity of the AR processes), tests for normality and serial correlation. Furthermore, both the rank of cointegration and parameter constancy are analyzed.

Beside time series techniques, panel techniques are applied to the panel composed of up to nine countries. Analogously to the time series analysis, stationarity is tested for by means of the panel unit root test proposed by Im et al. (2003) (IPS henceforth). The t-bar statistic is constructed as a mean of individual ADF statistics to test the null hypothesis of a unit root.

Subsequently, panel cointegration tests are employed to detect long-term relationships and to estimate the corresponding coefficients. For this purpose, the residual-based tests of the Engle and Granger type developed in Pedroni (1999) are used. Pedroni (1999) develops seven tests, of which the first four statistics are based on pooling along within-dimension whereas the last three tests rest on pooling along between-dimension. Only the last three tests (group rho-statistic, group pp-statistic, group ADF-statistic) will be employed because they allow for heterogeneity in the autoregressive term. According to Pedroni (1999), of the seven tests, the group ADF-statistic is the most powerful for small samples. Coefficients of the cointegrating vector are then determined using pooled OLS, fixed effect OLS, fixed effect DOLS, the Pooled Mean Group Estimator (PMGE) and the Mean Group Estimator (MGE) proposed by Pesaran et al. (1999). For DOLS, leads and lags are determined on the basis of the Schwarz and Akaike information criterion, and a lag structure of 1 is imposed alternatively (DOLS[1,1]). The same applies to the choice of the lag structure of PMGE and MGE (PMGE[1,1] and MGE[1,1]). [19]

6 Results

6.1 Time Series

Because conventional unit root tests, i.e. ADF and PP (Philips-Perron) tests, indicate that most of the series are not stationary in levels but turn out to be stationary in first differences, the cointegration techniques developed earlier appear to be the most appropriate approach to test for long-term relationships connecting the real exchange rate to the underlying fundamentals.

[19] For a discussion of panel unit root and cointegration tests and the estimation methods, see e.g. Banerjee (1999) and Baltagi and Kao (2000). For recent applications, see e.g. Crespo-Cuaresma et al. (2003) and Maeso-Fernandez et al. (2003).

We set out to test two sets of equations. First, the CPI-based real exchange is regressed on the gamut of variables described earlier. In this case, the productivity variable is likely to impact on the real exchange rate through three different channels: (a) the traditional B-S effect, (b) the indirect B-S effect through an increase in the service prices as inputs, and (c) tradable prices because of improved quality and reputation. Second, the PPI-deflated real exchange rate is regressed on the same set of variables. If labor productivity proves to be important in both relationships, the indirect B-S effect, and most importantly, the increase in tradable prices brought about by productivity changes, make the real exchange rate appreciate systematically. The theoretical framework developed earlier is supported if the two sets of equations yield similar results for labor productivity.

Employing the EG, DOLS, ARDL and Johansen cointegration techniques, estimations are performed for the period 1994–2002 for the Czech Republic, Hungary and Poland and for 1993–2002 for Slovakia and Slovenia.

6.1.1 The Czech Republic

Results obtained for time series are reported in tables 1 to 5. With regard to the Czech Republic, the specification including the difference in labor productivity, the differential in regulated prices and foreign debt is retained as the most reliable and economically the most compelling. This specification appears remarkably robust, given that all methods detect the presence of a cointegrating vector linking the aforementioned variables. It should be noted that although the Johansen trace statistic indicates the presence of two cointegrating vectors, the stability test on the number of cointegrating vectors shows only one stable vector. Moreover, all these variables are found to be statistically significant, have the expected sign, and the size of the estimated coefficients based on different techniques is fairly comparable. These observations apply not only to the equations including the CPI-based real exchange rate but also to those in which the PPI-deflated real exchange rate is used.

The fact that the estimated coefficients for the difference in productivity are very similar for the CPI- and PPI-based real exchange rate equations provides strong empirical support to the theoretical framework according to which real appreciation comes mainly through tradable prices. The coefficients tend to be lower for the PPI-based real exchange rate especially when the EG and ARDL techniques are employed. This may indicate that the CPI-based real exchange rate appreciates more than the PPI-based real exchange rate due to changes in the relative price of market nontradable items.

The differential in regulated prices enters both the CPI- and PPI-based specifications, and an increase in the differential results in an appreciation of the corresponding real exchange rates. Nonetheless, when the CPI-based real exchange rate is used, the estimated coefficients are clearly higher than in the case of the PPI-deflated real exchange rate. This may indicate that the difference between the CPI- and PPI-based real exchange rates may be partly explained by the differential in regulated prices.

As regards foreign debt, a rise (fall) induces a depreciation (appreciation) of the real exchange rate, and the estimated coefficients are rather similar for the CPI- and the PPI-based equations.

Table 1a. Cointegration tests for the CPI-based real exchange rate, Czech Republic, 1994-2002

	EG		DOLS				ARDL(1,1)		JOH.		
			SIC,HQ(0,1)		AIC(1,1)		SIC,AIC,HQ		M3,k=3		
SIC	1	-5.199**	3	-5.528**	3	-5.339**	6.84**		R=0	73.04***	RS ok
AIC	1	-5.199**	3	-5.528**	3	-5.339**			R=1	32.23***	AC ok
HQ	1	-5.199**	3	-5.528**	3	-5.339**			R=2	8.99	JB 0.016
									R=3	0.01	ST 1
	Coeff	t-stat	Coeff	t-stat	coeff	t-stat	Coeff	t-stat	coeff	t-stat	
PROD2	-0.701	-5.51	-0.948	-7.198	-1.021	-6.568	-0.793	-4.108	-0.649	-16.641	
REGD	-0.362	-6.713	-0.361	-3.674	-0.379	-2.667	-0.471	-3.066	-0.457	-32.643	
FDEBT	0.190	4.089	0.292	4.043	0.308	3.063	0.326	3.514	0.278	18.533	

Note: *,** and *** denote respectively the presence of cointegration at the 10%, 5% and 1% levels, respectively. EG represent the Engle and Granger residual based tests. SIC, AIC and HQ in the first column of the Table stand for the Schwarz, Akaike and the Hannan-Quinn information criteria based on which the lag length is selected for the ADF tests applied to the residuals of the EG and DOLS equations. The lag length is chosen so that it minimizes the information criteria. It is shown in the first column of each method (column 2 for EG, column 4 for DOLS etc.). Below DOLS and ARDL are shown the information criteria based on which leads and lags (DOLS) and lags for dY and dX (ARDL) are chosen (shown in parentheses). The test statistic shown below ARDL is the F-stat as in Pesaran et al. (2001). JOH represents the Johansen cointegration technique. k stands for the lag length chosen for the VAR. The trace-test statistics are given below. In the last column, RS and AC are roots of the model and autocorrelation. "ok" indicates that the inverse roots of the model are lower than 1 and the absence of serial correlation in the residuals. JB stands for the Jarque-Bera multivariate normality tests. A figure higher than 0.05 indicates that normality is accepted. Finally, ST indicates the number of cointegration relationship(s) that turn out to be stable over time.

Table 1b. Cointegration tests for the PPI-based real exchange rate, Czech Republic, 1994-2002

	EG		DOLS(1,1)		ARDL(1,1)		JOH.		
			SIC,AIC,HQ		SIC,AIC,HQ		M3,k=3		
SIC	1	-5.122**	4	-5.604**	6.163**		R=0	84.06***	RS ok
AIC	1	-5.122**	4	-5.604**			R=1	39.56***	AC ok
HQ	1	-5.122**	4	-5.604**			R=2	9.23	JB 0..012
							R=3	0.06	ST 1
	Coeff	t-stat	coeff	t-stat	coeff	t-stat	Coeff	t-stat	
PROD2	-0.632	-5.155	-0.974	-6.791	-0.716	-3.927	-0.699	-19.971	
REGD	-0.220	-4.227	-0.210	-1.596	-0.317	-2.334	-0.359	-25.643	
FDEBT	0.189	4.236	0.259	2.793	0.293	3.145	0.278	19.857	

Note: As for Table 1a.

6.1.2 Hungary

The results for Hungary are reported in tables 2a and 2b. They are less robust when compared with those of the Czech Republic in that the cointegration tests reach no clear consensus on whether or not the variables are linked through a long-term cointegration relationship. In particular, the EG and on some occasions the ARDL technique could not detect the presence of cointegration. However, the DOLS, the Johansen and in some cases the ARDL techniques reveal that both the CPI- and the PPI-deflated real exchange rates are connected to the difference in labor productivity, foreign debt and openness.

The coefficients are statistically significant and correctly signed. Thus, an increase (decrease) in labor productivity leads to an appreciation (depreciation) of both the CPI- and the PPI-based real exchange rate. This confirms indeed our conjecture stipulating the role of tradable prices in the appreciation of the real exchange rate. The estimated coefficients for the CPI-based specification are, in most cases, larger than those found for the PPI-deflated real exchange rate. This shows that the higher appreciation of the CPI-deflated real exchange rates may be a result of a rise in the price of market nontradables, i.e. the B-S effect.

The differential in regulated prices does not enter the equation. Because of possible multicollinearity between labor productivity and the differential in regulated prices, the coefficient may also capture the impact of regulated prices on the PPI- and CPI-based real exchange rates.

Foreign debt and the openness ratio work in the opposite direction, as they are positively related to both the CPI and PPI-based real exchange rates. Hence, an increase in these variables yields a depreciation of the real exchange rate.

Table 2a. Cointegration test for the CPI-based real exchange rate in Hungary, 1994-2002

	EG		DOLS				ARDL(1,2)		JOH		
			SIC(1,3)		AIC,HQ(2,3)		ARDL_SIC		M3,k=3		
SIC	0	-2.136	1	-4.848**	1	-6.825**	3.466[a]		R=0	74.14***	RS no
AIC	0	-2.136	4	-4.834**	4	-4.69**			R=1	20.46	AC ok
HQ	0	-2.136	4	-4.834**	4	-4.69**			R=2	7.77	JB 0.002
									R=3	1.18	ST 1
	Coeff	t-stat	Coeff	t-stat	coeff	t-stat	Coeff	t-stat	Coeff	t-stat	
PROD3			-2.344	-12.02	-2.489	-7.493	-2.099	-3.164	-2.099	-22.570	
FDEBT			0.811	9.482	0.908	6.795	0.622	2.551	0.730	19.211	
OPEN			0.590	6.855	0.633	4.052	0.434	2.346	0.511	13.447	

Note: As for Table 1a., (a) means that the ARDL test statistics cannot decide whether there is cointegration at the 10% significance level

Table 2b. Cointegration test for the PPI-based real exchange rate in Hungary, 1994-2002

	EG		DOLS				ARDL			JOH		
			SIC,HQ(2,3)		AIC(3,3)		SIC(1,0)	AIC,HQ(1,1)		M3,k=3		
SIC	0	-2.747	1	-5.936**	1	-8.101**	2.109	4.032*		R=0	45.09*	RS no
AIC	0	-2.747	1	-5.936**	3	-5.068**				R=1	20.24	AC ok
HQ	0	-2.747	1	-5.936**	3	-5.068**				R=2	8.16	JB 0.110
										R=3	3.58	ST 1?
	Coeff	t-stat	Coeff	t-stat	Coeff	t-stat		Coeff	t-stat	coeff	t-stat	
PROD3			-1.967	-5.821	-2.951	-2.735		-0.902	-2.077	-1.098	-7.572	
FDEBT			0.958	7.041	1.319	3.636		0.401	1.677	0.549	9.305	
OPEN			0.486	3.059	0.927	1.916		0.004	0.029	0.056	1.000	

Note: As for Table 1a.

6.1.3 Poland

As far as Poland is concerned, the long-term relationships include labor productivity, government debt, openness and the real interest differential. Cointegration is found with all methods except for the EG technique when applied to the CPI-based real exchange rate. Productivity is found to impact on both the CPI- and PPI-based real exchange rates. This supports our conjecture. The reason for the large differences in the size of the estimated coefficients in the case of the CPI- and the PPI-based equations are likely to be very similar to what we observed for Hungary, i.e. the influence of the B-S effect and regulated prices. The negative sign of the real interest differential shows that a rise (fall) in this variable results in the appreciation (depreciation) of the real exchange rate. This finding is in sharp contrast with the cases of the Czech Republic and Hungary, where the real interest differential is not found to enter the long-term relationship significantly. As shown in table 3, openness leads to a depreciation of the real exchange rate. A rise in government debt is found to cause a depreciation of the real exchange rate. However, in the PPI-based specification, it becomes significant only when the Johansen technique is employed.

Table 3a. Cointegration tests for the CPI-based real exchange rate in Poland, 1994-2002

	EG		DOLS(0,0)		DOLS(1,0)		ARDL(1,0)		JOH.		
			SIC,HQ		AIC		SIC,AIC,HQ		M3,k=2		
SIC	0	-4.057	0	-5.311**	2	-5.825**	6.144**		R=0	73.66**	RS no
AIC	3	-3.88	0	-5.311**	2	-5.825**			R=1	36.67	AC ok
HQ	0	-4.057	0	-5.311**	2	-5.825**			R=2	18.52	JB 0.102
									R=3	6.58	ST 1
									R=4	1.08	
	Coeff	t-stat	Coeff	t-stat	Coeff	t-stat	coeff	t-stat	Coeff	t-stat	
PROD1			-1.249	-9.958	-1.08	-7.966	-1.614	-5.281	-1.060	-12.990	
GOV			1.879	3.682	1.416	2.340	3.548	3.543	1.785	5.235	
OPEN			0.341	3.026	0.350	2.938	0.474	2.460	0.411	5.630	
INTCPI			-0.011	-5.063	-0.013	-5.680	-0.010	-2.222	-0.016	-12.308	

Note: As for Table 1a.

Table 3b. Cointegration tests for the PPI-based real exchange rate in Poland, 1993-2002

	EG		DOLS(0,0)		DOLS(0,1)		ARDL(1,1)		JOH.		
			SIC		AIC,HQ		SIC,AIC,HQ		M3,k=2		
SIC	0	-6.283**	2	-6.401**	2	-6.569**	7.935**		R=0	85.55**	RS no
AIC	0	-6.283**	2	-6.401**	2	-6.569**			R=1	39.85	AC ok
HQ	0	-6.283**	2	-6.401**	2	-6.569**			R=2	12.57	JB 0.296
									R=3	4.72	ST 1
									R=4	0.03	
	Coeff	t-stat	Coeff	t-stat	Coeff	t-stat	Coeff	t-stat	coeff	t-stat	
PROD1	-0.433	-4.054	-0.521	-5.067	-0.581	-5.069	-0.497	-4.753	-0.548	-6.683	
GOV	-0.568	-1.337	-0.156	-0.347	0.452	0.852	-0.047	-0.122	0.220	6.377	
OPEN	0.170	2.302	0.187	2.768	0.229	3.130	0.182	3.559	0.153	2.732	
INTCPI	-0.009	-6.450	-0.009	-6.82	-0.010	-7.048	-0.009	-5.23	-0.007	-5.833	

Note: As for Table 1a.

6.1.4 Slovakia

For Slovakia, it turned out to be highly complicated to find a relationship based on the reduced-form equation (13) that could be considered reasonable on economic and econometric grounds. Only real GDP, government debt and regulated prices enter the long-term relationship. It seems that government debt and GDP reflect similar developments: Until 1998, the reform process was rather sluggish in Slovakia, and public expenditures increased much faster than GDP.[20] The expansionary fiscal policy then became unsustainable; and the Slovak koruna had to be floated in 1998. After a period of turbulence in which the real exchange rate depreciated and government spending and GDP also decelerated, a more coherent reform strategy including the attraction of large FDI was implemented. This marked the return to higher growth and higher government spending. Therefore, the only relationship which appears to be stable over the whole period studied is the one including government spending to GDP and regulated prices.

Table 4a. Cointegration tests for the CPI-based real exchange rate in Slovakia, 1993-2002

	EG		DOLS(0,0)		ARDL(2,0)		Johansen	
			SIC,AIC,HQ		SIC,AIC,HQ		M3,k=1	
SIC	1	-3.710*	2	-3.851*	5.686**		R=0	10.67
AIC	2	-3.718*	2	-3.851*			R=1	2.54
HQ	1	-3.710*	2	-3.851*			R=2	0.03
	Coeff	t-stat	coeff	t-stat	coeff	t-stat		
GDP	-0.602	-5.58	-0.61	-5.361	-0.655	-2.863		
REGD	-0.343	-5.571	-0.346	-5.389	-0.333	-3.247		

Note: As for Table 1a.

[20] Real public consumption expenditure measured as in the national accounts increased by 50% between 1993–1997, compared with 25% growth of real GDP. See Beblavy (2002) for more details on Slovakia's exchange rate policy.

Table 4b. Cointegration tests for the CPI-based real exchange rate in Slovakia, 1993-2002

	EG		DOLS(0,0)		ARDL(2,0)		Johansen	
					SIC,AIC,HQ		M3,k=1	
SIC	2	-4.113**	2	-4.014**	4.654*		R=0	14.91
AIC	2	-4.113**	2	-4.014**			R=1	5.59
HQ	2	-4.113**	2	-4.014**			R=2	0.19
	Coeff	t-stat	Coeff	t-stat	coeff	t-stat		
REGD	-0.31	-3.922	-0.318	-3.78	-0.303	-2.512		
GOV	-1.305	-4.667	-1.284	-4.307	-1.312	-2.255		

Note: As for Table 1a.

6.1.5 Slovenia

In Slovenia, one relationship can be detected which connects the real exchange rate to the real interest differential and regulated prices. As expected, an increase (decrease) in regulated prices is found to bring about an appreciation (depreciation). However, the sign of the real interest differential does not correspond to our expectation, as an increase leads to a depreciation of the real exchange rate.

Table 5. Cointegration tests for the CPI-based real exchange rate in Slovenia, 1993-2002

	EG		DOLS(2,3)		ARDL(2,3)		Johansen	
			SIC,AIC,HQ		SIC,AIC,HQ		M3,k=2	
SIC	0	-5.041***	1	-6.695***	10.127**		R=0	63.26***
AIC	1	-4.092***	1	-6.695***			R=1	21.41***
HQ	0	-5.041***	1	-6.695***			R=2	6.18***
	Coeff	t-stat	Coeff	t-stat	Coeff	t-stat		
CONST	-0.107	-12.28	-0.144	-9.02	-0.111	-1.812	RS	Ok
REGD	-0.158	-16.225	-0.131	-8.946	-0.16	-3.281	AC	Ok
INTCPI	0.004	6.683	0.005	5.48	0.001	0.474	JB	0.504

Note: As for Table 1a.

This finding can be explained to a large extent by monetary and exchange rate policies in Slovenia (Caprirolo and Lavrac, 2003), which has aimed at a balanced current account and a corresponding real exchange rate position.

It should be noted that for Slovenia, much as for Slovakia, no meaningful relationship could be determined for the PPI-based real exchange rate. This suggests that contrary to the other countries, mainly to the Czech Republic, Hungary and Poland, the moderate appreciation could be largely attributed to factors other than productivity catching-up. It is worth mentioning that Slovenia has – deliberately – attracted the least FDI in terms of GDP during the period from 1993 to 2002.

6.2 Panels

The panel investigation is carried out on different panels to check for robustness of the results. First, the panel cointegration tests are performed on a panel composed of the five countries (panel 5) dealt with above, and this for the periods 1993 to 2002, 1994 to 2002 and 1995 to 2002. Subsequently, the three Baltic countries, Estonia, Latvia and Lithuania, are added to the panel (panel 8), for which econometric tests are performed for the periods running from 1994 to 2002, 1995 to 2002 and 1996 to 2002. Finally, the panel is enlarged to nine members with the inclusion of Croatia (panel 9) and is investigated for the periods 1995 to 2002, 1996 to 2002 and 1997 to 2002.

Seven specifications are estimated for each panel and for each time period. They are based upon the results of the time series analysis and are thus combinations of the variables found to be significant in the time series tests (see table 6). Note that each specification is estimated using the different productivity measures alternatively (PROD1, PROD2, PROD3, GDP), and for the CPI- and the PPI-based real exchange rate. For panels including eight and nine countries, only PROD1 and PROD3 are used because of the lack of data. As discussed in section 5.2, 11 different econometric specifications are estimated,[21] which leaves us with a total of 3,696 estimated equations.[22]

Table 6. Estimated Panel Specifications

	Y	X1	X2	X3	X4	X5
Eq1 :	RERCPI	PROD1/PROD2/PROD3/GDP	INTCPI	REGDIFF	FDEBT	OPEN
Eq2 :	RERCPI	PROD1/PROD2/PROD3/GDP	INTCPI	REGDIFF	FDEBT	GOV
Eq3 :	RERCPI	PROD1/PROD2/PROD3/GDP	INTCPI	REGDIFF	OPEN	GOV
Eq4 :	RERCPI	PROD1/PROD2/PROD3/GDP	INTCPI	FDEBT		
Eq5 :	RERCPI	PROD1/PROD2/PROD3/GDP	INTCPI	REGDIFF	FDEBT	
Eq6 :	RERCPI	PROD1/PROD2/PROD3/GDP	INTCPI	REGDIFF	GOV	
Eq7 :	RERCPI	PROD1/PROD2/PROD3/GDP	INTCPI	REGDIFF	OPEN	

After running the equations, Pedroni cointegration tests are applied to the residuals of the long-term relationship. In a score of cases, the cointegration tests find strong evidence for long-run relationships for specifications based on the CPI-based real exchange rate for all three panels. The productivity measures,

[21] Pooled OLS, fixed effect OLS and DOLS, PMGE and MGE based on three alternative lag structures.

[22] For each panel, 462 equations are estimated (3[periods] *2[CPI,PPI specification] *7[equations as in table 10] *11[econometric specifications: pooled OLS, fixed effect OLS, DOLS [AIC, SIC, HQ], PMGE [AIC, SIC, HQ] MGE [AIC, SIC, HQ]). For panel 5, four alternative measures for productivity are used whereas for panels 8 and 9, only two are used (462*[4+2+2]).

whether they be PROD1, PROD2, PROD3 or GDP, are always negatively related to the real exchange rate, i.e. an increase in productivity leads to a real appreciation based on the CPI index. And this holds true regardless of the time period, the number of countries included and the specification of the estimated equation.

Selected results based on panel DOLS estimates are shown in table 7 for panel 5. These reveal that the estimated coefficient for labor productivity is statistically significant and has the expected sign, irrespective of whether the CPI- or the PPI-based real exchange rate is employed. This strongly supports the view that for panel 5 the appreciation of the real exchange rate is to a large extent due to changes in tradable prices induced by productivity increases. The size of the coefficient seems to be systematically higher for the CPI-based real exchange rate when compared with that obtained for the PPI-based real exchange rate. Thus, productivity-induced service price inflation also contributes to real appreciation to some extent.

Table 7. Selected Panel Estimates for Panel 5, DOLS

	PROD	RIR	REG	FDEBT	OPEN	GOV	Cointegration test (p-value)		
Equation 3							P5	P6	P7
CPI, 1993-2002, PROD2	-0.60	-0.004	-0.07		0.13	-1.27	0.000	0.075	0.296
(1,1)	(-6.14)	(-4.73)	(-2.02)		(2.35)	(-7.64)			
PPI, 1993-2002, PROD2	-0.38	-0.003	-0.06		0.08	-0.65	0.001	0.012	0.025
(1,1)	(-4.78)	(-4.54)	(-2.08)		(1.82)	(-4.49)			
Equation 5									
CPI, 1993-2002, PROD 3	-0.47	-0.001	-0.17	0.23			0.000	0.000	0.001
(1,1)	(-4.00)	(-2.29)	(-4.13)	(3.40)					
PPI, 1993-2002, PROD3	-0.22	-0.002	-0.11	0.20			0.001	0.000	0.000
(1,1)	(-4.02)	(-2.70)	(-2.90)	(3.18)					
Equation 6									
CPI, 1995-2002, PROD1	-0.31	-0.004	-0.13			-1.38	0.001	0.040	0.091
(0,0)	(-3.58)	(-3.61)	(-3.48)			(-6.76)			
PPI, 1995-2002, PROD1	-0.17	-0.004	-0.13			-0.62	0.001	0.003	0.013

Note: PROD1 and PROD2 stand for labour productivity in industry measured by industrial production, PROD3 uses value added from national accounts. Leads and lags are shown in parentheses in column 1. Figures in columns 2-6 are estimated coefficients of the denoted variables in the tested relationship. T-stats are in parentheses below the estimated coefficients. p5, p6 and p7 denote respectively the Group rho-Statistics, the Group PP-Statistics (non-parametric) and the Group ADF-Statistics (parametric) proposed by Pedroni (1999)

Generally speaking and based on the whole set of estimations, similarly to labor productivity, regulated prices are also found to contribute to the real appreciation in all tested relationships. Moreover, an increase in openness most often leads to a real depreciation. The sign of foreign debt and government debt differs across specifications and applied methods. When foreign debt leads to a real appreciation, we do not consider this to be an equilibrium phenomenon. Rather, in the chosen time period the inflow of capital might have caused upward pressure on the exchange rate; and its negative impact on the exchange rate due to debt servicing will materialize only at a later point.

6.3 Real Misalignments

On the basis of the estimated time series and panel equations, the second step of the analysis consists in determining the estimated equilibrium real exchange rate. This is done using three sets of values of the fundamentals: (a) actual values, (b) long-term values obtained by means of the Hodrick-Prescott filter with the smoothing parameter set at the standard 1600 and (c) those computed by means of a smoothing parameter of 100. The latter distinction is done to see to what extent radically different smoothing parameters can affect the fitted value. Having done this, in a next step the total real misalignment is computed as the difference between the estimated equilibrium and the observed real exchange rates. First, in a rather "benign neglect" way, the fitted values and the derived real misalignments are taken as such. Nonetheless, given that some of the series used in the estimations are indexes, the question of the basis or reference year is to be addressed. Indeed, one needs to determine a year over the period under investigation during which the real exchange rate can be viewed as fairly valued. Judging from the external position of the countries, 1993 is taken as the reference year for the Czech Republic and Slovenia, whereas 1994 is chosen for Poland and Slovakia. For Hungary, two years, namely 1992 and 1997, are picked out. This enables us to check for the sensitivity of the base year assumption.

For the time series case, real misalignments could be determined only for the Czech Republic, Hungary and Poland because no useful specification was found for Slovakia and Slovenia. First, actual real misalignment is derived for the CPI-based real exchange rate on the basis of different econometric specifications as presented in section 6.1. Then, total real misalignment is computed by the substitution of long-term values of the fundamentals that are calculated by means of two different HP filters. The results are reported in tables 8a to 8c.

In the Czech Republic, actual real misalignment is very close to total real misalignment; both indicate an overvaluation of the real exchange rate by up to 12% in the last quarter of 2002. Results derived based on the reference year 1993 show a higher overvaluation than when no reference year is used. But more strikingly, substantial differences exist for the same specification estimated on the basis of alternative econometric techniques. For instance, when the base year is set to 1993 and an HP filter with a smoothing parameter of 1600 (line 6, table 8a) is used, a difference of 6 percentage points can be observed between the lower end, i.e. 4.01% (DOLS with leads and lags being chosen with the Akaike information criterion), and the higher end, i.e. 10.29% (obtained using the EG approach). Even more astonishing is the fact that using DOLS with a different structure of leads and lags yields two real misalignment figures, the difference between which is as high as over 3 percentage points. This is something that can also be observed for Hungary and Poland.

In Hungary, actual real misalignment ranges from –10% to +10%. Nevertheless, what we are really interested in is total real misalignment. Although apparently sensitive to the choice of the reference year, total real misalignment figures clearly indicate an overvaluation of the Hungarian currency in the fourth quarter of 2002.

Table 8a. Real Misalignments Based on Time Series in the Fourth Quarter of 2002, Czech Republic

BASE YEAR		EG	DOLS_SIC	DOLS_AIC	ARDL	Johansen
		Actual real misalignment				
None	ORIGINAL	7.81%	4.43%	3.61%	4.41%	5.16%
1993	ORIGINAL	12.94%	8.78%	5.76%	7.44%	11.17%
		Total real misalignment				
None	HP1600	6.03%	2.68%	0.00%	1.17%	4.28%
None	HP100	7.49%	3.73%	1.11%	2.10%	5.29%
1993	HP1600	10.29%	7.16%	4.01%	4.90%	8.51%
1993	HP100	11.35%	7.13%	3.92%	5.61%	9.63%

Table 8b. Real Misalignments Based on Time Series in the Fourth Quarter of 2002, Hungary

BASE YEAR		DOLS_SIC	DOLS_AIC	ARDL	Johansen
		Actual real misalignment			
None	ORIGINAL	-9.24%	-11.43%	-6.03%	-1.58%
1997	ORIGINAL	-0.01%	-1.77%	2.26%	2.65%
1992	ORIGINAL	7.54%	5.49%	7.87%	10.45%
		Total real misalignment			
None	HP1600	7.94%	6.23%	5.94%	10.64%
None	HP100	4.27%	2.10%	4.38%	7.47%
1997	HP1600	5.53%	3.82%	6.01%	7.66%
1997	HP100	2.52%	0.57%	4.57%	5.09%
1992	HP1600	19.33%	17.90%	16.22%	20.82%
1992	HP100	17.70%	16.04%	16.25%	19.51%

In Poland, the real exchange rate was overvalued according to figures shown in table 8c. The results appear relatively insensitive to the choice of the base year.

To sum up the extent of a possible overvaluation of the currencies, table 8d provides some descriptive statistics for the fourth quarter of 2002, namely the means, confidence intervals, mean ± confidence intervals, and Jarque-Bera normality tests for total real misalignment. The use of confidence intervals makes sense only if the sample follows normal distribution. The mean of the overvaluation is between 4% to 7% in the Czech Republic, amounts to 7% to 12% in Hungary and ranges from about 12% to 15% in Poland.

Table 8c. Real Misalignments Based on Time Series in the Fourth Quarter of 2002, Poland

BASE YEAR		DOLS_SIC	DOLS_AIC	ARDL	Johansen
		Actual real misalignment			
None	ORIGINAL	10.82%	13.43%	17.31%	4.83%
1994	ORIGINAL	18.47%	22.29%	25.91%	12.44%
		Total real misalignment			
None	HP1600	8.77%	13.86%	10.82%	9.71%
None	HP100	12.65%	16.97%	17.94%	9.93%
1994	HP1600	10.72%	15.84%	12.49%	11.24%
1994	HP100	14.81%	19.25%	19.91%	11.67%

Table 8d. Summary of Real Misalignments in the Fourth Quarter of 2002

	Czech Republic	Hungary	Poland
No. Obs	20	24	16
Mean	5.32%	9.52%	13.54%
Confidence interval (CI)	1.39%	2.60%	1.73%
Mean-CI	3.93%	6.92%	11.80%
Mean+CI	6.70%	12.12%	15.27%
Jarque-Bera (p-value)	0.727	0.264	0.510

A similar exercise is conducted for the panel setting. At the point of departure, we have nearly 2000 estimated equations for the CPI-based real exchange rate, which are based on (1) the specifications of table 8, (2) the alternative productivity measures, (3) different panel estimation techniques, (4) the three panels, i.e. panel 5, panel 8 and panel 9, and (5) different time periods for each panel (see footnote 23). Of these nearly 2000 equations, those that fulfilled the following two criteria: (1) the panel cointegration tests reject the null of the absence of cointegration, and (2) all coefficients are statistically significant were chosen. Of the nearly 2000 equations estimated, only a fraction appears to meet these selection criteria. We made sure that equations from panel 5, panel 8 and panel 9 are represented equally in the sample, leaving us approximately 80 equations. We used the selected equations to compute the actual and total real misalignments for the five acceding countries.

The observed series and the long-term values obtained by means of the two HP filters are substituted into the estimated equation. For each country, the simply fitted values and the reference year is used. As a result, six sets of real misalignments, each composed of roughly 80 observations, are derived for each country. Given the use of two different reference years, nine samples are derived for Hungary. Note that if an increase in foreign debt is found to cause an appreciation of the real exchange rate, foreign debt is not considered for the derivation of the real misalignment any longer (its coefficient is set to 0). The real interest differential is not considered when deriving actual and total real misalignment.

According to the Jarque-Bera tests shown in table 9, the Czech, Slovak and Slovene samples are all normally distributed. When no reference year is used, the mean of real overvaluation ranges from 17% to 27% for the Czech Republic for the last quarter of 2002. Note that results differ slightly depending on whether actual or long-term values of fundamentals (obtained using the HP filter) are used. However, when the reference year is set to 1993, the range of the real overvaluation shifts upwards to 29% to 33%. Also, the range diminishes from about 10 percentage points to 4.5 percentage points and the results appear neutral both for actual and total real misalignments. Similarly, sizeable overvaluation is detected for Slovakia. In the absence of a reference year, the real overvaluation lies between 20% and 30% and narrows to 24% to 31% when 1994 is employed as a base year.

In contrast to the Czech Republic and Slovakia, real undervaluation is found for Slovenia, the mean of which varies from 1% to 6.5% without reference year and from 6.5% to 12% with the base year set to 1993, and this for the last quarter of 2002.

For Hungary, the confidence interval around the mean does not indicate a clear undervaluation or overvaluation without a reference year or with 1997 being the base year. In the former case, real misalignment ranges from a 4.7% undervaluation to an 8% overvaluation, whereas in the latter case, the range is –6% to +1%. However, the use of 1992 as a reference year shifts the extent of real misalignment towards an undervaluation of –11% to –3%. But none of the total real misalignment samples and actual real misalignment when 1992 is used as a base year turn out to be normally distributed. Hence, the corresponding confidence intervals are difficult to be interpreted.

As for Poland, the means of the distributions indicate a slight overvaluation in the last quarter of 2002. Note that the results seem to be affected little by the reference year. The overvaluation around the sample mean amounts to 1% to 8%. Nevertheless, and once again, normality cannot be rejected at the 5% level only when the HP filter with a smoothing parameter of 1600 and the reference year of 1994 are used. In this case, the confidence interval indicates an overvaluation of 3% to 6.5%.

It is noteworthy that the results for the Czech Republic and Hungary are different to those obtained using time series estimates. As a matter of fact, panel results indicate an overvaluation of 17% to 33% whereas time series estimates yield an overvaluation of 4% to 7% for the Czech Republic. While panel estimates are indecisive regarding the direction of a possible real misalignment, time series estimates suggest a clear overvaluation of 7% to 12% for Hungary.

Table 9. Real Misalignments against the Euro, Panel Estimates, Fourth Quarter of 2002

	ACTUAL	TOTAL		ACTUAL	TOTAL	
	ORIG	HP1600	HP100	ORIG_BY	HP1600_BY	HP100_BY
No. Obs	83	83	83	83	83	83
			Czech Republic			
Reference year	--	--	--	1993	1993	1993
Mean	18.43%	24.95%	24.23%	30.42%	31.19%	31.10%
Confidence interval (CI)	2.10%	1.71%	1.62%	1.58%	1.78%	1.58%
Mean-CI	16.33%	23.24%	22.61%	28.84%	29.41%	29.52%
Mean+CI	20.53%	26.66%	25.85%	32.00%	32.97%	32.68%
Jarque-Bera (p-value)	0.295	0.185	0.314	0.394	0.185	0.346
			Hungary			
Reference year	--	--	--	1997	1997	1997
Mean	5.34%	-2.19%	-1.18%	-2.94%	-2.42%	-1.52%
Confidence interval (CI)	2.63%	2.54%	2.59%	3.00%	2.68%	2.81%
Mean-CI	2.71%	-4.73%	-3.76%	-5.93%	-5.10%	-4.33%
Mean+CI	7.97%	0.35%	1.41%	0.06%	0.25%	1.28%
Jarque-Bera (p-value)	0.831	0.002	0.000	0.127	0.043	0.041
Reference year				1992	1992	1992
Mean				-7.94%	-6.97%	-6.19%
Confidence interval (CI)				3.12%	2.85%	2.95%
Mean-CI				-11.07%	-9.82%	-9.14%
Mean+CI				-4.82%	-4.12%	-3.25%
Jarque-Bera (p-value)				0.001	0.000	0.000
			Poland			
Reference year	--	--	--	1994	1994	1994
Mean	3.30%	3.87%	4.94%	6.03%	4.78%	5.53%
Confidence interval (CI)	2.17%	1.66%	1.69%	1.84%	1.70%	1.82%
Mean-CI	1.13%	2.21%	3.25%	4.19%	3.08%	3.71%
Mean+CI	5.47%	5.53%	6.62%	7.88%	6.48%	7.34%
Jarque-Bera (p-value)	0.026	0.009	0.003	0.022	0.050	0.031
			Slovakia			
Reference year	--	--	--	1994	1994	1994
Mean	23.38%	26.73%	25.91%	26.43%	27.64%	27.20%
Confidence interval (CI)	3.35%	3.29%	3.16%	3.04%	3.25%	3.15%
Mean-CI	20.03%	23.44%	22.75%	23.39%	24.39%	24.06%
Mean+CI	26.73%	30.02%	29.08%	29.47%	30.89%	30.35%
Jarque-Bera (p-value)	0.0949	0.3867	0.6137	0.6220	0.5030	0.5971
			Slovenia			
Reference year	--	--	--	1993	1993	1993
Mean	-3.87%	-2.36%	-2.73%	-10.00%	-8.66%	-10.19%
Confidence interval (CI)	2.59%	1.88%	1.85%	2.30%	2.16%	2.24%
Mean-CI	-6.47%	-4.23%	-4.59%	-12.29%	-10.82%	-12.44%
Mean+CI	-1.28%	-0.48%	-0.88%	-7.70%	-6.50%	-7.95%
Jarque-Bera (p-value)	0.905	0.155	0.174	0.205	0.118	0.090

Note: Negative/positive figures represent an undervaluation/overvaluation. Confidence intervals at the 5% significance level.

This outcome may come about because panel estimates represent average long-term coefficients for the panel members and factors that could not be established to have systematically affected the real exchange rate for the time series case can turn out to be important, on average, for the panel. To put it another way, country-specific variables could be dampened, and at the same time, factors not important to individual countries may be emphasized (either by including new variables or by different size of the coefficient) within the panel framework.

Regulated prices are a case in point. Based on time series techniques, the differential in regulated prices is not included in the estimated relationship for Hungary and Poland. Nonetheless, regulated prices are always significant in the panel setting. Therefore, they are used to derive values of the equilibrium real exchange rate for all countries and thus affect the size of the real misalignment.

7 Conclusions

The issue of equilibrium exchange rates has produced a large echo in recent times. The new EU Member States can be expected to enter ERM II some time after EU accession, but not necessarily upon accession. For entering ERM II, an appropriate central parity should be set for which the equilibrium exchange rate could serve as a yardstick.

In this article, an attempt was made to compare estimates of the equilibrium real exchange rates of five acceding countries of Central Europe. In the choice and in the interpretation of the tested relationships, special attention was paid to the appreciation of the real exchange rate based on tradable prices. We developed a theoretical framework which provides a formal explanation for this. During the catching-up process and phases of higher growth, improvement in supply capacities and in the quality and reputation of goods produced in the home economy may result in a trend increase of both the CPI- and PPI-deflated real exchange rates, in addition to the traditional source of trend appreciation, namely productivity-fueled increases in market-based service prices (B-S effect).

Our results support the idea that the equilibrium appreciation of the real exchange rate in the transition economies is based not only on higher service prices, but also on higher prices of domestically produced tradable goods. Taking labor productivity in industry or in the overall economy as a proxy for increasing supply capacities, econometric tests show that labor productivity is found to be the most stable determinant not only of the overall inflation-based real exchange rate but also of the real exchange rate measured in terms of tradable prices, proxied by PPI.

A score of time series and panel cointegration techniques were employed to assess real exchange rate determination for the Czech Republic, Hungary, Poland, Slovakia and Slovenia. For time series estimates, it is possible to find long-term relationships between fundamentals and the real exchange rate vis-à-vis Germany for the Czech Republic, Hungary and Poland. Nonetheless, alternative measures for labor productivity are found to perform differently across countries and cannot be taken as equivalent to one another. Also, beside labor productivity, the included variables differ considerably across the three countries. In contrast to the aforesaid three economies, it is a very hard task to find any economically sound long-term relationships for Slovakia and Slovenia. These two countries could be considered economies for which it is difficult to establish the role of fundamentals in real exchange rate determination.

Going beyond the verification of the theoretical model, the size of total real misalignments is derived on the basis of time series estimates obtained on the basis of time series spanning from between 1993 and 1994 to 2002. Total real misalignments turn out to be sensitive to the econometric technique and the base year assumption in particular in Hungary. For all three countries, the results indicate a real overvaluation vis-à-vis the euro in the last quarter of 2002: by 4% to 7% for the Czech Republic, 7% to 12% for Hungary and 12% to 15% for Poland.[23]

Panel estimates based on different estimation techniques, panel sizes and model specifications leave us with a number of real misalignments that indicate an overvaluation of 16% to 30% for the Czech Republic, of 20% to 30% for Slovakia and of 1% to 8% for Poland in the last quarter of 2002. An undervaluation ranging from 1% to 12% is found for Slovenia, and real misalignments are between –5% (undervaluation) to 8% (overvaluation) for Hungary for the fourth quarter of 2002.

The conflicting results between time series and panel estimates regarding the size (Czech Republic and Poland) or partly even the direction of the real misalignment (Hungary) may be due to the fact that country-specific factors may be crucial, and their neglect in the panel framework can substantially change the derived real misalignment. Moreover, differences are also marked when comparing the results of different econometric methods or time periods.

To conclude, estimates of the equilibrium real exchange rates and the underlying real misalignments are fairly sensitive to the chosen econometric method, period and model specification and to differences in the included variables. Therefore, further research is needed to systematically evaluate the sources of different results. In particular, medium-size and large panels are needed, as is a structural model-based assessment.

References

Aglietta, M, C. Baulant and V. Coudert. 1999. Compétitivité et régime de change en Europe centrale. Revue économique 50(6). 1221–1236.

Aglietta, M, C. Baulant and S. Moatti. 2003. Les PECO devant la tentation de l'euro. Economie internationale. 93. 1er trimestre. 11–36.

[23] It should be noted that the real misalignment figures obtained for the last quarter of 2002 cannot be applied compared with the real and nominal exchange rates that prevail currently because both the prices and the nominal exchange rate (the real exchange rate) and the underlying fundamentals may have changed in a way that past misalignments are difficult to be interpreted today.

Baltagi, B. H. and C. Kao. 2000. Nonstationary Panels, Cointegration in Panels and Dynamic Panels: A Survey. In: Baltagi, B. H. (ed.): Nonstationary Panels, Panel Cointegration and Dynamic Panels. Advances in Econometrics 15. Elsevier Science. 7–51.

Banerjee, A. 1999. Panel Data Unit Root Tests and Cointegration: An Overview. Oxford Bulletin of Economics and Statistics. 61. Supplement 1. 607–629.

Benacek, V., L. Prokop and J. A. Visek. 2003. Determining factors of the Czech foreign trade balance: Structural issues in trade creation. Czech National Bank Working Paper 3.

Beblavy, M. 2002. Exchange Rate and Exchange Rate Regime in Slovakia: Recent Developments. ICEGEC Working Paper 5. Budapest

Campos. N. and F. Coricelli. 2002. Growth in Transition: What we know, what we don't and what we should. Journal of Economic Literature. 40(3). 793–836.

Caprirolo, G. and V. Lavrac 2003. Monetary and exchange rate policies in Slovenia, Ezoneplus Working paper 17G. (Working paper 17 Supplement)

Clark, P. and R. MacDonald. 1998. Exchange Rates and Economic Fundamentals: A Methodological Comparison of BEERs and FEERs. IMF Working Paper 67. May. Washington D.C.

Crespo-Cuaresma, J., J. Fidrmuc and R. MacDonald. 2003. The Monetary Approach to Exchange Rates: Panel Data Evidence for Selected CEECs. OeNB. Focus on Transition 2.

Csajbók, A. 2003. The Equilibrium Real Exchange Rate in Hungary: Results from Alternative Approaches. Paper presented at the 2nd Workshop on Macroecomic Policy Research. Magyar Nemzeti Bank. October 2 – 3, 2003.

Detken, C., A. Dieppe, J. Henry, C. Marin and F. Smets. 2002. Model Uncertainty and the Equilibrium Value of the Real Effective Euro Exchange Rate, ECB Working Paper 160. July.

Darvas, Z. and M. Sass. 2002. Changes in Hungarian Foreign Trade and Trade Balance with the European Union In: Pavlos Karadeloglou (ed.): Enlarging the EU: The Trade Balance Effect. 51–88. Hampshire. England: Palgrave Macmillan Publisher.

Dulleck, U., N. Foster, R. Stehrer and J. Wörz. 2003. Dimension of Quality Upgrading . Evidence for CEECs. University of Vienna Department of Economics Working Paper 14.

Duval, R. 2002. What Do We Know About Long-Term Equilibrium Real Exchange Rates? PPPs VS Macroeconomic Approaches. Australian Economic Papers. 41(4). 382-403

Égert, B. 2003a. Assessing equilibrium exchange rates in CEE acceding countries: Can We Have DEER with BEER Without FEER? A critical survey of the literature. Focus on Transition 2.

Égert, B. 2003b. Nominal and Real Convergence in Estonia: The Balassa-Samuelson (Dis)Connection – Tradable Goods, Regulated Prices and Other Culprits. Bank of Estonia Working Paper 4.

Engel, Ch. 1993. Real Exchange Rates and Relative Prices: An Empirical Investigation. Journal of Monetary Economics. 32. 35-50.

Halpern, L. and C. Wyplosz. 1997. Equilibrium Exchange Rates in Transition Countries. IMF Staff Papers 44(4). 430–461.

Im, K. S., M. H. Pesaran and Y. Shin. 2003. Testing for unit roots in heterogeneous panels. Journal of Econometrics. 115(1). 53–74.

Krajnyák, K. and J. Zettelmeyer. 1998. Competitiveness in Transition Economies: What Scope for Real Appreciation? IMF Staff Papers 45(2). 309–62.

MacDonald, R. 1997. What Determines Real Exchange Rates? The Long and Short of It. IMF Working Paper 21, January. Washington D.C.

MacKinnon, J. G. 1996. Numerical Distribution Functions for Unit Root and Cointegration Tests. Journal of Applied Econometrics. 11(6). 601–618.

Pedroni, P. 1999. Critical Values for Cointegration Tests in Heterogeneous Panels with Multiple Regressors. Oxford Bulletin of Economics and Statistics. 61. Supplement 1. 653–670.

Pesaran, M. H., Y. Shin and R. J. Smith. 2001. Bounds testing approaches to the analysis of level relationships. Journal of Applied Econometrics. 16(3). 289–326.

Rosati, D. 1994. Output decline during transition. Economics of Transition. 2(4). 419–441.

Rosati, D. 1996. Exchange rate policies during transition from plan to market. Economics of Transition. 4(1). 159–186.

Sgard, J. 2001. Direct foreign investments and productivity growth in Hungarian firms, 1992–1999. CEPII Working Paper 19. December.

Stock, J. and M. W. Watson. 1993. A simple estimator of cointegrating vectors in higher order integrated systems. Econometrica. 61(4). 783–820.

Comment on: Equilibrium Exchange Rates in the Transition: The Tradable Price-Based Real Appreciation and Estimation Uncertainty

Bernd Kempa

Égert and Lommatzsch analyse the determination of equilibrium exchange rates of transition economies both in a theoretical and in an empirical capacity. In terms of theory, the paper focuses on an explanation for trend increases of real exchange rates due to a catching-up process of supply capacities and the quality of tradables. In the empirical section, a variety of time series and panel cointegration techniques is employed to provide estimates of long-run equilibrium real exchange rates as well as real misalignments in the five transition economies Czech Republic, Hungary, Poland, Slovakia and Slovenia. The authors find robust evidence on the role of tradables price inflation in accounting for equilibrium real exchange rate appreciations in these countries, thus supporting their theoretical model. However, the extent of the total real misalignments turns out to be quite heterogeneous, even when averaged across various estimation designs.

The authors motivate their theoretical analysis by the empirical observation that real exchange rate appreciation in transition economies is brought about by price increases both in the tradables and the nontradables sectors. This observation does not conform to the much invoked Balassa-Samuelson effect which is based entirely on nontradables inflation. In contrast to the traditional argument, the model presented in the paper lays out a theory of technology-driven tradables-based real appreciation. Although the results of the model hinge crucially on the assumption of heterogeneous tradables, such that world demand for each good increases with its technological content, that assumption appears quite realistic, especially for the transition economies.

The assumptions of a balanced trade account and the complete disregard of the capital account appear more restrictive. But apart from not being stock-flow consistent, the model is in line with a long-run Behavioural Equilibrium Exchange Rate (BEER) specification as employed in the empirical part of the paper. Nevertheless, the model could easily be generalized to also conform to medium-run equilibrium concepts. According to Eq. (4) of the text, only *changes* in the trade account matter, so the model should go through for any trade account position. In particular, the model could be made compatible with a "sustainable" current account in the spirit of the Fundamental Equilibrium Exchange Rate (FEER) or the medium-term Natural Real Exchange Rate (NATREX).

The theory could also be extended to accomodate the capital account. Under the assumption that technological advances in tradables induce capital inflows, the results of the model would even be strengthened as the resulting surplus in the capital account allows the trade balance to be in deficit. Under such an extension, Eq. (6) turns into an inequality of the form $\hat{x} < \hat{e} + \hat{m}$, and the solution of the model presented in Eq. (13) implies the inequality

$$\frac{\hat{e}}{\hat{t}} < \frac{\varepsilon_T^x - \varepsilon_T^m - \varepsilon_Y^m}{1 + \varepsilon_E^m - \varepsilon_E^x} < 0 \tag{13'}$$

thus raising the issue of technology-induced appreciation. This medium run-appreciation is also a long-run equilibrium phenomenon as long as the capital account surplus is related to productive foreign investment. The resulting increase in the productivity of the domestic economy would then reinforce the technology-driven tradables-based real appreciation associated with supply capacities and the quality of tradables. Such an extended model would also more closely match the stylised facts of Section 3 of the text, where foreign direct investment (FDI) into the transition economies is associated with "economy-wide quality improvements of goods and services" (p. 214) such that "real appreciation may have been faster in countries where foreign investors contributed more to economic restructuring" (p. 215).

In the empirical part of the paper, the estimated coefficients for the productivity variables are significant for both the CPI- and PPI-based real exchange rate equations using either time series or panel cointegration techniques, with the size of the coefficients mostly higher for the CPI-based approach. This evidence suggests that both tradables and nontradables inflation contributed to the observed paths of real appreciations in the sample countries. The authors conclude that "the appreciation of the real exchange rate is to a large extent due to changes in tradable prices" (p. 226) while "service price inflation also contributes to real appreciation to some extent" (p. 226). This conclusion would be more convincing if it was buttressed by some formal investigation into the relative importance of these two channels. As a useful by-product of such an investigation, the empirical relevance of the Balassa-Samuelson effect could then also be established and assessed in a quantitative fashion.

In their reduced-form equation (12') on p. 216, the authors include a real interest rate differential based on one-year treasury bill yields relative to Germany as an explanatory variable of the real exchange rate. They argue that this variable "reflects imbalances between investment and savings and is expected to be negatively connected to the real exchange rate" (p. 216). However, this effect can only be established for Poland, while for the other countries it turns out to be either not significant (Czech Republic, Hungary and Slovakia), or wrongly signed (Slovenia). This evidence may be less puzzling than it appears as the capital flows into the transition economies have mostly taken the form of FDI, which itself may be rather insensitive to the size of these particular interest rate differentials. Also, the variability of risk premia, possibly associated with events such as the speculative attack on the Czech koruna in 1997, may have blurred the relationship between the interest rate differentials and the real exchange rates.

On the basis of the variables identified as being significant in the real exchange rate equations, the authors go on to estimate the equilibrium real exchange rates as well as the corresponding total real misalignments. While the latter vary substantially across the individual estimation designs, the authors average their results for the various specifications of the fundamentals, their actual and smoothed values, as well as the alternative econometric techniques employed. This way they are able to identify significant overvaluations for the Czech Republic, Hungary and Poland using the time series approach. However, when conducting a similar exercise for the panel setting, the results change dramatically, with a substantially stronger overvaluation for the Czech Republic and no apparent overvaluation for Hungary.

Despite these somewhat sobering results, this paper is a convincing piece of evidence of the sensitivity of empirical estimations of real misalignments in the transition economies. The fact that the existence and the extent of these misalignments can hardly be pinned down with any degree of accuracy raises the question whether such estimates have any usable implications for economic policy. The authors' call for further research on this question comes through loud and clear.

Innovation, Structural Change and Exchange Rate Dynamics in Catching-up Countries

Paul J.J. Welfens[1]

Contents

1 Introduction 246
2 Traditional and New Approaches to the Real Exchange Rate 251
2.1 A Short-Term Analysis of Financial Market Dynamics and Technology Shocks 251
2.2 Technology, Pricing and the Balassa-Samuelson Effect 256
2.3 Modifying Traditional Models and Looking at Economic Growth 259
3 Perspectives on Exchange Rate Research 271
Mathematical Appendix 1 273
Mathematical Appendix 2 275
References 277

[1] This paper is part of two projects: *EU fifth framework project "Changes in Industrial Competitiveness as a Factor of Integration: Identifying Challenges of the Enlarged Single European Market (Contract No. HPSE-CT-2002-00148); and* the Project Russia's Integration into the World Economy financed by the Alfried Krupp von Bohlen und Halbach Foundation, Essen. For technical support I am grateful to Albrecht Kauffmann, EIIW Center at the University of Potsdam, Martin Keim at the University of Wuppertal and to Dora Borbély, European Institute for International Economic Relations at the University of Wuppertal. The usual disclaimer applies.

1 Introduction

The exchange rate (price notation) is the relative price between two currencies and can be determined in various models which differ mainly according to their time horizon. From an economic perspective, the nominal exchange rate is relevant for aggregating nominal GDP figures, sales and asset values at the international level. The nominal exchange rate is quite important in a system with a fixed exchange rate or in a setting with a monetary union. In economic terms, the real exchange rate is (with P for price level and * for foreign variables) defined as $eP^*/P=q^*=(1/q)$ and is often the more relevant variable for economic analysis; e.g. as a factor affecting the quantity of exports and imports. The real exchange rate is also important for several reasons not always understood in the literature:

- World output in real terms (in terms of the home country good) is given by the expression $Y+ q^*Y^*$ (Y is national output); the higher q* is, the higher world real income in the perspective of the home country. In addition part of national income, namely net exports of goods and services depends on q* - a real appreciation will reduce exports and raise imports.
- There is also a link between the real exchange rate and capital flows, in particular foreign direct investment. A real appreciation, namely a fall of eP^*/P, implies that home firms will find it easier to acquire foreign assets. In imperfect capital markets (Froot/Stein, 1991), a fall of eP^*/P implies that at a given relative price of stocks (ratio of stock market price P' to output price level P) both home and abroad, foreign firms (in country II) can be acquired more easily than home country firms after an appreciation; firms from country I can put up more equity capital as expressed in terms of the foreign currency. Hence they will be able to obtain more loans in the target country than previously so that there is a higher likelihood to outbid rival firms in the target country. A rarely considered implication is that in open economies investment depends on the real exchange rate.
- There is a link between the real exchange rate and the burden of the debt. A real depreciation is particularly important for a country with foreign debt since it raises the burden of foreign debt; this effect offsets the stimulating effect of a depreciation of the currency on net exports of goods and services.

With respect to short-term analysis, with P and P* considered as sticky variables, nominal exchange rate changes are equivalent to real exchange rate changes. Over a long-term perspective price levels are flexible, however, so that discussing the real exchange rate requires us to take a look at both the nominal exchange rate as well as the price level at home and abroad. In a world with tradable (T) goods and (N) nontradable goods, the internal exchange rate is defined as P^T/P^N. It can be shown – we pick up on this point subsequently – that the real exchange rate, q, is related to both the internal exchange rate and relative international sectoral productivity differentials. Economic opening up and economic growth are associated with considerable sectoral changes and hence productivity shifts. Not all countries which have opened up to the world economy have achieved both high productivity growth and real income growth. It will be interesting to focus on this issue and to raise some issues related particularly to productivity growth and the nominal and real exchange rate.

While arbitrage in a two country model with homogeneous traded goods implies that $P^T = eP^{T*}$ the analysis looks different in a setup with product innovations and heterogeneous goods, respectively: It will hold $P^T = V'eP^{T*}$ where $V' \neq 1$ in equilibrium. In our analysis we are interested in looking into a world with Schumpeterian product innovations. Firms and countries differ in terms of product innovations. In certain countries the size of the market and consumer preferences might be particularly appealing for launching new products, and the large market with high per capita incomes in the US is therefore often an important lead market; this is all the more true since many US multinational companies have a strong record in product innovations and since in new niche markets innovative young firms can often be found. As regards Western Europe there are clearly differences across countries when it comes to per capita income and patenting per capita; and one may distinguish between large and small countries. However, there are also considerable differences in terms of response time to innovative products: time-to-takeoff in years (average time between product introduction on the national market and sales take-off) was found to be around four years in Denmark, Norway and Sweden, around five years in Finland, Ireland, Belgium, Switzerland and the Netherlands, about six years for Austria and Germany, seven years for Italy, Spain and France and roughly nine years for the UK, Greece and Portugal (Tellis/ Stremersch/ Yin, 2003).

Finland and Sweden also are among the leaders in the EU's European Innovation Scorebord (European Commission, 2003, p. 27) when it comes to questions such as:

- What is the percentage of "new to market products" of all turnover in manufacturing and of all turnover in services, respectively? In the 2003 scoreboard the EU-15 average (with missing data in the case of Ireland, Luxembourg and Netherlands) was 10.5 in manufacturing, while it was 27.2 for the top-leader Finland followed by Italy, Portugal and Denmark with 18.7, 16.0 and 14.3, respectively. In the field of services the EU-15 average was 7.4 (with missing data in the case of Ireland, Netherlands and the UK), while the leaders were Greece, Spain, Finland and Italy with 17.9, 13.7, 12.2 and 11.6, respectively. In the leader countries the price of tradables – in the field of manufacturing and services – should be higher than the EU average to the extent that novel products can fetch higher prices in the market. The data must be interpreted with caution since many products are newly introduced in the national market while this product does not necessarily stand for a global product innovation. If we concentrate on manufacturing products – typically all tradable – in high income countries where products new to the market normally should also mean new to the world market, Denmark has a clear lead, trailed by France and the UK with 9.5 for both countries, followed by Austria and Germany with 8.4 and 7.1, respectively. As a general hypothesis we expect that an increase in the share of new products to the market – relative to the EU average – will go along with a relative rise of the tradables price in the respective country. In a Schumpeterian perspective it is thus not adequate to assume the law of one price to hold strictly.

- What is the percentage of "new to the firm but not new to the market products", namely as a percentage of all turnover in manufacturing and of all turnover in services, respectively? In 2003 the EU-15 average in manufacturing (data missing for Ireland) was 28.6, while leaders were Germany, Sweden, Finland and Italy with 40.3, 32.1, 31.1 and 30.1, respectively, they are followed by Spain, Denmark and the Netherlands (25.8, 24.2 and 23.8, respectively). In services the EU-15 average (data missing for Ireland) was 18.8, while leaders were Greece, Spain, Sweden and Belgium scoring 37.1, 26.4, 23.7 and 23.5, respectively. Leading countries here indicate a high ability for imitation. It is, however, not ruled out that relatively poor countries have a relatively high score in the imitation index simply because they are catching up. As regards relatively poor countries one should not underestimate the role of diffusion in economic catching up. In the context of EU eastern enlargement this implies that firms in accession countries should perform well in imitation in the medium term. Over the longer term, the role of true innovations should gain importance, and this should become visible in international patent statistics.

The Innovation Scoreboard 2004 – see the subsequent table – gives figures for EU25, EU15 and individual member countries. Public R&D expenditures relative to GDP were relatively low in Poland and the Czech Republic (0.46% and 0.47%, respectively); France and Germany were leading economies in this field (0.83 and 0.77%, respectively). As regards R&D expenditures of the business community relative to GDP Poland reached only 0.13%, while EU 15 stood at 1.30% (Germany at 1.73%). Hungary seems to be a relatively week innovator as the score is only 1.4 (only 1.4% of all sales represents product innovations) compared to 7.2 for the Czech Repbulic and 5.9 for EU15. However, Hungary has reached 4.9 in new-to firm products, the Czech Republic 7.3. Expenditures on information and communication technology – here eastern Europe had a large gap vis-à-vis western Europe in the 1990s – reached a high score in Hungary (9.4 compared to 6.2 for EU-15) and the Czech Republic (9.2); Poland's ICT expenditures relative to GDP was 7.7% and thus still above the EU15 average of 6.2%. The share of high-technology manufacturing was 16% in Hungary which is more than twice the figures for Poland and the Czech Republic (14.1 is the average for EU15, the shares for the UK and France are a bit above 18%, much better than Germany – but Germany's share of manufacturing in GDP is higher than in the UK and France). The fact that Hungarian firms are not very strong in terms of product innovations – narrowly defined – but enjoy an excellent position in high-technology manufacturing can largely be explained by the relatively strong role of foreign direct investment in Hungarian industry. A strong position in cumulated foreign direct investment inflows lets us expect that Hungarian firms have improved over time in terms of product upgrading and high quality manufacturing exports. This in turn should show up in relatively rising export unit values for Hungary. As Hungary, Poland, the Czech Republic and other countries are catching-up technologically it is obvious that one cannot assume that the product mix on the export side and the import side remains constant. A straightforward application of the law of one price therefore is inadequate – Schumpeterian dynamics should be carefully taken into account. It also is clear that a rising share of product innovations in the tradables sector which will go along with higher export unit values should go along with an improvement of the nominal trade balance.

Table 1. European Innovation Scoreboard 2004: Current performance of selected countries

	EU 15	GER	FR	SPA	UK	NED	CZE	GRE	HUN	POL	POR
2.1 Public R&D exp	**0.69**	0.77	0.83	0.47	0.61	0.79	0.47	0.43	0.66	0.46	0.61
2.2 Business R&D exp	**1.30**	1.73	1.36	0.56	1.26	1.03	0.75	0.21	0.36	0.13	0.32
4.3.1 New-to-mark prods	**5.9**	6.2	5.7	8.3	1.9	5.6	7.2	2.9	1.4	--	10.8
4.3.2 New-to-firm prods	**17.1**	23.4	11.7	17.0	15.1	12.1	7.3	8.9	4.9	--	15.1
4.5 ICT exp	**6.2**	6.1	5.9	4.8	7.5	7.1	9.2	5.0	9.4	7.7	6.3
4.6 VA h-tech manuf	**14.1**	11.9	18.3	6.5	18.8	12.1	7.1	6.3	16.0	5.7	6.5

Source: European Commission (2004): European Innovation Scoreboard 2004, Brussels

In the literature the traditional analysis of the link between catching-up and relative price changes is the Balassa-Samuelson effect. This effect – narrowly defined – suggests that the relative price of nontradables will increase along with a rise in per capita income (Balassa, 1964; Samuelson, 1964). Basically, the reason could be that income elasticity for nontradables is higher than for tradables or that during economic catching-up productivity growth in the tradables sector is higher than in the nontradables sector. An alternative definition of the Balassa-Samuelson effect – broadly defined – is that the real exchange rate will rise along with the growth of per capita income. As is well known the two types of Balassa-Samuelson effect are linked to each other, and we will pick this up later.

Under flexible exchange rates the foreign exchange market determines – as part of an interdependent system of macro markets – the nominal equilibrium exchange rate. The short-term exchange rate is consistent with a long-term fundamental equilibrium exchange rate only if all other macro markets (including the goods market and the labor market) are also in equilibrium. Hence there are different analytical time horizons with respect to exchange rate analysis. Moreover, if we look at a given economy, it is important to consider the goods market and the labor market first; if these markets are in equilibrium and the exchange rate clears in a situation of a roughly balanced current account, we have an equilibrium real exchange rate.

Very short term models are based on the analysis of financial markets, where the Branson model is a standard approach. A well-known medium-term analytical framework is the Mundell-Flemming model for an economy with unemployment. A simple full employment model is the model from Mundell (1968), who emphasized the distinction between tradable goods and nontradable goods. More recent contributions to the literature with a particular focus on the Balassa-Samuelson effect, are from De Gregorio/Wolf (1994), Halpern/ Wyplosz (1997), Chin/ Johnston (1997), Maliszewska (1997), Krajnyak/ Zettelmeyer (1998), Canzoneri/ Cumby/ Diba (1999), Grafe/ Wyplosz (1999), Cipriani (2000), Rother (2000), Szapary (2000). It is worth mentioning that the real exchange rate can increase relatively fast during economic catching up, e.g., the case of Spain in the European Monetary System by 25% between 1986 und 1993. Several eastern European EU accession countries have also recorded phases of high real appreciation in the late 1990s. Many accession countries have also recorded a rise of the relative price of nontradables.

There are, however, no models considering the long-term link between growth/technology and the real exchange rate. As such, we will present the first such model. At the same time there is also no model dealing with very short-term financial market analysis and economic catching up which marks – along the time axis – the other extreme. Short-term exchange rate developments can have considerable effects, possibly including foreign debt problems if there is a strong short depreciation such as overshooting effects in a country with high foreign debt. Thus we will present both a very short-term financial market model (namely an augmented Branson model) and a long-term model of the real exchange rate. Additionally we will present some new ideas on the role between economic catching up and the exchange rate in the context of a modified perspective on Balassa-Samuelson effects related to the rise of the real exchange rate and the relative price of nontradables in the context of economic catching-up. We will first present the very short term financial market analysis, followed by a refined medium term model for Balassa-Samuelson effects in the context of product innovation; moreover, we suggest a basic approach for analysing the long term real exchange rate, where relative innovativeness also plays a key role. As a medium term approach we consider a modified Mundell Fleming model: we integrate product innovations into the model. We model innovativeness as changes in total factor productivity, product innovations and capital productivity changes. In the very short term model the focus is on productivity shocks, while the medium term and long term analysis put the focus, respectively, on product and process innovations.

The analysis suggests that relative international innovativeness is a crucial determinant for both the short term exchange rate, the medium term rate and the long term rate. As the medium term model suggests that the equilibrium nominal exchange rate could rise or fall as a consequence of a relative rise in per capita income (y/y^*; with y standing for per capita income) there are some doubts about a system of fixed exchange rates – in particular for countries catching up. As the ratio of research and development expenditures to GDP is increasing in OECD countries and Newly Industrializing Countries so that innovation dynamics intensify globally, one may indeed argue that in a world with stronger Schumpeterian innovation dynamics there are arguments for adopting more flexible exchange rate systems. As regards the 1980s und 1990s it is noteworthy that relative innovativeness – as proxied by patent applications per capita and other variables – has witnessed considerable shifts in Europe and across OECD countries (Jungmittag, 2003, 2003a). Section 2 will take a look first at familiar financial market models, additionally we will introduce capital productivity shocks within a modified Branson model, namely an approach which includes stock markets. This reflects our particular interest in better understanding the role of stock markets which have been important for more than a century for capitalist economic development. This means, of course, not to overlook the role of banking and interest rates. Section 2 also brings an innovation through taking a closer look at the role of product innovations in a modified Balassa-Samuelson model – with a focus on the relative price of tradables and the real exchange rate – of the real exchange rate. Moreover, we try to integrate the money market in a standard model and thus try to shed more light on the issue of how the relative change of per capita income will affect the real exchange rate. We argue that the ratio of domestic per capita income to foreign per capita income has ambiguous effects. We then integrate product innovations into the Mundell Fleming model and show that product innovations raise output and bring about a real appreciation of the currency so that the share of the respective country in world output will rise for two reasons (output effect plus exchange rate effect). Finally, we want to look at a long term model of the real exchange rate meaning a focus on the current account development, relative product innovations and the role of price elasticity. Section 3 looks at some further conclusions and perspectives on exchange rate research. This contribution takes a look to some extent at short term models, medium term approaches and long term approaches to the exchange rate and is mainly concerned with product innovations. It is quite interesting to show that indeed innovations can be included in familiar models and analysed with a rather simple approach. We do, however, not present a comprehensive model which would link the various models and time horizons. Also, we are considering the role of exchange rate policies and alternative exchange rate regimes.

2 Traditional and New Approaches to the Real Exchange Rate

2.1 A Short-Term Analysis of Financial Market Dynamics and Technology Shocks

A look at the effective real exchange rate of several countries shows that the real exchange rates show a long term rise – parallel to output per capita. This is true both for Asian NICs (until 1997, the year of the Asian crisis) and selected EU accession countries in the 1990s as is shown in the subsequent graph. Such a long term appreciation trend does, however, not rule out that there can be considerable short term depreciation periods; e.g. in the context of expansionary monetary policy and falling interest rates or as a consequence of investors' fears with respect to the sustainability of government debt policy. In addition to this, oil price shocks could affect short term nominal and real exchange rate development.

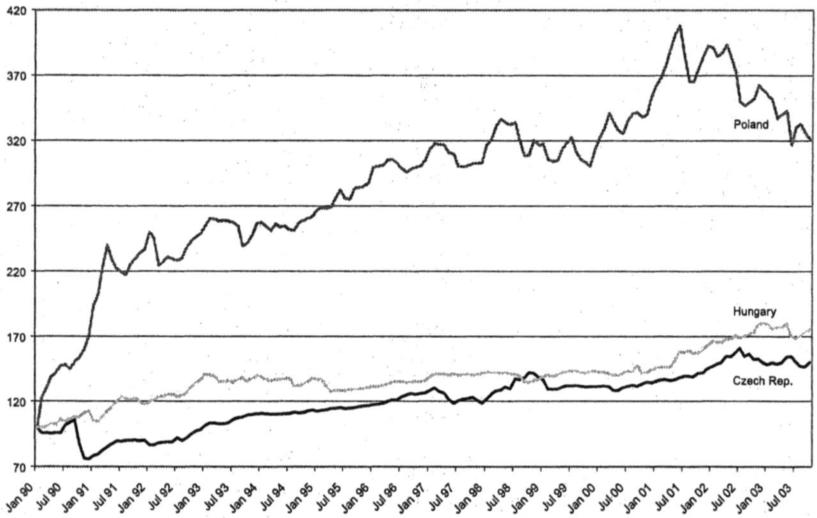

Fig. 1. Real Effective Exchange Rates for Selected EU Accession Countries in the 1990s, Jan 1990=100

Source: International Financial Statistics, IMF, 2003.

Now let us turn to some modelling analysis. Over the short-term, all stock variables – such as the capital stock K – and the price level P are given. There can however be productivity shocks, namely changes in the marginal or average capital productivity. As for a Cobb-Douglas production function, the marginal productivity is proportionate to the average productivity. Interesting cases to consider are changes in expectations and in productivity growth and in the price level, capital stock and the stock of money, whereas the latter is a policy variable.

Open Economy: Augmented Branson Model

A well known model of financial markets in open economies is the BRANSON model, which focuses on the money market as well as the short term domestic bonds market and the short term foreign bonds market, with foreign bonds being denoted as F* (in foreign currency). Essentially, the model allows for the simultaneous determination of the exchange rate and the nominal interest rate in a setting with a domestic bonds market (BB line), a foreign bonds market (FF line) and the money market (MM line). This model determines the nominal exchange rate e and the nominal interest rate i.

Subsequently we will modify the approach by dropping the domestic bonds market and adding the stock market. This allows for a convenient graphical exposition. The more complex augmented BRANSON model, which includes the original three markets of the seminal model and the stock market, could be discussed analytically.

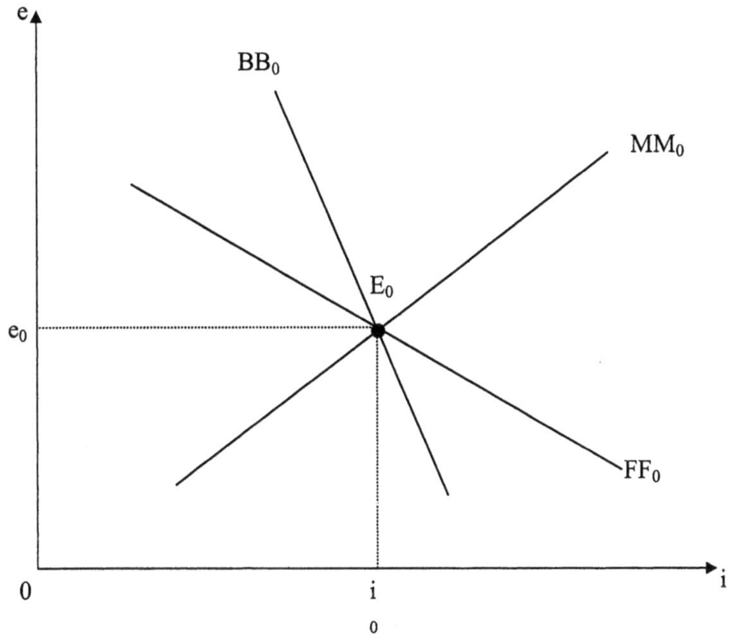

Fig. 2. Portfolio Equilibrium in the Simple Basic Branson Model

The simple augmented BRANSON model, with i* representing the foreign interest rate and a^E the exogenous expected exchange rate change, can be written as follows (with V representing the marginal utility of money, z capital productivity, ψ expected growth rate of the stock market price; M is the nominal money stock, K the capital stock, P' the stock market price and A'=[M/P] + [eF*/P] + P'K/P is overall real wealth):

$$A' = (M/P) + (eF^*/P) + P'K/P \qquad \text{[budget constraint]} \qquad (1a)$$

$$M/P = n(V, i^*+a^E, z, \psi)A';\ n_1>0,\ n_2<0,\ n_3<0,\ n_4<0 \qquad \text{[MM curve]} \qquad (1b)$$

$$eF^*/P = f(V, i^*+a^E, z, \psi)A';\ f_1<0,\ f_2>0,\ f_3<0,\ f_4<0 \qquad \text{[F*F* curve]} \qquad (1c)$$

$$P'K/P = h(V, i^*+a^E, z, \psi)A';\ h_1<0,\ h_2<0,\ h_3>0,\ h_4>0 \qquad \text{[KK curve]} \qquad (1d)$$

We have dropped the domestic bonds market for convenience; in principle there is no problem in also taking into account the domestic bonds market.

The system for equations (1c) and (1d) can be written in matrix form (remember that only two of the three equations (1b)-(1d) are independent as n+f+k=1) and determine – using Kramer's rule and taking into account the budget constraint equation (1a) – the multipliers for e and P'; while e and P' are endogenous variables, the other variables are exogenous. Thus we differentiate the system and look at interesting multipliers such as:

$de/dz \Leftrightarrow 0$	$dP'/dz > 0$
$de/d\psi \Leftrightarrow 0$	$dP'/d\psi > 0$
$de/dK = 0$	$dP'/dK < 0$
$de/dM > 0$	$dP'/dM > 0$
$de/di^* > 0$	$dP'/di^* \Leftrightarrow 0$

A rise of capital productivity will raise the stock market price level, and it – under certain parameter constellations – brings about a nominal depreciation. In such a case we cannot easily infer whether the domestic stock price has increased P' relative to the price of foreign stocks (eP'*). Only if the percentage rise of P' exceeds that of the nominal exchange rate this would be the case. One may dub such a case as an improvement in the international terms of capital where the latter is defined as P'/(eP'*); in an open economy with two-way foreign direct investment and portfolio investment in stocks a rise of the terms of capital implies that the amount of foreign real capital per unit of domestic real capital is increased. Such a perspective implicitly goes one step beyond the existing model in the sense that we would have to also consider foreign stocks – at a given price of stocks abroad – so that domestic investors can trade domestic stocks for foreign stocks.

In an e-P' diagram, we can display the equilibrium line (MM) for the money market, which has a negative slope since a rise in e (increase in the demand for money) must be combined with an adequate fall of the stock market price if money market equilibrium is to be maintained. The equilibrium line for the stock market (KK) has a positive slope, as a rise in P' (its impact is a net supply effect) must be combined with a rise in e, namely an increase in the demand for stocks if stock market equilibrium is to be maintained. The slope of the equilibrium curve for the foreign bonds market is also positive and smaller than that of the KK curve. A rise of e causes a net supply effect – indeed an excess supply – in the foreign bonds market. This excess supply is eliminated if the stock market price and hence the real value of wealth is adequately increased.

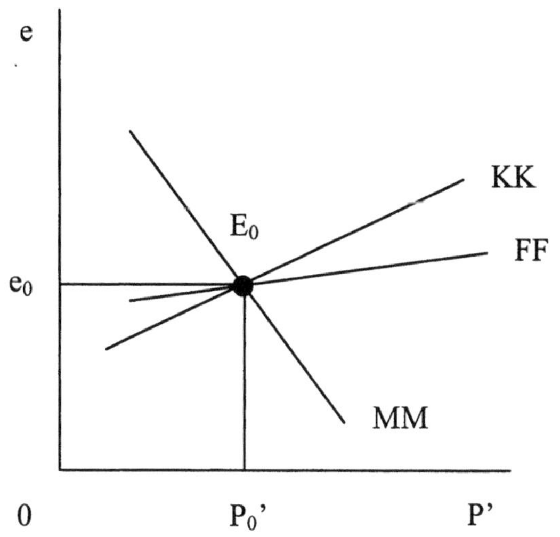

Fig. 3. Foreign Bonds Market, Stock Market and Money Market

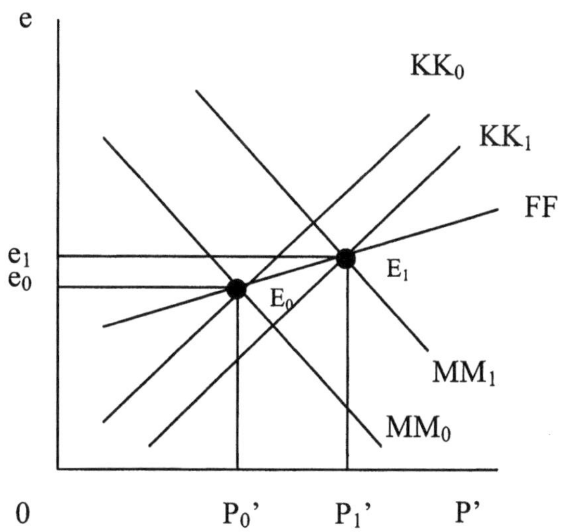

Fig. 4. Effects of an Increase in Capital Productivity in the Branson Model with Stock Market

An expansionary monetary policy implies an upward shift of the MM curve so that we observe depreciation and a rise in the stock market price. Net investment (i.e., a rise in K) will shift the KK curve upwards so that we can learn from the new intersection point with the MM curve that the nominal exchange rate will increase and the stock market price will fall. A rise in capital productivity (as occurs in the course of both structural change and economic catching-up) implies a downward (upward) shift of the KK (FF) curve and a rightward shift of the MM curve. The short-term result is nominal depreciation and a rising stock market price. In the medium-term, however, one must take into account that for foreign investors from country II, depreciation in country I is equivalent to an appreciation of the currency of country I, allowing the purchase of assets more cheaply. This, however, does not hold for either stocks or real capital if the percentage increase in stock prices is higher than the depreciation rate of the currency in country I. Based on this perspective, a modified Branson model suggests that foreign direct investment could fall over the medium-term. In the long run, the situation is different if one assumes that a relative rise of the stock market price will stimulate emission both of new stocks and net investment. The KK curve will shift upwards, thereby dampening the medium-term increase in stock market prices. This, in turn, will stimulate FDI inflows over the long run.

2.2 Technology, Pricing and the Balassa-Samuelson Effect

Economic catching up is associated with a rise in per capita income and structural change – these being interdependent – as well as a change of the real exchange rate. Real appreciation is expected in the sense that eP*/P will fall. This has traditionally been associated with the Balassa-Samuelson effect which implies that the ratio of the price of nontradeables (N) to the price of tradeables (T) – P^N/P^T, or φ – will rise along with per capita income. If the price level – with $0<a<1$ - is defined as

$$P=(P^T)^a(P^N)^{(1-a)} \tag{1}$$

and * representing a foreign variable, then:

$$P= (\varphi)^{(1-a)}P^T \tag{2}$$

$$P^*= (\varphi^*)^{(1-a^*)}P^{T*} \tag{3}$$

On the basis of the law of one price for homogenous tradable goods, we can denote the price for such goods as:

$$P^T=eP^{T}* \tag{4}$$

$$P= (\varphi)^{(1-a)}eP^{T*} \tag{5}$$

Dividing (5) by (3) we get:

$$P/(eP^*) = (\varphi)^{(1-a)}/(\varphi^*)^{(1-a^*)} \tag{6}$$

The real exchange rate, $q=P/(eP^*)$, positively depends on the ratio of the relative nontradables price. If the relative nontradables price at home is rising, there will be an increase in q. A rise in the relative price of nontradables can occur in the home country either because relative productivity growth in the fast growing (home) country is lower than abroad or because the demand for nontradables is rising in the growth process faster than that for tradables. Thus income elasticity of nontradables would be higher than for tradables.

In the following analysis, we will not focus on the standard Balassa-Samuelson effect, rather we assume heterogenous tradable goods and see the price of exported tradables as rising relative to that of tradables abroad, as the home country is pursuing relatively more product innovations (v) than the foreign leader country. International price arbitrage thus does not imply $P^T=eP^{T*}$, rather we will have for a world with differentiated products and quality index V':

$$P^T=V'eP^{T*}, \tag{7}$$

where we assume that the relative product innovativeness – or quality index – V' is determined according to:

$$V'= V'(v/v^*) \tag{8}$$

Variable V' is a relative product innovation variable which will become unity once both countries have achieved the same level of technology, assuming that they have an equal share of Schumpeterian talents in populations of equal size.

$$P^T= V'(v/v^*)eP^{T*} \tag{9}$$

P^T is the tradables export price index of country I, and it rises relative to world market prices of imported goods (eP^{T*}) along the relative quality index variable h (note: once the poor country has fully caught up with the foreign leader country, the law of one price will indeed hold in the form V'=1: this implies that all existing product varieties existing in the original lead country are also produced in the follower country). This view implies a modified equation (6'):

$$P/[V'(v/v^*)eP^*] = (\varphi)^{(1-a)}/(\varphi^*)^{(1-a^*)} \tag{10}$$

One may note that product innovations can also occur in the nontradables sector. A poor country which opens up to the world economy could be affected in the nontradables sector by technology spillovers from the tradables sector – possibly process innovations which then will allow the production of better quality products and more product varieties – as well as foreign direct investment in the N-sector. Foreign investment in the nontradables sector will be associated with a rise of product quality and product innovations. In the early stage of economic opening up an observed rise of the relative price of nontradables could indeed reflect the impact of product innovations in the nontradables sector. The traditional literature assumes that the relative rise of the nontradables price in the course of economic catching up is mainly due to relative productivity differentials (low productivity in the nontradables sector) and effects from the income elasticity in the N-sector and the T-sector, respectively. This view is incomplete.

Assume that money market equilibrium exists in both countries I and II in the following equations (with M signifying the stock of money, m the real money demand, Y output, and I the nominal exchange rate):

$$M=Pm(Y, i) \tag{11}$$

$$M^*=P^*m^*(Y^*, i^*) \tag{11'}$$

The nominal exchange rate is thus determined as follows:

$$e = [(\varphi^*)^{1-a^*}/(\varphi)^{1-a}][M/M^*][m^*(Y^*, i^*)/m(Y,i)]/[V'(v/v^*)] \tag{12}$$

If interest rate parity is holding, namely $i=i^* + a^E$, where a^E is the expected devaluation rate assumed to be exogenous, we have:

$$e = [(\varphi^*)^{(1-a^*)}/(\varphi)^{(1-a)}][M/M^*][m^*(Y^*, i^*)/m(Y,i^*+a^E)]/[V'(v/v^*)] \tag{13}$$

Denoting e' as the Euler number, we can specify money demand functions in a simple way, namely: $m= Ye'^{-\sigma i}$ and $m^*= Y^*e'^{-\sigma^* i^*}$. Assuming that the interest elasticity for the demand for money is identical in both countries and that relative product innovation lnω (ω = v/v*) positively depends on y/y*, we get (with Y=Ly, where y denotes per capita income for e):

$$e = \{[\varphi^* (y^*)^{1-a^*}/[\varphi(y)]^{1-a}\}[M/M^*][L^*y^*/Ly]/[V'(\omega(y/y^*))] \tag{14}$$

How will the nominal exchange rate develop over time if the growth rate of the money stock is equal in both countries whereby M/M* is constant? Here we find:

$$\ln e = [1-a^*][\ln\varphi^*(y)]- [1-a] \ln[\varphi(y)]+\ln[M/M^*]+\ln(L^*/L)+\ln[y^*/y]-\ln V'(\omega(y/y^*)) \tag{15}$$

Under the simplifying assumption of a=a* and φ=φ* and denoting M/L as M', we observe the following result from differentiation (with E' denoting a semielasticity):

$$d\ln e = [(1-a^*)E_{\varphi,y/y^*} -1 - E_{V',\omega} E'_{\omega,y}]d\ln[y/y^*] + d\ln(M'/M'^*) \tag{16}$$

A rise in the relative per capita money supply will cause a depreciation in the currency. Disregarding for the moment the money supply side, we observe the following multiplier:

$$d\ln e/d\ln[y/y^*] = [(1-a^*)E_{\varphi,y/y^*} -1 - E_{V',\omega} E'_{\omega,y}] \tag{17}$$

The elasticity is negative if:

$$(1-a^*)E_{\varphi,y/y^*} <1 + E_{V',\omega} E'_{\omega,y} \tag{18}$$

It seems quite feasible that the multiplier is indeed negative so that there will be nominal (and real) appreciation in the course of economic catching up: According to the above equation, we have to consider several effects, namely the internal Balassa-Samuelson effect (reaction of P^N/P^T to a rise of y/y*) on the left hand side of equation (18) and a technological catching-up effect (RHS of (18)) which is a new aspect introduced here. If the product innovation effect is sufficiently strong, there will be a real appreciation. Note that the technology effect in turn could have long-term effects on foreign direct investment. Finally, we observe from (16) that the elasticity of the nominal exchange rate with respect to M/M* is unity.

2.3 Modifying Traditional Models and Looking at Economic Growth

2.3.1 Internal and External Exchange Rate

Subsequently we will look at a setting with tradable and nontradable goods where quantities produced are both N (nontradable) and T (tradable). Nominal national output is $Y^n=P^T T + P^N N$, whereby national output (in terms of tradables) is given by: $Y" = T + [P^N/P^T] N$. If the relative price of nontradables should rise over time, Y' rises, even if T and N are constant. We will denote P^T/P^N as φ' – this is the inverse of φ – so that Y"=T+ (1/φ')N. If φ' <1, Y" will rise for the given T and N.

A simple alternative analytical framework for understanding real exchange rate movements where the real exchange rate is defined as q=P/(eP*)=Pe*/P* is as follows (MacDonald, 1998), with p representing lnP:

$$p=ap^T + (1-a)p^N \tag{1'}$$

$$p^*=a^*p^{T^*} + (1-a^*)p^{N^*} \tag{2'}$$

$$\ln q = \ln e^* + p - p^* \tag{3'}$$

$$\ln q = p-p^*-\ln e \tag{4'}$$

The external exchange rate with respect to the price of tradables q^T is thus defined as:

$$\ln q^T = \ln e^* + p^T - p^T{}^* = p^T-p^T{}^*-\ln e \tag{5'}$$

The logarithmic internal real exchange rate, namely $\xi = \ln P^T - \ln P^N$ and ξ*, can be expressed as follows:

$$\xi = p^T - p^N \tag{6'}$$

$$\xi^* = p^{T^*} - p^{N^*} \tag{7'}$$

$$\ln q = \ln q^T - (1-a)\xi + (1-a^*)\xi^* \tag{8'}$$

If there are constant returns to scale in production and full factor mobility across sectors as well as integration of capital markets (with real interest parity holding), we can state that the relative price of tradables depends on the logarithmic ratio of productivity (α) in both sectors, or:

$$\xi = - \alpha^T + \alpha^N \tag{9'}$$

$$\xi^* = -\alpha^{T^*} + \alpha^{N^*} \tag{10'}$$

Substituting (10') and (9') into (8') gives:

$$\ln q = \ln q^T + (1\text{-}a)(\alpha^T\text{-}\alpha^N) - (1\text{-}a^*)(\alpha^{T*}\text{-}\alpha^{N*}) \quad (11')$$

If we assume for simplicity that a=a*, we observe the following:

$$\ln q = \ln q^T + (1\text{-}a)[(\alpha^T\text{-}\alpha^{T*}) - (\alpha^N\text{-}\alpha^{N*})] \quad (12')$$

This is the traditional perspective of the literature, suggesting that the real exchange rate will appreciate (rise of q):

- if the external exchange rate is rising; this indeed cannot be ruled out; a possible case would be a relatively high domestic production innovation rate which so far is not considered in the literature;
- if the relative productivity growth advantage, the differential $(\alpha^T\text{-}\alpha^{T*})$ for the domestic tradables sector, is higher than that of the nontradables sector. While poor countries catching up may indeed record a high rate of technological progress in the tradables sector one cannot rule out that there is an even relatively strong productivity growth advantage in the nontradables sector – the latter might be related to broader deregulation and privatisation in the nontradables sector or to high sector specific technological progress in the nontradables-sector which might be related to high sector FDI inflows. Another possibility is that there could be strong spillover effects from stong productivity dynamics of the tradables sector going to the nontradables sector.

To the extent that the relative advantage of the tradables productivity differential depends positively on per capita income, one may run a regression not of q on relative productivity but on relative per capita income. De Broek/ Slog (2001) find for a large sample of non-transition countries that based on per capita figures, catching up by one percent is associated with a real appreciation of 0.4 percent.

What can we say about relative productivity growth in the tradables sector and the nontradables sector? As regards the technological catching up of poor countries vis-à-vis advanced countries, we may assume that productivity growth in the domestic tradables sector will be relatively high. It is rather unclear, however, whether productivity growth in the nontradables sector abroad could be higher than in the poor country. This is particularly likely if there are barriers to import competition or to foreign direct investment inflows or if there are impediments for strong competition. Why exactly should relative productivity growth in the T-sector be high? This is a question we will examine in greater detail later.

First, however, we wish to raise serious objections to the above equation. The above equation is considered here to be interpreted in an inappropriate manner. To see this, we can rewrite the equation as follows:

$$\ln q^T = \ln q + (1\text{-}a)[(\alpha^N\text{-}\alpha^{N*}) - (\alpha^T\text{-}\alpha^{T*})] \quad (13')$$

According to the view developed here, the real exchange rate q=P/(eP) is mainly a monetary phenomenon. Interpreted in this fashion, it is not the relative productivity differential combined with the real exchange rate which determines q^T, rather it is q^T and relative productivity differentials that determine the relative price of tradables.

Consider a money demand function (with m denoting the real demand for money and M^d the nominal money demand) where the real money demand depends on real income Y, the nominal interest rate I and real wealth A':

$$M^d = Pm(Y,I,A') = [P^T]\varphi^{1-a}\, m(Y,I,A') \tag{14'}$$

$$M^{d*} = P^*m^*(Y^*,i^*,A'^*) = [P^{T*}]^{a*}\, \varphi^{*\,1-a*}\, m^*(Y^*,i^*,A'^*) \tag{15'}$$

Under the assumption of money market equilibrium $M=M^d$ and $M^*=M^{d*}$ and the modified arbitrage condition $P^T=V'eP^T*$, we have the equation:

$$e = (1/V')(M/M^*)(m^*/m)\,[\varphi^*]^{1-a^*}/[\varphi]^{1-a} \tag{16'}$$

Using a rather simple money demand function, taking into account that m depends on real income, the nominal interest rate and the real value of stocks (Welfens, 2001, p.43), we have (with e' denoting the Euler number, σ the semi-interest elasticity and P' the stock market price):

$$m = Ye'^{-\sigma i}\, KP'/P \tag{17'}$$

$$m^* = Y^*e'^{-\sigma^* i^*}K^*P'^*/P^* \tag{18'}$$

Here we use a simple perspective in the sense that real wealth coincides with the real value of stocks. The nominal equilibrium exchange rate then assumes that $\sigma = \sigma^*$:

$$e = (1/V')(M/M^*)[\varphi^*]^{1-a^*}/[\varphi]^{1-a}\,[(Y/Y^*)(K/K^*)(P'/P'^*)(P/P^*)e'^{-\sigma(i-i^*)} \tag{19'}$$

and hence the real exchange rate is:

$$q = P/(eP^*) = (1/V')(M^*/M)\,[\varphi]^{1-a}/[\varphi^*]^{1-a^*}\,[(Y^*/Y)(K^*/K)(P'^*/P')e'^{-\sigma(i^*-i)} \tag{20'}$$

Using logarithms, we can write:

$$\begin{aligned}\ln q = -\ln V' + \ln(M^*/M) + (1-a)\ln\varphi - (1-a^*)\ln\varphi + \ln(Y^*/Y) \\ + \ln(K^*/K) + \ln(P'^*/P') - \sigma(i^*-i)\end{aligned} \tag{21'}$$

The interesting point here is that the relative stock of money, relative capital productivity $(Y^*/K^*)/(Y/K)$, the relative stock market prices and relative nominal interest play a role for q. Clearly, money is not neutral here. We should also note that V' is a parameter which might effectively be a function of relative per capita income and capital intensity and hence capital productivity. Comparing 21' to 13' we obtain that

$$\begin{aligned}\ln q^T = -\ln V' + \ln(M^*/M) + [\ln(Y^*/K^*) - \ln(Y/K)] + \ln(P'^*/P') \\ - \sigma(i^*-i);\end{aligned} \tag{13''}$$

This suggests that the external exchange rate is influenced by macroeconomic factors, including y/y^* if one takes into account that $V'=V'(y/y^*)$ and that $Y=yL$ and $Y^*=y^*L^*$.

Considering the fact that output consists of tradables and nontradables, we can argue that aggregate relative capital productivity will depend on weighted capital productivities in both the tradables and the nontradables sector. What determines capital productivity? In a simple neoclassical model with a standard production function, it is a positive function of the ratio L/K, which is the inverse of capital intensity K/L=k. Relative capital intensity also depends on the level of technology. Assume that in the home country $Y=K^{\beta}(AL)^{1-\beta}$ with $0<\beta<1$, so that technological progress is Harrod neutral (i.e., labor augmenting). A similar production function holds abroad. Hence for average capital productivity we find:

$$Y/K= A^{(1-\beta)}k^{\beta-1} \tag{22'}$$

$$Y^*/K^*= A^{*(1-\beta^*)}k^{*\beta^*-1} \tag{23'}$$

Based on the standard McDougall model, it follows that the poor country – with a low capital intensity – will attract some FDI inflows once the country begins opening up. This effect in itself will raise capital intensity and reduce capital productivity. Yet this holds only for a given A*. However, one may assume that A(t) evolves over time as a positive function of the share of cumulated FDI inflows – K** being the stock of capital owned by foreigners in the poor home country – the technology gap (A*/A) and the share of skilled labor H' in overall labor L. The larger the ratio of foreign subsidiaries to overall capital K, the faster the international technology transfer. Moreover, the higher the ratio of skilled labor to overall labor input, the faster the learning processes and hence catching up. Thus we state the following function with positive elasticities:

$$A=A_0(K^{**}/K)^{\mu}(A^*/A)(H'/L)^{\rho} \tag{24'}$$

The higher the ratio between K**/K, the higher is A, whereby capital productivity can grow despite FDI inflows in the home country. Under the simple specification chosen here, the elasticity of A with respect to A* is ½. Moreover, we may assume that such a catching-up function is valid for both the tradables and the nontradables sector, where the relevant elasticity is μ' in the tradables and μ'' in the nontradables sector. We may assume that the catching-up effect in the tradables sectors is initially faster than in the nontradables sector since:

- FDI inflows are typically more likely to occur in the tradables sector in the first phase of economic opening up (the main reason being that foreign investors can sell both in the host country market and in the world market, thereby limiting investment risks);
- The fact that the global tradables sector is subject to more competition than the nontradables sector (take for example the construction sector) in every country implies that technological progress is relatively high. From the perspective of the poor country, this implies a high sectoral technological gap and hence a large opportunity for technological catching up.

We thus have to focus on both FDI policy and competition policy in poor countries if we are to understand technological catching-up processes.

2.3.2 Medium Term Issues of Product Innovations, Output and the Exchange Rate

As countries catch up, the export-GDP and the import-GDP ratio will grow while the share of intra-industrial trade will increase. Moreover, foreign direct investment inflows will rise – and in the long run there will typically be two-way FDI flows. Firms will become more innovative and will emphasize product innovations; the rate of product innovations will be denoted as v; note that the term product innovation is understood here in the sense that the respective product is new from the perspective of the respective catching-up country (from the perspective of a global technology leader country this looks like product imitation). The term v may be understood are the country's product innovations relative to that of foreign countries: v is a stock variable, that is the share of product innovations given the overall number of products n_0. In the following analysis we will raise the issue of how product innovations will affect output, the interest rate and the exchange rate. The following macroeconomic model set up is a "Schumpeter-Keynes" approach in the sense that product innovations are integrated into the familiar Mundell-Flemming model. Hence the price level at home and abroad is given.

As regards the goods market our basic assumption is that investment I is a function of the real interest rate at home I and abroad (r*), the real exchange rate q* - following the Froot/ Stein argument – and the product innovation rate v which is exogenous in the model. Hence we implicitly assume a model with foreign direct investment inflows. Moreover, we basically assume that new products can be produced only with new equipment so that investment is a positive function of v. Consumption also is assumed to be a positive function of v; and a positive function of disposable income Y(1-τ) and of real money balances M/P so that we have a real balance effect in the consumption function. Net exports X' are assumed to be positive function of Y*, q* and v, but a negative function of Y. As regards the money market we assume that the real demand for money m depends positively on Y and v – the latter as a higher rate of product innovations suggests that the marginal utility of holding liquidity is increasing for consumers looking for shopping opportunities of innovative goods; m depends negatively on the nominal interest rate I which is equal to r plus the expected inflation rate (assumed here to be zero).

The foreign exchange rate market equilibrium requires here that net capital imports Q(i/i*, v, q*) – with positive partial derivatives of Q with respect to both i/i*, q* and to v – plus net exports of goods and services are equal to zero. Net capital imports react positively to a real depreciation in line with the Froot/ Stein argument. Net capital imports are assumed to depend positively on v because a higher rate of product innovations will stimulate FDI inflows – foreign investors become more active as they are anticipating higher profit opportunities. Linearizing the consumption function as

$$C= c(1-\tau)Y + c'(M/P) + c''v \qquad \text{(Ia)}$$

and using a simple investment function

$$I= -hr - h'r^* + h''v + h'''q^* \qquad \text{(Ib)}$$

and a net export function

$$X' = xq^* + x'Y^*/Y + x''v \qquad \text{(Ic)}$$

we have the following three equations (I, II, III) as the equilibrium condition in the goods market, the money market and the foreign exchange market, respectively (G is real government expenditures):

$$Y = c(1-\tau)Y + c'(M/P) + c''v + G - hr - h'r^* + h''v + h'''q^* + xq^* + x'Y^*/Y + x''v \qquad \text{[IS]} \quad \text{(I)}$$

$$M/P = m(Y,r,v) \qquad \text{[LM]} \quad \text{(II)}$$

$$Q(i/i^*, v, q^*) + xq^* + x'Y^*/Y + x''v = 0 \qquad \text{[ZZ]} \quad \text{(III)}$$

Product innovations shift the IS curve to the right, the LM curve to the left and the ZZ curve downwards; the latter holds since net exports of goods and services will increase as a consequence of a higher v: an initial negative trade balance will thus be reduced so that required net capital imports will fall. If m_v is zero the LM curve is not directly affected by a change of v so that product innovations clearly raise both equilibrium output and the interest rate. Under flexible exchange rates there will be an appreciation of the currency in point E_1 – as this point is above the ZZ line – so that the IS_1 curve (driven by reduced net exports of goods and services) will shift a bit to the left (IS_2) while the ZZ_1 curve will shift upwards (ZZ_2). It remains true that product innovations raise the output level and the real interest rate, and contribute to a current account surplus. This situation could continue until there is a new intersection point in the initial equilibrium E_0 (note that in a system of fixed exchange rates point E_1 implies higher net capital inflows and an excess supply in the foreign exchange market, respectively. The stock of money M will increase, the LM-curve and the IS-curve, the latter due to higher consumption, will shift to the right).

This, however, does not mean that government promotion of policy innovation is inefficient since in a medium term perspective the capital stock K will increase as the consequence of net investment – actually increased net investment in the context of product innovations. Indeed, a modified simple medium term model could consider that consumption $C = c(1-\tau)Y + c'[(M/P)+(P'/P)K] + c''v$ where the term $c'[\ldots]$ is a broader real wealth effect in the consumption, namely including the real value of the capital stock; P'/P is the ratio of the stock market price index P' to the outputprice index P. A consistent medium term export function would read $X = xq^* + x'Y^*/Y + x''v + x'''K$ where the term $x'''K$ (with $x'''>0$) is a supply shift variable in the export sector. This term will then shift both the IS curve to the right and the ZZ curve downwards as K is raised. Thus the general equilibrium point in our diagram will shift to the right over time where we assume that monetary policy raises the money supply in parallel with the capital stock K, so that medium term money supply equilibrium is given for the case of an income elasticity of output of unity by the simple equation $(M/P)/K = [Y/K]m'(i,v)$. In a noninflationary economy it is equal to the real interest rate r which under profit maximization and a Cobb Doublas production function $Y=K^{ß}AL^{1-ß}$ (with L standing for labor and A for Harrod-neutral technological progress) is equal to ßY/K so that Y/K=r/ß. Hence a monetary policy strategy which aims at a constant ratio [M/P]/K is then consistent with a constant money demand {[r/ß]m'(i,v)} – assuming that v and i and r, respectively, are constant; read: have reached an equilibrium value. An interesting long term question concerns the relation between product innovations v and the process innovations A. If A is a positive function of v – since new products can often be produced only on new equipment (and the innovation system may be assumed to be responsive to the higher demand for A) – an exogenous rate of product innovations dv/dt>0 would indeed generate a continuous growth process. A more realistic picture would emerge if we would also consider a quasi-depreciation rate of the stock of product innovations or a vintage type approach to product innovations so that in each period the oldest product generation is removed from the shelf and production, respectively.

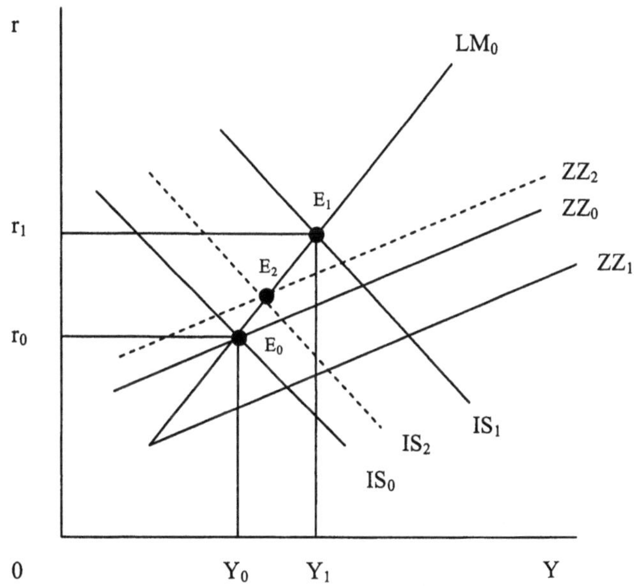

Fig. 5. Rise of Product Innovations in the Mundell-Fleming Model

As endogenous variables we have Y, r and e (changes in e stand for a real exchange rate change as long as P or P* are not changing). So we are interested in the medium term multipliers for Y, r and e with respect to v, the product innovation rate. Using Kramer's rule we obtain (with $\zeta = i/i^*$) after differentiation of (I), (II), (III):

$$dY/dv > 0 \text{ (sufficient condition is } m_v=0) \qquad \text{(IV)}$$

$$dr/dv > 0 \text{ (sufficient condition is } m_v = 0) \tag{V}$$

$$de/dv < 0 \tag{VI}$$

if (see appendix; the system determinant is negative; the following expression shows the nominator expression of the multiplier de/dv) Q_ζ and m_r are sufficiently small, so that

$$\left\{\left(1 - c'(1-\tau) + \frac{x'Y^*}{Y^2}\right) m_r \left(Q_{q^*} + x\right) - h m_Y \left(Q_{q^*} + x\right)\right\} > \left\{\left(h''' + x\right)\left(m_Y Q_\zeta - m_r \frac{x'Y^*}{Y^2}\right)\right\} \tag{VII}$$

and Y^* exceeding Y_0^* (home country is relatively small). Product innovations will bring about a real appreciation. One also may note that it raises equilibrium output. This is much in line with original reflections of Schumpeter who has argued that firms facing the pressure of economic recession will launch new products in order to generate more sales. From a policy perspective our analysis suggests that government could stimulate product innovations in recessions in order to raise output; indeed one may split government expenditures G into government consumption G' plus government R&D support (G") for product innovations. Such an approach certainly is rather appropriate in countries catching-up since for them a higher rate of product innovations largely means to accelerate the speed of international imitations of foreign product innovations; as regards advanced countries one may doubt that higher government R&D subsidies could stimulate product innovations in the short term strongly so as to overcome a recession easily. At the bottom line the model presented clearly suggests that the structural breakdown of government expenditures is crucial. Since the ratio of R&D expenditures to GDP has increased in the long run OECD countries it is obvious that innovation issues have become more important – while standard macroeconomic modelling largely ignores innovation issues.

Total Multiplier Effect

The distinction between different types of government expenditures is crucial as we will show subsequently and is totally ignored in the traditional macro models. Real government expenditure G is split here into government consumption G' and expenditures G" on the promotion of product innovations:

$$G = G' + G'' \tag{VIII}$$

Expenditures on the promotion of product innovations mean in the case of leading OECD countries that development of true product innovations is stimulated; and no short-run results can be expect. However, for catching-up countries this could mean mainly acceleration of imitation of foreign product innovations which in many cases should be possible within one or two years. We assume subsequently that there is a link between government expenditures on research & development – with a focus on product innovations – that can described by

$$v = \Omega G'' \tag{IX}$$

Hence we have a link between two exogenous variables. As regards multipliers for G" they clearly differ from that for G' since a change in G" will not only affect aggregate demand (direct impact) but also the product innovation rate v (indirect impact) so that the overall multiplier for any endogenous variable Z_i (=Y, r, e) can be written as

$$dZ_i/dG" = [dZ_i/dG] + \Omega dZ_i/dv \qquad (X)$$

The first RHS term in brackets is the same for dG=dG' and dG=dG", but the second term is relevant only with respect to a change of G". The output multiplier dY/dG" for a rise of G" clearly is larger than that for a rise of government consumption G'.

There is another link between exogenous variables in the context of product innovations which imply an effective fall of the price level P – a problem which theoretically comes under the heading of hedonic price measurement. Using a simple approach – with the hedonic parameter H (H>0) - we thus can write

$$dP = -Hdv \qquad (XI)$$

Product innovations are indeed a nonmonetary aspect of the price level. At the bottom line the complete multiplier analysis for the impact of a rise of G" is given by

$$dZ_i/dG" = [dZ_i/dG] + \Omega dZ_i/dv - HdZ_i/dP \qquad (XII)$$

The following graphical analysis shows both the direct effect of a rise in government expenditures promoting product innovations and the indirect effects of this policy which consists of a double rightward shift of the IS curve related to the impact of G" on v and of v on P and M/P, respectively; the effective rise of M/P amounts to a hedonic real balance effect. Moreover, there will be a rightward shift of the LM curve which is to say that product innovations are equivalent to a rise of M/P unless there is a dominant money demand effect.

In a more general perspective it is true that the impact of v on P must be considered with respect to all multipliers dZ_i/dv so that these multipliers are composed of a direct effect and an indirect effect related to a change of the price level. Thus a consistent analysis of the multipliers for Y, r and e is achieved. As regards the change in the "hedonically adjusted" real exchange rate one has to take into account that d(eP*/P) is given for a constant foreign price level P* normalized to unity by $(1/P)de/dv - (e/P^2)dP/dv$. Our analysis offers a new and broader analytical picture of important policy issues (for more details see appendix).

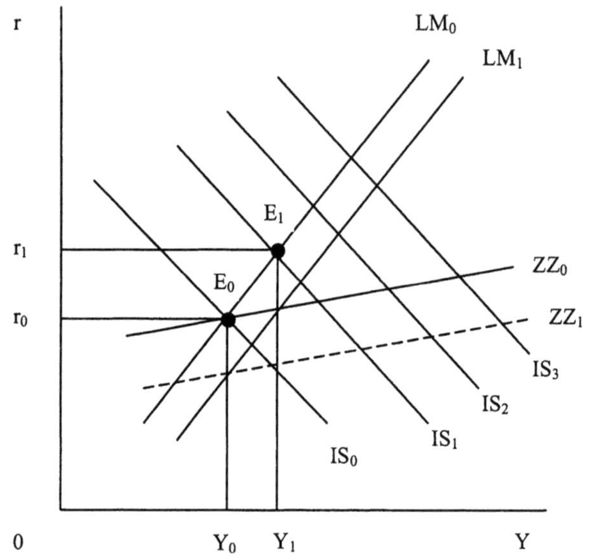

Fig. 6. Direct and Indirect Effects of Product Innovation

2.3.3 Economic Catching-up and Long Term Real Exchange Rate Dynamics

From a theoretical perspective, we expect a long-term real appreciation of the currency of accession countries which are assumed to catch up in economic and technological terms with EU-15. Thus, the Balassa-Samuelson effect would work. However, how will this effect indeed be realized? One may ask whether it is mainly a nominal appreciation which brings about the BS effect thereby requiring flexible exchange rates or whether it is a rise of the price level relative to the foreign price level (in a setting with a constant or stable nominal exchange rate). A rise in the domestic price level could bring problems with respect to the inflation convergence criterion and the interest rate convergence criterion of European Economic and Monetary Union. From this perspective, it is clear that countries eager to join quickly the monetary union might prefer an extended period of flexible exchange rates and enter the Euro zone only after a transition period of several years.

A Simple Long-Term Approach

In the following approach, we assume that net exports X' positively influence the real exchange rate q=:[P/(eP*] (parameter b>0) and that it is a negative function of the relative innovation differential a*". On the link between the real exchange rate and the current account, consistent models are available. A relative rise of innovativeness abroad (country II) – we focus here mainly on product innovations – will lead to relatively lower export prices of country I. The prospects for technological catching-up depend on technology policy and education policy, and both can be expected to negatively depend on the share of the natural resource sector in the overall economy. As regards the link between q and a*", one may also note that net capital exports will be larger the higher our a*" is (i.e., a technological progress differential in favor of the foreign country). Here we assume a*" to be an exogenous variable. Hence we find the following:

$$dq/dt = bX' - a^{*\prime\prime}q \qquad \text{(I)}$$

We furthermore assume that net exports negatively depend on q where the elasticity η is negative. Hence, we have:

$$X' = q^{\eta} \quad (\text{with } \eta \leq 0) \qquad \text{(II)}$$

This leads to the following Bernoullian differential equation for q(t):

$$dq/dt = bq^{\eta} - a^{*\prime\prime}q \qquad \text{(III)}$$

In the subsequent graph, we have drawn the first right hand side expression as the BB line and the second expression as the AA line. For given parameters, there will be a monotonous real appreciation (see the QQ-line). With C_o determined from initial conditions and e' denoting the Euler number, the solution of the differential equation is:

$$q(t) = \{C_o e'^{-a^{*}(1-\eta)t} + b/a^{*\prime\prime}\}^{1/(1-\eta)} \qquad \text{(IV)}$$

This equation is convergent for q. Hence we have an equation for the long-term real exchange rate with q converging and thus has the steady state value (for t approaching infinity) q#:

$$q\# = (b/a^{*\prime\prime})^{1/(1-\eta)} \qquad \text{(V)}$$

For a small, open – non-innovative (!) – economy facing an infinite price elasticity in export markets, the equilibrium real exchange rate is clearly unity (see equation V). If the export demand elasticity is zero, thereby reflecting the extreme case of a country exporting a very large share of high technology goods, we find that:

q# = b/a"* (case of high technology dominance in exports)

If the absolute value of η is unity, we would get as the steady state value $q\#=(b/a''^{*})^{1/2}$. Clearly, technological catching-up with a*' being reduced will lead to downward rotation of the AA curve (AA_1 in Fig. 7b). Technological upgrading could also go along with a fall in the absolute value of the price elasticity. Both elements could occur simultaneously.

Take E_o as the starting point. If there is only a fall in price elasticity (in absolute terms), the rotation of the hyperbola indicates that there will be a real depreciation effect. Next we take a look at the fall of a*". Taking E_0 as the starting point, we observe a real appreciation in point E_{01}. Catching-up of the home country is also associated with a rise in the share of technology intensive goods. Should catching-up go along with a higher share of (medium-) technology intensive goods (e.g., due to foreign investors increasingly producing product cycle goods in modern plants for exports to world markets), we find a rotation of the BB curve, since the price elasticity – in absolute terms – of exports is falling (BB_1). This elasticity effect will dampen the real appreciation so that E_1 is the final equilibrium point. If, however, the reduction of the technology gap is relatively strong (intersection point of AA is to the right of point F), the reduction of the absolute price elasticity will reinforce the real appreciation effect. Note that there may be cases when a*'' rise and the price elasticity falls in absolute terms.

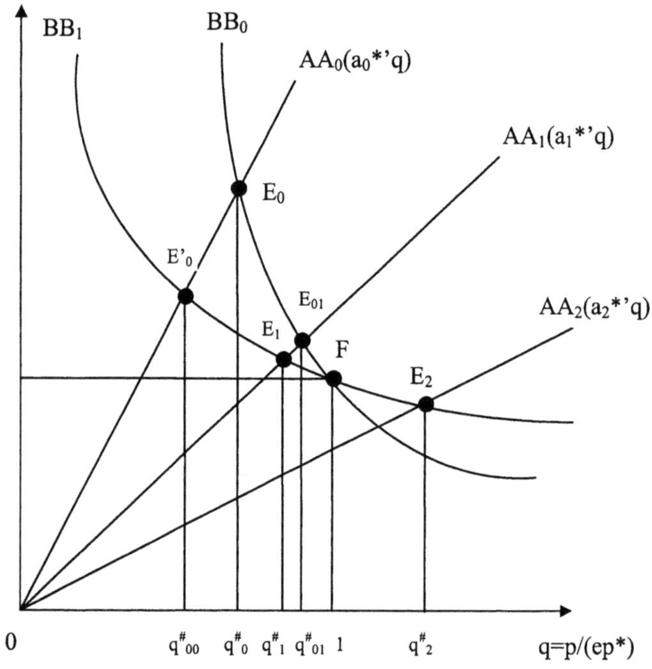

Fig. 7. Model of the Long Term Real Exchange Rate ($dq/dt=bq^{\eta} - a^{*\prime}q$)

From an empirical perspective, we may expect that countries opening up will liberalize trade and adopt internal modernization measures which help to raise per capita income in the medium term. This would help to stimulate capital inflows (in particular FDI inflows) so that per capita output will further increase. (Per capita GNP might increase more slowly than per capita GDP, however, since rising FDI inflows could raise the share of profit transfers relative to GDP.) As per capita income y rises, the share of intra-industrial trade should increase, accompanied by intensified competition. The latter, in turn, should stimulate static efficiency gains as well as innovation, and government policy may then stimulate innovation through subsidies for research and development.

3 Perspectives on Exchange Rate Research

We have shown that issues pertaining to economic catching-up and exchange rate dynamics are riddled with many unanswered questions and issues. Some of those issues have been analysed here in an innovative way. Essentially, we have offered new insights for both short-term financial market perspectives and a more long-term analysis, but we have also added some refinements to the existing theory. Clearly, there is need for more research. It will be important to shed light on some of the crucial empirical issues raised here.

There are strong theoretical arguments which suggest that there will be a medium term appreciation if there is increasing product innovation. Government policies can affect the rate of product innovations by adequate emphasis in procurement policies and by adequate focus of R&D policy – including a long term rise of R&D expenditures which, however, should take into account the size of positive external effects associated with product innovations and process innovations, respectively. Government may also stimulate product innovations through higher expenditures on education where the assumption is that this will raise the share of skilled labor which in turn will stimulate foreign direct investment and technological upgrading, respectively. At the same time we may assume that people with better education have a stronger preference for differentiated products so that the domestic market for differentiated products will rise along with the level of education.

The analysis presented is particularly relevant for transition countries and newly industrialized countries as well as for countries catching-up within regional integration blocks (e.g. Ireland, Spain, Portugal in the case of the EU or Thailand and Indonesia in the case of ASEAN). At the bottom line it is clear that in periods of a widening cross-country innovation differential – e.g. the 1990s with an acceleration of the US innovativeness as measured by patent applications – there is a need for increased nominal and real exchange rate flexibility.

As regards the medium term analysis it is interesting to note that the nominal exchange rate could increase or fall as a consequence of a change in relative per capita income. If monetary policy should have a bias in the sense that the central bank's propensity to adopt noninflationary policy is higher in a country with a high per capita income (compared to a low income country) – probably because the ratio of assets to income is relatively high which makes people more sensitive to inflation and because high income countries will not have to rely on the inflation tax as a source of government revenue – the course of the real exchange rate is not clear. If there is a nominal appreciation and the domestic price level is growing more slowly than the foreign price level, there could be a real depreciation. These and other issues can be clarified only in the context of empirical analysis.

A low inflation rate is rather likely if stability-oriented monetary policy goes along with a continuing nominal appreciation. Low inflation rates are useful for nurturing capital markets, namely to raise the average maturity of debt. The latter implies that there are more opportunities for long term domestic financing. Availability of more long term financing opportunities will go along with more long term and with higher aggregate investment (and possibly more innovation projects) which in turn raises the growth rate. If there is more long term debt financing, the demand for foreign long term borrowing will fall and hence net capital imports will fall. In a system of flexible exchange rates the implication then is that net imports of goods and services will fall. While a wise central bank will pursue strict anti-inflationary policies it should not adopt deflationary policies. To avoid an excessively rigid monetary policy will not be easy in an economy with a high rate of product innovations since part of the rise of the aggregate price increase is reflecting better product quality. Adequate hedonic price measurement therefore seems to be quite important. If the central bank adopts a policy which leads to relatively high short term interest rates and relatively modest long term interest rates there also is the risk that the country will have a high share of short term capital inflows which exposes the country to potentially strong international reversals of short term capital flows.

If there is a short and medium term real appreciation of the currency in the context of economic and technological catching up there is some risk that there will be a rise of the unemployment rate; mainly unskilled workers will become unemployed if one assumes that a rising share of quality products and more technology intensive production, respectively, go along with a rising relative demand of skilled labor. The fall in the demand for unskilled labor will be largely due to labor saving technological progress on the one hand, on the other hand to structural change in the sense that more (human)capital intensive and technology intensive technologies will be employed. The price level of nontradables and the overall price level will rise in the course of economic catching up – unless a strong nominal appreciation would depress the price of tradables in such a way that the overall price level remains constant. If economic catching up implies that the wage ratio of unskilled labor to skilled labor will fall unskilled workers face three problems:

- there will be a fall of the real unskilled wage level as the price level is rising while the unskilled nominal wage rate is falling;
- in line with the fall of unskilled wages there could be pressure on unskilled workers to work more hours so that labor supply is increasing;
- there could be a higher risk of unemployment for unskilled workers where trade union pressure not to allow a rise of the wage ratio skilled labor to unskilled labor could aggravate the problem.

From this perspective retraining of unskilled labor and higher expenditures on education are crucial. Government pressure on collective bargaining partners to make labor markets more flexible is often useful, but it can also bring serious problems: If regulations and laws undermine incentives for long term employment there will be reduced incentives for firms to invest in retraining and human capital formation; in an environment with reduced job tenure there is an increasing risk that a company's investment in retraining will be lost in the future as mobile workers – including unemployed workers – find later a job with competitors.

If high unemployment rates – along with a high share of long term unemployment – should be a sustained problem there could be political instability which will raise the risk premium in capital markets and will reduce net capital inflows which in turn undermines investment dynamics and growth. In a system of flexible exchange rates there is also the risk that there will be considerable nominal and real exchange rate overshooting (in line with the standard Dornbusch model). Such overshooting could bring about serious problems, including higher instability of the business cycle; and in the case of a temporary depreciation there could be liquidity problems for countries with high foreign debt.

Integrating the analysis of product innovations and process innovations into short term, medium term and long term macroeconomic models seems to be an important task in a world in which there is intensified global technological competition. The policy implications seem to be important. Moreover, the rapid growth of foreign direct investment (in OECD countries and several Asian countries) in the period 1985-2003 suggests that FDI should also be included into standard macro models. Foreign direct investment in turn is crucial for international technology transfer.

Mathematical Appendix 1

Multipliers of the extended Branson model

$$A' = (M/P) + (eF^*/P) + P'K/P \qquad \text{[budget constraint]} \tag{1a}$$

$$M/P = n(V, i^*+a^E, z, \psi)A';\ n_1>0,\ n_2<0,\ n_3<0,\ n_4<0 \qquad \text{[MM curve]} \tag{1b}$$

$$eF^*/P = f(V, i^*+a^E, z, \psi)A';\ f_1<0,\ f_2>0,\ f_3<0,\ f_4<0 \qquad \text{[F*F* curve]} \tag{1c}$$

$$P'K/P = h(V, i^*+a^E, z, \psi)A';\ h_1<0,\ h_2<0,\ h_3>0,\ h_4>0 \qquad \text{[KK curve]} \tag{1d}$$

Because of n+f+h=1 eq. 1b) – 1d) are linearly dependent. To solve the system we confine ourselves to the use of eq. 1b) and 1c). Inserting eq. 1a) into 1b) we get

$$M = n(V, i^*+a^E, z, \psi)(M + eF^* + P'K) = n^{\#}(\cdot)(eF^* + P'K) \tag{1b'}$$

$$eF^* = f(V, i^*+a^E, z, \psi)(M + P'K) = f^{\#}(\cdot)(M + P'K) \tag{1c'}$$

herein $n^{\#}(V, i^*+a^E, z, \psi) = n(\cdot)/(1-n(\cdot))$; $f^{\#}(V, i^*+a^E, z, \psi) = f(\cdot)/(1-f(\cdot))$; with $dn^{\#}/dn > 0$ for $0 < n < 1$; $df^{\#}/df > 0$ for $0 < f < 1$.

Differentiating eq. 1b' and 1c', we get the system

$$dM = \sum_i n^{\#}_{x_i} dx_i + n^{\#}(de + dF^* + dP' + dK) \tag{1e}$$

$$de + dF^* = \sum_i f^{\#}_{x_i} dx_i + f^{\#}(de + dF^* + dP' + dK)$$

Rearranging eq. 1e, we get the matrix system

$$\begin{pmatrix} -n^{\#} & -n^{\#} \\ 1 & -f^{\#} \end{pmatrix} \begin{pmatrix} de \\ dP' \end{pmatrix} = \begin{pmatrix} n_v^{\#} & n_{i*}^{\#} & n_z^{\#} & n_{\psi^{\#}}^{\#} & n^{\#} & n^{\#} & -1 \\ f_v^{\#} & f_{i*}^{\#} & f_z^{\#} & f_{\psi^{\#}}^{\#} & -1 & f^{\#} & f^{\#} \end{pmatrix} \begin{pmatrix} dv \\ di^* \\ dz \\ d\psi \\ dF^* \\ dK \\ dM \end{pmatrix} \qquad (1f)$$

with its system determinant $|\mathbf{A}| = n^{\#} f^{\#} + n^{\#} > 0$.

The multipliers referring the endogenous variables e and P' amount to

$$\frac{de}{dz} = \frac{-n_z f^{\#} + f_z n^{\#}}{|A|} > 0$$

$$\frac{de}{d\psi} = \frac{-n_\psi f^{\#} + f_\psi n^{\#}}{|A|} <=> 0$$

$$\frac{de}{dK} = \frac{-n^{\#} f^{\#} + n^{\#} f^{\#}}{|A|} = 0$$

$$\frac{de}{dM} = \frac{f^{\#} + n^{\#} f^{\#}}{|A|} = \frac{f^{\#}\left(1 + n^{\#}\right)}{|A|} > 0$$

$$\frac{de}{di^*} = \frac{-n_{i*}^{\#} f^{\#} + f_{i*}^{\#} n^{\#}}{|A|} > 0$$

$$\frac{dP'}{dz} = \frac{-n^{\#} f_z^{\#} - n_z^{\#}}{|A|} > 0$$

$$\frac{dP'}{d\psi} = \frac{-n^{\#} f_\psi^{\#} - n_\psi^{\#}}{|A|} > 0$$

$$\frac{dP'}{dK} = \frac{-n^{\#} f^{\#} - n^{\#}}{|A|} < 0$$

$$\frac{dP'}{dM} = \frac{-n^{\#} f^{\#} + 1}{|\mathrm{A}|} = \frac{h/((1-n)(1-f))}{|\mathrm{A}|} > 0$$

$$\frac{dP'}{di^{*}} = \frac{-n^{\#} f_{i*}^{\#} - n_{i*}^{\#}}{|\mathrm{A}|} <=> 0$$

Mathematical Appendix 2

$$dY = c'(1-\tau)dY + c'd(M/P) + c''dv - hdr + c'm_r dr + h''dv + h'''de + xde - \frac{x'Y*}{Y^2}dY + x''dv \tag{Ia}$$

$$(1-c'(1-\tau) + \frac{x'Y^{*}}{Y^2})dY + (h - c'm_r)dr - (h'''+x)de = c'd(\frac{M}{P}) + (c''+h''+x'')dv \tag{Ib}$$

$$d(\frac{M}{P}) = m_Y dY + m_r dr + m_v dv \tag{IIa}$$

$$m_Y dY + m_r dr = d(\frac{M}{P}) - m_v dv \tag{IIb}$$

$$Q_{\xi} dr + Q_v dv + Q_{q^{\cdot}} de + xde + \frac{x'Y^{*}}{Y^2} dY + x''dv = 0 \tag{IIIa}$$

$$\frac{x'Y^{*}}{Y^2} dY + Q_{\xi} dr + (Q_{q^{\cdot}} + x)de = -(Q_v + x'')dv \tag{IIIb}$$

The equation system in matrix notation is:

$$\begin{pmatrix} 1-c'(1-\tau)+\frac{x'Y^{*}}{Y^2} & h-c'm_r & -(h'''+x) \\ m_Y & m_r & 0 \\ \frac{x'Y^{*}}{Y^2} & Q_{\xi} & Q_{q'}+x \end{pmatrix} \begin{pmatrix} dY \\ dr \\ de \end{pmatrix} = \begin{pmatrix} c' & c''+h''+x'' \\ 1 & -m_v \\ 0 & -(Q_v+x'') \end{pmatrix} \begin{pmatrix} d\left(\frac{M}{P}\right) \\ dv \end{pmatrix}$$

Define $a = 1 - c'(1-\tau) + \frac{x'Y*}{Y^2}$, then we have the system determinant:

$$|A| = \left\{ am_r \left(Q_{q^*} + x \right) - \left(h - c' m_r \right) m_Y \left(Q_{q^*} + x \right) \right\} + \left[-\left(h''' + x \right) \left(m_Y Q_\xi - m_r \frac{x' Y^*}{Y^2} \right) \right]$$

If {...} exceeds [...]: $|A| < 0$; if Q_ξ and $|m_r|$ are sufficiently small, then $|A| < 0$.

$$\frac{de}{dv} = \frac{1}{|A|} \begin{vmatrix} a & h - c' m_r & c'' + h'' + x'' \\ m_Y & m_r & -m_v \\ \frac{x'' Y^*}{Y^2} & Q_\xi & -(Q_v + x'') \end{vmatrix} = \frac{1}{|A|} \cdot$$

$$\left\{ a \left[m_r (-Q_v - x'') + m_v Q_\xi \right] - (h - c' m_r) m_Y \left[-m_Y (Q_v + x'') + \frac{x' Y^*}{Y^2} m_v \right] \right.$$
$$\left. + b' (m_Y Q_\varphi - m_r \frac{x' Y^*}{Y^2}) \right\} < 0$$

where $b' = c'' + h'' + x''$.

For Y* > critical Y_0* (implicitly: home country is relatively small), the second term in squared brackets then is positive.

$$\frac{dY}{dv} = \frac{1}{|A|} \begin{vmatrix} c'' + h'' + x'' & h - c' m_r & -(h''' + x) \\ -m_v & m_r & 0 \\ -(Q_v + x'') & Q_\xi & Q_{q^*} + x \end{vmatrix}$$
$$= \frac{1}{|A|} ((c'' + h'' + x'') m_r (Q_{q^*} + x) + h m_v (Q_{q^*} + x) + (h''' + x)(m_v Q_\xi - m_r (Q_v + x'')))$$

Sufficient condition for $\frac{dY}{dv} > 0$ is that $|m_r Q_v - m_v Q_\xi| > |m_r x''|$.

$$\frac{dr}{dv} = \frac{1}{|A|} \begin{vmatrix} a & c'' + h'' + x'' & -(h''' + x) \\ m_y & -m_v & 0 \\ \frac{x' y^*}{y^2} & -Q_v - x'' & Q_{q^*} + x \end{vmatrix}$$

$$= [-am_v (Q_{q^*} + x) - b m_Y (Q_{q^*} + x) + (h''' + x)[m_Y (Q_v + x'') - m_v (x'' + \frac{x' Y^*}{Y^2})]$$

References

Balassa, B. (1964), „The Purchasing Power Parity Doctrine: A Reappraisal", Journal of Political Economy, Vol.72, No.6, pp.584-596.

De Broeck, M. and T. Sloek (2001), "Interpreting Real Exchange Rate Movements in Transition Countries", IMF Working Paper 01/56 (Washington: International Monetary Fund).

M.Canzoneri, R.Cumby and B. Diba (1999), "Relative Labor Productivity and the Real Exchange Rate in the Long Run: Evidence for a Panel of OECD Countries", Journal of International Economics, Vol.47, pp.245-266.

Chinn, M. and L. Johnston, 1997, "Real Exchange Rate Levels, Productivity and the Real Exchange Rate in long Run: Evidence for a Panel of OECD Countries", IMF Working Paper 97/66 (Washington: International Monetary Fund).

European Commission (2003). European Innovation Scoreboard, SEC (2003) 1255, Brussels.

European Commission (2004). European Innovation Scoreboard, Brussels.

Frenkel, J. and M. Mussa (1985), "Asset Markets, Exchange Rates, and the Balance of Payments", Chapter 14 in Gene Grossman and Kenneth Rogoff (eds.), Handbook of International Economics, Vol.2 (Amsterdam: North Holland), pp.679-747.

Froot, K. A. and J.C. Stein (1991), Exchange Rates and Foreign Direct Investment: An Imperfect Capital Markets Approach, Quarterly Journal of Economics, November, 1191-1217.

Grafe, C. and C. Wyplosz (1999), "A model of the Real Exchange Rate Determination in Transition Economies", in Mario Blejer and Marko Skreb, Balance of Payments, exchange Rates, and Competitiveness in Transition Economies (Boston: Kluwer Academic Publishers), pp.159-184.

De Gregorio, J. and H. Wolff (1994), "Terms of Trade, Productivity, and the Real Exchange Rate", NBER Working Paper No.4807 (Cambridge, MA: NBER).

Halpern, L. and C. Wyplosz (1997), "Equilibrium Exchange Rates in Transition Economies", IMF Staff Papers, Vol.44 (December), pp.430-61.

International Financial Statistics (2003). IMF, Washington.

Jungmittag, A. (2003), "Internationale Innovationsdynamik, Spezialisierungsstruktur und Außenhandel – Empirische Befunde und wirtschaftspolitische Implikationen", in: T. Gries, A. Jungmittag and P.J.J. Welfens (eds.), Neue Wachstums- und Innovationspolitik in Deutschland und Europa, Physica-Verlag Heidelberg, 183-214.

Jungmittag, A. (2003a), "Innovations, Technological Specialization and Economic Growth in the EU", Economic Papers, DGII Economic and Financial Affaires, European Commission, (forthcoming).

Krajnyak, K. and J. Zettelmeyer (1998), "Competitiveness in Transition Economies: What Scope for Real Appreciation?" IMF Staff Papers, Vol.45 (June), pp.309-62.

MacDonald, R. (1998), "What Do We Really Know About Real Exchange Rates?" Oesterrechische Nationalbank Working Paper No. 28.

Maliszewska, M. (1997), "Modelling Real Exchange Rate in Transition: The Case of Poland and Pomania", CASE Foundation, S&A No. 131.

Rother, P. (2000), "The Impact of Productivity Differentials on Inflation and the Real Exchange Rate: An Estimation of the Balassa-Samuelson Effect in Slovenia", IMF Staff Country Report 00/56 (Washington: International Monetary Fund), pp.26-38.

Szapary, G. (2000), "Maastricht and the Choice of Exchange Rate Regime in Transition Countries During the Run-up to EMU", NBH Working Paper 2000/7.

Tellis, G.UJ. and S. Stremersch, E. Yin (2003), The International Take-off of New Products: the Role of Economics, Culture and Country Innovativeness, *Marketing Science*, Vol. 22, 188-208.

Welfens, P.J.J. (2000), European Monetary Union and Exchange Rate Dynamics, New Approaches and Application to the Euro. Springer-Verlag Berlin Heidelberg New York.

Comment on: Innovation, Structural Change and Exchange Rate Dynamics in Catching-up Countries

Krzysztof Marczewski

The paper discusses the impact of innovations and technological catching-up on the determination of the nominal and the real exchange rate. It consists of five etudes on the topic differing in time horizon of the analysis. For each etude an adequate model of the exchange rate determination is selected ranging from the augmented Branson S/T portfolio approach through dependent economy and Mundell-Fleming classes of models to the long-term Schumpeterian approach.

Product innovations and capital productivity changes are taken as representatives of technological innovativeness. As both of them are treated as exogenous factors, the process of generation of innovations and their proliferation to a catching-up economy is apparently left aside the heart of the analysis. Of course, this focus on impact effects of innovations is reasonable from a technical point of view as it makes modelling less complicated but it simultaneously squeezes a room for a discussion of policy implications of the presented models.

For the short-term analysis a version of the Branson model was chosen in which the domestic bonds market was replaced by the domestic stock market. In this context, Welfens finds that an exogenous rise of capital productivity will raise the stock market price level and possibly bring about a nominal depreciation of the domestic currency. Depending on the differential between the percentage rise of the stock price and the nominal exchange rate, domestic assets could become more or less expensive in terms of foreign currency. If the rate of depreciation was low enough to contribute to a rise in the relative price of domestic assets, foreign direct investment could fall over the medium-term. Welfens argues that in the long run, this increase in stock market prices will be dampened due to emission of new stocks. These medium and long-term considerations are not necessary convincing as they are out-of-the model conclusions.

The second etude deals with the tradeables-nontradeables model with a coexistence of the Balassa-Samuelson effect and catching-up process in terms of product innovation. Welfens proves that if we assume that the product innovation positively depends on per capita income convergence we will identify a parallel, to the B-S effect, channel for the real exchange rate to appreciate. Technically, from very beginning, reasoning presented in equations (1)-(18) isolates productivity changes from structural changes (cf. equations (6)-(7)). It could be disputed to what extent such isolation is empirically justified assumption.

The third etude stresses the role of FDI and import competition as vehicles for international technology transfer. Welfens develops an idea of labour augmenting technological progress supported by a cumulation of FDI inflows. This assumption allows for a capital productivity growth despite FDI inflows in the home country. The underlying model of the real exchange rate determination is very similar to one presented in the second etude.

In the fourth etude medium-term economic conditions are modelled in the Mundell-Fleming manner extended to cover product innovation issue. Under this framework Welfens comes to the conclusion that product innovations will raise the equilibrium output and real interest rate simultaneously bringing about a real appreciation. A derivation of total multiplier effect gives a valuable insight into the combined impact of government expenditure volume and structure on the equilibrium output. However, some policy implications drawn from the model look rather dubious even in a case of catching-up economies e.g. the idea to use government R&D supporting expenditures as a stabilisation policy tool in the periods of recession.

The last etude provides a long-term approach with the real exchange rate movements being positively influenced by net exports and negatively influenced by the economy relative innovation backwardness. The model offers a brilliant discussion of a trade-off between the effects of progress in technological catching-up and the effects of changes in the price elasticity of exports.

Summing up the results of these model considerations we should agree with Welfens that technological catching-up requires an increased nominal and real exchange rate flexibility. However it is still not clear how strong are these technological effects as compared with traditional productivity differentials effects. Policy recommendations of the paper are rather loosely rooted in the presented models. It is especially relevant for a discussion of anti-inflationary policies (almost all models are based on assumption of the money neutrality) and labour market policies. Allowing for import competition and application of FDI attracting measures are rightly identified as crucial elements of any successful innovation promotion policy in catching-up countries.

Finally, it should be stressed that recommendations concerning government R&D supporting expenditures do not fit to conditions prevailing in accession countries. These economies are characterised by budget financing shortages, inefficient R&D sectors and disrupted education systems. So, these societies simultaneously experience a lack of sources and vision of the rational governmental policy stimulating product and process innovations.

List of Contributors

DORA BORBÉLY
European Institute for International Economic Relations (EIIW) at the University of Wuppertal, Germany.

ROLAND DÖHRN
Rheinisch-Westfälisches Institut für Wirtschaftsforschung, Essen, Germany.

BALÁZS ÉGERT
Oesterreichische Nationalbank, Austria, and University of Paris X-Nanterre, France.

FEDERICO FODERS
Kiel Institute for World Economics and University of Cologne, Germany

SIMON GÖRTZ
University of Wuppertal, Germany.

JUTTA GÜNTHER
Halle Institute for Economic Research, Germany.

ULLRICH HEILEMANN
University of Leipzig, Germany.

ANTJE HILDEBRANDT
Oesterreichische Nationalbank, Austria.

ANDRE JUNGMITTAG
University of Wuppertal, and European Institute for International Economic Relations (EIIW), Germany

ALBRECHT KAUFFMANN
University of Potsdam, Germany.

BERND KEMPA
University of Duisburg-Essen, Germany.

KIRSTEN LOMMATZSCH
German Institute for Economic Research, DIW Berlin, Germany.

KRZYSZTOF MARCZEWSKI
Foreign Trade Research Institute, Poland.

ANDREAS PYKA
University of Augsburg, Germany.

KERSTIN SCHNEIDER
University of Dortmund and University of Wuppertal, Germany.

DIETER SCHUMACHER
German Institute for Economic Research, DIW Berlin, Germany.

CHRISTOPHER SCHUMANN
European Institute for International Economic Relations (EIIW) at the University of Wuppertal, Germany.

PAUL J.J. WELFENS
European Institute for International Economic Relations (EIIW) at the University of Wuppertal, Germany.

DARIUSZ WINEK,
Higher School of Commerce and International Finance, Poland.

JULIA WÖRZ
Vienna Institute for International Economic Studies (wiiw), Austria.

ANNA WZIĄTEK-KUBIAK,
Institute of Economic Research, Polish Academy of Science, Poland.

Index

Accession Countries 37, 73, 252
AGHION, P. 173, 197
AGLIETTA, M. 237
AGRAWAL, A. 178, 197
Agriculture 104
AIGINGER, K. 71, 145
AITKEN, B. 150, 164
Allocation of Resources 80
AMITI, M. 120, 145
ANDERSON, B. 178, 197
Apparent Consumption 18
ARCHIBUGI, D. 173, 197
AURDRETSCH, D.B. 98, 99

BALASSA, B. 10, 31, 113, 277
Balassa-Samuelson Effect 109, 207, 211, 249, 256, 279
Balassa-Samuelson Model 211
BALTAGI, B. H. 222, 238
BANERJEE, A. 222, 238
BARFIELD, C. 98, 99
BARRIOS, S. 150, 164
BARRO, R. J. 194, 197
BAULANT, C. 237
Baumol Modell 110
BEBLAVY, M. 238
BEHRMANN, J. N. 164
BELITZ, H. 33, 35
BENACEK, V. 238
BERNARD, A.B. 173, 197
BLIND, K. 180, 198
BLOMSTRÖM, M. 150, 164
BLUNDELL, R. 178, 197
BORBÉLY, D. 4, 37, 41, 71, 73
BOSCO, M. G. 151, 156, 164
BRANSON, W. H. 12, 31
Branson Modell 253, 255
BRÜLHART, M 39, 71, 120, 145
BURGER, B. 153, 164

CABALLERO, R. 178, 197
CAMPOS. N. 238
CANTNER, U. 203, 204
CANTWELL, J. A. 178, 197
CANZONERI, M. 250, 277
CAPPELEN, A. 202, 203
Cash Flow 27
CASSON , M. 13, 31
CEEC 2, 88, 107, 119, 121, 132, 147, 156, 169
CHEN, S. S. 178, 197
Chenery Hypothesis 4, 80, 90, 97, 108
CHENERY, H. B. 80, 95, 108, 113, 115
CHINN, M. 250, 277
CLARK, C. G. 104, 113
CLARK, P. 207, 238
Classification 15, 20, 41, 60, 106, 179
Closed Economies 110
Cobb-Douglas Function 111
COCKBURN, I. 178, 197
COLLINS, S. 80, 95
COMBES, P.-P. 145
Competitive Advantages 9, 33
Competitiveness 3, 10, 33
Competitiveness Policy Council 35
Competitive Pressure 6, 35
Composition of Output 107
Concentration 123, 124, 135, 137
Convergence 111, 177
Convergence Decompositions 190
Copenhagen Criteria 2
CORDEN, W. M. 109, 113
CORICELLI, F. 238
COUDERT, V. 237
Council of Mutual Economic Assistance 102
Creative Destruction 13
CRESPO-CUARESMA, J. 222, 238
CROOKELL, H. 166
Cross Section Regression 84
CSAJBÓK, A. 206, 238
CUMBY, R. 250, 277
Czech Republic 40, 76, 83, 156, 206, 217, 223, 252

DALUM, B. 172, 197
DAMIJAN, J. P. 152, 164
DARVAS, Z. 238
DE BROECK, M. 277
DE GREGORIO, J. 250, 277
DE GROOT, H. L. F. 111, 114
DE LA FUENTE, A. 175, 197
DETKEN, C. 206, 238
Developed Market Economies 14

DIBA, B. 250, 277
DIE WELT 170
DIEPPE, A. 238
Diffusion 5
DJABLIK, M. 125, 145
DJANKOV, S. 152, 164
DÖHRN, R. 4, 79, 80, 95, 97, 113
Domestic Apparent Consumption 18
DOWRICK, S. 172, 198
DRIFFIELD, N. 150, 164
DULLECK, U. 238
DUNNING, J. H. 152, 154, 164
DUSHNITSKY, G. 178, 198
Dutch Disease 85, 109, 111
DUVAL, R. 238

Eastern Europe 80, 121, 141
Eastern Enlargement 79, 97, 248
EBERSBERGER, B. 203
ECHEVARRIA, C. 111, 113
Economic Gonvergence 171, 201
Economic Dynamics 101, 117
Economic Integration 79, 97
ÉGERT, B. 6, 205, 238, 241
ELLISON, G. 120, 145
EMERSON, M. 166
ENGEL, CH. 238
ENGEL, E. 104, 113
ERM-II 6, 206
ESTRIN, S. 164
ETHIER, W. J. 131, 145
EU 15 5, 107, 120, 169, 180, 202, 248
EU 25 98, 248
EUROPEAN COMMISSION 74, 75, 247, 277
European Innovation Scoreboard 249
EUROSTAT 83, 95, 202, 220
Exchange Rate 6, 86, 205, 206, 241, 245, 246, 279
Expert Interviews 162
Export Specialization Patterns 37, 73

FAGERBERG, J. 202, 203
FASSING, G. 82, 83, 96
FDI 73, 74, 76, 77, 78, 133, 149, 150, 167
Federal Ministry of Education and Research 35
FEENSTRA, R. C. 12, 31
FELS 82, 95
FIDRMUC, J. 119, 125, 145, 238
FISHER, A. G. B. 104, 113, 114
FODERS, F. 8, 167, 170
FORSLID, R. 131, 132, 146
FOSTER, N. 238
FOURASTIE, J. 104, 114
FRENKEL, J. 277
FRIETSCH, R. 34, 35
FROOT, K. A. 246, 277
FUCHS, V. R. 105, 114
FUJITA, M. 146

GALLAIS-HAMONNO, G. 166
GALLI, G. 13, 31
GAMBARDELLA, A. 178, 198
GDP 74, 82, 178, 189, 202, 208
Generaly Equilibrium Analyses 12
Geographical Concentration 4, 121
GERN, K. J. 41, 71
GERSCHENBERG, I. 164
GERSCHENKRON, A. 111, 114
GERSHUNY, J. 85, 95
GIRMA, S. 150, 165
GLAESER, E. 120, 145
GLOBERMAN, S. 150, 165
GOMORY, R. E. 11, 31
GÖRG, H. 152, 165
GÖRGENS, E. 82, 95, 114
GÖRTZ 8, 147
GRAFE, C. 250, 277
GREENAWAY, D 39, 72, 152, 165
GRIES, T. 111, 114
GRIFFITH, R. 178, 197
GRILICHES, Z. 178, 197
GROSSMAN, G. M. 165, 170, 198
Growth 84, 108, 173, 259
Growth Decompositions 186
Grubel-Lloyd Index 4, 40, 56, 57, 58
GRUPP, H. 180, 198
GUGLER, K. 146
GUNDLACH, E. 110, 114
GÜNTHER, J. 5, 149, 165, 167
GWARTNEY, J. 169, 170

HAALAND, J. I. 120, 146
HALL, B. H. 178, 198
HALL, R. 14, 32
HALPERN, L. 212, 238, 250, 277
HAMILTON, C. 80, 95
HANSON, G. 120, 146
HARE, P. 80, 95
HARRIGAN, F. 110, 114

HARRISON, A. E. 150, 164
HAUSMAN, J. A. 132, 146
HAVRYLISHYN, O. 80, 95
HECKSCHER, E. 39, 72
Heckscher-Ohlin-Modell 39, 44, 102, 130
HEELEY, M. B. 178, 198
HEIDUK, G. 98, 99
HEILEMANN, U. 4, 79, 95, 97, 113
HELLER, W. 95
HELPMAN, E. 131, 146, 165, 198
HENDERSON, R. 178, 197
HENRY, G. 146
HENRY, J. 238
HESTON, A. 203, 204
HILDEBRANDT, A. 4, 119, 148
HILL, H. 165
HINE, R. C., 39, 72
HINKLE, L. E. 109, 114
HO, K. W. 178, 197
HOEKMAN, B. 152, 164
HOWITT, P. 173, 197
HSIAO, C. 83, 95
HUGHES, G. 80, 95
HUGHES, K. 164
Human Capital 138
HUNGARIAN PATENT OFFICE 159, 165
Hungary 16, 35, 40, 77, 83, 156, 206, 217, 225, 252
Hungarian Manufacturing 22, 25, 125
HUNYA, G. 130, 146, 165

IK, K. H. 178, 197
IM, K. S. 222, 238
Imperfect Competition 39
Industrial Output 97
Industrial Revolution 103
Industrial Specialization 119, 147
Innovation 5, 171, 173, 201, 245, 248, 279
INOTAI, A. 80, 95
Intellectual Property Rights 169
International Financial Statistics 252, 277
Inter-Industry Specialization 7
Intra-Industry Trade 56
Investment Intensity 27, 82
Iron Curtain 73
ISIC Classification 105, 106, 179

JAFFE, A. 178, 197
JENSEN, C. 156, 165
JOHNSTON, L. 250, 277
JONES, C. I. 173, 197
JUNGBLUT, S. 111, 114
JUNGMITTAG, A. 5, 171, 177, 198, 201, 277

KALOTAY, K. 130, 146
KAO, C. 222, 238
KATHURIA, V. 150, 165
KAUFFMANN, A. 4, 101, 109, 117
KEMPA, B. 8, 241
Kernel Density 202
KHORANA, A. 178, 198
KIND, H.J. 146
KINOSHITA, Y. 151, 165
KIRZNER, I. 12, 32
KLODT, H 80, 96
KNELL, M. 152, 164
Knowledge Spillover 5
KOKKO, A. 150, 164
KONGSAMUT, P. P. 111, 114
KONINGS, J. 151, 165
KORNAI, J. 80, 96
KRAJNYÁK, K. 212, 238, 250, 277
KRAWCZYK, O. 34, 35
KRÜGER, J. 203, 204
KRUGMAN, P. 33, 35, 39, 72, 131, 146
KUGLER, M. 150, 165
KUZNETS, S. 105, 114

Labor Mobility 153, 159
Labor Productivity 104
LACH, S. 178, 198
LAMNEK, S. 159, 165
LANDESMANN, M. A. 145
LAURSEN, K. 172, 197
LAVRAC, V. 238
LAWSON, R. 169, 170
LEGLER, H. 198
LENOX, M. J. 178, 198
LIPTON, D. 85, 96
Lisbon Strategy 2
Logit Estimation 28
LOMMATZSCH, K. 6, 205, 241
LOVE, J. H. 150, 164
Love of Variety 39
LUCAS, R. E. 173, 198

LUNDVALL, B.-Å. 201, 204
LUTZ, S. H. 152, 166

MACDONALD, R. 207, 238, 277
MACKINNON, J. G. 239
MADDALA, G. S. 32
MAJCEN, B. 152, 164
MALISZEWSKA, M. 250, 277
MANKIW, N. G. 173, 198
MANSFIELD, E. 178, 198
Manufacturing 18, 40, 91
MARCZEWSKI, K. 8, 279
MARIN, C. 238
Market Economie 73
Market Performance 16, 17, 22
Market Share 13
Marxist Idiology 104
MATSUYAMA, K. 111, 114
MATUSIK, S. F. 178, 198
MECKL, J. 111, 114
MEIẞNER, W. 82, 96
MEUSER, M. 159, 166
MIDELFART-KNARVIK, K. H. 119, 122, 146
MILNER, CH 39, 72
MOATTI, S. 237
MOHNEN, P. 153, 166
Monetary Union 246, 268
MONTIEL, P. J. 109, 114
MUSSA, M. 277

Nace Classification 48, 106
NAGEL, U. 159, 166
NEARY, J. P. 109, 113
NELSON, R. R. 201, 204
Neoclassical Growth Theory 173
New Economic Geography 4, 39, 132, 134
New Trade Theory 39, 131

OECD 83, 91, 96, 152, 166, 220
OECD Countries 103, 108
OHLIN, B. 39, 72
OPEC 83
Open Economies 111
OVERMAN, H. 145, 146

Panel Estimation 4, 6
Panel Cointegration Methods 207
Partial Equilibrium Analysis 12
Patent Stocks 178
PEDRONI, P. 222, 239
PENG, M. W. 12, 32
Per Capita Income 88, 94
PESARAN, M. H. 221, 238, 239
PFAFFERMAYR, M. 146
PIANTA, M. 173, 197
PIATKOWSKI, M. 98, 99
PIAZOLO, D. 170
PISCITELLO, L. 178, 197
Poland 16, 35, 40, 78, 83, 156, 206, 217, 226, 252
Polish Manufacturing 20, 21, 24, 25
Population 94
PORTER, M. E. 12, 32
POSNER, M. V. 146
Post-Socialist Transformation 102
PRATTEN, C. 131, 146
President's Commission on Industrial Competitiveness 35
PRITCHETT, L. 80, 95
Privatization Strategy 1
Product Differentiation 28
Productivity Differences 185
Product Innovation 265, 268
PROKOP, L. 238
PUGA, D. 39, 72, 146
Purchasing Power Parity 86, 208
PYKA, A. 8, 201, 203

QUAH, D. 203, 204
QUIBRIA, M. G. 110, 114

R&D 4, 5, 34, 44, 181, 280
RAISER, M. 108, 114
RAMASWAMY, R. 110, 114
RAYNAULD, A. 12, 32
RAYP, G. 32
RCA 4, 40, 51, 52, 56
REDDING, S. R. 146
REUBER, G. L. 166
Revealed Comparative Advantage 40, 51
Ricardian Specialization 172, 179, 201
RICARDO, D. 39, 72
RICHTER, S. 120, 146
RIES, J. 165
RODRIK, D. 80, 95
ROJEC, M. 152, 164
ROMER, P. M. 173, 198
RONNING, G. 82, 96
ROSATI, D. 212, 239

ROTHER, P. 250, 277
ROWTHORN, R. 110, 114
RUANE, F. 150, 166
Russia 117

SACHS, J. 85, 96
SALA-I-MARTIN, X. 194, 197
SASS, M. 238
SCHNEIDER, K. 8, 73
SCHOORS, K. 156, 166
SCHUMACHER, D. 8, 33, 34
SCHUMANN, CH. 8, 117
Schumpeter 13, 44, 249, 279
SCHWARTZ, M. 178, 198
SCHWEICKERT, R. 170
Sectoral Change 79, 97
Sectoral Economic Structure 89
Sectoral Growth Functions 84-87
SGARD, J. 239
SHIN, Y. 238, 239
SJÖHOLM, F. 150, 164, 166
SLOEK, T. 277
Slovakia 83, 156, 206, 217, 227
Slovenia 156, 206, 217, 228
SMARZYNSKA, B. K. 151, 156, 166
SMETS, F. 238
SMID, S. 159, 166
SMITH, A. 32, 104, 114
Smithian Specialization 172, 180, 201
SPATAREANU, M. 156, 166
Specialization 129, 173
Spillover Effects 150
STEHRER, R. 238
STEIN, J. C. 246, 277
STEINER, M. 82, 96, 114
STOCK, J. 239
STRAßBERGER, F. 33, 35
STREMERSCH, S. 247, 278
STROBL, E. 150, 164
Structural Adjustment 109
Structural Change 2, 83, 92, 101, 105, 111, 117, 245, 279
Structural Convergence 92
Structur of Manufacturing 43, 44, 91
SUMMERS, R. 203, 204
SYRQUIN, M. 108, 113, 115
System of National Accounts 88
SZAPARY, G. 250, 278

TALAVERA, O. 152, 166
TANSINI, R. 165
TAYLOR, L. 80, 95
TAYLOR, W. E. 132, 146
Technological Change 16
Technological Differences 138
Technological Specialization 5, 171, 201
Technology Spillovers 149, 152, 167
TELLIS, G.UJ. 247, 278
Three-Sector-Hypothesis 85
Time Series 6
TONDL, G. 74, 75
TORRISI, S. 178, 198
TORSTENSSON, J. 146
TRABOLD, H. 33, 35
Trade Coverage Index 40, 48, 49, 50, 51
Traditional Trade Theory 4, 39, 131
Transition Economies 9, 33, 101, 117, 149, 167, 205, 241
TRAJTENBERG, M. 178, 198
TSOUKALIS, L. 32

UGUR, A. 150, 166
UNCTAD 153, 166
UNECE 170
United Nations 83, 96

Value Added 107
VAN ARK, B. 98, 99
VAN DER TOL, B. 156, 166
VAN RENEN, J. 178, 197
VAN WIJNBERGEN, S. 109, 115
VENABLES, A.J. 39, 146
VERSPAGEN, B. 172, 197, 202, 203
VERTINSKY, I. 165
VIDAL, J. P. 32
VISEK, J. A. 238
VUKSIC, G. 74, 75

WAGNER, S. 178, 198
WALLENDER, H. W. 164
WALSH, V. 178, 197
WATSON, M. W. 239
WEIL, D. N. 173, 198
WELFENS, P. J.J. 6, 97, 99, 109, 115, 198, 278, 279
Western Europe 98, 103
WIGGER, B. 111, 114
WIIW 146, 151
WINEK, D. 3, 34
WINIECKI, J. 80, 96

WINTERS, A. 80, 95
WOLFE, M. 105, 115
WOLFF, H. 250, 277
WOLFMAYR-SCHNITZER, Y. 72, 146
World Bank 105, 108, 112, 115
WÖRZ, J. 4, 119, 146, 148, 238
WYPLOSZ, C. 212, 238, 250, 277
WZIĄTEK-KUBIAK, A. 3, 32, 34

YIN, E. 247, 278

ZACHARIADIS, M. 178, 199
ZEJAN, M. C. 165
ZETTELMEYER, J. 212, 238, 250, 277
ZUKOWSKA-GAGELMANN, K. 151, 157, 166

Further Publications by *Paul J. J. Welfens*

P. J. J. Welfens
Market-oriented Systemic Transformations in Eastern Europe
Problems, Theoretical Issues, and Policy Options
1992. XII, 261 pages. 20 Figs., 29 Tab.,
Hardcover, ISBN 3-540-55793-8

M. W. Klein, P. J. J. Welfens (Eds.)
Multinationals in the New Europe and Global Trade
1992. XV, 281 pages. 24 Figs., 75 Tab.,
Hardcover, ISBN 3-540-54634-0

P. J. J. Welfens (Ed.)
Economic Aspects of German Unification
Expectations, Transition Dynamics and International Perspectives
1996. XV, 527 pages. 34 Figs., 110 Tab.,
Hardcover, ISBN 3-540-60261-5

R. Tilly, P. J. J. Welfens (Eds.)
European Economic Integration as a Challenge to Industry and Government
Contemporary and Historical Perspectives on International Economic Dynamics
1996. X, 558 pages. 43 Figs.,
Hardcover, ISBN 3-540-60431-6

P. J. J. Welfens (Ed.)
Economic Aspects of German Unification
Expectations, Transition Dynamics and International Perspectives
2nd revised and enlarged edition
1996. XV, 527 pages. 34 Figs., 110 Tab.,
Hardcover, ISBN 3-540-60261-5

P. J. J. Welfens
European Monetary Integration
EMS Developments and International Post-Maastricht Perspectives
3rd revised and enlarged edition
1996. XVIII, 384 pages. 14 Figs., 26 Tab.,
Hardcover, ISBN 3-540-60260-7

P. J. J. Welfens (Ed.)
European Monetary Union
Transition, International Impact and Policy Options
1997. X, 467 pages. 50 Figs., 31 Tab.,
Hardcover, ISBN 3-540-63305-7

P. J. J. Welfens, G. Yarrow (Eds.)
Telecommunications and Energy in Systemic Transformation
International Dynamics, Deregulation and Adjustment in Network Industries
1997. XII, 501 pages. 39 Figs.,
Hardcover, ISBN 3-540-61586-5

P. J. J. Welfens, H. C. Wolf (Eds.)
Banking, International Capital Flows and Growth in Europe
Financial Markets, Savings and Monetary Integration in a World with Uncertain Convergence
1997. XIV, 458 pages. 22 Figs., 63 Tab.,
Hardcover, ISBN 3-540-63192-5

P. J. J. Welfens, D. Audretsch, J. T. Addison, H. Grupp
Technological Competition, Employment and Innovation Policies in OECD Countries
1998. VI, 231 pages. 16 Figs., 20 Tab.,
Hardcover, ISBN 3-540-63439-8

P. J. J. Welfens, G. Yarrow, R. Grinberg, C. Graack (Eds.)
Towards Competition in Network Industries
Telecommunications, Energy and Transportation in Europe and Russia
1999. XXII, 570 pages. 63 Figs., 63 Tab.,
Hardcover, ISBN 3-540-65859-9

P. J. J. Welfens
EU Eastern Enlargement and the Russian Transformation Crisis
1999. X, 151 pages. 12 Figs., 25 Tab.,
Hardcover, ISBN 3-540-65862-9

P. J. J. Welfens
Globalization of the Economy, Unemployment and Innovation
1999. VI, 255 pages. 11 Figs., 31 Tab.,
Hardcover, ISBN 3-540-65250-7

P. J. J. Welfens, J. T. Addison, D. B. Audretsch, T. Gries, H. Grupp
Globalization, Economic Growth and Innovation Dynamics
1999. X, 160 pages. 15 Figs., 15 Tab.,
Hardcover, ISBN 3-540-65858-0

R. Tilly, P. J. J. Welfens (Eds.)
Economic Globalization, International Organizations and Crisis Management
Contemporary and Historical Perspectives on Growth, Impact and Evolution of Major Organizations in an Interdependent World
2000. XII, 408 pages. 11 Figs., 20 Tab., Hardcover, ISBN 3-540-65863-7

P. J. J. Welfens, E. Gavrilenkov (Eds.)
Restructuring, Stabilizing and Modernizing the New Russia
Economic and Institutional Issues
2000. XIV, 516 pages. 82 Figs., 70 Tab., Hardcover, ISBN 3-540-67429-2

P. J. J. Welfens
European Monetary Union and Exchange Rate Dynamics
New Approaches and Applications to the Euro
2001. X, 159 pages. 26 Figs., 12 Tab., Hardcover, ISBN 3-540-67914-6

P. J. J. Welfens
Stabilizing and Integrating the Balkans
Economic Analysis of the Stability Pact, EU Reforms and International Organizations
2001. XII, 171 pages. 6 Figs., 18 Tab., Hardcover, ISBN 3-540-41775-3

P. J. J. Welfens, B. Meyer, W. Pfaffenberger, P. Jasinski, A. Jungmittag
Energy Policies in the European Union Germany's Ecological Tax Reform
2001. VII, 143 pages. 21 Figs., 41 Tab., Hardcover, ISBN 3-540-41652-8

P. J. J. Welfens (Ed.)
Internationalization of the Economy and Environmental Policy Options
2001. XIV, 442 pages. 57 Figs., 61 Tab., Hardcover, ISBN 3-540-42174-2

P. J. J. Welfens
Interneteconomics.net
Macroeconomics, Deregulation, and Innovation
2002. VIII, 215 pages. 34 Figs., 30 Tab., Hardcover, ISBN 3-540-43337-6

D. B. Audretsch, P. J. J. Welfens (Eds.)
The New Economy and Economic Growth in Europe and the USA
2002, XII, 350 pages. 28 Figs., 59 Tab., Hardcover, ISBN 3-540-43179-9

C. E. Barfield, G. Heiduk, P. J. J. Welfens (Eds.)
Internet, Economic Growth and Globalization
Perspectives on the Digital Economy in Europe, Japan and the U.S.
2003. XII, 388 pages. 34 Figs. 67 Tab., Hardcover, ISBN 3-540-00286-3

J. T. Addison, P. J. J. Welfens (Eds.)
Labor Markets and Social Security
Issues and Policy Options in the U.S. and Europe, 2nd edn.
2003. X, 402 pages. 56 Figs., 52 Tab., Hardcover, ISBN 3-540-44004-6

T. Lane, N. Oding, P. J. J. Welfens (Eds.)
Real and Financial Economic Dynamics in Russia and Eastern Europe
2003. XII, 293 pages. 50 Figs., 63 Tab., Hardcover, ISBN 3-540-00910-8

J. E. Gavrilenkov, P. J. J. Welfens, R. Wiegert (Eds.)
Economic Opening Up and Growth in Russia
2004. IX, 298 pages. 61 Figs., 70 Tab., Hardcover, ISBN 3-540-20459-8

MIX
Papier aus verantwortungsvollen Quellen
Paper from responsible sources
FSC® C105338

If you have any concerns about our products,
you can contact us on
ProductSafety@springernature.com

In case Publisher is established outside the EU,
the EU authorized representative is:
Springer Nature Customer Service Center GmbH
Europaplatz 3, 69115 Heidelberg, Germany

Printed by Libri Plureos GmbH
in Hamburg, Germany